THE ANNALS

of The American Academy of Political
and Social Science

What Census Data Miss about American Diversity

Special Editors:
RICHARD ALBA
City University of New York
KENNETH PREWITT
Columbia University

Los Angeles | London | New Delhi
Singapore | Washington DC | Melbourne

The American Academy of Political and Social Science

202 S. 36th Street, Annenberg School for Communication, University of Pennsylvania,
Philadelphia, PA 19104-3806; (215) 746-6500; (215) 573-2667 (fax); www.aapss.org

Board of Directors
KENNETH PREWITT, *President*
REBECCA MAYNARD, *Chair*

ANDREW J. CHERLIN
SHELDON DANZIGER
GREG DUNCAN
JACOB HACKER
ROBERT HAUSER
JAMES JACKSON

SHERMAN JAMES
DAVID LEONHARDT
ARTHUR LUPIA
MARY ANN MEYERS
DOROTHY ROBERTS
THEDA SKOCPOL

Editors, THE ANNALS
THOMAS A. KECSKEMETHY, *Executive Editor*
EMILY W. BABSON, *Managing Editor*
PHYLLIS KANISS, *Editor Emerita (deceased)*   RICHARD D. LAMBERT, *Editor Emeritus*

Editorial Advisory Board

MAHZARIN BANAJI, *Harvard University*
FRANCINE BLAU, *Cornell University*
FELTON EARLS, *Harvard University*
PAULA ENGLAND, *New York University*
LEE EPSTEIN, *Washington University, St. Louis*
ROBERT GREENSTEIN, *Center on Budget and Policy Priorities*

ROBERT KEOHANE, *Princeton University*
DOUGLAS S. MASSEY, *Princeton University*
SEAN REARDON, *Stanford University*
ROGERS SMITH, *University of Pennsylvania*
THOMAS SUGRUE, *University of Pennsylvania*

Origin and Purpose. The Academy was organized December 14, 1889, to promote the progress of political and social science, especially through publications and meetings. The Academy does not take sides in controverted questions, but seeks to gather and present reliable information to assist the public in forming an intelligent and accurate judgment.

Meetings. The Academy occasionally holds a meeting in the spring extending over two days.

Publications. THE ANNALS of The American Academy of Political and Social Science is the bimonthly publication of the Academy. Each issue contains articles on some prominent social or political problem, written at the invitation of the editors. These volumes constitute important reference works on the topics with which they deal, and they are extensively cited by authorities throughout the United States and abroad.

Subscriptions. THE ANNALS of The American Academy of Political and Social Science (ISSN 0002-7162) (J295) is published bimonthly—in January, March, May, July, September, and November—by SAGE Publishing, 2455 Teller Road, Thousand Oaks, CA 91320. Periodicals postage paid at Thousand Oaks, California, and at additional mailing offices. POSTMASTER: Send address changes to The Annals of The American Academy of Political and Social Science, c/o SAGE Publishing, 2455 Teller Road, Thousand Oaks, CA 91320. Institutions may subscribe to THE ANNALS at the annual rate: $1129 (clothbound, $1275). Individuals may subscribe to the ANNALS at the annual rate: $126 (clothbound, $185). Single issues of THE ANNALS may be obtained by individuals for $39 each (clothbound, $54). Single issues of THE ANNALS have proven to be excellent supplementary texts for classroom use. Direct inquiries regarding adoptions to THE ANNALS c/o SAGE Publishing (address below).

Copyright © 2018 by The American Academy of Political and Social Science. All rights reserved. No portion of the contents may be reproduced in any form without written permission from the publisher.

All correspondence concerning membership in the Academy, dues renewals, inquiries about membership status, and/or purchase of single issues of THE ANNALS should be sent to THE ANNALS c/o SAGE Publishing, 2455 Teller Road, Thousand Oaks, CA 91320. Telephone: (800) 818-SAGE (7243) and (805) 499-0721; Fax/Order line: (805) 375-1700; e-mail: journals@sagepub.com. *Please note that orders under $30 must be prepaid.* For all customers outside the Americas, please visit http://www.sagepub.co.uk/customerCare.nav for information.

Printed on acid-free paper

THE ANNALS
© 2018 by The American Academy of Political and Social Science

All rights reserved. No part of this volume may be reproduced or utilized in any form or by any means, electronic or mechanical, including photocopying, recording, or by any information storage and retrieval system, without permission in writing from the publisher. All inquiries for reproduction or permission should be sent to SAGE Publishing, 2455 Teller Road, Thousand Oaks, CA 91320.

Editorial Office: 202 S. 36th Street, Philadelphia, PA 19104-3806
For information about individual and institutional subscriptions address:
SAGE Publishing
2455 Teller Road
Thousand Oaks, CA 91320

For SAGE Publishing: Peter Geraghty (Production) and Mimi Nguyen (Marketing)

From India and South Asia, write to:
SAGE PUBLICATIONS INDIA Pvt Ltd
B-42 Panchsheel Enclave, P.O. Box 4109
New Delhi 110 017
INDIA

From Europe, the Middle East, and Africa, write to:
SAGE PUBLICATIONS LTD
1 Oliver's Yard, 55 City Road
London EC1Y 1SP
UNITED KINGDOM

International Standard Serial Number ISSN 0002-7162
ISBN 978-1-5443-4206-1 (Vol. 677, 2018) paper
ISBN 978-1-5443-4205-4 (Vol. 677, 2018) cloth
Manufactured in the United States of America. First printing, May 2018

Information about membership rates, institutional subscriptions, and back issue prices may be found on the facing page.

Advertising. Current rates and specifications may be obtained by writing to The Annals Advertising and Promotion Manager at the Thousand Oaks office (address above). Acceptance of advertising in this journal in no way implies endorsement of the advertised product or service by SAGE or the journal's affiliated society(ies) or the journal editor(s). No endorsement is intended or implied. SAGE reserves the right to reject any advertising it deems as inappropriate for this journal.

Claims. Claims for undelivered copies must be made no later than six months following month of publication. The publisher will supply replacement issues when losses have been sustained in transit and when the reserve stock will permit.

Change of Address. Six weeks' advance notice must be given when notifying of change of address. Please send the old address label along with the new address to the SAGE office address above to ensure proper identification. Please specify the name of the journal.

THE ANNALS
OF THE AMERICAN ACADEMY OF POLITICAL AND SOCIAL SCIENCE

Volume 677   May 2018

IN THIS ISSUE:

What Census Data Miss about American Diversity
Special Editors: RICHARD ALBA and KENNETH PREWITT

Introduction

The Census Race Classification: Is It Doing Its Job? .... *Kenneth Prewitt*   8

I: The Significance of Ethno-Racial Mixing

The Rise of Mixed Parentage: A Sociological and Demographic
Phenomenon to Be Reckoned With. . . . . *Richard Alba, Brenden Beck, and Duygu Basaran Sahin*   26

Ethnic/Racial Identity: Fuzzy Categories and Shifting
Positions. . . . . *Kay Deaux*   39

Establishing the Denominator: The Challenges of Measuring Multiracial,
Hispanic, and Native American Populations. . . . . *Wendy D. Roth*   48

The Generational Locus of Multiraciality and Its Implications for
Racial Self-Identification . . . . *Ann Morning and Aliya Saperstein*   57

Multiracial Identification and Racial Gaps: A Work in
Progress . . . . *Jenifer L. Bratter*   69

Boundary Blurring? Racial Identification among the Children of
Interracial Couples. *Daniel T. Lichter and Zhenchao Qian*   81

II: Change across the Generations after Immigration

Finding the Lost Generation: Identifying Second-Generation Immigrants
in Federal Statistics . . . . *Douglas S. Massey*   96

Social Mobility across Immigrant Generations: Recent Evidence and
Future Data Requirements. . . . . *Van C. Tran*   105

Tracking a Changing America across the Generations after
Immigration . . . . *Tomás R. Jiménez*   119

Identifying the Later-Generation Descendants of U.S. Immigrants:
Issues Arising from Selective Ethnic Attrition . . . . *Brian Duncan
and Stephen J. Trejo* 131

III: Diversities within Major Populations

Measuring Hispanic Origin: Reflections on Hispanic Race
Reporting. . . . . *Sonya R. Porter and C. Matthew Snipp* 140

Latinos, Race, and the U.S. Census . . . . *Edward Telles* 153

Estimating the Characteristics of Unauthorized Immigrants Using U.S. Census
Data: Combined Sample Multiple Imputation . . . . *Randy Capps,
James D. Bachmeier, and Jennifer Van Hook* 165

Counting America's First Peoples . . . . *Carolyn A. Liebler* 180

Accurately Counting Asian Americans Is a Civil Rights Issue . . . . *Jennifer Lee,
Karthick Ramakrishnan, and Janelle Wong* 191

IV: Some Ramifications of Diversity

Racial and Political Dynamics of an Approaching "Majority-Minority"
United States . . . . *Maureen A. Craig, Julian M. Rucker,
and Jennifer A. Richeson* 204

Racial Population Projections and Reactions to Alternative News
Accounts of Growing Diversity . . . . *Dowell Myers and Morris Levy* 215

Growing U.S. Ethnoracial Diversity: A Positive or Negative Societal
Dynamic? . . . . *Frank D. Bean* 229

Editors' Note

Editors' Note . . . . *Kenneth Prewitt and Richard Alba* 242

FORTHCOMING

Evidence-Based Social Policy: The Promise and Challenges of a Movement
Special Editor: RON HASKINS

Regulating Crime: The New Criminology of Crime Control
Special Editors: JOSHUA D. FREILICH and GRAEME R. NEWMAN

Introduction

The Census Race Classification: Is It Doing Its Job?

By
KENNETH PREWITT

Aligning census ethnoracial categories with America's changing demography is a never-ending task and becomes more difficult when identity claims are rationales for altering categories. We examine four current problems: (1) the Census Bureau projects a population more nonwhite than white by midcentury—social demographers document trends pointing to a different racial future; (2) the census inadequately measures second- and third-generation Americans, limiting the nation's understanding of why some immigrant groups are "racialized" while others are "whitened"; (3) on health, education, and employment, there is more intrarace than between-race variability, which is better measured for Asians and Hispanics than it is for whites and blacks; and (4) consistency in racial self-identification is stronger for whites, blacks, and Asians than for Hispanics, Native Americans, and biracial groups, lowering the reliability of race data. These measurement problems weaken policy choices relevant to economic growth, social justice, immigrant assimilation, government reforms, and an enlightened public.

Keywords: majority-minority; assimilation; intrarace variability; identity rationales; white nationalism; statistical races

America's racial classification can be traced to 1735, when Carl Linnaeus, the father of taxonomy, briefly shifted his attention from flora and fauna—he was a botanist—and fearlessly divided the human species into four subspecies: *Americanus, Asiaticus, Africanus, Europeaeus.* A few decades later, the classification was slightly modified by a German doctor, Johan Blumenbach, in his influential *On the Natural Varieties of Mankind.* He divided the Asians into the Mongolian and Malaysian; he

Kenneth Prewitt is the Carnegie Professor at Columbia University, President of the American Academy of Political and Social Science, past director of the Census Bureau, and author of What Is Your Race? The Census and Our Flawed Effort to Classify Americans *(Princeton University Press 2013).*

Correspondence: kp2058@columbia.edu

DOI: 10.1177/0002716218756629

also took care to rank-order the races, Europeans being superior as the most civilized, and Africans inferior and uncivilized.

These five races—though not the rank-order—structure America's racial numbers today. Few are happy with this straitjacket, and for a half century the U.S. Census Bureau has been adding fixes big and small to better align eighteenth-century race science to changing social and demographic realities and public uses. It added an ethnic category—Hispanic—though that tripped over the *other* category, which, nonsensically, then became the fastest growing race in the country.[1] It invited Native American Indians to write in their tribal affiliation, which mixed up a civil status (membership in a federally recognized tribe) with culture (community belonging). It made extensive use of national origin subcategories for two races—Asians and Pacific Islanders—but neither whites nor blacks have subcategories. The latter two races are uniquely denoted by color, which, of course, has never been measured by the census. I doubt that it ever will be.

The "fix the race question" pace picked up as we entered the twenty-first century. One change was, on the face of it, more tinkering than transforming. It was in the 2000 census that Blumenbach's Mongolian and Malaysian subspecies were finally counted as separate races in the American census. The story merits retelling. In the mid-1990s, Hawaii's Senator Daniel K. Akaka successfully argued that the Native Hawaiians and Pacific Islanders (NHPI) should be a race separate from the Asian category. He cited statistics demonstrating that the NHPI were disadvantaged compared to the larger Asian population; he wanted these disadvantages separately tabulated and government programs targeted accordingly. In this Akaka was emphasizing the social justice reasoning so central to the civil rights era a half century earlier. Akaka, however, was not finished. In congressional testimony, he also argued that the current classification *"denies us our identity* as indigenous peoples" (U.S. House 1998, 263, italics added). Self-esteem rationales were not entirely new to the census (Schor 2005), but never had they led to such a radical change—adding to the census a new primary race category. Akaka's bold identity claim kept intact the eighteenth-century race science category scheme, but pushed aside its rationale. Races are not biologically meaningful; they are what groups of people claim—or reject as the case might be—as their rightful identity.

It was a short step to an even more radical assertion. The first census of the new millennium made clear that treating us as if we all belonged to pure mono-races was badly mistaken. Racial mixture occurs, in numbers large enough to merit counting.[2] This was officially announced in an understated option on the 2000 census form: respondents could, if they wished, "mark one or more" of the five primary races. This option is traced to the 1968 Supreme Court ruling that interracial marriage was constitutionally protected, which of course led to biracial children. Again, this was hardly new, but a long-standing demographic reality the census would finally take into account. In 2000, mark-one-or-more entered census history with these children in mind. It had a bumpy beginning.

The National Association for the Advancement of Colored People (NAACP) insisted that because race statistics existed for "the enforcement of civil rights laws," the move to multiracial census categories would reduce the size of discrete minority races, "diluting benefits to which they are entitled as a protected class under civil rights laws and under the Constitution itself" (Williams 2006, 308). In a show of racial solidarity, Asian and Hispanic advocacy groups agreed that the census categories were not called on "to provide vehicles for self-identification" (Williams 2006, 308).

But self-identification and self-esteem were exactly what Senator Akaka argued for, and what multiracial advocates sought. The Association of Multiethnic Americans demanded "choice in the matter of who we are, just like any other community. We are not saying that we are a solution to civil rights laws or civil rights injustices of the past." It is ironic that "our people are being asked to correct by virtue of how we define ourselves all of the past injustices [toward] other groups of people" (U.S. House 1998, 383).

This rationale notwithstanding, the Census Bureau is not in the self-esteem business. It does not produce *identity* races; it produces *statistical* races. The Bureau's website emphasizes that statistical races are used "to assess fairness in employment practices, meet legislative redistricting requirements by knowing the racial make-up of the voting age population, learn who may not be receiving medical services, determine disparities in health and environmental risks" and other similar purposes, as required by ten key executive agencies.

Nowhere on the Bureau's website, or those of the ten executive agencies, will you find attention to self-esteem, recognition, or identity expression. Instead, you will find programmatic reasons for *statistical* races, linked to concerns about disparities and discrimination, but also to city planning, transportation policy, and related government tasks and commercial uses—all drawing on census race and ethnic statistics. Stated differently, Akaka started with disparities and tagged on identity. The Office of Management and Budget (OMB) ran statistics on the former, concluding that the evidence justified NHPI as a separate race. Had Akaka offered only a self-esteem rationale, the OMB and Census Bureau would not have known how to measure it. NHPI would not today be a separate race.

But that was two decades ago. Do we not now have a broader array of identity claims and a richer understanding of, especially, the multiracial population? Yes, and much that is relevant is on display in this volume, starting with the fact that a multiracial emphasis turns out to have unexpected political consequences.

To understand those consequences, I briefly trace familiar history, dating to America's founding fathers. The War of Independence they led was justified as a war against tyranny and a proclamation of liberty and equality. This posed a tricky question: How could a new nation reject tyranny but simultaneously impose it on the indigenous Native Americans in forceful removal from their homelands and, even more comprehensively, on the African slave? The answer—impose a citizenship test in the new republic, conveniently tethered to who was civilized and who was not. The Europeans wrote the rules, declaring themselves civilized and fit for citizenship, but of course not the uncivilized Indian and African. A white superiority narrative was born (Parkinson 2017). It haunts our history, very often finding in the census a convenient tool: a Jim Crow apartheid regime, a whites-only melting pot, second-class citizenship for Asian and Hispanic labor, continuing in current times in gerrymandering and voter suppression, and, today, unexpectedly, in the revival of white nationalism that shows traces of the eighteenth-century fixation on white superiority.

The civil rights era took on the white superiority narrative when the census, previously an aid to exclusion, shifted 180 degrees to serve as a tool of racial inclusion. Its most telling early achievement was statistical proportionality—groups matter proportionate to their share of the total population. This idea was anticipated by the constitutionally protected decadal census reapportionment process, but in 1787 none could have imagined its mid-twentieth-century application.

Statistical proportionality began its official life in the Kerner Commission Report (National Advisory Commission on Civil Disorders 1968), a response to the mid-1960s epidemic of urban race riots. The commission introduced an idea new to public discourse—*unintentional* discrimination, the kind that flows not from a racially prejudiced employer or realtor but from how the labor and housings markets are structured. Soon the phrase *institutional racism* caught on, and from that it was a short step to preferential hiring. Institutional discrimination required institutional solutions (Knowles and Prewitt 1969). Statistical proportionality slipped into government policy and public usage in the late 1960s, later named *affirmative action* or, today, the widely established practice of *diversity hiring*. The white superiority narrative faded from public usage, its rejection further hastened by a demographic transformation as America again opened its door to immigration, this time overwhelmingly from non-European regions. This gave the nation a new multicultural narrative.

The census, still anchored to an eighteenth-century classification and heavily constrained by path dependency, struggled to match the new demography and discourse. Mark-one-or-more was an awkward response to the hundreds of national origins, ethnic, and language groups confused about what census box to tick. Mark-one-or-more applied to only the five primary races. The part white and part Asian could find a census home, but not the part white and part Hispanic. But change was still in the air. A few years after the partial fix represented by mark-one-or-more in 2000, the Census Bureau went at it again. It mounted a research project on racial categories unprecedented in its ambition and scale—comparing seventeen different ways to count races and ethnicity, with two control panels; adding in fifteen experimental treatments and focus groups; as well as assembling expert panels and presenting in dozens of professional settings.

The research led to various mode, wording, and framing improvements and then, much more consequentially, to two ambitious category recommendations: (1) the 2020 census should introduce a race category that the botanist and the doctor had missed—Middle-Eastern North African (MENA); and (2) it should merge what had been a separate Hispanic question into a single ethnoracial classification with the primary races. Mark-one-or-more stays in place, though now applied to seven primary categories (if MENA is accepted). The census form also offers space to write in specific ancestry, ethnicity, tribe, or national origin identities for each of the basic categories. As of this writing, these recommendations are before the statistical policy office of the OMB, the controlling executive agency.[3]

Are the proposed 2020 changes an improvement? Yes, is the general answer in this volume. Does this mean that the country will finally have a coherent set of categories? Not exactly. Problems persist and are pointed out in the articles that follow. The reader will find many sentences with some variant of "the census should...." with specific recommendations as well as sweeping complaints. Telles, for example, says that the Census Bureau is "out of step with popularly held notions of race and ethnicity." If the Census Bureau accepted all the recommendations found in this volume, would it then be in-step, would we have a coherent set of categories? Not likely. As Lopez (2005) observes, incoherent census categories are inevitable because they "arise out of (fundamentally irrational) social practices" (p. 50).

Repeated effort to fix the census classification system is welcome, but it will never completely fix what is inescapably an incoherent classification scheme. There is a racial reality independent of the reality captured in the census; and as academic research points out, that reality is more complex, nuanced, changeable than what census statistics capture. This is *not* for lack of intelligence, imagination, or effort in the Census Bureau—all present in abundance. It is because the Bureau is not a free agent. Its purpose is decided elsewhere, starting with the first Article of the U.S. Constitution. Its past, present, and future cannot escape the "fundamentally irrational" task imposed in law and practice—count America's races.

Academic research is not so constrained. Consider a simple example. Social scientists find implicit bias and racial stereotyping, and find that phenotypic attributes are in play. Skin color matters. Perhaps it would be useful if the American census measured color (Brazil does). This will not happen. Academic research, with its experiments, in-depth interviews, and tailored surveys, will always probe corners not reachable by the census.

This volume, under four headings, reviews research that draws primarily on census data but also brings other data into the picture. The back and forth between census measures and academic unpacking, aided by other measures, inevitably reveals measurement flaws, some that are, at least in principle (first two), fixable; others less so (second two).

I.   The *majority-minority future* now being much discussed, with significant political consequences, is highly likely to be more distant than has been asserted. Under reasonable assumptions, it may be postponed indefinitely as assimilation "whitens" some nationality groups. It did so for the once alien Irish, Italian, and Polish "races" and is now under way, if very selectively, among Asians (especially the Chinese, Japanese, and Korean-Americans), Hispanics (especially from the Caribbean Islands), Native Americans (especially those living in cities rather than on reservations), well-educated African immigrants who started arriving in the 1970s, and multiracials.

II. The *inadequately measured generational differences*, especially where place-of-birth gets tangled up with the dynamics of racializing immigrants, that is, where color-line and nativity-line overlap. This is a nontrivial

matter; in 2016, nearly one in five Americans were immigrants (43.7 million) or first generation (16.6 million).
III. The difficulty of assessing and responding to disparities and inequalities because *within-group variability* (detected by comparing the national origin groups that belong to one or another primary race group) is greater in magnitude than that between the primary race groups, which are generally used in policy design and evaluation.
IV. The *low reliability of ethnoracial statistics*, across settings and over time, when compared to other population characteristics measured by the census, playing havoc with trend lines.

The Majority-Minority Projection

In 2015, the Census Bureau projected that three decades hence America will be majority-minority, defined as fewer whites than nonwhites, as is already the case of babies being born. A Census Bureau Report—*Non-Hispanic Whites May No Longer Comprise over 50 Percent of the U.S. Population by 2044*—compared non-Hispanic whites (European decent) to all other racial groups, including white Hispanics and all multiracial respondents (U.S. Census Bureau 2015). The report generated a media storm.

Hold on, said demographers and sociologists, several of the best represented in this volume. This projection is misleading, dangerously so as reflected in the angry white vote demanding that "we want our country back." Alba commented on the census projection in the journal *American Prospect*, tellingly titled: "The Likely Persistence of a White Majority: How Census Bureau Statistics Have Mislead Thinking about the American Future" (Alba 2016). The journal editor asked me to provide a comment, from the perspective of an ex-director of the Census Bureau. I wrote, "Richard Alba's analysis is a service to the country. I write to urge the Census Bureau and its various oversight agencies and committees to take his message seriously" (Prewitt 2016).[4] What Alba characterized as misleading thinking, and what I described as his service to the country, was projecting a nonwhite majority that was not supported by sociological theory based on more nuanced analysis of the full range of census data (discussed in more detail in this volume). This, of course, was before the nation experienced a presidential campaign that aggressively labeled immigration as a threat, and an aftermath of the election that strikes many as hospitable to angry white nationalism. Certainly the phrase "majority-minority" is now common in national political discourse, with consequences examined in a Russell Sage workshop, and now continued in this volume of *The ANNALS*.[5]

I take a detour to place the majority-minority phrase in a more general context. It is well established that official statistics shape social realities. Bourdieu writes that struggles over racial definitions and classification are "struggles over the monopoly of the power to make people see and believe, to get them to know and recognize, to impose the legitimate definition of the divisions of the social world and, thereby, to *make and unmake groups*" (Bourdieu 1991, 306, emphasis in original).

Bourdieu's influential line of reasoning is persuasive but is not the entire story. Certainly the making and unmaking of groups are located in power centers, but they are increasingly also found in how people self-identify on the census forms. The population itself can make and unmake groups. Alba reports that interracial marriage is predominantly between white and nonwhite, and results in "social identities, affiliations, and contexts of Americans … [as] on the whole *closer to those of whites than to those of minorities*" (italics added). Moreover, and of great importance, there is nothing in the conduct of the American census preventing these "closer to whites" from ticking *only* the white box. Because this is happening in substantial numbers, the arrival of a majority-minority America is continually being postponed.

Alba adds that partly black persons are an exception, either remaining multirace or identifying as black only. There is a prominent example, underscoring that inviting identity expression in census practice has consequences for the making and unmaking of groups.

The Obama rule

When President Obama returned his census form in 2010, the *New York Times* reported:

> It is official: Barack Obama is the nation's first black president.
> A White House spokesman confirmed that Mr. Obama, the son of a black father from Kenya and a white mother from Kansas, checked African American on the 2010 census questionnaire. (Roberts and Baker 2010)

The phrase, "It is official," is hyperbole. Ticking a census box does not make anything about an individual "official"—it is just a tick on a form that is then aggregated with millions of other ticks to give an estimate, in this case, of the size of the African American population group. Other ticks, biracial black and white ticks, for instance, in that same census give us an estimate of the size of a mixed-race population group—now, we see in Obama's census decision, one person fewer than it might have been (and the black race one person more).

The Census Bureau did not say of Obama "we know this person to have a white mother and African father, making him (and his daughters) biracial and will so be recorded statistically." No such thing happened or was even contemplated. This was not timidity because Obama was president. His census self-identification stands because, in the census, you are in the category you choose, or in the case of children, is chosen for you. If you are in some other category a decade later, and millions are, you have changed your mind. *Racial identity* in the census is not whether a taxi stops for you, or what is on your birth certificate, or what your grandparents thought they were. It is a tick in a box. Call that the Obama rule, and recognize that statistical races are every bit as real as socially constructed or identity races. And in the arena of public policy, only statistical races are real, and we cannot be surprised if they then are forcefully deployed in political battles over those policies.

If Obama was signaling that he feels closer to his African than to his European heritage, he is joined by many African Americans. Alba presents relevant data, as he does for the fact that other mixtures, especially white-Asians and white-Hispanics, tend to relate more easily to their European than their minority heritage. We see that similar patterns occur when mixed-race parents, for various reasons, describe their children as monoracial.

Myers and Levy carefully unpack the different ways that census race counts can be presented depending on how the multirace count is handled; one version, no less plausible than the majority-minority projection, indicates a white majority well into the century and perhaps indefinitely if children of white-Hispanic or white-Asian parents migrate to the white-only census option.

But that story has been drowned out by the majority-minority media story, now treating the presumed decline of the white population to minority status as an inevitable and official fact. For example, more than a third of the white population now describe their racial identity as extremely or very important to them (American National Election Study 2016). We do not have trend data on that number, but it is unlikely that "my white identity is important to me" response would have been so numerous two decades ago.

The current beliefs and behaviors of white Americans are affected. As reported by Craig, Rucker, and Richeson, there is "clear evidence that white Americans … experience the impending 'majority-minority' shift as a threat to their dominant (social, economic, political, and cultural) status." Whites who believe they will lose their place "at the top" of various status hierarchies are drawn to "politically conservative policy positions, including on policies most relevant to societal racial equity (e.g., affirmative action, immigration policy, harsh criminal justice policies)."

The emergence of a politically assertive white identity occurs to the extent that the binary white/nonwhite narrative gets traction. Bean, however, emphasizes that this narrative and the new forms of identity politics it spawns are inconsistent with powerful social-demographic transformations simultaneously under way. He reports on the social mobility of various nonwhite groups, whose members "have been gaining in average education and income and are experiencing less residential segregation from whites, often as a result of geographic mobility."

This finding underpins a narrative counter to the binary majority-minority framing. "Rather than emphasizing that newcomers are essentially people of color whose mobility is limited by discriminatory treatment," which supports anxiety narratives and underscores the weakening of social cohesion, there is substantial evidence on the positive impact of diversity, including ways in which it strengthens social cohesion.

For Bean and others, the most effective way to move away from the white-nonwhite picture of America's population and its majority-minority framing is to emphasize what is going on *within* the primary race groups. There we find a more nuanced and differentiated population, which we consider in Section III.

A takeaway lesson from Section I. The majority-minority projection is problematic in two respects: it will not happen by 2044, and it will possibly be postponed indefinitely. It is based on a binary framework of whites versus all other Americans, which seriously distorts the demographic realities and the lived experience of millions of Americans.

A caution about this takeaway. Of course a Census Bureau report did *not* cause an insurgent white racism, which dates to the early Crusades targeting Jews, and was then deepened by the Atlantic slave trade and colonization (Fredrickson 2002). Its twenty-first-century political traction stems from the anti-immigrant sentiment that swept across Europe and the United States. In brief, white nationalism and the specific majority-minority framing has multiple sources, all of which predate a 2015 Census Bureau Report to which we have drawn your attention. With that caution emphasized, I also underscore that political discourse has never hesitated to lift statistically grounded phrases out of context and to deploy them to shape and even deliberately mislead public opinion. We are in a heightened phase of such political practice. The final takeaway lesson is that

> it matters if America measures races, and then, of course, how the government decides what those races are. It matters because law and policy are not about an abstraction called *race* but are about races *as they are made intelligible* and acquire their numerical size in our statistical system. When we politically ask why black men are jailed at extraordinarily high rates, whether undocumented Mexican laborers are taking jobs away from working-class whites, or whether Asians have become the model minority in America, we start from a count of jailed blacks, the comparative employment patterns of Mexicans and whites, and Asian educational achievements. When our political questions are shaped by how many of which races are doing what, and when policies addressing those conditions follow, we should worry about whether the "how many" and the "which races" tell us what we need to know about what is going on in our polity, economy, and society. (Prewitt 2013, 7–8)

The Color Line, the Nativity Line

> Why should the Palatine Boors [Germans] be suffered to swarm into our Settlements, and by herding together establish their Language and Manners to the Exclusion of ours? Why should Pennsylvania, founded by the English, become a colony of *Aliens*, who will shortly be so numerous as to Germanize us instead of us Anglifying them, and will never adopt our Language or Customs, any more than they can acquire our Complexion. (Labaree 1961, 234)

Thus anxiously pondered Benjamin Franklin, 266 years ago. Obviously the alien immigrant has long been with us, always with a complexion darker than the superior English.

When in 1903 Du Bois famously wrote that "the problem of the 20th century is the problem of the color-line," Jim Crow white racism was in full stride. He correctly anticipated that the white-black color line would persist, even as the then-immigrant populations began to melt, losing their alien identities as German, Irish, Polish, or Italians. Intermarrying across nationality and religious lines, these outsiders Franklin found so threatening, would "whiten."

And what of our times? The color-line has not disappeared but it is permeable, the one-drop rule was discarded midcentury, and interracial marriages and biracial children increase their number with each census. What about the nativity-line? The nation needs to know if assimilation of the alien proceeds today, as it did for the Palatine Boors, when Germanizing the Anglos (from Christmas trees to soccer) and Anglifying the Germans (from Thanksgiving to baseball) jointly strengthened the nation.

We know less than we can and should about the pace of assimilation today, especially as it differs across the many national origin and linguistic groups that constitute today's population. Readers will know the reason—"the absence of reliable data on the children of immigrants remains the single greatest weakness in the U.S. statistical system," writes Massey. The resurgence of mass immigration starting in the 1970s was itself captured in a place of birth question, but did not statistically survive as a second generation (where were your parents born?). We now are on the verge of an unmeasured third generation.

Yet the third generation—grandchildren of the post-1965 immigrants—"will write the next chapter in the contemporary American immigrant assimilation story," writes Jimenez. Their "social, political, and economic fortunes will reveal the extent and kind of assimilation among the descendants of today's largely non-European immigrants." Tran, like Massey, emphasizes "ongoing data limitations" that have "created unique challenges for empirical assessments of second-generation decline or progress," and also draws attention to the way in which today's immigrants confront a color-line even as they navigate social and economic barriers confronting those born of foreign parents. We know from academic surveys that the nativity-line is selectively racialized, but we lack a nation-wide, detailed grasp of the scope and durability of this racialization. We are blindfolded, and open up a space for misleading exaggerations that have political consequences.

Duncan and Trejo, handicapped as well by the absence of census data, make do with the much more limited Current Population Survey (CPS) to tease out patterns of ethnic attrition, that is, the rate at which the children and grandchildren of immigrants cease to self-identify with the ethnicity of their immigrant ancestors. They report that for the third generation, "ethnic attrition predominately occurs in children with mixed parental origins." This finding is of course an important indicator of whether today's immigrants, like their nineteenth-century predecessors, are assimilating, and whether multiraciality hastens that assimilation.

I have written elsewhere (Prewitt 2013, 189–90), echoing Bean and many others, that assimilation can fail, leading to a xenophobic politics, a disillusioned and angry second generation, and heightened fears in white enclaves about the incursion of nonwhite "non-Americans." Or it can succeed, leading to cultural, economic, and political achievements similar to those produced by the successful assimilation of white ethnics in the twentieth century. More likely, there will be a mixed pattern. Some nonwhite population groups are assimilating into an America broadly understood as multiracial. But not every group is learning English, graduating from high school, naturalizing, finding a job, and buying a home at the same rate. There are second- and even third-generation Americans being left behind, often being racialized in the process. The scope and distribution of this disparity determines what kind of America is in store for us.

Realistic policy and law—on school conditions, job training, language acquisition, and homeownership—can tilt the country away from failure and toward success. Accurate statistics cannot in themselves ensure the right kind of policy and law, but the primary race framework hides variation, and is a weak basis on which to understand, let alone manage, the demographic transformation now unfolding in America.

A takeaway lesson from Section II. To again cite Massey: "the absence of reliable data on the children of immigrants remains the single greatest weakness in the U.S. statistical system." We apply Du Bois's classic prediction of the twentieth century to twenty-first-century conditions: the problem of the twenty-first century is the problem of the color line *as it* intersects and interacts with the nativity line. The census is less help than it can be to our understanding of this dynamic.

Variability within the Primary Race Categories

Though variability within America's broad race categories is a long-standing research interest, its relevance to public understanding and to policy was muted in the melting pot decades, when European nationality groups gradually assimilated, adding numeric strength to the white population and reinforcing the white/black color line. The second wave of immigration, 1970s to today, forced more attention to the nativity line—where were you, your parents, your grandparents born?—and the obvious growth of a multiracial and multiethnic population. It is in these population groups that we find substantial "within-race" variability.

Porter and Snipp, for example, note that only a few Asian countries—China, Japan, South Korea—supply the high percentage of technology workers immigrating with H1(B) visas, whose language skills, education levels, and career opportunities significantly differ from Vietnamese or Laotian immigrants. Today's immigrants from Ghana or Ethiopia differ from, and in some cases try to avoid contact with, African Americans whose ancestors arrived as slaves. Telles's complaint, cited above, that the Census Bureau is "out of step with popularly held notions of race and ethnicity," is developed in his analysis of Latinos, where he emphasizes a racial hierarchy based on "phenotypic and color gradients." This hierarchy leads some to treat their "blackness as an identity to be avoided."

A less familiar within-group variation is described by Liebler, who reports that self-identification as American Indian-Alaskan Native (AIAN) is conditioned by any number of factors, including their tribal affiliation, whether they are responding to the term ancestry or race, and their level of trust in government (and its census-takers).

Scholars emphasize that Asian Americans are significantly more likely to identify with their national origin than the "Asian race," a pattern especially prevalent in the first generation. Moreover, as noted by Lee, Ramarkrishnam, and Wong, national origin groups vary in income, occupational status, education, and health.

Consequently, data disaggregation is "a civil rights issue." Preserving the higher number of subgroup census options for the Asian race is strongly urged by academics and advocacy groups.

With approximately 11 million unauthorized persons living in the country, there are numerous policy issues relevant to how they differ from the remainder of the population. Capps, Bachmeier, and Van Hook take advantage of multiple datasets: the CPS that in a once-a-year supplement asks a question on parental place of birth and the Survey of Income and Program Participation (SIPP) that asks a question on legal status. The American Community Survey (ACS) asks neither of these questions, but has respondents' place of birth and other characteristics permitting statistical modeling that can be used to assign legal status to immigrants in this much larger survey. By combining legal status information from the SIPP with the greater statistical power of the larger ACS, researchers have been able to derive estimates of small unauthorized immigrant populations in certain locations. They have been able to model the characteristics of Deferred Action for Childhood Arrivals (DACA) participants—a group of unauthorized immigrants receiving protection from deportation under the Obama administration policy.[6] Another instance was Hurricane Harvey (August 2017) flooding large sections of Houston, where the number of unauthorized immigrants is approximately 17 percent of Houston's population of four hundred thousand—estimates critical to disaster response and communication strategies.

A takeaway lesson from Section III. Policy tied to the primary race categories, whether five or seven, makes little difference, seriously misses what a more granular measurement system provides, one making greater use of national origin categories and immigration status. Particularly problematic is the absence of African American and white subcategories in the current census classification scheme. This results, for example, in forcing recent immigrants from Ethiopia, Ghana, and Nigeria into the all-inclusive black category, despite significant educational, employment, or family structure differences from the African Americans whose ancestors most certainly did not voluntarily migrate to America (Prewitt 2013, 165–66). It is equally important to unpack white nationalism. When and how does it vary by national origin, religion, social class, or geography, and with what consequences?

The Reliability Problem

America's first census racial classification system, administered in 1790, produced counts of three races: the Europeans, soon to be recognized as citizens of the new nation; the Native Indians in the new thirteen states, separately counted and taxed, but not slated for citizenship; and the enslaved, counted as three-fifths of a person and totally excluded from civic life. It was taken for granted that this racial classification produced reliably consistent results. It was unimaginable that a large number of Americans might be recorded differently from one census to the next.

Much history separates that 1790 starting point from what we know to be true of today's census, when we routinely note the shifts in how Americans record themselves from one census to another, and across different information platforms and settings. We acknowledge and accept high levels of inconsistent and unreliable data in our race statistics. This was vividly demonstrated in the first application of mark-one-or-more. Forty percent of those who marked more than one race in the 2000 census did not give the same answer to a Census Bureau follow-up survey conducted a year later. Many had become monorace. The reverse was also true, as respondents shifted from single race in 2000 to more-than-one a year later (Bennett 2003). There is now a large research literature on multirace as a flexible identity. The self-esteem rationale invites this flexibility. Race is not biological; it is attitudinal.

Or, as Bratter notes, at any given time, those "who choose to mark more than one box are a nonrandom subset of *those who could do so*" (italics added). Those "who could do so" constitute a denominator that is not captured in the census. Roth makes a similar observation when she calls for "determining the denominator," that is, all the people who could identify in the multiracial group. However useful this might be for the research community, there is no realistic way the Census Bureau could determine that hypothetical denominator. Should the bureau have coded Obama as black and white so he would be in the correct denominator? If so, what of the unknown number of the multiracial who reported only one race in the 2010 census, but neglected to tell the *New York Times* they had done so.

How mixed-race couples identify their children adds a further level of complexity and confusion. Lichter and Qian find that a sizable share "of America's children from mixed-race marriages are identified by their parents as monoracial." More than 25 percent of the black-white and Asian-white couples do so. And there is negotiation by parents in deciding which race to favor, with various factors having an influence: the educated parent prevails or the composition of the neighborhood serves as a reference point. Overall, there is a drift in favor of whiteness, underscoring Alba's doubts about the majority-minority future.

Compounding this problem is the tendency for people to make strategic choices. Deaux writes that people present different racial identities as their social settings shift. The extent to which this occurs varies from one racial group to another. We are beginning to understand that race groups differ in the strength of their respective classification norms. Whites, blacks, and Asians have comparatively stronger, more stable norms. Hispanics and Native Americans have weaker norms and, thus, are more likely to shift depending on context. The multiracial identifiers are least likely to give consistent responses across time or settings.

Morning and Saperstein note yet another inconsistency in the data. They start with the census report that America's multirace population is approximately 2.5 percent, then, drawing on the Pew Survey of Multiracial Adults, warn that the 2.5 percent estimate is seriously misleading. It does not take into account the possibility of multiracial ancestors earlier in the family tree, before multiracial was recognized by the census. I offer a personal example. When I was five or so years old, on a visit to my paternal grandparents, an older cousin shared a hush-hush family secret; my grandmother was part Cherokee. If true (to a five-year-old she looked the part), my father was multiracial, as then am I, though both of us appear in the census record as white only—an identity that mark-one-or-more now invites me to reconsider. Morning and Saperstein write that the "multiracial population is not solely a 'first-generation' community, but rather a layered collective including second, third, and further generations." America's assimilation patterns and census practice have historically erased multirace ancestors. Morning and Saperstein, taking advantage of the Pew survey data, report a current multiracial rate of 18 percent. This, they write, is a more accurate multiracial denominator than the 2.5 percent, an argument that gives further support to the Bratter and Roth pieces.

A takeaway lesson from Section IV. There is fluidity in race statistics, prominently visible in the multirace data but not limited to that population group. Trend lines on health and employment disparities or analysis of the hardening/softening of racial boundaries or understanding rates and patterns of immigrant assimilation will vary in their accuracy as classification norms vary in their stability. The direction and scope of the bias are difficult to detect. It is another strong signal that our ancient classification categories do not adequately capture the social and demographic realities of the nation—a misalignment that frustrates the academic, misinforms the policy-maker, and confuses the public.

What Is Fixable?

The first and second conditions discussed—the majority-minority problem and the inadequacy of measuring generational differences—have easy technical fixes but face political and bureaucratic challenges. The majority-minority storyline is now too embedded in the surge of white nationalism to be easily erased. We can expect it eventually to fade if, as expected by demographic sociologists, there is a steady shift toward the white category. But that is at least a generation away. Adding parental place of birth to the ACS is technically easy. The barrier is the paper reduction act, which works to keep census questions to a minimum. Adding a question would probably require dropping a question now on the form, and every question has its constituency.[7]

The third and fourth conditions—variability within and between different race and national origin labels and less than reliable ethnoracial statistics—are substantively very different from the first two. They are embedded in the census numbers and cannot be whisked away with a technical fix. But academic research using census and federal statistics more generally should be alert to what authors in this volume emphasize: within-group variability is high, often greater than between the primary races, and there are serious reliability issues in our race statistics.

Conclusion

Is the census racial classification doing its job? Obviously "yes" is the answer but, of course, with the always present qualifier: "there is room for improvement."

The Census Bureau launched its major 2010 research, on the promise that the results of that research would help to improve the accuracy and reliability of census statistics.

With improvement in mind, I published a book with the subtitle *The Census and our Flawed Efforts to Classify Americans* (Prewitt 2013). The Princeton University Press editor asked why not "failed" instead of "flawed." Because, I replied, the census only fails if its numbers go unused, clearly not the case for any census-produced counts, least of all for its race and ethnicity numbers. What, then, to do about its flaws? The core of my argument is incremental change—take one step in 2020, another step a generation or so later, and yet another later in the century.[8]

When we reach the endpoint, the census will be making less use of the eighteenth-century primary races, with the possible exception that the African American and Native American populations will still be better served by retaining their identity as such. They uniquely experienced centuries of punitive and cumulative disadvantage; it does not get fixed in decades, even when there is a will to do so.

The Hispanics, Asians, Native Hawaiian Pacific Islanders, and, if a separate race, the Middle-Eastern North Africans, will, I suggest, benefit from measurement more attuned to their variability and diversity based on national origin and linguistic differences. They also, more recently arrived, will assimilate differently from one national origin to another, a process that will occur across the rest of the century (maybe beyond, depending on immigration rates in the decades ahead).

My guides in reaching this conclusion are Michael Omi and Howard Winant, who ask whether America is best understood through a more cultural or more racial lens (Omi and Winant 1994). Critics of the cultural focus claim that it ignores the persistent color line that was and remains racist in its construction, including the American instinct to racialize any newly arrived nonwhite immigrant groups. The counterargument is that the racial lens hides too much about the highly varied way in which different immigrant groups have made a place for themselves in American society.

Census statistics are not a neutral bystander. Insofar as they are structured as Blumbachian primary races, they favor the more racial interpretation and, in their lack of detail about national origin and the importance of generational differences, they miss much of importance to a cultural interpretation. I want to loosen the grip of the primary race classification.

David Hollinger has made clear that this loosening need not come at the expense of robust racial measurement. The design can be sufficiently flexible that the analyst, advocate, and policy-maker can have it both ways (Hollinger 2005). The proposal now under review in the OMB is a major step in this direction. It allows data to be disaggregated by national origin/tribal affiliation. It also allows the data to be reaggregated into the primary races, be they five or seven. It also allows special purpose groups to be constituted for academic or policy purposes. For example, all national origin/tribal groups with limited education could be assembled—white Appalachians, inner-city African Americans, Hispanic migrant workers, Native American Indians on impoverished reservations, selected Asian nationalities. Today's race borders need to be porous. This is happening in the lived experience of millions of Americans; it needs to happen in the statistics that try to capture the lived experience. The articles that follow make a compelling case for greater granularity and flexibility in federal statistics, led by the Census Bureau.

Notes

1. Do not blame the Census Bureau for the "other" category. It is imposed by Congress. The Hispanic members of Congress would do Americans a favor by withdrawing that now anachronistic requirement.

2. A gesture in this direction was the mulatto count in late nineteenth-century censuses, and even once adding quadroon and octoroon. The data were ignored.

3. As of this writing, December 2017, these are Census Bureau proposals being reviewed by the Trump administration and awaiting congressional attention and action. If, as is possible, Census 2020 does not modify the Hispanic and race questions as indicated by the Bureau's research, all is not lost. The recommended change need not wait for 2030; it could be incorporated in the ACS much earlier if a different administration were to support it.

4. Following the "mark-one-or-more" option in the 2000 census, it was the Department of Justice (DoJ) that decided how the 2.4 million Americans who ticked more than one racial box in 2000 would be allocated (OMB 2000). Mindful of the resistance to the mark-one-or-more option by the NAACP and other advocacy organizations, DoJ decided that in cases resting on a claim of racial discrimination, the complaining minority would be allocated all those who have indicated they are any part of that racial minority. There was scattered grumbling that this echoed the one-drop rule, but the allocation was politically possible because it protected the minority groups disadvantaged by the multiple-race option. The practice was retained by the Bush administration, continued by the Obama administration, and remains on the books today. Whether, and in what direction, the Trump administration might change this practice is, as I write, uncertain.

5. This issue of The ANNALS compiles the papers from a conference hosted by the Russell Sage Foundation on December 9, 2016. The editors are grateful for the financial and administrative support of the conference by the Foundation and especially to Sheldon Danziger, its President; Aixa Cintrón-Vélez, Program Director; and Leana Chatrath, Program Officer. The coeditors also express appreciation to Katherine Wallman, then the nation's OMB-based Chief Statistician of the United States, for encouraging us to explore issues now addressed in this volume. We appreciate as well the candor and responsiveness of senior staff of the Census Bureau who participated in the workshop, patiently explaining the reasons for and conclusions reached in the extensive study of the Hispanic and race questions following the 2010 census. Finally, I, though listed as a coeditor, emphasize that Richard Alba organized the workshop, carefully reviewed and edited each contribution, and in every important respect deserves credit for this volume.

6. As of this writing, the Trump administration is taking action to have that protection revoked.

7. There was a major effort to add the place of birth in time for the 2010 census, when it was assumed by many that the ancestry question—because the data are not used in government programs—could be easily dropped. However, ancestry data are highly valued by Americans who want to trace their ancestors. Opposition from this group, coupled with a brewing congressional effort to convert ACS into a voluntary survey (which would have substantially reduced the ACS response rate), weighed against initiating action at the time.

8. This sentence oversimplifies a complex argument. Essentially, the civil rights generation (1940–2010) needed the primary race categories, especially of course comparing the African American and white disparities, but they are aging out of the population. The multirace generation (1970–2040) needs to understand the assimilation and intermarriage of the immigrant surge. The expected (hoped for) changes for the 2020 census will help, but the next generation (2020–2070?) needs more detailed national origin measures, as well as second- and third-generation counts, which will give us a "national origin" generation stretching to the next century. Or something along these lines (see Prewitt 2013, 197–201).

References

Alba, Richard. 11 January 2016. The likely persistence of a white majority: How Census Bureau statistics have mislead thinking about the American future. *The American Prospect*, Winter.
American National Election Study. 2016. *Pilot study*. Available from http://www.electionstudies.org/study-pages/anes_pilot_2016/anes_pilot_2016.htm.
Bennett, Claudette. 2003. Exploring the consistency of race reporting in Census 2000 and the Census Quality Survey. Paper presented at the Joint Meetings of the American Statistical Association, San Francisco, 3–7 August.
Bourdieu, Pierre. 1991. *Language and symbolic power*, ed. John B. Tompson, trans. Gino Raymond and Matthew Arnold. Cambridge, MA: Harvard University Press.
Fredrickson, George. 2002. *Racism: A short history*. Princeton, NJ: Princeton University Press.
Hollinger, David. 2005. *Post-ethnic America: Beyond multiculturalism*, 3rd ed. New York, NY: Basic Books.
Knowles, Louis L., and Kenneth Prewitt, eds. 1969. *Institutional racism in America*. Englewood Cliffs, NJ: Prentice Hall.
Labaree, Leonard W., ed. 1961. Observations concerning the increase of mankind, people of counties, etc. In *The paper of Benjamin Franklin*, vol. 4. New Haven, CT: Yale University Press.
Lopez, Ian Haney. 2005. Race on the 2010 Census: Hispanics and the shrinking majority. *Daedalus* 134:42–52.
National Advisory Commission on Civil Disorders. 1968. *Our nation is moving toward two societies, one black, one nation—Separate and unequal*. New York, NY: Bantam Books.
Office of Management and Budget. 2000. *Guidance on aggregation and allocation of data for use in civil rights monitoring and enforcement*. Bulletin 00-02. Washington DC: Office of Management and Budget.
Omi, Michael, and Howard Winant. 1994. *Racial formation in the United States*, 2nd ed. New York, NY: Routledge.
Parkinson, Robert. 2017. *The common cause: Creating race and nation in the American Revolution*. Chapel Hill, NC: University of North Carolina Press.
Prewitt, Kenneth. 2013. *What is your race? The census and our flawed effort to classify Americans*. Princeton, NJ: Princeton University Press.
Prewitt, Kenneth. 2016. Reframing race in the census. Comment on "The likely persistence of a white majority," by Richard Alba. *The American Prospect*, Winter.
Roberts, Sam, and Peter Baker. 2010. Asked to declare his race, Obama checks "black." *New York Times*. Available from http://www.nytimes.com/2010/04/03/us/politics/03census.html.
Schor, Paul. 2005. Mobilizing for pure prestige? Challenging federal census categories in the USA (1850–1940). *International Social Science Journal* 183:89–101.
U.S. Census Bureau. 2015. *Non-Hispanic whites may no longer comprise over 50 percent of the U.S. population by 2044*. Washington, DC: U.S. Census Bureau.
U.S. House of Representatives, 150th Cong., 1st sess. 1998. *Federal measures of race and ethnicity and the implications for the 2000 Census: Hearings before the Subcommittee on Government Management, Information, and Technology of the Committee on Government Reform and Oversight, April 23, May 22, and July 25, 1997*. Washington, DC: Government Printing Office.
Williams, Kim. 2006. *Mark one or more: Civil rights in multiracial America*. Ann Arbor, MI: University of Michigan Press.

I: The Significance of Ethno-Racial Mixing

The Rise of Mixed Parentage: A Sociological and Demographic Phenomenon to Be Reckoned With

By
RICHARD ALBA,
BRENDEN BECK,
and
DUYGU BASARAN SAHIN

Ethno-racially mixed parentage is rising in frequency, creating a strong challenge to both census classification schemes and, indeed, to common conceptions of ethnicity and race. Majority (white) and minority (nonwhite or Hispanic) parentage predominates among individuals with mixed-family backgrounds. Yet in public presentations of census data and population projections, individuals with mixed backgrounds are generally classified as nonwhite. We analyze 2013 American Community Survey data and summarize the results of important studies to argue that individuals from mixed majority-minority backgrounds resemble whites more than they do minorities in terms of some key social characteristics and experiences, such as where they grow up and their social affiliations as adults. Those with a black parent are an important exception. An implication of this analysis is that census classification practices for mixed individuals risk distorting conceptions of the current population, especially its youthful portion, and promoting misunderstandings of ethno-racial change.

Keywords: ethnicity and race; ethno-racial mixing; population change; diversity; census data; population projections

Ethno-racial mixing is nothing new in the United States—it was observed as early as the colonial era (Gordon 1964). In the

Richard Alba is distinguished professor of sociology at the Graduate Center of the City University of New York. His most recent book, coauthored with Nancy Foner, is Strangers No More *(Princeton University Press 2015).*

Brenden Beck is a PhD candidate in sociology at the Graduate Center of the City University of New York. His dissertation analyzes low-level policing in the contexts of suburbanization, gentrification, and fiscal crises. His research has appeared in Social Forces *and* Crime & Delinquency.

Duygu Basaran Sahin is a PhD candidate in sociology at the Graduate Center of the City University of New York (CUNY) and a research fellow at the CUNY Institute for Demographic Research. Her work centers on race/ethnicity and housing and urban inequality.

Correspondence: ralba@gc.cuny.edu

DOI: 10.1177/0002716218757656

post–World War II period, the rise of marriage on a large scale across ethnic and religious lines among whites played a leading role in the story of mass assimilation, which forged a white mainstream that included the descendants of late-nineteenth- and early-twentieth-century immigrants from Ireland and southern and eastern Europe (Alba and Nee 2003). Throughout American history, moreover, whites' dominant status has been expressed in sexual encounters across racial lines, particularly between white men and minority women, which have produced children. When these children were mixed white and black, they were consigned to the African American population by the so-called one-drop rule. When the children were mixed white and American Indian, they had a greater chance of being absorbed into the white population (see Liebler, this volume).

The level of ethno-racial mixing—now across the major lines of race and Hispanic ancestry—is rising again. A recent analysis by the Pew Research Center found that 17 percent of the newlyweds of 2015 had married across these lines (Livingston and Brown 2017; see also Frey 2015). Intermarriage has been increasing steadily since the 1967 *Loving v. Virginia* decision of the U.S. Supreme Court invalidated the remaining state-level antimiscegenation laws; at that time, the rate of interracial marriage was just 3 percent. The growth of interracial and interethnic marriage reflects also the surging diversity of the U.S. population, itself a product of post-1965 mass immigration. Intermarriage is accordingly more common in those regions of the country that are more diverse (Lee and Bean 2010; Livingston and Brown 2017). Despite the apparent meaning of diversity in the burgeoning of different minority groups, however, the predominant pattern of intermarriage takes the form of a majority-minority couple, that is, where one partner is white and the other minority. According to the Pew report, such marriages are about 80 percent of the total; about half of these marriages involve non-Hispanic whites with Hispanic partners.

The rising level of mixing—specifically, the growing number of young people coming from mixed-family backgrounds—poses a potent challenge to our conventional statistical schemes for ethnicity and race and to our perceptions of the present and near future of American society. The current situation seems novel in the degree of social recognition accorded mixed ethno-racial parentage as an independent status, rather than one that must be amalgamated to one group or another (as in the "one-drop" rule). The Census Bureau's important decision to allow multiple-race reporting starting in 2000 is an acknowledgement of this new reality but also has contributed to it by creating statistical "facts" concerning racial mixture that permeate into public consciousness (Perlmann and Waters 2002).

Nevertheless, the public presentation of census data about ethno-racial change is generally cast in terms of two mutually exclusive categories, whites and nonwhites, the latter usually taken as synonymous with members of minority groups. Thus, the Census Bureau declared that in 2011, for the first time, nonwhite babies outnumbered white ones (although a subsequent revision showed the claim to be mistaken; see Cohn 2016). Likewise, its report on its 2014 projections of the U.S. population foresaw that "by 2044 more than half of all Americans are projected to belong to a minority group" (Colby and Ortman 2015, 1). This binary conception of the population would seem on its face inadequate to comprehend the new social realities associated with ethno-racial mixing on a substantial scale.

In this article, we examine Census Bureau statistical practices in light of these new realities. We ask whether the practices relevant to ethnic and racial data distort important population changes and convey to demographers and the public a misleading picture of ethno-racial divisions. Of course, to understand the relationship of statistical categories to social realities, we also need to know more than the mere frequencies of ethno-racial mixing and parentage. A substantial part of what follows therefore is taken up with a summary of what is known about the characteristics of Americans coming from ethno-racially mixed-family backgrounds—the circumstances in which they are raised, along with their adult identities and social affiliations. Though much more research into this rapidly growing, predominantly youthful, group is needed, the evidence in hand is sufficient to allow us to conclude that Census Bureau statistical practices need revision to better take into account the new social realities.

A Statistical Paradox

A rarely noted demographic paradox signals unresolved issues in our official statistical systems: according to Census Bureau estimates, the majority of babies born in the United States since 2013 have been nonwhite (Cohn 2016); but the National Center for Health Statistics (NCHS; 2015) finds that so far, in each year of the new century, non-Hispanic white mothers continue to bear the majority of births—about 54 percent in 2014.

The apparent contradiction revolves around the treatment of infants with ethno-racially mixed parentage, whom the Census Bureau classifies according to the way they are identified on the American Community Survey (ACS) by their parents, with children of reported mixed race or any Hispanic ancestry categorized as nonwhite or minority, even when one of their parents is non-Hispanic white. The NCHS, meanwhile, uses the mother's ethno-racial group as recorded on the birth certificate.

Census Bureau classification practices are affected both by the way that ethno-racial data are collected, as well as by decisions made when more than one race is reported. Since 1980, the information has been recorded in a two-question format, one for race (with multiple responses allowed since 2000) and one for Hispanic origin (single response only). (The two-question format used on the 2010 census is shown in Figure 1; the Bureau considered merging the two questions for 2020 but has now rejected this option.) This format excludes the possibility of reporting mixed Hispanic/non-Hispanic origins: anyone reporting a Hispanic origin is regarded as unmixed Hispanic, regardless of what reported on the race question (since Hispanics may be "of any race," according to the common formulation). Multiple races are recorded and thus available for analysis in most census datasets; however, the most widely available tabulations report race in mutually exclusive

FIGURE 1
Questions about Race and Hispanic Origin Used on the 2010 Census

→ **NOTE: Please answer BOTH Question 5 about Hispanic origin and Question 6 about race. For this census, Hispanic origins are not races.**

5. **Is this person of Hispanic, Latino, or Spanish origin?**
   - ☐ **No,** not of Hispanic, Latino, or Spanish origin
   - ☐ Yes, Mexican, Mexican Am., Chicano
   - ☐ Yes, Puerto Rican
   - ☐ Yes, Cuban
   - ☐ Yes, another Hispanic, Latino, or Spanish origin — *Print origin, for example, Argentinean, Colombian, Dominican, Nicaraguan, Salvadoran, Spaniard, and so on.*

6. **What is this person's race?** *Mark ☒ one or more boxes.*
   - ☐ White
   - ☐ Black, African Am., or Negro
   - ☐ American Indian or Alaska Native — *Print name of enrolled or principal tribe.*

   - ☐ Asian Indian   ☐ Japanese   ☐ Native Hawaiian
   - ☐ Chinese   ☐ Korean   ☐ Guamanian or Chamorro
   - ☐ Filipino   ☐ Vietnamese ☐ Samoan
   - ☐ Other Asian — *Print race, for example, Hmong, Laotian, Thai, Pakistani, Cambodian, and so on.*   ☐ Other Pacific Islander — *Print race, for example, Fijian, Tongan, and so on.*

   - ☐ Some other race — *Print race.*

SOURCE: U.S. Census Bureau.

categories, with individuals having both white and nonwhite ancestries classified usually in a mixed category that is regarded as part of the minority population (see also Myers and Levy, this volume). "Whites" in these tabulations are therefore individuals who report solely "white" on the race question.

These classification practices lie behind the growing difference between the figures from the Census Bureau and the NCHS for the ethno-racial composition of the infant population. This difference demonstrates that the magnitude of ethno-racially mixed parentage among young children is now large enough to affect substantively the way that we think about the American population and the changes occurring to it. This is not only the case for our assessment of the current state of the population, but even more so, for our projections of it in the future. The category classifications of individuals in the census data that provide the starting point for population projections ramify through them. That is, individuals who in reality are partly white but are classified as not white remain in that category in future years and have children who are not white (in the great majority, a qualification made necessary by the technicalities of the procedure that assigns ethno-racial status to projected children).

Quite obviously, then, to understand better the consequences of classifying individuals from mixed-family backgrounds, we need to know more about them to reflect on the most appropriate ways to take the new mixing into account. We draw three main conclusions in what follows.

The mixed-parentage group is sizable among young Americans and complex in its composition, but mixed majority-minority backgrounds dominate

We begin by looking at infants (children under one year of age), because they provide the best opportunity to unravel the complexities of parentage and ethno-racial background as reported on the census. That is, we have the greatest chance with infants of finding both parents (whether married or not) in the same household. Accordingly, we have analyzed 2013 ACS data, examining what parents say about their own ethno-racial backgrounds as well as what they say about the infant's. For the quarter of infants who reside with only one parent, we have compared the report for the child against that for the parent, presuming that many single parents will acknowledge the background of the other, even if that other parent is nonresident.

We find that 14 to 15 percent of U.S.-born infants have parents of different races or one Hispanic and one non-Hispanic parent (for a more detailed discussion of the results, see Alba, Beck, and Sahin 2018). The 2013 figure represents an increase, albeit not large, from that in 2000, when 11 percent of infants had mixed parentage. As Figure 2 (limited to children with two coresident parents because of the greater certainty about their backgrounds) shows, the large majority—almost four-fifths—of the mixed infants of 2013 have one non-Hispanic white parent and one minority one. Those where the minority parent is Hispanic form by far the largest portion—these partly Anglo, partly Hispanic infants make up more than 40 percent of all infants from mixed-family backgrounds. Children who are white and Asian or white and black are each about a ninth of the total. Among the remaining majority-minority mixtures, the dominant combination involves a white parent paired with a partly white (i.e., mixed-race) parent—in other words, these are children who may have three white grandparents. This combination constitutes about an eighth of the total.

The fifth or so of mixed infants without a non-Hispanic white parent display a more heterogeneous set of patterns. Overall, children with one Hispanic and one non-Hispanic parent are almost 60 percent of this group. The largest portion

FIGURE 2
Ethno-Racial Mixes among 2013 Infants (Only Infants in Two-Parent Families)

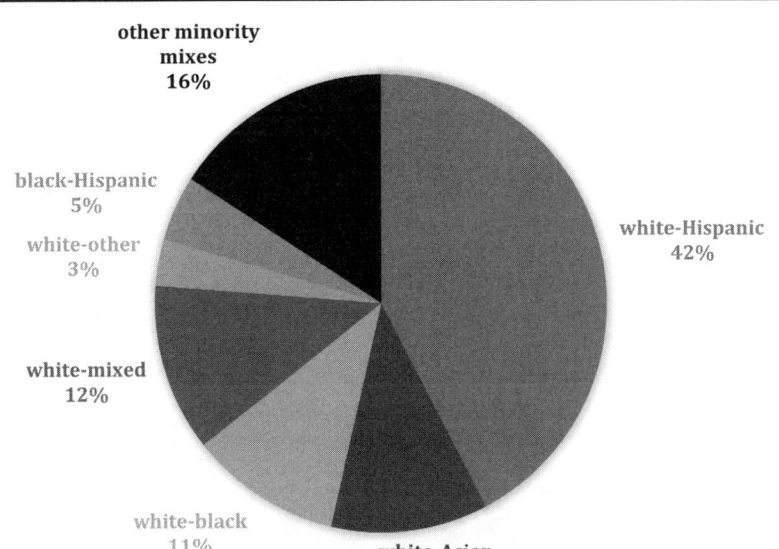

among them is made up of infants whose other parent is non-Hispanic black—they are about 5 percent of all mixed infants. Another group encompasses the children of two parents who each have mixed race—they are about 3 percent of all mixed infants, and most of them have some white ancestry on both sides (but they are classified in Figure 1 as minority in keeping with census categorization conventions).

The mixed-family backgrounds of these infants are not always reflected in the ways their parents report them on the census or the Census Bureau treats them in their reports. As already noted, one of the major problems of census data concerns the oversimplification of mixtures involving some Hispanic ancestry: a tick mark indicating that an individual is Hispanic means that he or she will be regarded as exclusively Hispanic, regardless of what is reported on the race question. In the case of children who have one white and one Hispanic parent, more than three-quarters therefore are reported in a way that results in categorization as Hispanic; 22 percent are classified as non-Hispanic and white. In the case of children who are black and Hispanic, the distribution is even more lopsided: more than 80 percent appear as Hispanic, and 13 percent are reported as non-Hispanic black.

For the infants with one white and one nonwhite, non-Hispanic parent, almost three-quarters are reported as having mixed race by their parents, with the remainder divided between the white and a minority category (17 percent white, 12 percent minority, respectively). The children who have a white and a black parent are the least likely to be reported as white. Children who have one white and one partly white parent are the most likely to be reported as white, but only 30 percent are.

The growing population of mixed children is creating heterogeneity within major ethno-racial populations, especially the minority ones. For instance, of the children with an Asian parent, about 30 percent also have a non-Asian parent. The figures are similar for children with black or Hispanic parents. For children with an American Indian parent, the percentage is much higher: more than two-thirds have a non–American Indian parent.

The social identities, affiliations, and contexts of Americans from mixed majority-minority backgrounds are on the whole closer to those of whites than to those of minorities, with partly black persons an exception

Given the high proportion of ethno-racial mixtures that involve majority and minority parents, we have to ask whether it is reasonable to regard mixed individuals in wholesale fashion as minorities, or even to impose the majority/minority dichotomy on them in the first place. The term *minority* can invoke multiple meanings, engendering confusion about how to understand statements such as the Census Bureau's claim that "most children younger than age 1 are minorities" (U.S. Census Bureau 2012). One meaning of *minority* could be: not solely non-Hispanic white. But this is a rather technical understanding. In common parlance, *minority* connotes a person who is not white or is Hispanic or, alternatively, is a member of a disadvantaged group. One of the latter meanings appears often in the public translation of Bureau statements, as in NPR's July 1, 2016, article titled, "Babies of Color Are Now the Majority, Census Says."

The data that we possess about individuals from mixed backgrounds are admittedly on the thin side, but with important qualifications they do not support the notion that those who are partly white (non-Hispanic understood) generally should be viewed as members of ethno-racial minorities. The data we discuss come partly from analyses of ACS data and partly from surveys such as the Pew surveys of Multiracial Americans (2015) and of Americans with Hispanic ancestry (Lopez, Gonzalez-Barrera, and López 2017), as well as from studies by Edward Telles and Vilma Ortiz (2008) and by Jennifer Lee and Frank Bean (2010).

To begin, partly white infants appear on the whole to be growing up in circumstances similar to those of infants with only white parents; infants of white and black parentage are the major exceptions to this generalization. (The discussion that follows focuses again on the three-quarters of infants with two co-resident parents.) In terms of family income (see Figure 3), the mixed families with one white parent generally have an average level of affluence more like that of white families than they do that of families with two parents belonging to the same group as the minority partner. This is especially the case when the white parent is the father. For instance, the median family income when the father is white and the mother is Hispanic ($70,000) is scarcely distinguishable from that for white families ($72,800) and is much higher than that in Hispanic families ($34,800). The median household income when the father is Hispanic and the other is white ($57,600) is decidedly lower than that of the reverse pairing but is still much higher than that in Hispanic families.

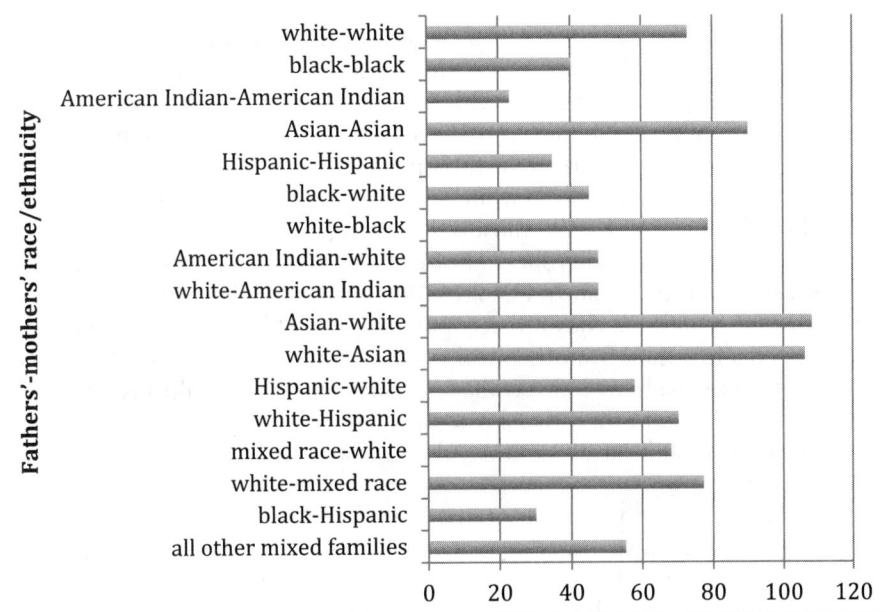

FIGURE 3
Median Family Incomes for Infants with Different Mixed and Unmixed Parentage (Only for Infants in Two-Parent Families), 2013

Families with the combination of white and Asian parents are the most affluent of all types, with median family incomes (above $100,000 regardless of which parent is white and which Asian) higher than those of either white- or Asian-only families ($72,800 and $90,000, respectively). By contrast, families with black fathers and white mothers, the most common black-white pairing, are only slightly advantaged in income terms compared to families of two black parents ($45,000 vs. $40,000).

Since income is related to housing, this broad profile of similarity to the situations of white families, with variations according to the precise mix of the parents of the infants, carries over into residential space. Distinguishing crudely between "outer-urban and suburban homeowners" versus "inner-city renters" (we are limited by the categories available in microdata; see Alba, Beck, and Sahin 2018), we find that white families are much more concentrated in the former—about half there versus a fifth in the latter category. For the black and Hispanic families with infants, the proportions are reversed.

The mixed white and Asian families are even more concentrated in the outer-urban and suburban owner category than are the all-white families. White and Hispanic families and also white and racially mixed ones are found considerably more in these advantaged contexts than in urban renter ones, but their distribution between the two is not as lopsided as in the all-white case. White and black families are more often in the urban renter category than in the other, and when the father is black—the more common case—their distribution between the two is no different from that of all-black families.

For insight into the identities and experiences of individuals with multiracial backgrounds, we can turn to the Pew multiracial survey, although it has the limitation that the sample is dominated by individuals of mixed white and American Indian ancestry (because its operationalization of multiraciality extended several generations back [see Morning and Saperstein, this volume]). In particular, the sample of individuals of mixed white and Asian background is small ($n = 88$). However, the results are consistent with other studies, especially that by Lee and Bean (2010). Another limitation: it does not consider mixed ethnicity (non-Hispanic ancestry) for those who are also Hispanic.

These data indicate that partly white adults possess more fluid social identities than unmixed adults but for the most part appear comfortable with the white or European sides of their backgrounds. For instance, individuals who are white and Asian or white and American Indian are likely to feel that they have a lot in common with whites and that they are accepted by them. Their social distance from whites appears less than from the groups of their minority heritage. These individuals are more likely to believe that a casual observer would take them for white than for another ethno-racial category. Nevertheless, those who are white and Asian favor a multiracial identity, while those who are white and American Indian do not.

Individuals who are partly black are quite distinct in these ways (see also Rocquemore and Brunsma 2007). Individuals who are white and black show a stronger sense of identity and affiliation with blacks than with whites. These mixed black individuals believe they have a lot in common with other blacks and feel very accepted by them. They think that casual observers are more likely to see them as black than as white or multiracial. The distinctiveness of black ancestry for mixing highlights the continuing power of antiblack racism in the United States (Alba and Foner 2015).

For data about the identities and experiences of individuals who are partly Hispanic and partly white, we can turn to two sources: one is the intergenerational survey of Mexican Americans first conducted in the 1960s and then updated for the next generation in the 1990s by Telles and Ortiz. In their conclusion, Telles and Ortiz (2008, 281; see also Duncan and Trejo [2007, this volume]) lay out the impact of mixed ancestry very clearly: "The ... children with a non-Hispanic parent were less likely to know Spanish, were more likely to intermarry themselves, identified less with their Mexican origin, and were more likely to call themselves American. Such children were often perceived as and understood themselves as less Mexican." The other source, Pew's complementary surveys of Americans with Hispanic ancestry (Lopez, Gonzalez-Barrera, and López 2017), adds additional confirming detail. It reveals a weakening of Hispanic identity across generations, as the frequency of mixed backgrounds rises. By the fourth generation, half no longer identify as Hispanic.

The Pew Survey of Multiracial Adults is also informative about social milieus of adults from mixed racial backgrounds. Most individuals who are white and American Indian live in white-dominated social worlds. Almost three-quarters say that all or most of their friends are white, and two-thirds live in largely white neighborhoods. Those who are white and Asian appear to inhabit more diverse worlds, but ones in which whites still are likely the majority. Nearly half say that most or all their friends are white, compared to just 7 percent who say this about Asians; and nearly two-thirds say that all or most of their neighbors are white. Individuals who are white and black are in rather different milieus. Half of them say that all or most of their friends are black. However, just a third claim to live in mostly black neighborhoods; more than 40 percent live in mostly white neighborhoods.

The marriage patterns of individuals of mixed race can be studied in census data, though with considerable uncertainty about how fully adults report racial mixture. Individuals who report being partly white most often take white partners. In a recent analysis, Miyawaki (2015) shows that white–American Indian and white-Asian individuals have high rates of marriage to whites—around 70 percent. Most white-black persons also marry whites. In all cases, the rates of marriage to someone from their same minority background are much lower. These results seem consistent with other analyses, such as Qian and Lichter (2011). The gap in choice of a white or minority partner can be expected to subside somewhat as the white proportion of the marriageable population declines.

In one key respect—stability of ethno-racial reporting over time—the demographic behavior of individuals of mixed parentage is quite distinct

The social identities of individuals from mixed backgrounds are more fluid and contingent than those of other Americans, and consequently their reports on census race and Hispanic-origin questions are much less stable over time. (We do not know, obviously, whether these reports are made by them or by other household members, but almost always the individuals who make them have intimate knowledge of the family backgrounds involved.)

This inconsistency emerges powerfully from the analysis by Carolyn Liebler et al. (2017) of a matched 2000–2010 census file. The largest shifts between censuses, apart from changes in the race reporting of Hispanics (typically, between the white and other race categories), involve individuals who appear as mixed on one of the censuses. Large movements, for example, occur between the non-Hispanic white and the white Hispanic categories, implying that a sizable portion in the latter group comes from mixed backgrounds. Another big shift occurs between the mixed white and American Indian and the unmixed white categories, and a similar one involves the mixed white and Asian category (Liebler et al. 2017, Table 4).

This inconsistency over time makes mixed-race reporting especially unstable; moreover, when it shifts to a single race, that race is most likely to be white. For instance, of those who are reported as mixed white and Asian on either census, 63 percent are reported as being single race on the other; and white responses outnumber Asian ones by 60 percent in this group (see Table 1). An even more extreme version of this pattern appears for individuals who are reported as white and American Indian on either census. Among the almost 90 percent who appear as single race on the other census, whites outnumber American Indians by a

TABLE 1
Ethno-Racial Turnover among Individuals Who Are Reported as Mixed
White and Asian on 2000 or 2010 Censuses

2000 Category	2010 Category	N (1,000s)	Percentage
White & Asian	White & Asian	280.1	37.4
White & Asian	White	102.9	13.7
White & Asian	Asian	86.5	11.6
White	White & Asian	186.2	24.9
Asian	White & Asian	93.1	12.4

SOURCE: Liebler et al. (2017), Table 4.

margin of four to one. A mixed-race combination that shows a different pattern is—unsurprisingly—that of white and black. The inconsistency between the 2000 and 2010 censuses is about 60 percent. However, the single race chosen on the other census is much more likely to be black than white.

Given the substantial representation of ethno-racial mixture among the U.S.-born children with at least one minority parent—roughly 30 percent among Asians and Hispanics, it will be remembered—this "churning" (as Liebler et al. [2017] describe it), should it continue, is likely to have as-yet-undetermined future effects on the measured characteristics of U.S.-born minority groups in census data. It also carries powerful implications for the population projections, which start from estimates that rely on these unstable ethno-racial reports. The risk—and it seems sizable—is that Census Bureau projections exaggerate the decline of the non-Hispanic white majority and convey to Americans a distorted picture of population change.

Any exaggeration should not be regarded as neutral in its implications. As two articles in this volume demonstrate (by Craig, Rucker, and Richeson; and Myers and Levy), predictions of a demographic shift to a majority-minority society by the middle of this century alarm many whites, stoking anxieties about their future loss of status. As a result, these predictions appear to have political consequences: by stimulating zero-sum thinking, they encourage some whites to take more conservative positions on questions of racial justice and immigration.

Conclusion

Although ethno-racial mixing in the United States is nothing new, the social recognition granted to the mixed backgrounds of young Americans with parents from different groups makes contemporary mixing something different. This mixing presents a strong challenge to common conceptions and statistical accountings of ethno-racial group membership, which tend still to reflect older social realities of mutually exclusive groups, with every individual belonging to one, and only one, of them.

Also consistent with older social realities is a binary division of the population between majority (white) and minority, a division that guides many public presentations of demographic data about the growing diversity of the United States. The classification practices of the Census Bureau, which assign all individuals who report ethno-racially mixed backgrounds (whether these involve multiple racial origins or mixes of Hispanic and non-Hispanic ancestries) to the minority side of this division, distort the social realities of contemporary mixing. As we have shown, most ethno-racial mixing involves both white and minority parentage. The available evidence strongly suggests that individuals from majority-minority backgrounds—with the important exception of those with black parentage—resemble whites more than they do minorities in key social characteristics and experiences.

This is not in any respect an argument that these individuals should be classified on the majority side of a binary division. It is rather an observation about the futility of imposing a binary division on social realities that increasingly puncture such a neat compartmentalization. At this moment, given the beginning state of our knowledge, it is critical, first, to measure ethno-racial backgrounds as accurately as possible, although the fluidity of their social identities creates challenges (see also Morning and Saperstein, this volume; Roth, this volume). Especially important given the limitations of existing census data is to be able to identify individuals who are partly Hispanic and partly non-Hispanic, since they make up by far the largest subgroup of the mixed population. The proposed merger of the two questions used to collect ethno-racial data for the 2020 Census could have provided a solution, but a recent Census Bureau decision has taken it out of consideration. Second, it is critical to avoid presenting the data in highly simplified ways that amalgamate individuals from mixed backgrounds to conventional ethno-racial categories. The classification, for instance, of individuals who report being partly white as nonwhite—current Census Bureau practice—seems absurd on its face.

Our statistical categories for comprehending growing diversity need to acknowledge the novelty and importance of the rising levels of ethno-racial mixing in American families. This mixing is engendering ever larger numbers of individuals whose ties of kinship span wide majority-minority divides. In a society where ethno-racial inequalities remain large and seem intractable, this mixing is a phenomenon to be reckoned with.

References

Alba, Richard, Brenden Beck, and Duygu Basaran Sahin. 2018. The U.S. mainstream expands—again. *Journal of Ethnic and Migration Studies* 44:99–117.

Alba, Richard, and Nancy Foner. 2015. *Strangers no more: Immigration and the challenges of integration in North America and Western Europe*. Princeton, NJ: Princeton University Press.

Alba, Richard, and Victor Nee. 2003. *Remaking the American mainstream: Assimilation and contemporary immigration*. Cambridge, MA: Harvard University Press.

Cohn, D'Vera. 23 June 2016. *It's official: Minority babies are the majority among the nation's infants, but only just*. Pew Research Center brief. Washington, DC: Pew Research Center.

Colby, Sandra, and Jennifer Ortman. 2015. *Projections of the size and composition of the U.S. population: 2014 to 2060*. Census Population Reports. Washington, DC: U.S. Census Bureau.

Craig, Maureen, Julian Rucker, and Jennifer Richeson. 2018. Racial and political dynamics of an approaching "majority-minority" United States. *The ANNALS of the American Academy of Political and Social Science* (this volume).

Duncan, Brian, and Stephen Trejo. 2007. Ethnic identification, intermarriage, and unmeasured progress by Mexican Americans. In *Mexican immigration to the United States*, ed. George Borjas, 229–67. Chicago, IL: University of Chicago Press.

Duncan, Brian, and Stephen Trejo. 2018. Identifying the later-generation descendants of U.S. immigrants: Issues arising from selective ethnic attrition. *The ANNALS of the American Academy of Political and Social Science* (this volume).

Frey, William. 2015. *The diversity explosion: How new racial demographics are remaking America*. Washington, DC: Brookings Institution.

Gordon, Milton. 1964. *Assimilation in American life*. New York, NY: Oxford University Press.

Lee, Jennifer, and Frank Bean. 2010. *The diversity paradox: Immigration and the color line in twenty-first century America*. New York, NY: Russell Sage Foundation.

Liebler, Carolyn. 2018. Counting America's First Peoples. *The ANNALS of the American Academy of Political and Social Science* (this volume).

Liebler, Carolyn, Sonya Porter, Leticia Fernandez, James Noon, and Sharon Ennis. 2017. America's churning races: Race and ethnicity response changes between Census 2000 and the 2010 census. *Demography* 54:259–84.

Livingston, Gretchen, and Anna Brown. 18 May 2017. *Intermarriage in the U.S. 50 years after Loving v. Virginia*. Pew Research Center brief. Washington, DC: Pew Research Center.

Lopez, Mark Hugo, Ana Gonzalez-Barrera, and Gustavo López. 20 December 2017. *Latino identity fades across generations as immigrant connections fall away*. Washington, DC: Pew Research Center.

Miyawaki, Michael. 2015. Expanding boundaries of whiteness? A look at the marital patterns of part-white multiracial groups. *Sociological Forum* 30:995–1016.

Morning, Ann, and Aliya Saperstein. 2018. The generational locus of multiraciality and its implications for racial self-identification. *The ANNALS of the American Academy of Political and Social Science* (this volume).

Myers, Dowell, and Morris Levy. 2018. Racial population projections and reactions to alternative news accounts of growing diversity. *The ANNALS of the American Academy of Political and Social Science* (this volume).

National Center for Health Statistics. 2015. *Births: Final data for 2014*. National Vital Statistics Reports. Washington, DC: National Center for Health Statistics.

Perlmann, Joel, and Mary Waters. 2002. *The new race question: How the census counts multiracial individuals*. New York, NY: Russell Sage Foundation.

Pew Research Center. 2015. *Multiracial in America: Proud, diverse and growing in numbers*. Washington, DC: Pew Research Center.

Qian, Zhenchao, and Daniel Lichter. 2011. Changing patterns of interracial marriage in a multiracial society. *Journal of Marriage and Family* 73:1065–84.

Rocquemore, Kerry Ann, and David Brunsma. 2007. *Beyond black: Biracial identity in America*. Lanham, MD: Rowman & Littlefield.

Roth, Wendy. 2018. Establishing the denominator: The challenges of measuring multiracial, Hispanic, and Native American populations. *The ANNALS of the American Academy of Political and Social Science* (this volume).

Telles, Edward, and Vilma Ortiz. 2008. *Generations of exclusion: Mexican Americans, assimilation, and race*. New York, NY: Russell Sage Foundation.

U.S. Census Bureau. 17 May 2012. Most children younger than age 1 are minorities, Census Bureau reports. Press release. Available from https://www.census.gov/newsroom/releases/archives/population/cb12-90.html.

Ethnic/Racial Identity: Fuzzy Categories and Shifting Positions

By
KAY DEAUX

Demographic changes and increasing diversity in the United States bring about changes in how people define themselves and how they categorize others. I describe three issues that are relevant to the labeling and self-definition of ethnic groups in U.S. society: (1) the creation and definition of identity categories, (2) the subjectivity of self-definition, and (3) the flexibility of identity expression. In each case, substantial research from social psychology and related disciplines supports a socially constructed definition and use of ethnic categories, wherein identities are subject to the influence of local and national norms and are amenable to change across situations and over time.

Keywords: categorization; ethnic identity; identity expression; multiple identities; social construction

In an advertisement for Ancestry.com, a user named Lezlie describes the curiosity she encountered from others concerning her ethnicity: What was she? Not certain herself, she found an answer to questions about her heritage in the online service: 35 percent Great Britain, 24 percent Ghana and Ivory Coast, 22 percent Congo and Cameroon, 2 percent Asian, and 17 percent unknown other. Knowing those constituent parts, how would Lezlie respond to a U.S. census inquiry? Can a limited category system capture this ethnic combination, or that of millions of Americans whose lineage has multiple strands, rather than a single clear path?

The challenge of representing race and ethnicity in an increasingly diverse nation is considerable, and it is one not limited to a

Kay Deaux is a distinguished professor emerita at the Graduate Center of the City University of New York and a visiting research scholar in the Department of Psychology at New York University. She is the author of To Be an Immigrant *(Russell Sage Foundation 2009).*

Correspondence: kdeaux@gc.cuny.edu

DOI: 10.1177/0002716218754834

single disciplinary perspective. Ethnic and racial categories have a history, as well as a contemporary usage. They are embedded in the norms and practices of a society, as well as internalized in those who reside in the society. And perhaps most importantly, they are subject to continual change.

From the perspective of a social psychologist, I organize my comments in terms of three areas of psychological research that are relevant to categorization and racial/ethnic identity: (1) the creation and definition of identity categories, (2) the subjectivity of identity claims and self-definition, and (3) the flexibility of identity expression and presentation.

Creation and Definition of Identity Categories

Diversity in a population makes a multiplicity of identity categories available, both to those who occupy the diverse positions and those who want to classify a larger group into smaller, presumably more homogeneous, units. The U.S. decennial census represents one approach to this classification task. The history of the U.S. census (see Prewitt 2013) provides a fascinating look at how changing demographics, understandings, and priorities have defined and redefined the adopted principles of categorization over time. From an early quantification rule used in the first 1790 census, that is, that blacks would be counted as three-fifths of a white, to later revisions that were concocted to deal with an increasing number of immigrants from Asia and later from Latin America, the census has represented the current thinking of those responsible for counting the citizenry. Many of the incorporated options suggest deep-rooted beliefs about race (or at least seemingly unbreakable habits) whose origin can be traced back to the Swedish botanist Linnaeus. However, the ways in which these beliefs are represented in the census varies with the demographic and social context. From 1850 to 1920, for example, *mulatto* was an official census category, reflecting both the increased recognition of interracial unions (many the repercussion of the slavery system) and an unsupported belief that those of mixed race were inferior to pure cases of either race, and thus needed to be separately identified. Steady increases in immigration from Latin America in the latter part of the twentieth century spurred a move to distinguish immigrants and their descendants from established whites of European heritage; hence the term *non-Hispanic white* emerged to characterize the "true whites" from a sometimes browner version.

Changes of this sort in the census are consistent with a social constructionist perspective, whereby categories are not inherent but rather reflect and substantiate a particular set of assumptions about the world or a particular agenda for addressing issues in the society. These categories are adopted for a variety of reasons. Psychologically, categories are used to simplify and manage the complexity of information available and as a shorthand for communication; in broader social and political terms, categories can be a means of control and definition of status boundaries.

However, the match of category to person is not always a good fit. The person answering "Black, African American, or Negro" on the census form, for example, might be an immigrant from Haiti, Jamaica, or Senegal, or could be a native-born black with generations of U.S.-born ancestors. Unless that person went on to specify a country of origin when asked to provide "some other race," the distinctive linguistic, cultural, and historical differences between members of those various groups would not be captured.

Categories can also be a poor fit when the nature of those being categorized changes. Just as discoveries of new planets or plant species typically require new astronomical or botanical categories, so too can changes in the demographics of a population or the salience of a particular group within the existent population impel a reconstruction of categories. In some cases, the perceived need is for broader, more encompassing categories (e.g., Hispanic, Asian); in other cases, greater differentiation of categories is proposed (e.g., the multiple subcategories of Asian and Native Hawaiian/Pacific Islander in the 2010 census). For many people, however, the provided categories still seem unsuitable. For people of Latino heritage, for example, answering the Hispanic question either does or does not provide a specifically relevant membership category (e.g., Mexican/Puerto Rican/Cuban), but does offer the option of identifying a country of origin (e.g., Guatemala) or a particular ethnic culture (e.g., Mixtec). However, the subsequent question on race may seem irrelevant to them (and indeed, 90 percent of those using "some other race" are Hispanic; see Prewitt 2013).

In the United States (and elsewhere), increasing rates of intermarriage represent another challenge to standard categories. According to a recent Pew report, one in six people who married in 2015 (17 percent) had a spouse of a different race or ethnicity (Pew Research Center 2017). Rates of intermarriage, although rising for all groups, are greatest for newlyweds of Asian (29 percent) and Hispanic (27 percent) heritage. As in the example offered at the beginning of this article, mixed parentage challenges the standard assumptions of clear category placement—a challenge that has, historically, created elaborate systems for defining race (apartheid South Africa is an example of the contortions that may be required to maintain clear demarcations). Allowing people to mark more than one box on a question about race is a partial solution to this problem, but it does not address all the possible combinations of race and ethnicity that exist in the United States today or the weightings that may be associated with each race/ethnicity.

Thus, in an ethnically diverse society, a multiplicity of identity definitions and combinations is almost inevitable. Which categories are to be included in the equation is not a given, however, and depends on the agenda of those setting the categories. Certainly the census form is evidence of that plasticity, insofar as the basic categories and the distinctions within categories have changed frequently over the years (Prewitt 2013). Adding the option to check more than one box on the race question reflects a recognition of some forms of multiplicity. At the same time, "more than one" is not presented as an option on the Hispanic question, suggesting a lack of interest in combinations of, for example, Puerto Rican and Cuban.

Of course, categories emerge and gain traction even without policy considerations, and observers generally feel free to use or ignore some categorizations in favor of others. Visibility of a category marker increases the likelihood of that category being used. But even with equivalent markers, category boundaries may be defined differently. As an example, a "one drop of blood" rule can be the basis of a dichotomous categorization system, although that general rule can be applied differently from one society to another (e.g., compare the United States to Brazil; see Telles 2004). Further, dichotomous monoracial categorization has been found to persist even when a multiracial category is available. Research findings indicate that people in the United States rely on categories of black versus white and are less prone to use a multiracial category even when the available physical evidence supports the use of that combination (Chen and Hamilton 2012).

Categories based on place of birth or parental heritage are not currently included in the decennial census form, although this information is part of the American Community Survey. Strong arguments can be made for including parental heritage questions in the census as well, thus allowing analysis of generational differences in a variety of outcomes (see articles by Jiménez; Massey; Tran; and Duncan and Trejo, this volume). Studies of both health-related behaviors and more basic social psychological processes reveal important generational differences within the same ethnic group that have significant policy implications. Social psychological research has shown generational differences, for example, in the performance of West Indian immigrants on academic tasks (Deaux et al. 2007), in Latinos' beliefs in meritocracy (Wiley, Deaux, and Hagelskamp 2012), and in patterns of self-esteem in both black and Latino immigrant groups (Wiley, Perkins, and Deaux 2008). Analyses of health and illness typically show that immigrants have better outcomes than do native-born Americans (Waters and Pineau 2015). That advantage diminishes over time, however, and members of the second generation on average are far less healthy than their first-generation counterparts (Abraido-Lanza, Chao, and Flórez 2005; Waters and Pineau 2015). Thus, rather than policy having dictated categories, in this case it would appear that research attests to the policy relevance of categories and argues for the inclusion of generational indicators.

It is important to recognize that a system of classification, once developed and applied, can have self-fulfilling consequences. Thus, categories will not only be used by those who initiated the classification, but can also become part of the identity of those who respond to the questions. The immigrant from Jamaica, for example, may shift from an identification with specific country/ethnic origin to a more general West Indian or black label when presented with or assumed to be part of a larger generic group (Waters 1999). Individuals from Vietnam, China, or the Philippines may accept the more general label of Asian American, either because it is the most frequently available option or because they see strategic value in adopting a panethnic identity (Okamoto 2014). Similarly, Dominican immigrants may use the readily available panethnic category of Hispanic as a way of placing themselves in a category distinct from black and white (Itzigsohn 2009).

In sum, category labels are, fundamentally, choices that people make from an array of alternatives, not an objective drill into the essential nature of a person. Further, these choices are not limited to the use of a particular label but also invoke networks of association and meaning that are associated with the label (Ashmore, Deaux, and McLaughlin-Volpe 2004). These associations allow a category to be not just a self-descriptive term but also to have implications and consequences for one's own actions as well as alliances with others.

Subjectivity of Identity Claims

Given that identity categories are not essential realities but rather are to a large extent social constructions, it follows that individuals themselves have some latitude in deciding what label to apply to themselves. These choices can emerge from the particular heritage and experiences of the person; they can also be influenced by the attitudes of and pressures from others, as well as the degree to which a category is "in the air," that is, in common usage by the people and media one regularly encounters. This variability raises the questions of what category—or categories—people choose for themselves and why they might make that choice.

In a modern complex society, people are likely to have more than one meaningful identity, such as nationality, ethnicity, religion, gender, and age. Some of these categories can be quite distinct from one another; others can overlap substantially (for example, ethnicity and religion are often closely connected in both meaning and strength of endorsement; cf. Verkuyten 2014). Identities vary in the importance that a person attaches to them, and level of importance is predictive of the likelihood that a person will act in ways consistent with that identity label. For example, a person with a strong religious identity is more likely to observe ritual practices than those whose religious identities are less important to them; similarly, someone who strongly identifies as a Democrat or Republican is more likely to engage in political activities than one with a weaker political identity (Deaux 2015).

Even limiting the focus to ethnicity and race allows for multiplicity of identity. Since 2000, this multiplicity has been recognized in the census race item. In the 2000 census, 6.8 million people chose more than one race to identify themselves; in 2010, that number increased to 9 million (U.S. Census Bureau 2012), and the likelihood of that number increasing substantially in the 2020 census is high. It is important to note that the "more than one" option is available only on the race question, and does not readily capture the multiplicity of ethnic group combinations that might be considered as distinctive from one another by those who possess them, as is the distinction based on societal definitions of race.

The likelihood that people will opt for multiple identities and the particulars of what identities they claim are influenced by a variety of factors. In a survey of adults who had one white and one nonwhite parent, respondents were asked how strongly they identified as white, as the relevant nonwhite ethnic group, and as multiracial; they were also asked to assess the ethnic identification of each parent. In general, these respondents showed a pattern of identification that matched the strength of the perceived parental identification, and more so to the degree that they felt close to a particular parent (Cheney, Sanchez, and Handy 2015). Presumably during childhood, the intermarried parents also have a direct influence on their children, choosing and using the ethnic label that they consider to be most appropriate for their children (see Lichter and Qian, this volume). Other people who the multiethnic person encounters in her or his life course can also be influential. Individuals who look more prototypical of their ethnic group in terms of physical features, for example, are more likely to be assigned to that ethnic category by others and to identify with that category themselves (Wilkins, Kaiser, and Rieck 2010). Some work also suggests that multiracial identity is more likely to be claimed by those who belong to higher- versus lower-status groups (Gaither 2015).

Although the multiplicity of identity is an increasingly available option for people, the process of making such decisions is not without stress, and individuals differ considerably in the way they handle possible multiplicity. Research on what has been termed *bicultural identity integration* (Benet-Martínez and Nguyen, forthcoming) documents variations in how people who have two different cultural backgrounds deal with possible differences between the two: Are they more likely to see them as integrated and compatible, or do they find it difficult to integrate the two in any satisfactory way? Not only do these different patterns have implications for psychological adjustment, but they also are associated with differential sensitivity to cultural cues in the environment and shifting claims of identity. In short, people may share the same ethnic profile, in terms of combining basic demographic categories, but their way of defining and dealing with the combinations can vary considerably.

All these characteristics of social identity add variability and nuance to the decisions about what categories should be included on a census form, as well as to the subsequent interpretation of data obtained from those forms.

Flexibility of Identity Presentation

Because categories are multiple and people have options in the identities they claim, we cannot assume that a category endorsed on one occasion will be constant over time. Some evidence of this variability is provided by Liebler and her colleagues (2017), who used matched 2000/2010 census files to determine the extent to which self-selected ethno-racial categories remained stable or changed over the 10-year period. Not only did they find an overall rate of 6 percent of respondents who showed a difference in self-labeling between the two time periods, but they also were able to point to particular groups and combinations that were most likely to show variations in their responses. Not surprisingly, greater instability was often associated with combination categories, endorsed either at time 1 or time 2, suggesting the flexibility with which people manage their identity options.

There are numerous possible reasons for the change in the identity category over a 10-year period (even assuming that the person completing the census form was the same from time 1 to time 2). They range from methodological issues (e.g., unreliability in the assessment of categories that may not be common-use terms for the respondents) to variations in personal experience (e.g., a person's social network could change substantially during that time period and in turn make one ethnic identity category more salient or relevant than another). Certainly, more longitudinal research on the self-labeling of identity would be helpful to sort out possible causes.

At the same time, social psychological research provides ample evidence that people can easily shift from one identity to another in shorter, more situationally dependent circumstances. Both cognitive and behavioral evidence for these shifts exists. In what is termed *cultural frame-switching* (Benet-Martínez and Nguyen, in press), the availability of cognitive cues relevant to one or another identity can affect the thoughts and expressions of multicultural persons, often in wholly nonconscious and automatic ways. For example, if a Chinese-Anglo bicultural person is asked to explain an ambiguous social event in the presence of Chinese cultural material (e.g., a picture of the Great Wall of China), they are more likely to offer external causes, consistent with what has been shown to be an Asian attribution style. In contrast, the presence of U.S. cultural material (e.g., a photo of the White House) is likely to precipitate more internal, person-centered explanations, consistent with the Western attributional style (Hong et al. 2000). On a behavioral level, in a process that has been termed *bicultural (or multicultural) identity performance* (Wiley and Deaux 2011; see also Klein, Spears, and Reicher 2007), people will strategically make choices among possible identities to present to others in a given situation.

Numerous factors influence these choices. For example, a person will be more likely to present a version of self that is consistent with the situation or with the characteristics of those around them, such as identifying as a student in a classroom or as a Muslim when in a mosque. Norms and social pressures influence many of these choices: for instance, the American-born daughter of Chinese immigrant parents is apt to express her Chinese identity more strongly and more often when at home, while perhaps emphasizing her identity as an American when in a diverse school setting. People can also assert a preferred identity to counter the perceived assumptions of others. As shown by Sapna Cheryan and her colleagues, for example, Asian-American students are more likely to stress their American identity than their Asian heritage when asked by an interviewer if they speak English (Cheryan and Monin 2005), or to indicate a preference for American food over Asian food when similarly challenged (Guendelman, Cheryan, and Monin 2011). Individual differences in the importance of a particular identification, or allegiance to an ethnic group, also moderate presentational choices. Not surprisingly, those who strongly identify with a category membership are more likely to show consistency across situations than are those whose subjective investment in the category is weaker (Wiley and Deaux 2011).

These situational variations in identity presentation provide fertile soil for social psychological research and theory. At the same time, evidence of this variability in identity claims suggests that researchers should use some caution in the interpretation of data gathered in any one set of circumstances. Survey data, such as the census, which is gathered at a particular point in time and reported to a specific interviewer, is generally assumed to be a relatively stable indicator of category membership. Yet if the identity categories reported on that single occasion are influenced by, for example, the presence of others when the form is being filled out or the political climate at the time of reporting, biases can enter the process. Some of these could be random circumstances that might be assumed to even out over a large dataset; others, however, could be more systematic in their influence.

Concluding Thoughts

Substantial research from social psychology and related disciplines supports a socially constructed definition and use of racial/ethnic categories, wherein identities are subject to the influence of local and national norms and amenable to change across situations and over time. This view contrasts with those that might assume an essentialism to categories that would show minimal variation over different historical and cultural contexts. In a time when societies are becoming more ethnically diverse and when intermarriage and interethnic unions are becoming more common, it would seem difficult to argue against a more constructionist perspective.

Acceptance of a more dynamic perspective, in which categories can be arbitrary and subject to revision over time and circumstances, certainly creates a new set of challenges for those seeking to assess and to interpret the variations and combinations that have emerged. Almost certainly, race and ethnicity will continue to be used as a key aspect of describing and differentiating among individuals, on the census as well as in various other forms of surveys and descriptions. Yet as the basic demographics of the population show change over time, so too is there likely to be change in the social definitions that individuals select. With specific reference to the census, both the construction of the forms and the interpretation of data derived from the forms need to take possible variation and change into account. General processes of identification and labelling will surely persist, but variations in the use of specific categories and the possibilities of flexibility and change are inevitable as well.

References

Abraido-Lanza, Ana F., Maria T. Chao, and Karen R. Flórez. 2005. Do healthy behaviors decline with greater acculturation? Implications for the Latino mortality paradox. *Social Science & Medicine* 71:1243–55.

Ashmore, Richard D., Kay Deaux, and Tracey McLaughlin-Volpe. 2004. An organizing framework for collective identity: Articulation and significance of multidimensionality. *Psychological Bulletin* 130:80–114.

Benet-Martínez, Veronica, and Angela-MinhTu D. Nguyen. Forthcoming. Multicultural identity and experiences: Cultural, social, and personality processes. In *The Oxford handbook of personality and social psychology*, 2nd ed., eds. Kay Deaux and Mark Snyder. New York, NY: Oxford University Press.

Chen, Jacqueline M., and David L. Hamilton. 2012. Natural ambiguities: Racial categorization of multiracial individuals. *Journal of Experimental Social Psychology* 48:152–64.

Cheney, Cesalie T., Diana T. Sanchez, and Phillip E. Handy. 2015. Perceptions of parents' ethnic identities and the personal ethnic-identity and racial attitudes of biracial adults. *Cultural Diversity and Ethnic Minority Psychology* 21:65–75.

Cheryan, Sapna, and Benoit Monin. 2005. "Where are you really from?" Asian Americans and identity denial. *Journal of Personality and Social Psychology* 89:717–30.

Deaux, Kay. 2015. Social identity in sociology. In *International encyclopedia of the social & behavioral sciences*, 2nd ed., ed. James D. Wright, 319–24. Philadelphia, PA: Elsevier.

Deaux, Kay, Nida Bikmen, Allwyn Gilkes, Ana Ventuneac, Yvanne Joseph, Yasser Payne, and Claude Steele. 2007. Becoming American: Stereotype threat effects in Afro-Caribbean immigrant groups. *Social Psychology Quarterly* 70:384–404.

Gaither, Sarah E. 2015. "Mixed results": Multiracial research and identity explorations. *Current Directions in Psychological Science* 24:114–19.

Guendelman, Maya D., Sapna Cheryan, and Benoit Monin. 2011. Fitting in but getting fat: Identity threat and dietary choices among U.S. immigrant groups. *Psychonomic Science* 22:959–67.

Hong, Ying-yi, Michael W. Morris, Chi-yue Chiu, and Verónica Benet-Martínez. 2000. Multicultural minds: A dynamic constructivist approach to culture and cognition. *American Psychologist* 55:709–20.

Itzigsohn, José. 2009. *Encountering American faultlines: Race, class, and the Dominican experience in Providence*. New York, NY: Russell Sage Foundation.

Klein, Olivier, Russell Spears, and Stephen Reicher. 2007. Social identity performance: Extending the strategic side of SIDE. *Personality and Social Psychology Review* 11:1–18.

Liebler, Carolyn A., Sonya Rastogi, Leticia E. Fernandez, James M. Noon, and Sharon R. Ennis. 2017. America's churning races: Race and ethnicity response changes between Census 2000 and the 2010 census. *Demography* 54:259–84.

Okamoto, Dina G. 2014. *Redefining race: Asian American panethnicity and shifting ethnic boundaries*. New York, NY: Russell Sage Foundation.

Pew Research Center. May 2017. *Intermarriage in the U.S. 50 years after* Loving v. Virginia. Washington, DC: Pew Research Center.

Prewitt, Kenneth. 2013. *What is your race? The census and our flawed efforts to classify Americans*. Princeton, NJ: Princeton University Press.

Telles, Edward E. 2004. *Race in another America: The significance of skin color in Brazil*. Princeton, NJ: Princeton University Press.

U.S. Census Bureau. 2012. *The two or more races population: 2010*. Washington, DC: U.S. Census Bureau.

Verkuyten, Maykel. 2014. *Identity and cultural diversity*. New York, NY: Routledge.

Waters, Mary C. 1999. *Black identities: West Indian immigrant dreams and American realities*. New York, NY, and Cambridge, MA: Russell Sage Foundation and Harvard University Press.

Waters, Mary C., and Marisa Gerstein Pineau. 2015. *The integration of immigrants into American society*. Washington, DC: National Academies Press.

Wiley, Shaun, and Kay Deaux. 2011. The bicultural identity performance of immigrants. In *Identity and participation in culturally diverse societies: A multidisciplinary perspective*, eds. Assaad Azzi, Xenia Chryssochoou, Bert Klandermans, and Bernd Simon, 49–68. Chichester, UK: Wiley-Blackwell.

Wiley, Shaun, Kay Deaux, and Carolin Hagelskamp. 2012. Born in the USA: How ethnic generation shapes meritocracy and its relation to ethnic identity and collective action. *Cultural Diversity and Ethnic Minority Psychology* 18:171–80.

Wiley, Shaun, Krystal Perkins, and Kay Deaux. 2008. Through the looking glass: Ethnic and generational patterns of immigrant identity. *International Journal of Intercultural Relations* 32:385–98.

Wilkins, Clara L., Cheryl R. Kaiser, and Heather Rieck. 2010. Detecting racial identification: The role of phenotypic prototypicality. *Journal of Experimental Social Psychology* 46:1029–34.

Establishing the Denominator: The Challenges of Measuring Multiracial, Hispanic, and Native American Populations

By
WENDY D. ROTH

For multiracial, Hispanic, and Native Americans, norms for racial and ethnic self-identification are less well established than they are for other population groups. There is considerable variation and fluidity in how multiracial, Hispanic, and Native Americans self-identify, as well as how they are classified by others. This presents challenges to researchers and analysts in terms of consistently and accurately estimating the size and population dynamics of these groups. I argue that for analytic purposes, racial/ethnic self-identification should continue to be treated as a statistical numerator, but that the challenge is for researchers to establish the correct denominator—the population that *could* identify as members of the group based on their ancestry. Examining how many people who could identify with these groups choose to do so sheds light on assimilation and emerging racial classification processes. Analyses of the larger potential populations further avoid bias stemming from nonrandom patterns of self-identification with the groups.

Keywords: race; ethnicity; measurement; mixed race; identity; census; statistics

Ethno-racial mixture is on the rise in the United States. This is occurring not only because of a growing population of children born from interracial unions (U.S. Census Bureau 2010), but also because of the growth of the Hispanic population (Krogstad and Lopez 2015), where racial mixture is so common over

Wendy D. Roth is an associate professor of sociology at the University of British Columbia. She is the author of Race Migrations: Latinos and the Cultural Transformation of Race *(Stanford University Press 2012).*

NOTE: The author would like to thank Richard Alba, Mary Waters, the Russell Sage Foundation, and the participants in its 2016 workshop on "What the Census Bureau Needs to Know to Improve Ethnic, Racial, and Immigration Statistics." This work was supported by a University of British Columbia Killam Research Fellowship.

Correspondence: wendy.roth@ubc.ca

DOI: 10.1177/0002716218756818

generations that relatively few consider themselves not to have any mixed-race origins. Native Americans are another population in which ethno-racial mixing is so common historically that large portions of the population consider themselves racially mixed (Snipp 1997). The Office of Management and Budget's 1997 decision to allow people to mark more than one race was an important recognition of the ways that population trends and ethno-racial classification norms are changing (U.S. Office of Management and Budget 1997; Wallman, Evinger, and Schechter 2000). These changes reflect an understanding that people with multiple racial ancestries often identify with more than one of them, but they also reveal that the norms for how these populations self-identify are less well established than for those who consider themselves solely Black or White.[1] There is considerable variation in how these groups identify their race and ethnicity, as well as how they are classified by others (Alba, Insolera, and Lindeman 2016; Liebler et al. 2014; Porter, Liebler, and Noon 2016; Roth 2010, 2016). This presents challenges for estimating and analyzing these populations based on their ethno-racial self-identification alone. When group identification is fluid, self-identification is itself a dependent variable. I argue that for analytic purposes, racial/ethnic self-identification should be treated as a statistical numerator, but that the challenge is for researchers to establish the correct denominator—the population that *could* identify as members of the group based on their ancestry. Examining how many people who could identify with these groups choose to do so sheds light on assimilation and emerging racial classification processes. Analyzing the larger potential populations, by avoiding bias from nonrandom patterns of self-identification with the groups, is important for statistical accuracy and consistency and is crucial for academic progress and informed policy.

Estimates of Populations Miss People Who Could Identify with the Group

Current estimates of ethnic and racial groups from the U.S. Census are based on individuals' ethno-racial self-identification or classification by a member of their household who fills out the census form, presumably a relative or someone who knows them well. Yet relative to White, Black, and Asian populations,[2] there is considerable fluidity in how multiracial, Hispanic, and Native American populations self-identify. In their comparison of individually linked responses in the 2000 and 2010 censuses, Liebler and colleagues (2014) found that 97 percent of non-Hispanic Whites, 94 percent of non-Hispanic Blacks, and 91 percent of non-Hispanic Asians had the same self-identification in both censuses, but all other groups had much greater fluidity in their responses. Only 53 percent of American Indians or Alaska Natives and 48 percent of Native Hawaiians or Pacific Islanders were consistent in both censuses. Similarly, based on calculations of their data, we see that only 23 percent of all non-Hispanic multiracials and 41 percent of all Hispanics listed the same race and Hispanic origin responses in 2000 and 2010.[3]

These findings are consistent with a number of other studies that show much greater fluidity in racial self-classification for multiracial, Hispanic, and Native American individuals, and greater stability in self-classification for non-Hispanic Whites, Blacks, and Asians (Doyle and Kao 2007; Liebler and Ortyl 2014; Saperstein and Penner 2012). Furthermore, this fluidity is seen not only over time, but also across contexts. Harris and Sim (2002) found that 12.4 percent of the non-Hispanic adolescents in the first wave of the National Longitudinal Survey of Adolescent Health (Add Health) survey gave different racial identifications in an in-school questionnaire and an in-home interview; most of these adolescents revealed multiracial origins in at least one of their responses. Although Harris and Sim's study focused only on non-Hispanic adolescents, when both Hispanic and non-Hispanic adolescents were included, about 15 percent answered the race question differently across these contexts (Brown, Hitlin, and Elder 2006).

In general, Hispanics reveal greater fluidity in their racial identification than in their identification as Hispanic. Although only 41 percent of Hispanics answered the race and Hispanic origin questions in the same way in 2000 and 2010, 87 percent of Hispanics consistently identified as Hispanic (of any race) at both times (Liebler et al. 2014). However, there seems to be greater fluidity in Hispanic identification among younger people and those who are less immersed in a Hispanic community. Among adolescents who identified as Hispanic in the Add Health in-school survey, 80 percent identified as Hispanic in the in-home interview as well (Brown, Hitlin, and Elder 2006). In a study of Hispanic high school students from 1980 to 1982, 68 percent consistently identified as Hispanic at both times, and inconsistent identifications were more likely for those who were monolingual English speakers or attended schools with smaller percentages of Hispanic students (Eschbach and Gómez 1998).

There is also greater inconsistency between self-identity and observation by others for the multiracial, Hispanic, and Native American populations (Roth 2016). Several studies in the health fields examined inconsistencies between individuals' self-reports and the observations of others on medical records, in interviewer classifications, or on death certificates (Hahn, Truman, and Barker 1996; Kressin et al. 2003; West et al. 2005). These studies found the highest rates of consistency among self-reported Whites (91–98 percent) and Blacks (90–99 percent), and typically moderate to high rates among Asians (76–95 percent). Rates of consistent observations by others were lower for self-reported Hispanics (64–83 percent), and extremely low for Native Americans (0–23 percent). Studies of people who self-identify as multiracial also find relatively low rates of consistency in observers' classifications of their race. Observers tend to classify multiracial individuals as monoracial (Herman 2010). More observers classify those with mixed Black backgrounds as only Black, while there is greater diversity in how they classify those with any other racial mixtures (Feliciano 2016).

What is particularly notable is that inconsistencies persist even when the observer knows the person he or she is classifying. In one study, people who previously self-identified their ancestry but died before a follow-up study were identified by both a proxy—a next of kin or a nonrelative who knew them—and by funeral directors. Only 20 percent of those who had self-identified as Native American were classified as such by the proxies who knew them (and none of them were classified as Native American by the funeral directors) (Hahn, Truman, and Barker 1996). Porter, Liebler, and Noon (2016) also examined racial classifications by proxies in the individually linked data from the 2000 and 2010 censuses. They examined cases that had a proxy report in one decennial census (usually from a neighbor) and a report from the individual or someone in her or his household in the other census. They found high consistency between the household reports and proxy reports for Whites (98 percent), Blacks (94 percent), and Asians (88 percent). They also found high consistency for a Hispanic designation, with 86 percent of household reports of Hispanic identity confirmed by proxies. However, the proxy reports matched household reports at lower rates for Native Americans (62 percent), Pacific Islanders (62 percent), and multiracial people (8–36 percent, depending on the mix of races reported). About half of Hispanics were classified as a different race by proxies than that reported by their households.

Although the proxies in the Porter, Liebler, and Noon (2016) study typically had some knowledge of the individual, their classifications were guided by external cues, such as the racial and ethnic composition and class composition of the neighborhood and the person's age. Proxy classifications were more likely to match household reports if the person was living in an area where many others reported the same race. This suggests that observers relied on the racial composition of the area to guide their assessments. Proxies more frequently reported children as multiple-race and adults as single-race, which may reflect a common perception that younger people are more likely to identify themselves as multiracial, or may stem from a greater tendency to see these young people with their parents and to draw upon this information in assigning their race.

The greater fluidity of multiracial, Hispanic, and Native American self-identification, and greater inconsistency between their self-identification and observation by others, indicates that norms of classification are less well formed for these groups than they are for Whites, Blacks, and Asians. These racial and ethnic designations are relatively flexible, and their salience is more dependent on the situational context. This means that estimates of multiracial, Hispanic, and Native American populations in the census, American Community Survey (ACS), and many other surveys will miss people who *could* identify as members of these populations and may in some circumstances but do not do so at data collection. Furthermore, when the individual in question is not the one filling out the household report for the census or ACS, there is likely to be greater discrepancy between what the household member reports and the individual's self-identification than for groups with more established norms of racial classification, such as Whites, Blacks, and Asians. Unfortunately, information about whether it is the individual himself or herself who is answering the questions or another member of the household is not available in ACS or census data.

Assimilation and Emerging Racial Classification Processes: Analyzing Everyone Who Could Identify in These Populations

Noting the fluidity in multiracial adolescents' identifications, Harris and Sim argued that the 2000 census provided "a count of *a* multiracial population, not *the* multiracial population" (2002, 625; see also Morning and Saperstein, this volume). The same could be said for Hispanics and Native Americans, reflecting patterns of widespread interracial mixing across many generations. In this sense, when determining a population based on ethno-racial self-identification, one needs to recognize that individuals self-select into the group. One of the most important issues for scholars of race and immigration then becomes the ability to detect everyone who *could* identify in these populations, whether or not they do. Analyzing these patterns can reveal how racial classification processes unfold and what identities people choose under what circumstances. In the case of Hispanics, this type of analysis can reveal which individuals have assimilated into the American mainstream by dropping a Hispanic identity.

Scholars have attempted various strategies to consider everyone who could potentially identify in these populations by garnering information on the ethno-racial identity or origins of their parents and grandparents. One approach is to focus on children from interracial marriages by aggregating census data to the household level and compiling information about the race and ethnicity of the parents and the children. Several studies have used this approach, focusing on how these children who could potentially be labelled as multiracial are in fact racially classified on the census (Brunsma 2005; Kana'iaupuni and Liebler 2005; Liebler 2004, 2010; Qian 2004; Roth 2005; Xie and Goyette 1997).[4] In general, this research shows that many of these children are not classified as part of the two or more races population, despite having parents of two or more races. In 2000, only 43 percent of children with parents of different single races were identified as multiracial, while the remainder were identified as the race of one of their parents (Roth 2005).[5]

There are limitations to this approach due to the survey structure and available information in the census, however. It can only focus on interracial couples where one member is "Person 1," and it focuses on children (rather than the adult multiracial population) because the only way to get information about the race of individuals and their parents is for them to be living in the same household. This approach also has to rely on assumptions about the biological relatedness of the child and parents. The distinction made beginning in the 2000 census between "natural-born son/daughter" and "adopted son/daughter" in the question on each person's relationship to Person 1 is extremely valuable to this type of analysis. But researchers still have to assume that the child is also the natural-born child of the spouse or partner of Person 1. These studies typically focus only on married households for this reason, which limits our knowledge of the potential multiracial population further and yet still draws on assumptions about relatedness rather than on data to confirm it.

These studies are also limited by the lack of information on the person filling out the form, as well as valuable information about the context of survey completion. We cannot tell who in the household is completing the form, although this is likely to be an important aspect of how the child is classified. The parent completing the form may be more likely to emphasize his or her own racial background in the child's designation (Roth 2005). Analysis of Current Population Survey (CPS) data on Mexican Americans showed that when children's Mexican ancestry derives from the mother's side of the family, the children are more likely to be identified as Mexican if their mother completes the survey form (Duncan and Trejo 2011).

Another aspect of the context that we are currently unable to evaluate is whether the survey is self-completed and mailed in or completed by an enumerator or with an enumerator present. Since some adolescents will identify their race differently when completing the questions on their own or in an in-home interview (Harris and Sim 2002), we might expect this context to influence some household members' classification of their multiracial children as well. And since the race of the interviewer or observer can influence how they perceive the respondent (Feliciano 2016; Hill 2002), it is possible that there could be race-of-enumerator effects in how multiracial children are classified in cases where an enumerator is present or helping to complete the form. These types of contextual factors are likely to matter more in the racial classification of ethno-racially mixed populations than for Whites, Blacks, or Asians because of the greater fluidity in their identification and in the norms for how enumerators might classify the person.

Another approach to analyzing all those who potentially *could* identify as multiracial, Hispanic, or Native American focuses on ancestry data. By identifying people who list ancestries of multiple races, or Hispanic or Native American origins, scholars can analyze which individuals have chosen to identify with these groups or to simplify their ethno-racial identities in ways that shed light on broader processes of assimilation and racial boundary formation. Gullickson and Morning (2011), for example, used the census ancestry question to identify adults who report having ancestry in more than one racial group. They found that individuals with part-Asian ancestry were the most likely to identify themselves as multiracial in 2000; and for those with no Asian ancestry, part-Black ancestry groups were more likely to identify themselves as Black rather than multiracial. Those with White and Native American ancestry were much more likely to identify their race as White than as any other option. Similarly, Emeka and Vallejo (2011) used the ancestry question on the ACS to identify adults with Latin American ancestry, and found that 6 percent of them did not identify as Hispanic. A non-Hispanic identification was most common among those who listed Latin American and non-Latin American ancestries, suggesting intermarriage in earlier generations, as well as those who speak only English. These studies attempt to portray the individuals' self-identification but are again limited by the lack of information about who is completing the survey. Gullickson and Morning (2011) restricted their analysis to the household head on the assumption that this is most likely the person completing the form, but it is not clear that the household head is always the person answering the questions.

To study ethnic attrition among Mexican Americans, Duncan and Trejo (2011) took advantage of the question on parents' place of birth in the CPS. They examined whether the children of Mexican-born parents identified themselves as Mexican and found that 90 percent of U.S.-born individuals aged 25 to 59 with a Mexican-born parent did identify as Mexican on the Hispanic origin question. However, those who did not self-identify as Mexican had more education than those who did, showing that estimates of socioeconomic status that rely on self-identification will underestimate the achievements of people of Mexican descent. Furthermore, by using the household aggregation approach described above and focusing on children in their parents' households, the authors were able to determine the places of birth of the children's grandparents. When three or four of their grandparents were born in Mexico, these children were identified as Mexican nearly all the time (95 percent and 96 percent, respectively). But only 79 percent of those with two grandparents born in Mexico and 58 percent of those with one grandparent born in Mexico were identified as Mexican on the Hispanic-origin question. And children who were not identified as Mexican had parents with much higher levels of educational attainment than those who retained a Mexican identification. The question on parents' place of birth in the CPS offers one of the best ways to study those who could identify as Hispanic, but the relatively small sample size of the CPS, even when pooled over many years, limits the use of these data to study other Hispanic subgroups.

Further information about the ethno-racial identities and places of birth of individuals' parents and grandparents are central to expanding research on the identity choices of adults who could consider themselves part of the multiracial, Hispanic, and/or Native American populations. The challenge is to not define these populations by individuals' ethno-racial identification (or ethno-racial classification by someone in the household) but to recognize that this identification is a dependent variable to a much greater extent than with other population groups. Accurately estimating and analyzing these groups therefore requires new strategies for determining the denominator—all the people who could identify in these populations—and treating self-identification as a numerator. With less-established classification norms for multiracial, Hispanic, and Native American populations, current measures of racial and ethnic identification—the numerator—will increasingly fail to serve as stable measures that reliably delineate these populations.

Notes

1. A grammatical note: Throughout this article, I have deliberately capitalized the racial categories "Black" and "White." Common grammatical usage does not capitalize these terms, even though other racial categories such as "Asian" and "Native American" are capitalized, as are ethnicities, nationalities, religions, and other social constructions. I believe this grammatical exception reflects a conception of race, and particularly of Whiteness and Blackness, as natural and generic, much like age and sex (also not capitalized). Yet it is clear that the categories "Black" and "White" are just as socially constructed as other racial terms. I believe it is appropriate for these labels to take their rightful place in our language with other proper nouns.

2. White and Black self-identifications are regularly found to be the most consistent over time and context; Asian self-identifications are also quite stable, generally showing rates of consistency just slightly below those of Whites and Blacks (Liebler et al. 2014). The rates for inconsistency between Asian self-identification and classification by others as Asian is similar, with Asians typically falling slightly below Blacks and Whites but higher than Hispanics or Native Americans in consistency (Hahn, Truman, and Barker 1996; Kressin et al. 2003; West et al. 2005).

3. These percentages are based on my calculations of the figures in Liebler et al.'s (2014) Table 2.

4. Studies have also used this analytical approach with other datasets, including Add Health (Bratter and Heard 2009), Brazilian national household surveys (Schwartzman 2007), and the Chilean census (Valenzuela and Unzueta 2015).

5. This percentage is my calculation based on data in Roth (2005), Tables 4 and 5.

References

Alba, Richard D., Noura E. Insolera, and Scarlett Lindeman. 2016. Is race really so fluid? Revisiting Saperstein and Penner's empirical claims. *American Journal of Sociology* 122 (1): 247–62.

Bratter, Jenifer, and Holly E. Heard. 2009. Mother's, father's, or both? Parental gender and parent-child interactions in the racial classification of adolescents. *Sociological Forum* 24 (3): 658–88.

Brown, J. Scott, Steven Hitlin, and Glen H. Elder. 2006. The greater complexity of lived race: An extension of Harris and Sim. *Social Science Quarterly* 87:411–31.

Brunsma, David L. 2005. Interracial families and the racial identification of mixed-race children: Evidence from the Early Childhood Longitudinal Study. *Social Forces* 84 (2): 1131–57.

Doyle, Jamie Mihoko, and Grace Kao. 2007. Are racial identities of multiracials stable? Changing self-identification among single and multiple race individuals. *Social Psychology Quarterly* 70 (4): 405–23.

Duncan, Brian, and Stephen J. Trejo. 2011. Intermarriage and the international transmission of ethnic identity and human capital for Mexican Americans. *Journal of Labor Economics* 29 (2): 195–227.

Emeka, Amon, and Jody Agius Vallejo. 2011. Non-Hispanics with Latin American ancestry: Assimilation, race, and identity among Latin American descendants in the U.S. *Social Science Research* 40 (6): 1547–63.

Eschbach, Karl, and Christina Gómez. 1998. Choosing Hispanic identity: Ethnic identity switching among respondents to High School and Beyond. *Social Science Quarterly* 79 (1): 74–90.

Feliciano, Cynthia. 2016. Shades of race: How phenotype and observer characteristics shape racial classification. *American Behavioral Scientist* 60 (4): 390–419.

Gullickson, Aaron, and Ann Morning. 2011. Choosing race: Multiracial ancestry and identification. *Social Science Research* 40 (2): 498–512.

Hahn, Robert A., Benedict I. Truman, and Nancy D. Barker. 1996. Identifying ancestry: The reliability of ancestral identification in the United States by self, proxy, interviewer, and funeral director. *Epidemiology* 7 (1): 75–80.

Harris, David R., and Jeremiah Joseph Sim. 2002. Who is multiracial? Assessing the complexity of lived race. *American Sociological Review* 67 (4): 614–27.

Herman, Melissa R. 2010. Do you see what I am? How observers' backgrounds affect their perceptions of multiracial faces. *Social Psychology Quarterly* 73 (1): 58–78.

Hill, Mark E. 2002. Race of the interviewer and perception of skin color: Evidence from the Multi-City Study of Urban Inequality. *American Sociological Review* 67 (1): 99–108.

Kana'iaupuni, Shawn Malia, and Carolyn A. Liebler. 2005. Pondering poi dog: Place and racial identification of multiracial Native Hawaiians. *Ethnic and Racial Studies* 28 (July): 687–721.

Kressin, Nancy R., Bei-Hung Chang, Ann Hendricks, and Lewis E. Kazis. 2003. Agreement between administrative data and patients' self-reports of race/ethnicity. *American Journal of Public Health* 93 (10): 1734–39.

Krogstad, Jens Manuel, and Mark Hugo Lopez. 2015. *Hispanic population reaches record 55 million, but growth has cooled.* Washington, DC: Pew Research Center. Available from www.pewresearch.org.

Liebler, Carolyn A. 2004. Ties on the fringes of identity. *Social Science Research* 33 (4): 702–23.

Liebler, Carolyn A. 2010. Homelands and indigenous identities in a multiracial era. *Social Science Research* 39 (4): 596–609.
Liebler, Carolyn A., and Timothy Ortyl. 2014. More than one million new American Indians in 2000: Who are they? *Demography* 51 (3): 1101–30.
Liebler, Carolyn A., Sonya Rastogi, Leticia E. Fernandez, James M. Noon, and Sharon R. Ennis. 2014. America's churning races: Race and ethnic response changes between Census 2000 and the 2010 census. Revision of Center for Administrative Records Research and Applications (Census Bureau) Working Paper 2014-09, Washington, DC.
Porter, Sonya R., Carolyn A. Liebler, and James M. Noon. 2016. An outside view: What observers say about others' races and Hispanic origins. *American Behavioral Scientist* 60 (4): 465–97.
Qian, Zhenchao. 2004. Options: Racial/ethnic identification of children of intermarried couples. *Social Science Quarterly* 85:746–66.
Roth, Wendy D. 2005. The end of the one-drop rule? Labeling of multiracial children in Black intermarriages. *Sociological Forum* 20 (1): 35–67.
Roth, Wendy D. 2010. Racial mismatch: The divergence between form and function in data for monitoring racial discrimination of Hispanics. *Social Science Quarterly* 91 (5): 1288–1311.
Roth, Wendy D. 2016. The multiple dimensions of race. *Ethnic and Racial Studies* 39 (8): 1310–38.
Saperstein, Aliya, and Andrew M. Penner. 2012. Racial fluidity and inequality in the United States. *American Journal of Sociology* 118 (3): 676–727.
Schwartzman, Luisa Farah. 2007. Does money whiten? Intergenerational changes in racial classification in Brazil. *American Sociological Review* 72 (6): 940–63.
Snipp, C. Matthew. 1997. Some observations about racial boundaries and the experiences of American Indians. *Ethnic and Racial Studies* 20 (4): 667–89.
U.S. Census Bureau. 2010. *Households and families: 2010*. 2010 Census Brief. Available from www.census.gov.
U.S. Office of Management and Budget. 30 October 1997. Revisions to the standards for the classification of federal data on race and ethnicity. Federal Register Notice. Available from http://www.whitehouse.gov/omb.
Valenzuela, Eduardo, and M. Belén Unzueta. 2015. Parental transmission of ethnic identification in mixed couples in Latin America: The Mapuche case. *Ethnic and Racial Studies* 38 (12): 2090–2107.
Wallman, Katherine K., Suzann Evinger, and Susan Schechter. 2000. Measuring our nation's diversity: Developing a common language for data on race/ethnicity. *American Journal of Public Health* 90:1704–8.
West, Carmen N., Ann M. Geiger, Sarah M. Greene, Emily L. Harris, In-Lu A. Liu, Mary B. Barton, Joann G. Elmore, Sharon Rolnick, Larissa Nekhlyudov, and Andrea Altschuler, et al. 2005. Race and ethnicity: Comparing medical records to self-reports. *Journal of the National Cancer Institute Monographs* 35:72–74.
Xie, Yu, and Kimberly Goyette. 1997. The racial identification of biracial children with one Asian parent: Evidence from the 1990 census. *Social Forces* 76 (2): 547–70.

The Generational Locus of Multiraciality and Its Implications for Racial Self-Identification

By
ANN MORNING
and
ALIYA SAPERSTEIN

Estimates of the size of the multiracial population in the United States depend on what prompts people to report multiple races on censuses and surveys. We use data from the 2015 Pew Survey of Multiracial Adults to explore how racial self-identification is shaped by the generational locus of an individual's multiracial ancestry—that is, the place in one's family tree where the earliest interracial union appears. We develop the theoretical rationale for considering generational heterogeneity and provide its first empirical demonstration for U.S. adults, by estimating what shares of the population identify multiracial ancestry in their parents' or grandparents' generation, or further back in their family tree. We find that multiracial generation is related to—and likely confounded with—the ancestry combinations that individuals report (e.g., white-Asian, black–American Indian). Finally, we show that later generations are less likely than their first-generation counterparts to select multiple races when they self-identify. Consequently, we argue that generational locus of multiracial ancestry should be taken into account by demographers and researchers who study outcomes for multiracial Americans.

Keywords: demography; racial classification; multiracial population; generation; ancestry

The projected decline in the white share of the U.S. population over the next 50 years regularly garners media interest, but an equally striking demographic projection that has drawn much less attention concerns the multiple-race

Ann Morning is an associate professor of sociology at New York University and a member of the U.S. Census Bureau's National Advisory Committee on Racial, Ethnic and Other Populations. Her research focuses on racial classification and conceptualization, both in the United States and abroad.

Aliya Saperstein is an associate professor of sociology at Stanford University. Her research focuses on how categories of perceived difference such as race/ethnicity and sex/gender are recorded in censuses and surveys, and the consequences of those measurement decisions for studies of social mobility and inequality.

Correspondence: ann.morning@nyu.edu

DOI: 10.1177/0002716218754774

population. By far, the count that the U.S. Census Bureau expects to grow most rapidly between 2014 and 2060 is the number of Americans who choose "more than one race" (Colby and Ortman 2015).

Whether this expectation for mixed-race Americans is realized will depend not just on the familiar variables of fertility, mortality, and net migration, but also on a factor that has not traditionally figured into demographic analysis: individuals' decisions about how to classify themselves (Perez and Hirschman 2009). Recent research has made it clear how flexible racial self-reporting can be (Liebler et al. 2017; Saperstein and Penner 2014), and both quantitative and qualitative evidence suggests this malleability is particularly true for respondents who report multiple races (see their relatively low consistency rates in Matthews et al. 2017, 57; note also Doyle and Kao 2007; Hitlin, Brown, and Elder 2006; Khanna 2011; Rockquemore and Brunsma 2007). Consequently, making informed projections of population growth requires an understanding of the characteristics associated with, and the mechanisms behind, multiple-race reporting. In other words, research on the racial self-identification of mixed-ancestry people is essential because their choices underpin the estimates and projections for one of the most dynamic segments of the U.S. population.

Sustained academic attention to "the multiracial experience" (Root 1996) emerged in the 1990s, making it a fairly new (though vibrant) area of scholarly inquiry. The availability of large-scale data for such research has also been rather limited until recently. The U.S. government formally recommended the collection of multiple-race responses in the census in 1997, and thus only two decennial censuses (2000 and 2010) so far have included this information. (Multiple-race reporting has also been included on the annual American Community Survey as well as on other federal, state, local, and private-sector forms.) And it was only in 2015 that a random sample of adults nationwide was employed to produce a large survey of multiracial respondents: the Pew Research Center's Survey of Multiracial Adults, which we use below. Accordingly, there is still considerable work that can be done to understand the factors that influence individuals' decisions to identify with more than one race.[1]

As part of this effort, we draw attention to a factor in multiracial self-identification that has received little attention to date: the "generational locus" or "genealogical locus" of one's mixed-race ancestry (Morning 2000; see also Song 2017a), that is, the place in one's family tree when the earliest interracial union appears. Researchers in the past were well aware of the existence of mixed-race Americans (U.S. Census Bureau 1918; Frazier 1957/1997; Nobles 2000), yet multiraciality is often presented as a recent phenomenon, attributed to the Supreme Court's 1967 decision striking down state bans on interracial marriage. As a result, the mixed-race population is usually treated as a novel, "first-generation" community of young people with parents of different races—the "Brave New Faces" (Alaya

---

NOTE: The authors wish to thank Rich Morin and Elaine Patten at the Pew Research Center, as well as our research assistants Anna Boch, Janet Xu, and Sarah Iverson. We are also grateful for the valuable feedback received after presentations at Princeton, UC Santa Barbara, the Russell Sage Foundation, Brown, and Fordham.

2001) or "The New Face of Race"(Meacham 2000) of U.S. media headlines. In reality, interracial unions have been a feature of our society ever since the Spanish, French, and British first established colonies in North America (Sollors 2000). This long history of hybridity makes the mixed-race population of the United States a multigenerational one, including millions of Americans of all ages who are descended from interracial unions that took place in the generation of their grandparents, great-grandparents, or beyond. In other words, the multiracial population is not solely a first-generation community, but rather a layered collective including second, third, and further generations—not unlike how scholars differentiate people in terms of how genealogically close they are to the (im)migrant experience (Rumbaut 2005; Lieberson 1973). As we show, this generational status is associated with individuals' likelihood of identifying with more than one race.[2]

Enumerating the Multiple-Race Population

How the multiracial population is delimited has implications for the generational structure that we discern in it, which makes it especially important to attend to how multiraciality is defined and measured. In an early article exploring young people's choices to identify with more than one race, Harris and Sim (2002) pointed out that when we try to enumerate mixed-race people, we are capturing "a" multiracial population, not "the" multiracial population. Different data-collection methods or question formats lead to different counts, as do different definitions or inclusion rules.[3]

Moreover, the same questions and categories can yield different counts, depending on the circumstances in which individuals encounter them. As Harris and Sim (2002) reported, the same student who identifies as multiracial on a self-completion survey at school might not do so when answering an interviewer's questions at home. Multiracial self-identification on the census or surveys may also be particularly unstable because it depends on multiple-race responses being salient and conceptually available to respondents. Given the long reach of the "one-drop rule," a custom by which Americans with any African ancestry are considered solely as black, there are many Americans for whom "mixed race" is not a plausible identity, regardless of their ancestral background. In short, the sensitivity of multiracial counts to definitions, instrument design, and the malleability of mixed-race identity makes the estimation, projection, and description of the multiple-race population especially challenging.

To investigate mixed-race Americans' self-identification, we first identify a potential multiracial population, comprising all the individuals who could be considered mixed race regardless of whether they identify themselves as such. To borrow the model of political scientist Kanchan Chandra (2012), this "nominal" pool includes all individuals who possess the "descent-attribute(s)" required for membership. More specifically, we assign to the potential mixed-race population any person who descends from ancestors who are considered members of more than one race, whether or not these kin self-identify (or would have self-identified) as such.

To be sure, this theoretical construct of the nominal multiracial population is not without drawbacks. For one thing, the source of ancestry data used will affect the size (and other characteristics) of the population. Following Goldstein and Morning (2000) and Gullickson and Morning (2011), we use individuals' ancestry reports as indicators of multiple-race descent, which brings with it problems of recall and variation in knowledge of one's ancestors. In addition, this approach means that individual respondents' notions of racial categorization introduce variation into the reporting of multiracial ancestry. Finally, our labelling as mixed a person whose ancestors "are considered" members of distinct races is a present-oriented one that entails shifting definitions of multiraciality over time, as cultural beliefs about which groups constitute races change. For example, today "Hispanic or Latino" may be considered a distinct race (at least by some), and thus a potential element of multiraciality, but that may not always have been the case. Despite the challenges of data quality and the ever-shifting terrain of racial boundary-marking (Wimmer 2012), however, the construct of a nominal multiracial population offers a parsimonious way to delimit—at a given point in time—the pool of individuals whose racial self-identification we wish to explore.[4]

Factors Shaping Multiracial Self-Identification: The Importance of Generation

Once we have delimited our potential mixed-race population, the next step is to ask: What prompts a person in that nominal pool—that is, someone who could potentially claim multiraciality—to actually do so? Or to use Chandra's (2012) language, what prods an individual to "activate" a nominal category? Previous research has explored factors as varied as appearance (Khanna 2011); neighborhood composition (Rockquemore and Brunsma 2007); parental characteristics (Xie and Goyette 1997); interview setting (Harris and Sim 2002); and gender, class, and religion (Davenport 2016) in multiple-race self-reporting. However, the multigenerational nature of the mixed-race population has been largely overlooked. All too often, researchers apply terms like "multiracial," "biracial," and "mixed-race" solely to the offspring of racially discordant couples (see for example Khanna 2011). Indeed, demographers have often studied the multiracial population solely by looking for people who are reported as having parents of different races (see for example Xie and Goyette 1997). Even when later-generation multiracials are included—for example, by sampling individuals who select multiple races for themselves—we rarely ask respondents about the genealogical locus of their mixed ancestry.

Such approaches ignore both theory and evidence that suggest that the generational locus of one's mixed-race heritage matters for racial self-identification, as well as for other outcomes such as attitudes or socioeconomic status. For one thing, there are likely to be *period* effects related to multiracial generation, whereby the era in which an interracial union formed mattered for a couple's socioeconomic outcomes and for those of their descendants. The consequences of multiracial status have varied in the United States, as attitudes, legal discriminations, and classificatory practices toward interracial couples, mixed-race people, and nonwhites generally have changed over time (Davis 1991; Lee 1993; Schuman et al. 1997; Sollors 2000). The legal persecution, media interest, and social opprobrium that Mildred and Richard Loving faced for their 1958 marriage, for example, would not be the lot of a white man and black woman married in 2008. Moreover, the children of these unions would likely face a different range of choices for their self-racial identification.

The period effects related to the generational locus of multiracial ancestry also likely contribute to what are usually interpreted as effects of specific racial combinations (e.g., white-black, white-Asian, etc.). Gullickson and Morning (2011) suggested as much after finding that individuals reporting mixed Asian ancestry were more likely than those reporting mixed African ancestry to self-identify using more than one race; they hypothesized that this reflected the more generationally recent characteristic of mixed Asian people, as opposed to the more genealogically distant source for mixed blacks, which was grounded in earlier beliefs about "one-drop" racial classification. In short, the period-specific social treatment of both interracial unions and their multiracial offspring is likely to have implications for later generations and should not be conflated with the impact of particular combinations of racial ancestry.

In addition to the *period* effect associated with the genealogical locus of one's multiracial ancestry, there is also likely to be a *generational effect* due to the "genealogical distance" (Lieberson 1973, 561) between a person and the earliest (i.e., original) interracial union in his or her family tree. Broadly speaking, we expect that a first-generation experience of growing up with two parents who identify differently in racial terms is distinct from a later-generation experience of associating one's multiracial heritage with much more distant ancestors, with whom one has had little or no personal contact. More precisely, we anticipate two dimensions of the generational effect, involving the loss over time of (1) genealogical knowledge and (2) direct kinship ties. The loss of information about one's ancestors over generations is a general condition hardly limited to mixed-race people, and research on European Americans provides ample evidence that the dissipation of genealogical knowledge has a real impact on individual identity (Nahirny and Fishman 1965; Alba 1990; Waters 1990). It is no accident that Gans (2014) labels this condition the plight of "late-generation" European ethnics. Regarding the second dimension, we hypothesize that genealogical distance is associated with weakened or broken kinship ties, particularly those that span perceived racial divides. Accordingly, we expect that in the contemporary United States, being the "biracial" daughter of a white father and black mother entails stronger social ties to the white community than does being the seventh-generation "black" descendant of a white slave owner and black slave.[5]

Although the literature on multiracial generations is sparse, as we have suggested previously, there are two important studies that lend support to our hypothesized relationship between genealogical distance, on one hand, and racial identification on the other. In the United States and the United Kingdom, respectively, Bratter (2007) and Song (2017b) found that parents who identified as mixed-race did not necessarily apply that label to their children. Using data from the 2000 U.S. Census, Bratter discovered that monoracial parents in interracial unions were more likely than couples including a mixed-race parent to select multiple races for their offspring. Put differently, first-generation multiracial children were more likely to be labelled by their parents as multiple-race than were second- or later-generation offspring. Song's interview study of sixty-two mixed-race parents found that just 65 percent of the respondents said they would identify their children with multiple races. Her interviews, moreover, documented a variety of reasons for selecting other kinds of racial identities, including a child's physical appearance, the parent's familiarity with particular racial branches of the family tree, or what Bratter termed racial "overlap" (i.e., shared racial ancestry) with the nonmixed parent. Although these studies explore parents' racial classification of their children, rather than the latter's self-identification, and they do not go beyond a two-generation parent/child comparison, they offer important evidence of the impact of the generational locus of multiracial ancestry on a person's racial categorization.

Evidence from the 2015 Survey of Multiracial Adults

We have begun a project to explore empirically the relationship between the genealogical locus of one's multiracial ancestry and his or her racial identity, attitudes, social networks, and socioeconomic status, drawing on the Pew Research Center's 2015 Survey of Multiracial Adults.[6] In this article, we present several initial findings that pertain to the topic we have developed theoretically above: the association between multiracial generation and racial self-identification, and how the former can confound associations between ancestry combination and the latter.

The Pew Research Center's 2015 Survey of Multiracial Adults was conducted online by the Gfk Group using its nationally representative KnowledgePanel, whose respondents were recruited through either random-digit dialing or address-based sampling. Through KnowledgePanel, Pew screened 21,224 U.S. adults for the races of their parents, grandparents, and earlier ancestors as well as for their own racial self-identification (Pew Research Center 2015). It is these screening data—along with those collected by Pew from a smaller comparison sample ($n = 1,495$)—that we analyze here.

We identify 18 percent of the individuals sampled as being (potentially) multiracial, according to our nominal definition of a multiracial person as one who descends from ancestors of different races, regardless of how genealogically distant (see Table 1). This in itself is a striking finding, because it is so much higher than the roughly 2.5 percent of the U.S. population that selects more than one race on Census Bureau forms (Colby and Ortman 2015).[7] It speaks volumes about the difference that recognizing multigenerational depth makes when thinking about multiraciality. It also suggests that census mixed-race counts are

TABLE 1
Estimated Population Shares of U.S. Adults by Multiracial Generation

	Percent	Frequency
Multiracial generation		
First generation	2.5%	547
Second generation	5.8%	1,296
Third+ generation	10.1%	2,241
No multiracial ancestry	81.7%	18,214
Total	100%	22,298

SOURCE: Pew Survey of Multiracial Adults, 2015.
NOTE: Unweighted counts. Restricted to respondents with no missing data on race/ancestry measures. Third+ generation multiracial respondents indicate that their great-grandparents or earlier ancestors could be described as a different race than themselves, their parents, or their grandparents. Second-generation multiracials report mixed racial ancestry beginning in the grandparents' generation. First-generation multiracials report different single races for their parents and do not report any additional races for their earlier ancestors.

just the tip of the proverbial iceberg, with a much larger multiracial population potentially coming into view as classification and identification norms change over time.

Table 1 also presents what are, to our knowledge, the first estimates of the generational composition of the American adult mixed-race population. By drawing on the screening questions about the "race(s) or origin(s)" of respondents and their mothers, fathers, grandparents, and "great grandparents or earlier ancestors," we are able to distinguish "first-generation" multiracials (i.e., those who describe their mother and father as monoracial members of different races) from later-generation multiracials (whose interracial mixture stems from the generation of their grandparents or earlier).[8] Our estimate of the nominal multiracial population is quite generationally heterogeneous, as the historical record suggested. Notably, the first-generation offspring of interracial unions that are so often the poster children for multiraciality in fact make up only a small share of all the people in the Pew sample who reported two or more races in their family tree (13 percent, or 547 out of 4,084).

In Table 2, we take up the variation in ancestral racial combination commonly highlighted in studies of the multiracial population, to reveal its relationship to generational structure. As Gullickson and Morning (2011) hypothesized, people who report white and American Indian descent differ from people reporting white and Asian descent not only because of the races with which they are associated, but also because they have very different generational composition. More generally, we see that groups combining white, black, and/or American Indian ancestry have the largest third-generation shares, likely reflecting many seventeenth-, eighteenth-, and early-nineteenth-century unions under conditions of slavery and territorial conquest. Although this colonial history is equally applicable to Latinos, the generational structure of the part-Latino population, like that

TABLE 2
Generational Structure by Reported Racial Ancestry

	Multiracial Generation			
	First Generation	Second Generation	Third+ Generation	Row N
Reported ancestry				
Black-Indian	2%	35%	62%	234
Black-Latino	27%	20%	53%	49
Latino-Indian	10%	49%	41%	51
White-Asian	62%	14%	23%	111
White-Black	13%	15%	72%	241
White-Indian	8%	39%	53%	1,612
White-Latino	36%	34%	30%	771
2 other races	24%	28%	49%	72
White-Black-Indian	–	30%	70%	263
White-Latino-Indian	–	54%	46%	105
3 other races	–	47%	53%	110
4+ races	–	37%	63%	57
Third+ generation, no specifics	–	–	100%	408
Total	13%	32%	55%	100%
Column N	547	1,296	2,241	4,084

SOURCE: Pew Survey of Multiracial Adults, 2015. Row percentages may not sum to 100 due to rounding. Cells that represent structural zeros are denoted by an en-dash (–).

of the part-Asian group, is also influenced by significant recent (post-1965) immigration. In other words, differences in generational structure mean that different period and generational effects (as we defined them above) are likely at work in shaping outcomes for people with different racial ancestry combinations, and researchers must take these historical processes into account when making comparisons across populations.

Finally, Table 3 illustrates that both the generational locus of one's multiracial ancestry and the specific components of that ancestry are related to racial self-identification. Overall, we find generational distance to be negatively associated with reporting more than one race: just 7 percent of third- or later-generation respondents selected more than one race to describe themselves, even though they reported having ancestors of different races, compared to 46 percent of first-generation respondents. The pattern is broadly consistent with our hypothesis that greater genealogical distance weakens attachment to aspects of one's heritage, in this case not through a loss of information (because they are able to report having ancestors of different races) but perhaps through broken or otherwise more distant ties to the differently racialized branches of their family tree. The pattern is repeated across most of the specific ancestry combinations that we examined. Yet the breakdown by ancestry combination also demonstrates how variation in overall propensities to identify with more than one race—say, 58

TABLE 3
Multiple-Race Self-Identification, by Generation and Reported Racial Ancestry

	% Selecting More than One Category for Racial Self-Identification				
	First Generation	Second Generation	Third+ Generation	No Multiracial Ancestry	Total
All respondents	46%	50%	7%	0.2%	5%
Reported ancestry					
White-Asian	77%	56%	8%	–	58%
White-Black	66%	31%	3%	–	15%
Latino-Indian	60%	48%	0	–	29%
White-Latino	44%	62%	14%	–	41%
Black-Latino	38%	30%	4%	–	18%
White-Indian	35%	45%	5%	–	23%
Black-Indian	0	22%	2%	–	9%
2 other races	18%	30%	0	–	13%
White-Latino-Indian	–	74%	33%	–	55%
White-Black-Indian	–	60%	19%	–	31%
3 other races	–	65%	24%	–	44%
4+ races	–	86%	33%	–	53%
3+ generation, no specifics	–	–	1%	–	1%
Monoracial	–	–	–	0.2%	0.2%
Column N	547	1,296	2,241	18,214	22,298

SOURCE: Pew Survey of Multiracial Adults, 2015.
NOTE: All ancestry combinations reported include at least forty-nine cases total (see Table 2), and none of the reported frequencies by generation is based on fewer than five cases. Cells that represent structural zeros are denoted by an en-dash (–).

percent for respondents with white-Asian ancestors versus 15 percent for those reporting white-black ancestors—may not reflect ancestry combination-specific tendencies so much as distinct generational compositions. In this example, first-generation white-Asian and white-black respondents are more similar in their propensity to identify with more than one race (at 77 and 66 percent, respectively), so the different shares of the first generation in each population is likely a key factor that explains the wide divergence in multiple-race self-identification overall.

Conclusion

As our discussion of the confluence of generation with racial ancestry and self-identification shows, we cannot fully understand the mixed-race population—or the processes that shape it—until we recognize the legacy and heterogeneity of its generational depth. Given our empirical findings, we urge researchers to consider the role of generation in influencing the counts and characteristics of the multiracial population beyond the usual forces of fertility, mortality, and migration. Changes in the generational structure of the mixed-race population are likely to affect individuals' self-identification as multiracial and thus future census enumeration of the multiple race population.

Notes

1. For useful overviews of the existing literature, see Bratter (2007), Khanna (2012), and Song (2017b).
2. As we hope to have made clear, we use *generation* in the sense promoted by Ryder (1965) and Kertzer (1983): namely, as "a relational concept bound to the realm of kinship and descent" (Kertzer 1983, 128). On the frequent confusion between generation and age, cohort, life stage and/or period, however, see Kertzer (1983) and Alwin and McCammon (2007).
3. See Roth (2016) for application of this observation to racial classification in general.
4. Note that just as our definition of *multiracial* refers to socially constructed understandings of racial groupings and membership—which may or may not include beliefs about biological difference—our definition's reference to *descent* (i.e., with ancestors of more than one socially recognized race) need not be limited to genetic lineage. If American notions of race were to evolve away from biologically essentialist views, then it might well become accepted that a person could be mixed-race by virtue, say, of having been adopted by an interracial couple. See Tuan and Shiao (2011) for a thoughtful discussion of how some Korean children adopted by white American parents at times regarded themselves as white as well.
5. Of course, a great deal would depend on how the other branches of their family trees were racially labeled. But given the period effect that is also at work in this example—namely, the one-drop rule that generally governed such historical unions involving blacks—it seems likely that, in the absence of passing, the descendants of this slave-era union would have been classified as black or mulatto, and married into families who were similarly designated, further attenuating kinship links to the white population.
6. As consultants on the survey design, the authors were granted early access to the resultant data.
7. It is also higher than the 6.9 percent multiracial that the Pew Research Center (2015) calculated, principally for two reasons. One is that we took into consideration the reported races of ancestors prior to the generation of grandparents; the other is that we treated "Hispanic or Latino" as a race for the purposes of multiracial designation. Our approach reflects the growing racialization of Latinos as a group distinct from—but akin to—blacks, whites, and other traditional racial categories, as is warranted by Census Bureau findings that most people who self-identity as Hispanic in the United States decline to identify with races like "white" and "black" when a Hispanic or Latino checkbox is available to them (Compton et al. 2012; Matthews et al. 2017). However, our substantive conclusion about the role of generation does not hinge on this coding decision (results available upon request).
8. Unfortunately, the survey design does not permit generational distinctions so clearly beyond the first. This is because rather than asking individually about the racial identities of each of a respondent's four grandparents, the survey asked about their "races or origins" *en masse*. This gives us an estimate of people who are second- or later-generation multiracial, but no information about the specific relative to whom the different race(s) might have applied. Accordingly, we emphasize here the difference between first- and later-generation multiracial Americans.

References

Alaya, Ana M. 27 May 2001. Brave new faces: The changing image of New Jersey: Multiraciality gaining prominence, acceptance. *Sunday Star-Ledger*.

Alba, Richard. 1990. *Ethnic identity: The transformation of white America.* New Haven, CT: Yale University Press.
Alwin, Duane F., and Ryan J. McCammon. 2007. Rethinking generations. *Research in Human Development* 4:219–37.
Bratter, Jenifer. 2007. Will "multiracial" survive to the next generation? The racial classification of children of multiracial parents. *Social Forces* 86:821–49.
Chandra, Kanchan, ed. 2012. *Constructivist theories of ethnic politics.* Oxford: Oxford University Press.
Colby, Sandra L., and Jennifer M. Ortman. 2015. *Projections of the size and composition of the U.S. Population: 2014 to 2060.* Washington, DC: U.S. Census Bureau.
Compton, Elizabeth, Michael Bentley, Sharon Ennis, and Sonya Rastogi. 2012. *2010 Census race and Hispanic origin alternative questionnaire experiment.* Washington, DC: U.S. Census Bureau.
Davenport, Lauren D. 2016. The role of gender, class, and religion in biracial Americans' racial labeling decisions. *American Sociological Review* 81:57–84.
Davis, Floyd James. 1991. *Who is black? One nation's definition.* University Park, PA: Pennsylvania State University Press.
Doyle, Jamie Mihoko, and Grace Kao. 2007. Are racial identities of multiracials stable? Changing self-identification among single and multiple race individuals. *Social Psychology Quarterly* 70:405–23.
Frazier, E. Franklin. 1957/1997. *The black bourgeoisie.* New York, NY: Free Press Paperbacks.
Gans, Herbert J. 2014. The coming darkness of late-generation European American ethnicity. *Ethnic and Racial Studies* 37:757–65.
Goldstein, Joshua R., and Ann J. Morning. 2000. The multiple-race population of the United States: Issues and estimates. *Proceedings of the National Academy of Sciences* 97:6230–35.
Gullickson, Aaron, and Ann Morning. 2011. Choosing race: Multiracial ancestry and identification. *Social Science Research* 40:498–512.
Harris, David R., and Jeremiah Joseph Sim. 2002. Who is multiracial? Assessing the complexity of lived race. *American Sociological Review* 67:614–27.
Hitlin, Steven, J. Scott Brown, and Glenn H. Elder Jr. 2006. Racial self-categorization in adolescence: Multiracial development and social pathways. *Child Development* 77:1298–1308.
Kertzer, David I. 1983. Generation as a sociological problem. *Annual Review of Sociology* 9:125–49.
Khanna, Nikki. 2011. *Biracial in America: Forming and performing racial identity.* Lanham, MD: Lexington Books.
Khanna, Nikki. 2012. Multiracial Americans: Racial identity choices and implications for the collection of race data. *Sociology Compass* 6:316–31.
Lee, Sharon M. 1993. Racial classifications in the U.S. census: 1890–1990. *Ethnic and Racial Studies* 16:75–94.
Lieberson, Stanley. 1973. Generational differences among blacks in the north. *American Journal of Sociology* 79:550–65.
Liebler, Carolyn A., Sonya R. Porter, Leticia E. Fernandez, James M. Noon, and Sharon R. Ennis. 2017. America's churning races: Race and ethnic response changes between Census 2000 and the 2010 Census. *Demography* 54:259–84.
Matthews, Kelly, Jessica Phelan, Nicholas A. Jones, Sarah Konya, Rachel Marks, Beverly M. Pratt, Julia Coombs, and Michael Bentley. 2017. *2015 national content test race and ethnicity analysis report: A new design for the 21st century.* Washington, DC: U.S. Census Bureau.
Meacham, Jon. 18 September 2000. The new face of race. *Newsweek.*
Morning, Ann. 2000. Who is multiracial? Definitions and decisions. *Sociological Imagination* 37:209–29.
Nahirny, Vladimir C., and Joshua A. Fishman. 1965. American immigrant groups: Ethnic identification and the problem of generations. *Sociological Review* 13:311–26.
Nobles, Melissa. 2000. *Shades of citizenship: Race and the census in modern politics.* Stanford, CA: Stanford University Press.
Perez, Anthony D., and Charles Hirschman. 2009. Estimating net interracial mobility in the United States: A residual methods approach. *Sociological Methodology* 39:31–71.
Pew Research Center. 2015. *Multiracial in America: Proud, diverse and growing in numbers.* Washington, DC: Pew Research Center.
Rockquemore, Kerry Ann, and David L. Brunsma. 2007. *Beyond black: Biracial identity in America.* Lanham, MD: Rowman & Littlefield.

Root, Maria P. P., ed. 1996. *The multiracial experience: Racial borders as the new frontier*. Thousand Oaks, CA: Sage Publications.
Roth, Wendy D. 2016. The multiple dimensions of race. *Ethnic and Racial Studies* 39:1310–38.
Rumbaut, Rubén G. 2005. Immigration, incorporation, and generational cohorts in historical contexts. In *Historical influences on lives and aging*, eds. K.Warner Schaie and Glen H. Elder Jr., 43–88. New York, NY: Springer Publishing.
Ryder, Norman B. 1965. The cohort as a concept in the study of social change. *American Sociological Review* 30:843–61.
Saperstein, Aliya, and Andrew M. Penner. 2014. Beyond the looking glass: Exploring fluidity in racial self-identification and interviewer classification. *Sociological Perspectives* 57:186–207.
Schuman, Howard, Charlotte Steeh, Lawrence Bobo, and Maria Krysan. 1997. *Racial attitudes in America: Trends and interpretations*. Cambridge, MA: Harvard University Press.
Sollors, Werner, ed. 2000. *Interracialism: Black-white intermarriage in American history, literature, and law*. Oxford: Oxford University Press.
Song, Miri. 2017a. Generational change and how we conceptualize and measure multiracial people and "mixture." *Ethnic and Racial Studies* 40:2333–39.
Song, Miri. 2017b. *Multiracial parents: Mixed families, generational change, and the future of race*. New York, NY: New York University Press.
Tuan, Mia, and Jiannbin Lee Shiao. 2011. *Choosing ethnicity, negotiating race: Korean adoptees in America*. New York, NY: Russell Sage Foundation.
U.S. Census Bureau. 1918. *Negro population 1790–1915*. Washington, DC: Government Printing Office.
Waters, Mary C. 1990. *Ethnic options: Choosing identities in America*. Berkeley, CA: University of California Press.
Wimmer, Andreas. 2012. *Ethnic boundary making: Institutions, power, networks*. Oxford: Oxford University Press.
Xie, Yu, and Kimberly Goyette. 1997. The racial identification of biracial children with one Asian parent: Evidence from the 1990 census. *Social Forces* 76:547–70.

Multiracial Identification and Racial Gaps: A Work in Progress

By
JENIFER L. BRATTER

For nearly 20 years, the U.S. Census has allowed respondents to report multiple races, offering new opportunities to assess the well-being of multiracial groups. Multiple-race reporting provides much-needed nuance for assessing the racial stratification of social outcomes as the distinctions between racial groups is less clear. Here, I explore the promises and the pitfalls of working with multiple-race data in studies of race inequality. I begin with a discussion of prior work using multiple-race data, showing how they inform our understanding of race-based patterns, and also consider issues raised by the conceptual and methodological fuzziness inherent in using multiple-race responses. I then provide a brief picture of current racial differences in adult poverty rates for single- and multiple-race groups, revealing that some multiracial groups experience parity with single-race groups while others occupy a space in between. While these patterns are meaningful, multiple interpretations are possible given the nature of multiple-race data.

Keywords: multiracial identity; racial inequality; U.S. Census; racial identification; poverty

The multiracial population represents a rapidly expanding share of the U.S. population. In the 2000 Census, 6.9 million people marked more than one race (Humes, Jones, and Ramirez 2011). This had grown to approximately 8.2 million

Jenifer L. Bratter is an associate professor in sociology at Rice University. Her work focuses on the implications of the continual intersection of racial and ethnic groups for families and individual identities. She has published several peer-reviewed journal articles in Demography, Social Forces, Race and Social Problems, *and* Ethnicity and Health.

NOTE: I wish to acknowledge Richard Alba and Kenneth Prewitt for including me in the conference, "What the Census Needs to Know about Measuring Race and Ethnicity," and all the participants from the conference for their useful feedback on earlier drafts. I also wish to extend a special thanks to Carolyn Liebler and Richard Alba for their tremendous help on previous drafts.

Correspondence: jbratter@rice.edu

DOI: 10.1177/0002716218758622

people as of 2013,[1] or close to 3 percent of the U.S. population. The U.S. Census Bureau projects that this population will grow to 26 million, representing 6.2 percent of the American population by 2060 (U.S. Census Bureau 2014). The expansion of this group signals an increased space for understanding identities as occurring in between categories and reflects changing norms around how one identifies and perceives race in a rapidly diversifying era (Hochschild, Weaver, and Burch 2012; Lee and Bean 2010; Perlmann and Waters 2002). Although the prevalence of this institutionally recognizable racial subgroup points to more flexibility in identification, its growth exists within a social landscape in which racial inequality continues to be durable. National data on life expectancy, incarceration, and several forms of economic standing consistently reveal disadvantages for racial minorities relative to (non-Hispanic) whites (Pettit 2012; Proctor, Semega, and Kollar 2016). Increasingly, scholars believe that racial progress may have stalled or even reversed since the gains made following the civil rights era (Lichter 2013; Sharkey 2008), portending an increasing tie between race and life chances. Where does an expanding multiracial population fit within a landscape characterized by pernicious and stable divides?

What we can know about racially mixed people in the context of race-based gaps has expanded, with self-reported multiracial status documented in the U.S. Census since 2000 and in a growing number of federal and social surveys since the Office of Management and Budget (OMB) revision of standards of ethnic and racial classification in 1997 (OMB 1997). Incorporating a "mixed-race presence" allows us to investigate whether well-established disadvantages endure and are equally shared within racially complex groups, or if such disadvantages may be lessened among mixed-race individuals (Lee and Bean 2010; Bonilla Silva 2004). Multiracial experiences can also reveal the rigidity and staying power of racialized distinctions (Currington, Lin, and Lundquist 2015) and may skew patterns of well-being of larger groups if multiracial distinction remains uncaptured (Bratter and Gorman 2011; Qian and Lichter 2007). However, tracking the demographic and socioeconomic profiles of the mixed-race population has historically been a challenge for several reasons. First, self-reporting of multiple race categories is conditioned on social, structural, and geographic factors (Davenport 2016). Additionally, reporting multiple races is notoriously unstable for individuals, with many of those who report multiple races shifting their responses in a later enumeration (Hitlin, Brown, and Elder 2006; Liebler et al. 2017). Analyses of ongoing racial stratification require a more complex classification scheme; unfortunately, the available public data to do so may not be up to the task.

In this article, I explore the promises and pitfalls of incorporating multiple-race responses into studies of racial inequality. I begin with an overview of recent work comparing the well-being of multiracial and single-race populations. This work reveals important variations in race-based gaps, but with few consistent patterns across all multiracial subgroups. I then discuss the many unresolved measurement issues when employing multiple-race responses to capture multiracial groups (Prewitt 2013; Roth 2016). Standard approaches to group-based demographic analyses, such as comparing and contrasting the same group over time or generalizing analyses to a larger population, are generally less precise when applied to groups reporting multiple races.

In the final section, I use multiple-race data to assess racial variation in the percent of the adult U.S. population living at or below the federal poverty line. This analysis examines poverty rates for the single- and multiple-race populations using the public data from the American Community Survey (ACS) and the U.S. Census. I find that on one hand, these patterns reveal how some multiracial individuals face a distinctive poverty risk compared to other groups; on the other hand, the variation in who selects multiple categories at any time period and over time suggests that poverty level may actually affect whether someone identifies as multiracial. In closing, I argue for the continued inclusion of multiracial groups in studies of racial inequality for the insights they can provide, while acknowledging that analysts must be aware of the limitations involved.

Racial Inequality in and between Groups: Multiracial versus Single-Race Well-Being

How do multiracial populations fare relative to their single-race counterparts? A small but growing literature has tackled this question with an important, though limited, set of dynamics used to assess multiracial life. While single-race identification remains most commonly studied (Davenport 2016), an expanding body of work examines the distinctive social experiences of mixed-race groups. Research on poverty (Bratter and Kimbro 2013; Bratter and Damaske 2013), residential segregation (Bennett 2011; Ellis et al. 2012), mate selection preferences and behaviors (Qian and Lichter 2007; Currington, Lin, and Lundquist 2015), and physical and mental health (Bratter and Gorman 2011; Tabb 2015) have focused on comparisons between single- and multiple-race groups. It is important to note that these studies define racially mixed status in various ways, including parental racial identification as well as self-reporting of racial identification with multiple categories. Much of what we know focuses on racially mixed children whose status is determined by their presence in interracial families (Bratter and Damaske 2013). Meanwhile, fewer studies focus on multiracial groups in adulthood. Those that do employ "two or more races" or other designations of racially mixed identification as the sole means to identify racially mixed groups of adults (Bennett 2011; Qian and Lichter 2007; Miyawaki 2015; Bratter and Gorman 2011). While placing racially mixed experiences in the context of families has tremendous value, our understanding of multiple-race groups across the life course is limited, particularly in mid- and late adulthood.

What we know about multiple-race groups defies any expectation of uniformity in how these individuals may either mirror or be distinct from their respective single-race populations. On one hand, there is evidence that boundaries of whiteness may be expanding to include nonblack groups who simultaneously identify as partly "white" (Alba, Beck, and Sahin 2017). Asian-white and American Indian–white multiracials are far more likely to reside in predominately white neighborhoods and have white spouses or partners than their same-race minority peers. Asian-white multiracials are uniquely advantaged in the online dating market as a group highly preferred by whites relative to other groups (Currington, Lin, and Lundquist 2015). Other work reveals that some multiracials continue to face disadvantages even if whiteness as an identity is embraced (see Kao and Burke 2013). American Indian–white multiracials have exceedingly poor health, even those who view white as a category that best describes them (Bratter and Gorman 2011). Overall, whiteness can convey advantages and disadvantages for multiracial adults.

Other groups' experiences reveal the continued salience of minority status. Some argue that blackness may operate as a master status in the lives of black-white individuals, reflecting a departure from the experiences of other multiracial groups (Lee and Bean 2010). The evidence for this is mixed. Multirace blacks stand apart from blacks in their lower exposure to segregated neighborhoods and lower rates of poor health and poverty (Bratter and Damaske 2013), pointing potentially to fewer racialized disadvantages. Black-white multiracials, like black-white interracial families, live in more integrated and diverse areas (Bennett 2011; Ellis et al. 2012). Also, while they are slightly more likely, compared to other multiracials, to partner with their single-race minority counterparts (i.e., other African Americans), most black-white adults have white partners (Miyawaki 2015). A similar pattern emerges in dating preferences (Currington, Lin, and Lundquist 2015). Ultimately, minority status remains salient for multiracial adults in the realm of mate selection (Song 2016); however, their experiences remain distinctive from minority counterparts.

Taken together, multiracial dynamics provide much insight into the evolving nature of racial stratification, but how might methodological and conceptual concerns affect our interpretation of trends for this group? We can learn much about the staying power of racially stratified systems from studies that fully account for the presence of multiple-race groups, but, as I discuss in the following section, serious methodological and conceptual challenges remain.

Conceptual and Methodological Challenges in Measuring Multiple-Race Groups

Capturing the social outcomes of multiple-race people relative to their single-race counterparts remains an ongoing challenge on several fronts. Conceptually, it is unclear what precisely is revealed when individuals report their race (Roth 2016). While we know that many racially mixed people communicate single-race affinities when reporting their race (Herman 2004; Campbell 2007), we are still unclear what is conveyed when multiple categories are reported. Some respondents who mark more than one box are reporting ancestral complexity (e.g., acknowledging interracial parentage), while for others, race responses reflect racial identification as "mixed" (e.g., experiential ties to more than one race group), and still others may be reporting an identity that is externally validated by others (e.g., being understood by outsiders as "mixed"). Not surprisingly, the majority of social science research on the multiracial population focuses on self-perception and the formation of identity (Charmaraman et al. 2014), indicating that "who is multiracial" in terms of ancestry and what that means in terms of social understanding are still unanswered questions.

Moreover, those who choose to mark more than one box are a nonrandom subset of those who could do so, given the mixing in parental and grandparental generations (Davenport 2016; Pew Research Center 2015) and their understanding of their ancestry (Gullickson and Morning 2011; Goldstein and Morning 2000). Different estimates of the mixed-race population's size and composition are calculated if based on (1) multiple races marked in one census (Bennett 2011), (2) parental racial origins of interracial couples (Brunsma 2005; Roth 2005; Xie and Goyette 1997; Qian 2004), (3) mixed heritage inferred through ancestry responses presumed to give racial information based on geographic regions of origin (Gullickson and Morning 2011), or (4) reports of multiple races in a past census (Liebler et al. 2017). Census information, unlike other surveys, is generally nonspecific about who in the household is reporting racial classification for its members. Racial identifications of minors are more than likely provided by their parents or adult guardians, but this is not explicit. This ambiguity presents clear problems given the general tendency to classify the racially mixed as members of single-race groups (Herman 2004; Lee and Bean 2010). Taken together, estimates of the two-or-more-race population reflect the dynamics of racially identifying individuals who, despite sharing an ancestral mix, can take on various classifications (e.g., Brunsma 2005; Burke and Kao 2013) as opposed to a specific (or stably understood) ethno-racial grouping.

Finally, people who mark multiple race responses do not always do so in every census or survey (Liebler et al. 2017), which makes cross-time comparison—and, thus, an appraisal of racial trends—extremely challenging. Shifting their race responses may be akin to the developmental arc of racial identification (Hitlin, Brown, and Elder 2006; Doyle and Kao 2007). Ultimately, the population that retains this classification stably is often distinctive from those who "enter" single-race groups or adopt this designation later in life (Tabb 2015; Kramer, Burke, and Charles 2015). In fact, response consistency is uncommon among people who mark multiple races (less than 50 percent reported multiple races in both the 2000 Census and the 2010 Census). Analysts wanting to know whether multiple-race individuals' circumstances improved or declined across a specific time frame run a serious risk of comparing groups that represent significantly different populations defined by conditions that are currently not understood.

Ultimately, these concerns are broadly reflective of race as a socially constructed concept (Nagel 1994; Roth 2016; Saperstein, Penner, and Light 2013). More than any single racial category, identification with two or more racial categories is affected by contextual factors at multiple levels. However, these issues are generally well beyond our current knowledge and, unless the research focuses explicitly on racial identification, are routinely absent from a discussion of racial gaps. These issues notwithstanding, we can learn much about the staying power of racially stratified systems from studies that account for the presence of multiple-race groups. Trend analyses operate as a "gold standard" for analyzing racial inequality, but multiple-race groups are rarely treated as distinct categories. Moreover, if these groups are included, what would those comparisons convey? We need to develop better language to describe what we have in our data and not make assumptions about what we do not have.

Multiracial Economic Well-Being, 2000–2015: What Can We Learn?

Given these methodological and conceptual concerns, what can be made of analyses of public data on multiple-race groups? Here, I use the U.S. Census and ACS data on separate multiple-race and single-race populations to investigate racial differences in adult poverty rates over a 15-year period (2000–2015). Poverty remains a heavily race-stratified indicator of economic well-being, and the Great Recession both enhanced poverty overall and intensified race/ethnic specific gaps (Thomas and Tucker 2015). We can gauge whether gaps between multiple-race and single-race groups are sensitive to these changes. While we cannot make any claims on the collective shifts in well-being across time for multiple-race groups (see above), we can surmise how individuals who occupy these categories experience poverty risk in specific years.

Methodology

The analysis draws on the public use microdata samples (PUMS) one-year estimates of the ACS for the years 2005, 2010, and 2015 and the 1 percent PUMS from the 2000 U.S. Census. These files were made available through the Integrated Public Use Microdata Sample series (Ruggles et al. 2017). The ACS is a year-long survey that was modelled after the U.S. Census, specifically the "long-form" questionnaire (National Research Council 2007), sampling roughly 1 percent of the U.S. population. This nationally representative sample employs a sampling frame aimed at providing census-based estimates. All statistical analyses are weighted employing person weights provided by the ACS for these patterns, within a margin of error, to reflect the U.S. population, despite that they are derived from a sample.

I construct the following race/ethnic groups: non-Hispanic white, black/African American, Asian, Pacific Islander, and American Indian/Alaskan Native, some other race, and Hispanic, including those who indicate "Hispanic origin" and one racial category. I then identify several multiple-race groups, including groups that represent combinations spanning (non-Hispanic) white and non-white categories and dual-minority categories, and allow for a category for Hispanic respondents who selected multiple races. The current structure of the race and Hispanic origin question leaves no possibility to enumerate persons who combine Hispanic with a non-Hispanic race/ethnic group (e.g., persons seeking to convey [non-Hispanic] white and Hispanic parentage). This represents a serious shortcoming given the high rates of intermarriage between Hispanic and non-Hispanic persons (Pew Research Center 2017) and the shifts in identifying as Hispanic among those from intermarried-family backgrounds (Duncan and Trejo 2011).

I present the poverty rates across various single- and multiple-race groups for each year. The poverty measure is constructed from a measure of family income as a percent of the federal poverty line, with values at or below 100 percent, indicating a family income that is at or less than the poverty line. Although the federal poverty line is heavily critiqued on a variety of fronts, and alternative measures have been introduced, it continues to be a widely used standard of economic well-being (Fisher 1992). Instead of raw percentages for the entire population, I focus the estimates on adult householders who represent families in poverty statistics (see Proctor, Semega, and Kollar 2016).

Racial Gaps in Poverty: Where Do Multiple-Race Groups Fit?

Table 1 shows baseline estimates of poverty rates across several single- and multiple-race groups for 2000, 2005, 2010, and 2015. This analysis focuses on the adult population spanning majority and minority groups to gauge the variation in poverty experiences across the most salient social divides. Additionally, to capture the groups most represented in racial statistics on income and poverty, the analysis is restricted to individuals who are designated as householders and aged 25 and older. I show predicted probabilities (or adjusted rates of poverty), as opposed to raw percentages, to account for basic demographic profiles: age, gender, and presence in a married-couple household, in addition to race/ethnicity. Models are estimated separately for each year (with appropriate weights). Although myriad factors impact poverty risk beyond these basic controls (e.g., employment, education, and nativity), these figures provide a useful baseline for appraising race-based gaps. I show two sets of statistically significant differences. As nearly all groups have significantly higher poverty than whites, I mark instances when differences are not significant (superscript "ns"), according to a two-tailed test ($p < .05$). I also test for differences between multiple-race and a corresponding single-race nonwhite group.

According to Table 1, the likelihood of living at or below the poverty line increased for all groups in 2005 and 2010, but varied by race/ethnicity. White (single race) and Asian (single race) householders had relatively lower likelihoods of poverty. White householders had an adjusted poverty probability of .083, or 8.0 percent, in 2000 that rose to 10.0 percent by 2010 and then declined somewhat by 2015 to 9.7 percent. The probability of poverty for Asians was higher at all years, ranging from 12 to 13 percent. Poverty probabilities are substantially higher for black, American Indian, and Hispanic householders, ranging from 15 to 21 percent, depending on the group and year. As of 2015, American Indians (single race) have the highest adjusted poverty probability, at 22 percent. These

TABLE 1
Predicted Probabilities of Adult Poverty by Race/Ethnic Category for
Single- and Multiple-Race Groups, 2000–2015

	2000	2005	2010	2015
White	0.083	0.085	0.102	0.097
Black/African American	0.184	0.173	0.186	0.179
Black-white	0.122	0.163	0.176	0.145[a]
Asian	0.131	0.123	0.130	0.127
Asian-white	0.127	0.099[ns]	0.116	0.106[ns]
American Indian/Alaskan Native	0.221	0.197	0.222	0.217
American Indian/Alaskan Native–white	0.159[b]	0.133[b]	0.192[b]	0.147[b]
Hispanic (single race)	0.221	0.198	0.215	0.202
Hispanic (two or more races)	0.208	0.142[c]	0.207	0.150[c]

SOURCE: 2000 1 percent Public Microdata Sample of U.S. Census; 2005, 2010, and 2015 American Community Survey, one-year estimates (Ruggles et al. 2017).
NOTE: With the exception of Hispanic respondents, all race/ethnic groups refer to non-Hispanic adults. Several groups are not reported here, including those identifying as "some other race," Pacific Islanders, and all other multiple-race groups. Predicted probabilities were generated from a model adjusting for age, sex, and household type for householders aged 25 and older. A superscripted "ns" indicates no statistically significant differences from whites. No statistical differences between Asian-white and Asians found.
a. Statistical differences between black-white and African Americans.
b. Statistical differences between American Indian-whites and American Indians.
c. Statistical differences between single-race and multiple-race Hispanics.

baseline figures align with research revealing that a substantial share of adults lived at or below the poverty line during the 2000s, with populations of color experiencing the greatest risk (Reardon and Bischoff 2011; Thomas and Tucker 2015).

Where do multiple-race adult householders fit into these patterns? Beneath each nonwhite single-race group are the patterns for adults who combine this group with white. Black-white adults have a poverty risk that trends below, but close to, single-race black/African Americans in 2005 (0.163 vs. 0.173), although this gap is significantly different by 2015 (0.145 vs. 0.179). Asian-white adults, meanwhile, are the only group whose adjusted poverty probability is sometimes not significantly different from that of whites, which is the case in 2005 and 2015 but not 2000 or 2010. Their poverty probability is only 10 percent in 2015, which is not significantly different from white adults at 12 percent. Single-race Asians, by contrast, have significantly higher poverty at each year relative to whites. American Indian–white householders complicate this pattern even further. Their probability of living in poverty is solidly in between both origin single-race groups, with adjusted percentages that are statistically higher than those of whites but lower than those of American Indians.

Ultimately, mixed-race groups experience a variety of gaps that are not neatly predictable given the experiences of either single-race group. Asian-white adults are the only group at near-parity with whites at any year, while black-white poverty risks reflect the relatively high poverty of blacks. American Indian–white households also face substantial poverty risks, largely falling between whites and American Indians. It is interesting to note that patterns remain highly consistent across the period of analysis despite the variations in who reports being multiracial and how stable that designation is across surveys. I consider the implications of these patterns for studies of race-based gaps, particularly in light of the considerable methodological concerns that affect year-to-year comparisons.

Concluding Thoughts: Does Mixed-Race "Matter" to the Study of Inequality?

Nearly 20 years out from the first count of the "two-or-more-races" population in the U.S. Census, we find ourselves with more questions than answers in the study of racial gaps in well-being among single- and multiple-race groups. The current analysis of adult poverty risks across race echoes prior work by revealing that multiple-race groups are not easily collapsible into broader racial categories. Black-white respondents face substantial poverty risk that is mostly (though not entirely) parallel to black adults; meanwhile, Asian-white adults face substantially less poverty than their Asian peers, at rates that parallel the experiences of whites in certain years. American Indian–white adults face a poverty risk that, while exceeding that of white adults, is still lower than that of American Indian adults. In all, these patterns yield various ways that racial mixture interacts with racially stratified patterns.

Yet the patterns lend themselves to multiple interpretations. On one hand, they add support to general contentions of simultaneous hardening and softening of racial boundaries. While racial boundaries appear more permeable for nonblack multiracials, black-white adults face a fairly rigid black/nonblack divide: their heightened poverty risks are generally commensurate with those of other black adults; this was true particularly around the time of the Great Recession. Additionally, we know that the nonrandomness of who is described as multiple race in census data may shape these patterns. Structural circumstances may determine whether individuals "leave," "stay," or "join" racial categories from one measurement moment to another (Liebler et al. 2017). This means that poverty risk, or other correlates of poverty, may operate as drivers of racial identification, either increasing or decreasing the likelihood of selecting multiple boxes from one year to the next. Moreover, broader norms concerning identifying may vary at specific time periods—for example, during the Obama administration—and may enhance the likelihood of employing multiple race categories overall. This response flux strongly suggests that poverty shifts in any direction do not immediately indicate a large-scale worsening or improvement of conditions. Ultimately, our ability to gauge if gaps are closing or widening over time is seriously compromised by the fluidity of multiple-race identification.

While measurement issues abound, much can be learned about the larger structure of well-being when multiple-race groups are included in surveys. Taken together, these patterns call for more data and more racial detail, not less. Currently, officials of the U.S. Census are proposing to alter the race question again to allow for, among other things, Hispanic origin to be listed alongside racial groups in a single format, with checkboxes and open-ended spaces to allow respondents to elaborate on their identity. This can add much to our understanding of socioeconomic profiles by allowing for further delineations of more specific segments of racially identified groups.

Note

1. U.S. Census Bureau (2014), Table 10.

References

Alba, Richard, Brenden Beck, and Duygu Basaran Sahin. 2017. The U.S. Mainstream expands-again. *Journal of Ethnic and Migration Studies* 44:1–19.
Bennett, Pamela. 2011. The social position of multiracial groups in the United States: Evidence from residential segregation. *Ethnic & Racial Studies* 34 (4): 707–29.
Bonilla-Silva, Eduardo. 2004. From bi-racial to tri-racial: Towards a new system of racial stratification in the USA. *Ethnic and Racial Studies* 27 (6): 931–50.
Bratter, Jenifer L., and Sarah Damaske. 2013. Poverty at a racial crossroads: Poverty among multiracial children of single mothers. *Journal of Marriage and Family* 75 (2): 486–502.
Bratter, Jenifer L., and Bridget K. Gorman. 2011. Does multiracial matter? A study of racial disparities in self-rated health. *Demography* 48 (1): 127–52.
Bratter, Jenifer, and Rachel Tolbert Kimbro. 2013. Multiracial children and poverty: Evidence from the early childhood longitudinal study of kindergartners. *Family Relations* 62 (1): 175–89.
Brunsma, David L. 2005. Interracial families and the racial identification of mixed-race children: Evidence from the Early Childhood Longitudinal Study. *Social Forces* 84 (2): 1131–57.
Burke, Ruth, and Grace Kao. 2013. Bearing the burden of whiteness: The implications of racial self-identification for multiracial adolescents' school belonging and academic achievement. *Ethnic and Racial Studies* 36 (5): 747–73.
Campbell, Mary E. 2007. Thinking outside the (black) box: Measuring black and multiracial identification on surveys. *Social Science Research* 36 (3): 921–44.
Charmaraman Linda, Megan Woo, Ashley Quach, and Sumru Erkut. 2014. How have researchers studied multiracial populations: A content and methodological review of 20 years of research. *Cultural Diversity & Ethnic Minority Psychology* 20 (3): 336–52.
Currington, Celeste Vaughn, Ken-Hou Lin, and Jennifer Hickes Lundquist. 2015. Positioning multiraciality in cyberspace. *American Sociological Review* 80 (4): 764–88.
Davenport, Lauren D. 2016. The role of gender, class, and religion in biracial Americans' racial labeling decisions. *American Sociological Review* 81 (1): 57–84.
Doyle, Jamie Mihoko, and Grace Kao. 2007. Are racial identities of multiracials stable? Changing self-identification among single and multiple race individuals. *Social Psychology Quarterly* 70 (4): 405–23.
Duncan, Brian, and Stephen J. Trejo. 2011. Intermarriage and the intergenerational transmission of ethnic identity and human capital for Mexican Americans. *Journal of Labor Economics* 19 (2): 195–227.

Ellis, Mark, Steven R. Holloway, Richard Wright, and Christopher Fowler. 2012. Agents of change: Mixed-race households and the dynamics of neighborhood segregation in the United States. *Annals of the Association of American Geography* 102 (3): 549–70.

Fisher, Gordan. 1992. Poverty guidelines for 1992. *Social Security Bulletin* 55 (1): 43–46.

Goldstein, Joshua R., and Ann J. Morning. 2000. The multiple-race population of the United States: Issues and estimates. *Proceedings of the National Academy of Sciences* 97 (11): 6230–35.

Gullickson, Aaron, and Ann Morning. 2011. Choosing race: Multiracial ancestry and identification. *Social Science Research* 40 (2): 498–512.

Herman, Melissa. 2004. Forced to choose: Some determinants of racial identification in multiracial adolescents. *Child Development* 75 (3): 730–48.

Hitlin, Steven, J. Scott Brown, and Glen H. Elder. 2006. Racial self-categorization in adolescence: Multiracial development and social pathways. *Child Development* 77 (5): 1298–1308.

Hochschild, Jennifer L., Vesla M. Weaver, and Traci Burch. 2012. *Creating a new racial order: How immigration, multiracialism, genomics and the young can remake race in America*. Princeton, NJ: Princeton University Press.

Humes, Karen, Nicholas Jones, and Roberto Ramirez. 2011. *Overview of race and Hispanic origin: 2010*. 2010 Census Briefs C2010BR-02. Washington, DC: U.S. Census Bureau.

Kao, Grace, and Ruth Burke. 2013. Bearing the burden of whiteness: The implications of racial self-identification for multiracial adolescents' school belonging and academic achievement. *Ethnic and Racial Studies* 36 (5): 747–73.

Kramer, Rory, Ruth Burke, and Camille Z. Charles. 2015. When change doesn't matter: Racial identity (in)consistency and adolescent well-being. *Sociology of Race and Ethnicity* 1 (2): 270–86.

Lee, Jennifer, and Frank Bean. 2010. *The diversity paradox: Immigration and the color line*. New York, NY: Russell Sage Foundation.

Lichter, Daniel. 2013. Integration or fragmentation? Racial diversity and the American future. *Demography* 50 (2): 359–91.

Liebler, Carolyn A., Sonya R. Porter, Leticia E. Fernandez, James M. Noon, and Sharon R. Ennis. 2017. America's churning races: Race and ethnic response changes between Census 2000 and the 2010 census. *Demography* 54 (1): 259–84.

Miyawaki, Michael H. 2015. Expanding boundaries of whiteness? A look at the marital patterns of part-white multiracial groups. *Sociological Forum* 30 (3): 995–1016.

Nagel, Joane. 1994. Constructing ethnicity: Creating and recreating ethnic identity and culture. *Social Problems* 41 (1): 152–76.

National Research Council. 2007. *Using the American Community Survey: Benefits and challenges*, eds. Constance F. Citro and Graham Kalton. Washington, DC: National Academies Press.

Office of Management and Budget (OMB). 1997. Revision to the standards for the classification of federal data on race and ethnicity. *Federal Register* 62 (210).

Perlmann, Joel, and Mary C. Waters. 2002. *The new race question: How the census counts multiracial individuals*. New York, NY: Russell Sage Foundation.

Pettit, Becky. 2012. *Invisible men: Mass incarceration and the myth of black progress*. New York, NY: Russell Sage Foundation.

Pew Research Center. 2015. *Multiracial in America: Proud, diverse, and growing in numbers*. Washington, DC: Pew Research Center.

Pew Research Center. 2017. *Intermarriage in the U.S. 50 years after* Loving v. Virginia. Washington, DC: Pew Research Center.

Prewitt, Kenneth. 2013. *What is your race: The census and our flawed efforts to classify Americans*. Princeton, NJ: Princeton University Press.

Proctor, Bernadette D., Jessica L. Semega, and Melissa A. Kollar. 2016. *Income and poverty in the United States: 2015*. U.S. Census Bureau, Current Population Reports, P60-256(RV). Washington, DC: U.S. Government Printing Office.

Qian, Zhenchao. 2004. Options: Racial/ethnic identification of children of intermarried couples. *Social Science Quarterly* 85 (3): 746–66.

Qian, Zhenchao, and Daniel T. Lichter. 2007. Social boundaries and marital assimilation: Interpreting trends in racial and ethnic intermarriage. *American Sociological Review* 72 (1): 68–94.

Reardon, Sean F., and Kendra Bischoff. 2011. Income inequality and income segregation. *American Journal of Sociology* 116 (4): 1092–1153.
Roth, Wendy D. 2005. The end of the one-drop rule? Labeling of multiracial children in black intermarriages. *Sociological Forum* 20 (1): 35–67.
Roth, Wendy D. 2016. The multiple dimensions of race. *Ethnic and Racial Studies* 39:1310–38.
Ruggles, Steven, Katie Genadek, Ronald Goeken, Josiah Grover, and Matthew Sobek. 2017. Integrated Public Use Microdata Series: Version 7.0 [dataset]. Minneapolis, MN: University of Minnesota.
Saperstein, Aliya, Andrew M. Penner, and Ryan Light. 2013. Racial formation in perspective: Connecting individuals, institutions and power relations. *Annual Review of Sociology* 39:359–78.
Sharkey, Patrick. 2008. The intergenerational transmission of context. *American Journal of Sociology* 113:931–69.
Song, Miri. 2016. Multiracial people and their partners in Britain: Extending the link between intermarriage and integration? *Ethnicities* 16 (4): 631–48.
Tabb, Karen M. 2015. Changes in racial categorization over time and health status: An examination of multiracial young adults in the USA. *Ethnicity & Health* 21 (2): 146–57.
Thomas, Kevin J., and Catherine Tucker. 2015. Child poverty during the years of the Great Recession: An analysis of racial differences among immigrants and U.S. natives. *Race and Social Problems* 7 (4): 300–314.
U.S. Census Bureau. 2014. Table 10. Projections of the Population by Sex, Hispanic Origin, and Race for the United States: 2015 to 2060 (NP2014-T10). Available from https://www.census.gov/data/tables/2014/demo/popproj/2014-summary-tables.html.
Xie, Yu, and Kimberly Goyette. 1997. The racial identification of biracial children with one Asian parent: Evidence from the 1990 census. *Social Forces* 76 (2): 547–70.

Boundary Blurring? Racial Identification among the Children of Interracial Couples

By
DANIEL T. LICHTER
and
ZHENCHAO QIAN

This article uses data, pooled annually, from the 2008 to 2014 American Community Survey (ACS) to document (1) recent fertility patterns among interracially married couples and (2) the racial or ethnic identification of the children from interracial marriages. We find that a sizable minority of America's children from mixed-race marriages are identified by their parents as monoracial, which suggests that mixed-race children are seriously underreported. Moreover, the assignment of race is highly uneven across interracial marriages comprising husbands and wives with different racial backgrounds. For America's children, their reported racial identities in the ACS reflect a kind of racial "tug-of-war" between fathers and mothers, who bring their own racial and cultural identities to marriages. The status or power of parents is often unequal, and this is played out in children's racial identification. For example, parents from minority populations in interracial marriages often have fewer claims on the race of their children. The racial and ethnic identities of children from these marriages, at a minimum, are highly subjective and complex.

Keywords: intermarriage; race; ethnicity; diversity; racial identity; family; children

The share of all U.S. marriages involving partners with different racial and ethnic backgrounds has risen sharply over the past few

Daniel T. Lichter is the Ferris Family Professor in the Department of Policy Analysis and Management, professor of sociology, and director of the Institute for the Social Sciences, all at Cornell University. His work focuses on changing racial boundaries, as measured by shifts in racial segregation in America's settlement system and by new patterns of interracial marriage and cohabitation during a period of massive immigration.

Zhenchao Qian is a professor of sociology and associate director of the Population Studies and Training Center at Brown University. His research focuses on changing patterns and consequences of marriage, cohabitation, and assortative mating. He is also interested in racial identification among children born to interracial couples, immigrant integration in the United States, and social and family change in China.

Correspondence: dtl28@cornell.edu

DOI: 10.1177/0002716218760507

decades (Qian and Lichter 2011; Lee and Bean 2010). According to a recent Pew Research Center report, 17 percent of all newly married couples were interracial or interethnic (Livingstone and Brown 2017). The clear implication of this finding is that racial and ethnic boundaries are weakening. In the case of interracial marriage, partners presumably define one another as equals, even if they occupy different places in America's racial or ethnic hierarchy. This has been defined historically along a white-black continuum (Frank, Akresh, and Lu 2010) or by a tripartite classification with America's nonblack, nonwhite populations occupying a middle category (Bonilla-Silva 2004). Rising interracial dating, cohabitation, and marriage are thus seen as evidence both of improving racial and ethnic relations and declining social distance between the white majority and different minority populations (Qian and Lichter 2007; Lichter, Qian, and Tumin 2015). The past several decades have been marked by a new openness in attitudes and receptivity to interracial marriages (Herman and Campbell 2012).

Rising rates of interracial marriage clearly reflect and reinforce growing racial and ethnic diversity in America. Increasing diversity itself creates more abundant demographic opportunities for interracial contact and intermarriage, while childbearing among interracial couples—both past and present—is expressed in new forms of racial diversity. Indeed, the children of interracial marriages have fueled the growth of America's multiracial population and the so-called biracial baby boom. In 2010, 9 million persons or nearly 3 percent of the U.S. population identified as multiracial (i.e., listing two or more racial or ethnic categories) (Jones and Bullock 2012). The recent growth among mixed-race children has been particularly striking. The share of multiracial babies (under age one and living with two parents) increased from 1 percent in 1970 to 10 percent in 2013 (Pew Research Center 2015). Whereas marriages involving partners with the same racial identity (e.g., Asian-Asian or black-black) contribute in obvious ways to growing diversity through differential fertility, racial diversity also takes demographic expression in the growth of multiracial children from interracial marriages. Yet many persons with intermarried parents do not identify as mixed-race, which is responsible for the so-called multiracial identity gap (Pew Research Center 2015). Mixed-race individuals are seriously undercounted, especially American Indians, who have a long history of substantial out-group marriage with whites (Liebler 2010; Perez and Hirschman 2009).

For these reasons, race today is often reflexively regarded as a "social construction" that reflects demographic and cultural processes that are rooted in color, nativity status, ancestry, and national origin, among other factors (Gullickson 2016; Liebler 2016; Qian, Lichter, and Tumin 2018). For mixed-race children, racial identity may not only reflect the phenotypes of both biological parents, but also be shaped by exposure to the competing or contested cultural influences of parents, extended kin, and the racially integrated or segregated communities in which they live (Davenport 2016). These children may serve as associational bridges connecting each side of the racial divide yet remain culturally isolated or only weakly embraced by the broader ethnoracial populations of their parents. By moving back and forth across racial boundaries, multiracial children quite literally blur the color line. In doing so, they make ambiguous their own racial identity, giving them unusual flexibility in how they present themselves but also placing them at risk of having their racial identity externally imposed and internalized.

In the case of America's children, the fluidity of racial and ethnic identity is further complicated by the fact that parents initially define their children's racial and ethnic identity (Brunsma 2005; Qian 2004; Gullickson and Morning 2011). Children's racial identity, at least how it is measured in government reports, may depend heavily on situational or contextual circumstances that have little or nothing to do with how children are perceived by others (on the basis of phenotype) or even how children see themselves as they grow up (Vargas and Kingsbury 2016). For example, the classification of children's racial identity may depend on the idiosyncratic race and sex combinations of parents (e.g., black male and white female parents as opposed to white male and black female parents). The commonplace reference to racial self-identification is a misnomer for children if parents assign racial designations. Who answers the race and Hispanic origin questions on government surveys clearly matters not only in defining whether the children of interracial couples are classified as monoracial or multiracial, but which racial group or groups are imposed upon them. This racial designation may or may not correspond to how these children define themselves later as adolescents or young adults (Liebler et al. 2017).

Specific Objectives and Empirical Approach

In this article we use data, pooled annually, from the 2008 to 2014 American Community Survey (ACS) to document (1) recent fertility patterns among interracially married couples and (2) the racial or ethnic identifications of the children from white-minority interracial marriages. Childbearing among interracial couples is the engine of growth in the mixed-race population of children (Fu 2008), who are defined as such (or not) by parents or other family members who fill out the race and Hispanic questions in the ACS on behalf of all household members. Perhaps surprisingly, nationally representative studies of fertility among intermarried couples are rare. To the extent that interracial couples bear children—or bear more children than in the past—the rise in interracial marriages will reinforce ethnoracial diversity by fueling the growth of America's mixed-race populations of all kinds.

The ACS includes information on marital status, year of marriage, and number of children born (along with their ages). It is important to note that the ACS includes information on recent births (i.e., whether a woman aged 15–50 had a birth in the past 12 months). This information can be used to determine whether interracial couples have fewer children than endogamous couples and whether the particular racial combination of interracial parents matters. Because the likelihood of having a birth in the past 12 months is conditional on marital duration, we limit the sample for this research to those who married in the past five years. As recently married couples, they are in their prime childbearing years, when annual fertility rates are highest. In addition, the ACS includes a count of own children in the household, which allows us to compare the number of residential children by marriage type. To maximize the likelihood that the children are the biological offspring of currently married couples and reduce the likelihood that couples have children living elsewhere, we limit the sample to couples in which both spouses are in first marriages and wives are aged 20 to 39 years. Our analyses are limited to heterosexual marriages.

We also restrict the sample to interracial couples, where ethnoracial categories include Hispanics, non-Hispanic whites (hereafter whites), non-Hispanic blacks (hereafter blacks), American Indians, Asians, and persons who self-identify as multiracial. For our purposes, we first distinguish Hispanics (of all races) from other racial groups as defined broadly by the Office of Management and Budget (OMB). These are parents who self-identify as Hispanic; the remaining non-Hispanic populations are defined as white, black, Asian, and American Indian. By cross-classifying the race of each parent in a 5×5 table, we compare the percentage having a child in the past year and number of children born by marriage type (defined by each cell of the table). The cells on the diagonal of the table comprise the children of racially homogamous unions, while the off-diagonal cells identify children of interracial marriages. Our sample is restricted to children who were born after their parents married (i.e., age of children is less than or equal to marital duration in years). This ensures that the children are the biological children of both spouses. The ACS provides a unique opportunity to evaluate how intermarried parents identify the race and ethnicity of their biological children.

Fertility among Interracially Married Couples

Our first objective is to provide baseline fertility estimates for couples comprising spouses with different racial backgrounds. We consider two competing hypotheses. One is that fertility will be comparatively low among interracial couples, a pattern perhaps reflecting fear of stigma (for their children) among interracial couples (Fu 2008). An alternative hypothesis assumes little or no racial stigma, implying instead that fertility rates among intermarried couples will assume the average fertility levels of the racial groups represented by each partner. For example, intermarriages between whites and Hispanics may be intermediate between the low fertility rates of whites and the much higher rates observed among Hispanics. Of course, fertility intentions also reflect selection into racially or ethnically heterogeneous marriages (e.g., Chinese who marry whites versus Catholic Mexicans who marry Catholic whites).

We begin by comparing past-year fertility of all racially homogamous and racially heterogamous married couples with wives aged 20 to 39 (see columns 1–5, Table 1). These results do not provide simple or straightforward conclusions. For whites, for example, differentials in fertility were small across racially homogamous marriages (i.e., white-white) and heterogamous marriages. There is little evidence that mixed-race couples—whether the husband is white (compare

TABLE 1
Percentage Who Had a Birth Last Year among Married Couples in Which the Wife Was Aged 20–39 by Couples' Racial Combination

All Husbands or Husbands Married Fewer than 5 Years	All Wives						Wives Married Fewer than 5 Years				
	White	Black	American Indian	Asian	Hispanic		White	Black	American Indian	Asian	Hispanic
White (%)	13.7	13.5	11.6	13.4	14.0		18.7	15.6	17.6	15.2	17.7
N	698,319	4,360	5,655	17,372	29,857		287,329	2,366	2,399	9,120	14,603
Black (%)	13.7	13.1	18.6	14.0	13.7		17.9	17.4	22.7	18.9	17.0
N	9,976	49,557	279	1,091	3,725		5,473	22,816	150	550	2,026
American Indian (%)	12.0	16.3	13.2	12.4	12.8		18.0	22.0	18.5	13.8	18.2
N	5,675	86	4,109	218	659		2,440	50	1,695	94	313
Asian American (%)	15.6	17.3	23.4	14.7	15.1		17.6	15.9	30.8	19.4	20.4
N	7,704	260	141	65,037	1,747		3,947	145	65	24,071	828
Hispanic (%)	14.6	15.5	13.1	15.7	13.6		19.4	19.5	19.6	18.3	19.3
N	28,886	1,527	865	2,382	141,244		14,117	860	418	1,222	50,292

across columns in each row) or the wife is white (compare down rows in each column)—represent statistical outliers with unusually low levels of fertility. In fact, for white women and men who marry Hispanics, past-year fertility is slightly higher than white-homogamous or Hispanic-homogamous marriages. The highest past-year fertility is observed among marriages involving American Indian women and Asian men (23.4 percent), but this race-sex combination represents a very small percentage of marriages.

We also compare past-year fertility among couples who have been married in the past five years (columns 6–10, Table 1). This restriction identifies a smaller subset of recently married couples who may be starting families. As expected, these analyses reveal somewhat higher percentages of past-year fertility than the estimates reported in Table 1 for all married couples. In some cases, especially for whites, interracial marriages appear to have lower fertility rates than white-homogamous marriages. For example, 18.7 percent of white-white couples had a baby in the past 12 months. This fertility rate is higher than any other white-heterogamous marriage considered here, except for marriages involving a white woman and a Hispanic man (19.4 percent).

Overall, these data suggest that fertility is moderately lower in white-minority marriages, except when white women marry men from high-fertility groups.[1] This pattern is also apparent among black women who intermarry. They have lower fertility than in black-black marriages, except in the case of marriages to Hispanic and American Indian men. Asian homogamous marriages have the highest rates of past-year fertility (19.4 percent). When Asian men are married to Hispanic women (20.4 percent) and American Indian women (30.8 percent), past-year fertility is especially high.[2]

At a minimum, these results clearly indicate that the proportion of intermarriages may overstate the frequency of racial mixture among children. Fertility rates are uneven across different types of interracial couples.

Racial Identification of Children Born to Interracial Couples

Our second objective is to highlight variation in how parents (i.e., the householder or another adult in the household who responds to the ACS) in interracial marriages identify the race or ethnicity of their coresidential children. We assume predictable patterns (e.g., patterns of hypo-descent, as determined by the one-drop rule, among black-white couples and their children) of identification, which we describe in this article. We also assume that racial identification is both fluid and situational, which we assess by examining whether children's racial identification reflects: (1) the comparative socioeconomic status (or earnings/education) of each parent, (2) the racial mix of the minority spouse (i.e., multiracial or monoracial), (3) the racial or ethnic composition of the metropolitan (or nonmetropolitan) area in which interracial couples and their children live, and (4) the nativity status of parents (i.e., native- versus foreign-born).

We hypothesize that the children of interracial couples are most likely to be identified with the ethnoracial background of the most educated parent, who may have more influence or power in the marital relationship. Reflecting America's racial hierarchy or racial stratification system, we also expect that mixed-race parents will be more likely to "defer" to their white spouse in identifying the race of their children. If racial identity is situational or fluid (Harris and Sim 2002), we expect that children of interracial marriages may also be more likely to be identified with the dominant ethnoracial share of the local area in which they live. Moreover, first-generation Hispanic-white couples will be more likely to indicate that their children are Hispanic or multiracial than will Americanized Hispanic-white couples who are native-born (Qian, Lichter, and Tumin 2018).

Information on who fills out the ACS questionnaire is unavailable in the public data. For our purposes, we instead identify how responses to questions on race and Hispanic origin vary by householder status. The householder is the first person listed on the survey; all family relationships (i.e., spouse of householder, child of householder, etc.) are measured in relation to the householder. If we assume that most householders are considered to be the "head" of household (i.e., who owns or rents the place), the householder may be regarded as the most influential person of the family, in which case the householder may dominate decisions in naming the race of children, regardless of who actually fills out the questionnaire. Another common assumption is that children take their father's surname, which may also be used by parents and others to assign the ethnoracial background or ancestry of children, regardless of the race of the householder (Waters 1989). Whether the minority spouse in the minority-white marriage is the householder or male arguably influences their children's racial classification, at least how it is measured in most survey research.

In fact, the data in Table 2 show that when minority spouses are listed as the householder or are male, the children of interracial marriages are more likely to be identified as minority than white. For example, among black-white couples, 17.8 percent of the children are identified as black when the minority spouse is male versus only 10.8 percent when the minority spouse is female. When the black spouse is listed as the householder, 19.1 percent of children are identified as black compared with only 12.8 percent when the householder is white. For children, marital power—as measured by householder status and gender—seemingly influences how children are identified and classified by their parents. This is a potentially important issue given that interracial pairings are asymmetrical in the shares of minority men (e.g., black men married to white women, versus the opposite pattern).[3]

Mixed-race minority spouses may have less personal stake in identifying their children's race, especially if they have a white spouse (the sample we focus on here). Indeed, biracial spouses (who are in most cases partially white) in interracial marriages are far more likely to identify their children as monoracial white than as a racial minority (columns 5–6, Table 2). In the case of black-white marriages, for example, 29.0 percent of the children were identified as white if their minority parent was biracial. This compares with only 8.3 percent if the black minority parent was monoracial. A similar pattern of racial identification was

TABLE 2
Racial Classification of Children Aged 0–17 Born to Interracial Married Couples (in percentages)

	Minority Spouse Is:						
Children's Race in:	Male	Female	Householder	Not Householder	Biracial	Monoracial	Total
Black-white couples							
Black	17.8	10.8	19.1	12.8	0.2	18.2	15.7
White	8.6	19.1	9.1	14.0	29.0	8.3	11.8
Mixed	73.7	70.0	71.8	73.2	70.8	72.9	72.5
Total	100.0	100.0	100.0	100.0	100.0	100.0	100.0
Indian-white couples							
Indian	23.2	23.6	22.9	24.0	0.6	54.2	23.3
White	28.2	28.3	29.3	27.0	32.6	22.5	28.3
Mixed	48.6	48.1	47.8	49.0	66.9	23.3	48.4
Total	100.0	100.0	100.0	100.0	100.0	100.0	100.0
Asian-white couples							
Asian	9.4	7.3	8.7	7.6	0.6	10.1	8.0
White	16.7	18.4	17.8	17.9	30.9	14.2	17.9
Mixed	73.9	74.3	73.5	74.6	68.5	75.8	74.2
Total	100.0	100.0	100.0	100.0	100.0	100.0	100.0
Hispanic-white couples							
Hispanic	17.2	13.5	14.2	16.0	0.5	62.7	15.2
White	19.7	30.1	23.2	26.6	27.7	16.8	25.1
Mixed	63.1	56.5	62.6	57.4	71.8	20.5	59.7
Total	100.0	100.0	100.0	100.0	100.0	100.0	100.0

evident regardless of white-minority pairings. In each racial pairing, roughly 30 percent of the children were identified as monoracial white. Still, biracial Indian and Hispanic parents are far more likely to report their children as mixed-race in comparison to their monoracial counterparts. This reporting pattern may have roots in the long history of conquest and oppression that has brought added racial and cultural awareness and sensitivity to miscegenation among America's Indian and Hispanic populations.

A more general lesson drawn from these data (last column, Table 2) is that surprisingly large shares of American children are identified by their interracially married parents as monoracial. By definition, these children should be reported as multiracial, with the races of both parents listed. However, 72.5 percent of children born to black-white interracial couples are identified as multiracial. The other 27.5 percent are classified as monoracial black (15.7) or monoracial white (11.8 percent). Whether these children will similarly define themselves as mixed-race as adults is an empirical question. Similarly, 25.9 percent of children born to Asian-white couples are classified as either monoracial Asian (8.0) or monoracial white (17.9). The contrast from black-white couples is that Asian-white couples are more likely to identify their children as white than as minority. In contrast, the children of Indian-white couples have the lowest percentage classified as biracial. More than one-half are either classified as American Indian or white only.

Hispanic is not a racial group. Still, 40 percent of children born to Hispanic-white couples are classified as only Hispanic (listing a racial category other than white) or only white (with no Hispanic classification).

Interracial Pairings and Variation in the Racial Identity of Children

In this section, we examine the ambiguous or fluid nature of racial identity of the children of interracially married couples. Our results suggest that children's racial and ethnic identity is "negotiated" by parents, who bring different racial backgrounds and interpersonal resources that influence assigning race or ethnicity to their children. Indeed, patterns of racial assignment of children differ across couples with different racial mixes. For example, the results in Table 3 highlight high percentages of black-white couples who identify their children as monoracial black rather than white, regardless of education level (a result consistent with the "one-drop" rule, whereby partly black Americans historically have been regarded as part of the black population). This pattern contrasts with other minority-white racial pairings, where children are more likely than the children of black-white couples to be identified as white at each education level (of the minority spouse).

It is nevertheless also the case that higher educational attainment of minority spouses (black and Asian spouses in particular) is associated with larger percentages of children classified as biracial rather than monoracial white or minority. For the children of Asian-white marriages, for example, roughly one-quarter are identified as monoracial white if the Asian spouse is poorly educated, compared with only 15 percent if the Asian parent has a postgraduate degree. This pattern is also true for blacks in interracial marriages with whites. More education of the black spouse is associated with larger percentages of children identified as biracial. There is little if any evidence that increases in education among the black spouses are associated with larger percentages of children identified as monoracial black. For Hispanics, a college education is strongly linked to identifying children as "white." This clear educational gradient in white racial reporting is also observed among American Indians who are married to whites.

Racial identity may also be contextual; that is, parental reports on race may depend on the racial composition of the cities and communities in which they live. Racial and ethnic diversity is much greater in metropolitan than nonmetropolitan areas, despite large increases in diversity throughout America (Lee and Sharp 2017). One possibility is that interracial couples may report their children as mixed-race or even monoracial minorities if they live in metropolitan areas. But evidence for this hypothesis is equivocal. For example, as expected, the

TABLE 3
Racial Classification of Children Aged 0–17 Born to Interracial Married Couples, by Education, Metro Status, and Nativity (in percentages)

Children's Race in:	Education of Minority Spouse Is:					Lives in:		Couple Nativity Pairing Is:			
	Less than High School	High School	Some College	College Graduate	Post-graduate	Metro	Nonmetro	Both Native	Minority Native	White Native	Both Immigrant
Black-white couples											
Black	21.9	17.0	16.1	14.1	14.1	15.4	17.5	14.8	18.1	18.8	21.4
White	14.0	13.5	11.2	12.2	10.1	11.4	15.8	11.1	12.0	13.3	25.6
Mixed	64.1	69.5	72.7	73.7	75.8	73.2	66.7	74.2	69.9	67.9	53.1
Total	100.0	100.0	100.0	100.0	100.0	100.0	100.0	100.0	100.0	100.0	100.0
Indian-white couples											
Indian	25.4	25.4	23.6	22.1	19.9	22.2	26.9	23.6	19.2	19.6	17.7
White	26.5	27.2	28.0	30.2	28.8	29.4	24.9	28.1	32.3	30.4	39.2
Mixed	48.1	47.4	48.5	47.7	51.3	48.4	48.2	48.3	48.6	50.0	43.1
Total	100.0	100.0	100.0	100.0	100.0	100.0	100.0	100.0	100.0	100.0	100.0
Asian-white couples											
Asian	9.9	9.5	8.5	8.0	6.8	7.9	9.3	6.7	7.7	9.3	7.2
White	25.9	25.4	19.3	16.5	15.0	17.5	23.2	18.3	14.3	17.3	27.0
Mixed	64.2	65.1	72.2	75.5	78.3	74.7	67.5	75.0	77.9	73.4	65.7
Total	100.0	100.0	100.0	100.0	100.0	100.0	100.0	100.0	100.0	100.0	100.0
Hispanic-white couples											
Hispanic	21.0	17.9	16.9	12.3	11.2	14.9	18.3	14.2	19.3	17.0	11.1
White	23.3	24.1	23.9	27.0	26.5	25.3	23.2	22.5	24.3	32.0	41.3
Mixed	55.7	57.9	59.2	60.7	62.3	59.8	58.5	63.3	56.4	51.0	47.6
Total	100.0	100.0	100.0	100.0	100.0	100.0	100.0	100.0	100.0	100.0	100.0

children of black-white marriages are more likely to be defined as mixed-race if they live in metropolitan areas; and among the children who are identified as monoracial, a slightly larger share in metropolitan than nonmetropolitan areas (i.e., 57 to 53 percent) were identified as black. Among Asian-white marriages, however, the opposite pattern was true: smaller shares of children were identified as monoracial in metropolitan areas than nonmetropolitan areas; and very similar percentages of all monoracial children in metropolitan area (7.9/25.4, or 31 percent) and nonmetropolitan areas (9.3/32.5, or 29 percent) are identified as Asian only.

Finally, immigrant minority spouses may be least well positioned to report their children as a monoracial minority, especially if they are married to a white native spouse. The data in Table 3 (last four columns) show that interracial couples with two immigrant spouses are less likely than their native counterparts to classify their children as biracial. On the other hand, Asian-white foreign-born couples are most likely to identify their children as white (27.0 percent) in comparison to other native-immigrant comparisons. For example, only 17.3 percent of couples with an Asian immigrant and a white native identified their children as white. Similar reporting patterns also occur for Indian-white and Hispanic-white couples. Why white foreigners dominate minority immigrants in reporting their children as monoracial rather than biracial is unclear, but points to a possible power differential between partners. Or, more benignly, divergent patterns of race reporting may simply reflect the lack of knowledge or familiarity with filling out the ACS question on race, that is, that their children can be listed as having multiple races.[4] Of course, these descriptive results, although informative, also are potentially confounded by many other unobserved factors.

Discussion and Implications

The growth of interracial marriages and childbearing is fueling population diversity in new ways. Indeed, Jiménez, Fields, and Schachter (2015, 110) claim that "no factor has been more important to ethnoracial identity in the last three decades than romantic partnerships across ethnoracial lines, and the children these unions produce." Diversity has proceeded most rapidly among America's children—"from the bottom up" (Johnson and Lichter 2010)—and rising interracial marriage and childbearing has played a large role in this regard. Recent government reports claim that the majority of all babies today are born to minority or mixed-race women. Of course, defining "minority" babies—or the U.S. population more generally—is a fraught issue (Alba 2016; Prewitt 2013). The race and ethnicity of America's children is determined subjectively by parents (often a single parent), not on the basis of some objective standard that all parents understand, accept, and act upon. Newborn babies do not have a racial or ethnic or cultural identity; this is something that unfolds as children make their way into adulthood as social beings.

Our analyses, based on data for newborn children from the ACS, suggest several specific conclusions. Interracial marriages—and subsequent fertility—are clearly making the measurement of mixed-race populations an increasingly important task. The mixed-race population of children is underestimated by conventional approaches based on parents' own reports. Indeed, as we have shown here, substantial shares of America's children from mixed-race marriages are identified by their parents as monoracial. On its face, this suggests that mixed-race children are seriously underreported, as it has always been in the past. The full extent, of course, is largely unknown because parents themselves often underestimate (e.g., the "one-drop" rule in the case of African Americans) or misrepresent racial mixing in their own family backgrounds or genealogies (Perez and Hirschman 2009). Moreover, how parents classify their children's race is highly uneven across intermarriages distinguished by the differing ethno-racial combinations of husbands and wives. Our results seemingly suggest that children's racial identity reflects a kind of racial "tug-of-war" between parents who bring their own racial and cultural identities to marriages. The status or power of parents is often unequal, and this is played out in how children are identified. Parents from some minority populations seemingly have fewer claims on the race of their children. The racial and ethnic identities of children of interracial marriages, at a minimum, are highly subjective and complex.

Our study tells us little if anything about the meanings that parents attach to the assigned racial classifications of their children or what identities the children will assume as adults. How parents identify their own biological children—as monoracial and biracial—nevertheless signals how parents (at least one of the parents) view or hope to shape their children's racial identity. These racial assessments or aspirations for their children are often consistent with historical patterns of hyper- and hypo-descent (Gullickson 2016; Gullickson and Morning 2011). Racial and ethnic identification can be fluid (for some racial and ethnic groups), perhaps even providing evidence of a kind of intergenerational racial mobility (Bratter 2007; Saperstein and Penner 2012). Parents' racial assignments at their child's birth or during early childhood are subject to change with the shifting social and economic circumstances of the family. Significant but currently unknown shares of American children also are likely to discard the racial identities assigned by their parents as they make their way to adulthood or when they have the opportunity to officially define themselves on government-sponsored surveys.

Census estimates indicate that the multiracial population of U.S. children was 4.2 million in 2010, up by nearly 50 percent since 2000. Under the circumstances, empirical claims about the changing prevalence and racial mix of monoracial and multiracial children are marked by uncertainty. And this is not likely to change anytime soon. Indeed, America's future is rooted in today's unprecedented diversity in the national origins of new immigrant groups, the rapid growth and aging of America's new second generation, increases in intermarriage (especially as cultural and economic integration continues apace), and relative declines in the majority white population (Frey 2014; Lichter 2013). Racial diversity in America will be expressed in new ways with the rise in multiracial children from interracial marriages. Common racial classification schemes of the past are unlikely to accurately represent the new American racial and ethnic mosaic.

Notes

1. To be sure, uneven rates of fertility among racially homogamous and heterogamous marriages may arise from differential selection into marriages involving partners with socioeconomic and demographic characteristics (e.g., educational attainment) commonly associated with higher or lower fertility. In some multivariate analyses, interaction terms include different racial combinations comprising interracial marriages, along with other control variables (e.g., age, education, etc.). Each of these interaction terms is negative-signed and statistically significant. This means that interracial marriages of all combinations are associated with lower past-year fertility, a result that is consistent with our descriptive results.

2. In some additional analyses of cumulative fertility, we also considered the average number of own children reported by couples in first marriages. These data again reveal some fertility suppression in white-heterogamous marriages, except when white women are married to black men and when whites are married to American Indians.

3. Our analysis shows that 69.4 percent of black-white couples (with children) consist of a black man and a white woman, while only 32.4 percent of Asian-white couples involve an Asian man and a white woman. In contrast, gender asymmetry is much smaller for Indian-white and Hispanic-white couples. Minority spouses in interracially married couple families represent less than 50 percent of all married couple families in our sample, except for American Indian/white couples.

4. In some additional analyses, we found that racial identity does not depend heavily on children's sex; that is, racial identity is not bestowed differently for boys and girls. However, older children are more likely than younger children to be classified as monoracial minorities than monoracial whites. It is unclear whether observed age pattern reflects cohort effects (e.g., older cohorts—those exposed to less tolerant racial environments—may be more likely to be defined as minority) or age effects (e.g., mixed-race children redefine themselves as minorities as they grow older, which are accepted by their reporting parents).

References

Alba, Richard. 11 January 2016. The likely persistence of a white majority: How Census Bureau statistics have misled thinking about the American future. *The American Prospect*, winter: 67–71.

Bonilla-Silva, Eduardo. 2004. From bi-racial to tri-racial: Towards a new system of racial stratification in the USA. *Ethnic and Racial Studies* 27:931–50.

Bratter, Jenifer. 2007. Will "multiracial" survive to the next generation? The racial classification of children of multiracial parents. *Social Forces* 86:821–49.

Brunsma, David L. 2005. Interracial families and the racial identification of mixed-race children: Evidence from the early childhood longitudinal study. *Social Forces* 84:1131–57.

Davenport, Lauren D. 2016. The role of gender, class, and religion in biracial Americans' racial labeling decisions. *American Sociological Review* 81:57–84.

Frank, Reanne, Ilana Redstone Akresh, and Bo Lu. 2010. Latino immigrants and the U.S. racial order: How and where do they fit in? *American Sociological Review* 75:378–401.

Frey, William H. 2014. *Diversity explosion: How new racial demographics are remaking America.* Washington, DC: Brookings Institution Press.

Fu, Vincent K. 2008. Interracial-interethnic unions and fertility in the United States. *Journal of Marriage and Family* 70:783–95.

Gullickson, Aaron. 2016. Essential measures: Ancestry, race, and social difference. *American Behavioral Scientist* 60:498–518.

Gullickson, Aaron, and Ann Morning. 2011. Choosing race: Multiracial ancestry and identification. *Social Science Research* 40:498–512.

Harris, David R., and Jeremiah Joseph Sim. 2002. Who is multiracial? Assessing the complexity of lived race. *American Sociological Review* 67:614–27.

Herman, Melissa R., and Mary E. Campbell. 2012. I wouldn't, but you can: Attitudes toward interracial relationships. *Social Science Research* 41:343–58.

Jiménez, Tomás R., Corey D. Fields, and Ariela Schachter. 2015. How ethnoraciality matters: Looking inside ethnoracial "groups." *Social Currents* 2:107–15.

Johnson, Kenneth M., and Daniel T. Lichter. 2010. Growing diversity among America's children and youth: Spatial and temporal dimensions. *Population and Development Review* 36:151–76.

Jones, Nicholas A., and Jungmiwha Bullock. 2012. *Two or more races population: 2010*. C2010BR-13. Washington, DC: U.S. Census Bureau.

Lee, Barrett A., and Gregory Sharp. 2017. Ethnoracial diversity across the rural-urban continuum. *The ANNALS of the American Academy of Political and Social Science* 672:26–45.

Lee, Jennifer, and Frank Bean. 2010. *The diversity paradox: Immigration and the color line in twenty-first century America*. New York, NY: Russell Sage Foundation.

Lichter, Daniel T. 2013. Integration or fragmentation? Racial diversity and the American future. *Demography* 50:359–91.

Lichter, Daniel T., Zhenchao Qian, and Dimtry Tumin. 2015. Whom do immigrants marry? Emerging patterns of intermarriage and integration in the United States. *The ANNALS of the American Academy of Political and Social Science* 662:57–78.

Liebler, Carolyn A. 2010. Homelands and indigenous identities in a multiracial era. *Social Science Research* 39:596–609.

Liebler, Carolyn A. 2016. On the boundaries of race identification of mixed-heritage children in the United States, 1960 to 2010. *Sociology of Race and Ethnicity* 2:548–68.

Liebler, Carolyn A., Sonya R. Porter, Leticia E. Fernandez, James M. Noon, and Sharon R. Ennis. 2017. America's churning races: Race and ethnicity response changes between Census 2000 and the 2010 census. *Demography* 54:259–84.

Livingston, Gretchen, and Anna Brown. 2017. *Intermarriage in the U.S. 50 years after* Loving v. Virginia. Washington, DC: Pew Research Center.

Qian, Zhenchao. 2004. Options: Racial/ethnic identification of children of intermarried couples. *Social Science Quarterly* 85:746–66.

Qian, Zhenchao, and Daniel T. Lichter. 2007. Social boundaries and marital assimilation: Interpreting trends in racial and ethnic intermarriage. *American Sociological Review* 72:68–94.

Qian, Zhenchao, and Daniel T. Lichter. 2011. Changing patterns of interracial marriage in a multiracial society. *Journal of Marriage and Family* 73:1065–84.

Qian, Zhenchao, Daniel T. Lichter, and Dmitry Tumin. 2018. Divergent pathways to assimilation? Local marriage markets and intermarriage among U.S. Hispanics. *Journal of Marriage and Family* 80:271–88.

Perez, Anthony D., and Charles Hirschman. 2009. The changing racial and ethnic composition of the U.S. population: Emerging American identities. *Population and Development Review* 35:1–51.

Pew Research Center. 2015. *Multiracial in America: Proud, diverse and growing in numbers*. Washington, DC: Pew Research Center.

Prewitt, Kenneth. 2013. *What is "your" race? The census and our flawed efforts to classify Americans*. Princeton, NJ: Princeton University Press.

Saperstein, Ariel, and Andrew M. Penner. 2012. Racial fluidity and inequality in the United States. *American Journal of Sociology* 118:676–727.

Vargas, Nicholas, and Jared Kingsbury. 2016. Racial identity contestation: Mapping and measuring racial boundaries. *Sociology Compass* 10:718–29.

Waters, Mary C. 1989. The everyday use of surnames to determine ethnic ancestry. *Qualitative Sociology* 12:303–24.

II: Change across the Generations after Immigration

Finding the Lost Generation: Identifying Second-Generation Immigrants in Federal Statistics

By
DOUGLAS S. MASSEY

This article underscores the importance of adding a question on parental birthplace to the American Community Survey (ACS). This question was removed from the long form of the U.S. Census after 1970 and replaced by a question on ancestry. While the former provides accurate information about a demographic fact that is critical to the identification of the children of immigrants, the latter refers to a subjective social construction that has limited utility for purposes of program administration, apportionment, or governance. At the time that the parental birthplace question was eliminated, the percentage of ACS respondents who were foreign-born had reached an all-time low, and the second generation was aging and shrinking, so the loss to the nation's statistical system was not immediately apparent. With the revival of immigration in the final quarter of the twentieth century, the inability to identify and study the second generation has become glaringly apparent. Immigrants and their children now constitute a quarter of the U.S. population: their non-white racial origins and a widespread lack of legal documents among them render their prospects for integration uncertain. Our current inability to accurately measure progress between first- and second-generation immigrants now constitutes a major weakness in the U.S. statistical system.

Keywords: immigrants; integration; second generation; assimilation

In the study of immigration and social integration, the second generation is conventionally defined as persons born in the United States with at least one foreign-born parent (although in recent years, analysts have coined the term *2.5 generation* to indicate persons with one U.S.-born parent; see Rumbaut 2004). To identify the second generation using census or survey data, a question on parental birthplace must be used, along with a question on the respondent's own

Douglas S. Massey is the Henry G. Bryant Professor of Sociology and Public Affairs at Princeton University, where he also directs the Office of Population Research.

Correspondence: dmassey@Princeton.edu

DOI: 10.1177/0002716218760506

place of birth. With answers to these questions, it is straightforward to define the first, second, and third or higher generations within any population. Intergenerational trends in social, economic, and demographic traits may then be analyzed to assess the extent and pace of immigrant integration into the host society over time.

In general, generation-to-generation increases in socioeconomic status, host language fluency, and residential integration are taken to indicate successful immigrant adaptation and assimilation. Unfortunately for scholars of contemporary immigration to the United States, the census question on parental birthplace was eliminated from the census questionnaire after 1970, making it impossible to distinguish the second generation from other native-born persons. Although a question on parental birthplace was added to the Current Population Survey (CPS) in 1996, the CPS sample of around 60,000 households is too small to produce reliable estimates of the size and characteristics of the second generation by national origin in states, counties, and municipalities, or even to derive stable national-level estimates for all but a few large national-origin groups.

The only way to overcome these problems is to insert a question on parental birthplace into the American Community Survey (ACS), which is administered by the Census Bureau annually to a large sample of approximately 2.4 million households. Since 2000, the ACS has served as a replacement for the old census "long form," which had formerly been administered to around a fifth of all U.S. households during each decennial census. Here I describe how and why the question on parental birthplace was dropped from the decennial census and the epistemological problems this exclusion has created. I then go on to explain why it is essential at this point in our national history to restore our ability to identify and study the second generation, a population that has largely been "lost" to analysts since 1970.

How the Second Generation Got "Lost"

The U.S. census is a political as well as a statistical undertaking, reflecting that demographic data inevitably carry political ramifications. Race, of course, has been measured since the first census in 1790. Its inclusion began not for demographic reasons, but to address political exigencies related to the three-fifths clause of the U.S. Constitution, which allocated congressional representatives to states by counting slaves as three-fifths of a person for purposes of apportionment (Waldstreicher 2009). Although the three-fifths rule is no longer with us today, the enumeration of race has remained a constant in American censuses and surveys over the years, and indeed the measurement of race acquired new importance after 1960 as researchers and policy-makers sought to assess progress toward racial equality in the wake of the civil rights revolution.

Civil rights legislation covers more than just African Americans, of course, and Hispanics also mobilized during the 1960s to advance their interests. A key element in their mobilization was the demand for the inclusion of a pan-ethnic Hispanic identifier on the decennial census, a demand that was vociferously articulated in the run-up to the 1970 census (Anderson 2015). Before this time, terms such as *Hispanic* and *Latino* were not in common usage, and people of Latin American origin were generally identified as belonging to one of three discrete, regional populations: Puerto Ricans in the Northeast, Mexicans in the Southwest, and Cubans in South Florida. Because of 1917 legislation, Puerto Ricans are U.S. citizens by birth (Glass 2008), though one can measure separate generations of mainland residence; and although Mexicans may be either native or foreign born, in 1970 the Mexican-origin population was overwhelmingly native born, having experienced little immigration since the onset of the Great Depression in 1929 (Grebler, Moore, and Guzman 1970). Cubans, meanwhile, had only begun coming to the United States in large numbers around 1959 and, in 1970, were almost entirely in their first generation of U.S. residence (Bean and Tienda 1987). Given the relatively small size, geographic segmentation, and tripartite division of the Latino population by national origin, the Census Bureau initially resisted the addition of an omnibus Hispanic identifier and only agreed to its inclusion very late in the process of census planning and preparation. As a result, the bureau was able to include it on only a 5 percent sample rather than on the "short form" of the census that went to all U.S. residents (Haub 2012). Nonetheless, provisions were soon made to include it as a short form item on the 1980 census (Bean and Tienda 1987).

The addition of a Hispanic identifier triggered demands from other national-origin groups for their own identifier, notably the descendants of southern and eastern European immigrants who had experienced exclusion and discrimination earlier in the twentieth century (Higham 2002). In reaction to the political mobilization of blacks and Latinos, many of them were in the process of mobilizing as self-identified "white ethnics" who were defiantly "unmeltable" (Novak 1972). Bowing to political pressure and with the approval of members of Congress with surnames such as Rodino, Rostenkowski, and Javitz, the Census Bureau added a new question on "ancestry" to the census long form, to which respondents could write in any national-origin combination they wished.

To make room for the new item, the Census Bureau deleted the question on parental birthplace, an item that for 100 years had been used both to identify the second generation and to study processes of intergenerational assimilation (Anderson 2015). Unlike parental birthplace, however, ancestry is a subjectively reported social construction, not an objective fact. Later analyses concluded that "because of ethnic intermarriage, the numerous generations that separate present respondents from their forebears, and the apparent unimportance of ancestry to many whites of European origin, responses appear quite inconsistent"; and "no simple census question will distinguish those who identify strongly with a specific European group from those who report symbolic or imagined ethnicity" (Farley 1991, 411).

Despite its lack of demographic efficacy, however, the ancestry question remained on subsequent census questionnaires and was carried over onto the ACS after 2000; but the parental birthplace question continued to be excluded. At the time of the original exclusion, both the first- and second-generation populations were small and rapidly aging; and in 1970, immigration was seen as a thing

FIGURE 1
First- and Second-Generation Immigrants as a Percentage of the U.S. Population

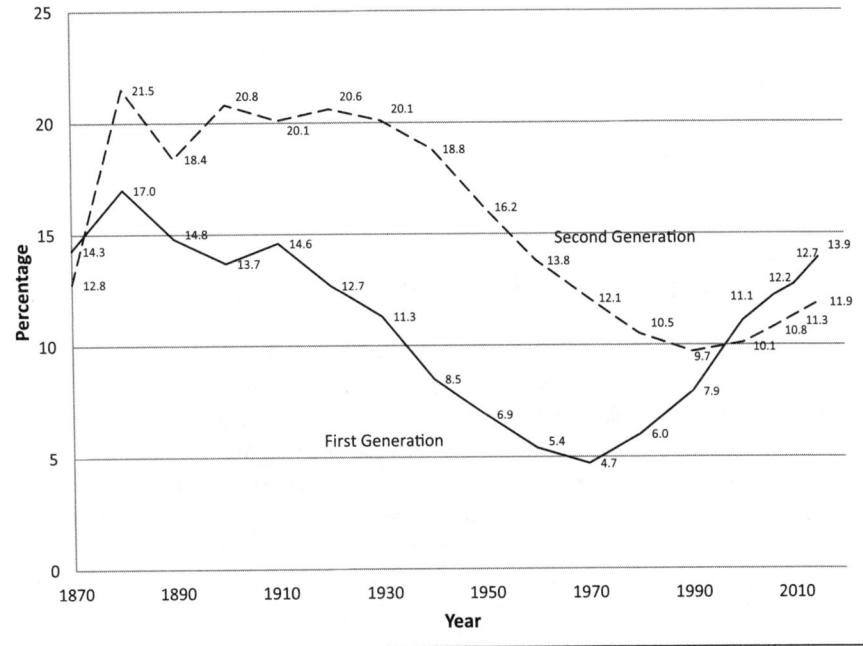

SOURCE: Pew Research Center on Hispanic Trends (2015) and Gibson (2017).

of the past and the status of an elderly second-generation immigrant as unimportant. The irony is that in 1970 the United States was on the verge of a resurgence of mass immigration that would hugely expand the second generation during a time of rising inequality, growing undocumented migration, and declining investment in public goods, all of which made the progress of second-generation immigrants a crucial issue for the future of American society (Waters and Pineau 2015).

Figure 1 draws on data from the Pew Research Center on Hispanic Trends (2015) and Gibson (2017) to show the percentage of first and second generations in the U.S. population from 1870 to 2015. The period leading up to 1920 was characterized by mass immigration from Southern and Eastern Europe, pushing the numbers in the first and second generations to historical records (Massey 1995). During this time, the foreign-born percentage ranged from a low of 13.7 percent to a high of 17 percent, while the share of the second generation ranged from 12.8 percent to 20.6 percent. As of 1920, one-third of all Americans were either first-generation immigrants (12.7 percent) or their children (20.6 percent).

With the imposition of restrictive immigration quotas in 1921 and 1924 and the onset of the Great Depression in 1929, however, immigration slowed to a trickle in the 1930s and remained low during the war years of the 1940s. As a result, the share of the first and second generations steadily fell in subsequent decades, with the foreign-born percentage reaching a nadir of 4.7 percent in 1970 and the second-generation percentage reaching a minimum of 9.7 percent in 1990. As a result, the consequences of eliminating the census question on parental birthplace were not appreciated right away. During the 1970s the average immigrant was someone's elderly Russian, Polish, or Italian grandparent; the typical second-generation person was well into middle age; and the third generation of European descent was disappearing into the American mainstream (Alba and Nee 2003).

Finding the Lost Second Generation

Although the ancestry question may have produced some interesting studies based on the 1980 census (cf. Lieberson and Waters 1988; Waters 1990), the item is now of very limited utility and could profitably be eliminated to return the parental birthplace question to census enumeration as part of the ACS. If ancestry is somehow considered important to retain for purposes of research and study, it could be added to the CPS; but it addresses no legislative mandate and serves no practical purpose for program administration, apportionment, or governance.

From the very beginning, demographers strongly opposed elimination of the parental birthplace question and long pressed for its insertion back onto the census long form (see Levine, Hill, and Warren 1985). In recent years, efforts have focused on including it on the ACS so that it can be used to generate reliable estimates centered on 2020, when the next census will occur. This action was explicitly recommended by the Census Scientific Advisory Committee and has been formally endorsed by two recent National Academy of Sciences (NAS) panels. According to the report of the Panel on the Integration of Immigrants into American Society, "the most serious current gap in the U.S. statistical system on immigration is the lack of a question on parental birthplace for a large representative sample of the U.S. population," and it explicitly recommended that "the U.S. Census Bureau should add a question on the birthplace of parents to the American Community Survey" (Waters and Pineau 2015, 429). Likewise, the Panel on the Economic and Fiscal Consequences of Immigration noted that the capacity to monitor progress of the second generation was "critical" to the nation's statistical infrastructure and likewise recommended that "the U.S. Bureau of the Census should add a question on the birthplace of parents to the American Community Survey" (Blau and Mackie 2016, 445).

As of this writing, the fate of the question is unknown but certainly not promising, and the absence of reliable data on the children of immigrants remains the single greatest weakness in the U.S. statistical system (Massey 2010). Although the resurgence of immigration after 1970 initially took Census Bureau demographers by surprise, we now know that the low-immigration epoch from 1950 to 1970 was the historical anomaly, not the current era. The 1965 amendments to the Immigration and Nationality Act abolished the old national-origins quota system and rescinded the bans on Asian immigration, replacing these prejudiced policies with a new preference system that granted permanent resident visas to people on the basis of U.S. labor market needs and family ties to U.S. residents while exempting immediate relatives of U.S. citizens from numerical limitations (Zolberg 2006).

Although Asians initially entered in small numbers through occupational preferences, high rates of naturalization enabled them to sponsor the subsequent entry of spouses, minor children, and parents without numerical restriction, as well as brothers, sisters, and adult children subject to numerical limitation, thus accelerating the course of Asian immigration through chain migration. During the 1970s, Asian immigration was further reinforced by the arrival of hundreds of thousands of Indochinese "boat people" who were admitted as refugees outside the formal quota system; and once established as permanent residents and later as U.S. citizens, they too were able to sponsor the subsequent entry of family members left behind.

In contrast to the case of Asians, Congress in 1965 imposed the first-ever numerical limits on the entry of legal immigrants from Latin America, capping immigration from the Western Hemisphere at 120,000 visas in 1968 and in 1976 folding it into a single worldwide cap of 290,000 visas, with no more than 20,000 going to any country in any year (Zolberg 2006). In 1965, Congress also unilaterally terminated a 22-year-old guest worker treaty with Mexico known as the Bracero Program, which at its height in the late 1950s sponsored the temporary entry of some 450,000 Mexican workers each year, who joined an annual inflow of some 50,000 Mexicans arriving as legal permanent residents.

When opportunities for legal entry were curtailed, the well-established inflows of Mexican workers and residents did not cease but simply reestablished themselves under undocumented auspices (Massey and Pren 2012). Through the mid-1980s the flows remained overwhelmingly circular, and the undocumented population grew slowly. In response to perceived "alien invasion" by "illegal migrants," however, border enforcement increased sharply beginning in 1986 and rose exponentially through the 1990s and early 2000s. This militarization of the border did not curtail undocumented entries, however; instead, it deterred undocumented departures by migrants who were loath to face the elevated costs and risks of unauthorized border crossing entailed by circular migration. As a result, the net volume of undocumented migration increased and undocumented population growth accelerated to peak at 12 million in 2008, with around 60 percent of all undocumented residents being Mexicans (Massey, Durand, and Pren 2016).

In addition to reinforcing the border, during the 1980s the United States intervened in Central America in an effort to topple the Sandinista government of Nicaragua and prevent the spread of communism, providing military aid to right-wing regimes in El Salvador, Guatemala, and Honduras; funding paramilitary organizations in these countries; and ultimately funding, supplying, and training a right-wing army of "contras" in Nicaragua. The resulting waves of violence and economic turmoil generated hundreds of thousands of refugees; but whereas Nicaraguans, like the Indochinese before them, were welcomed as refugees from communist tyranny, those fleeing Guatemala, Honduras, and El Salvador were not embraced and thus entered the United States without authorization, ultimately composing 15 percent of the undocumented population (Massey, Durand, and Pren 2014). At this point, roughly three-quarters of the resident population of undocumented migrants hail from Mexico or Central America (Passel and Cohn 2016).

Assessing the Future of the Lost Generation

In the years since 1970, the percentage of foreign born in the United States has risen back up to historically more typical levels, reaching 13.9 percent in 2015 compared to 14.6 percent in 1910. Likewise, after 1990, the percentage of persons in the second generation of U.S. residence also began to rise, reaching 11.9 percent in 2015 compared to its earlier nadir of 9.7 percent 25 years earlier. Since 1970 the average age of the second generation has dropped dramatically, and the composition has swung away from Europe toward Asia and Latin America. Currently, immigrants and their children compose 26 percent of the U.S. population, a figure that is projected to rise to 28 percent by 2025 and reach 30 percent by 2035. At this point, since the children of Latino and Asian immigrants are still very young and the offspring of earlier European immigrants are rapidly dying off, data on the second generation tell us much more about the future of the nation than they tell us about our past (Lopez, Passel, and Rohal 2015).

The inclusion of a question on parental birthplace on the ACS is thus essential for understanding the social, economic, and demographic future of the United States. The ability to identify and study progress between the first and second generations is essential not only by virtue of the second generation's increasing size, but also because two circumstances render their integration unusually fraught and uncertain: a predominance of nonwhite origins and a large share lacking legal documentation. Indeed, the NAS Panel on the Integration of Immigrants cited as serious "causes for concern … the role of legal status in slowing or blocking the integration of not just the undocumented but also their U.S.-citizen children [and] racial patterns in immigrant integration and the resulting racial stratification in the U.S. population" (Waters and Pineau 2015, 8–9).

Among the children of immigrants in the United States today, 58 percent are Hispanic, 21 percent are Asian or Middle Eastern, and 8 percent are African, with only 12 percent coming from Europe, Canada, or Australia (Fortuny et al. 2009). Moreover, among these children, 5.1 million (nearly a third of the total) have undocumented parents, with more than 4 million of them being native-born U.S. citizens (Passel and Taylor 2010). Recent research suggests that both skin color and legal status are powerful determinants of immigrant socioeconomic status (Hersch 2008, 2011; Massey and Gentsch 2014) and that the children of the undocumented display lower access to health care and poorer health and developmental outcomes than others (Capps et al. 2005; Yoshikawa and Kalil 2011; Delva et al. 2013; Gelatt 2016). Thus, accurate information about the progress of the second generation is even more important today than it was in the past.

As the Baby Boom generation increasingly moves into retirement and is replaced in the labor force by younger cohorts of Americans, the economic well-being of the nation will increasingly depend on the productivity and performance of the second generation. Not only must the children of immigrants help to support a bulging retirement population with their labor and taxes, they will also shoulder a large share of the responsibility for the nation's future economic growth and prosperity. In this context, tracking the progress of the second generation with respect to its health, education, employment, earnings, and mobility is critical to social planning, economic forecasting, and policy formulation. Relying on data from the CPS, demographers can assess this generational progress at the national level and for certain large origin groups, but without a parental birthplace question on the ACS, policy-makers working at the state, county, and municipal levels and those interested in the well-being of specific origin groups at particular localities will be left in the dark. In a very real way, the future of the United States depends on the welfare of immigrant-origin children now completing their educations and entering the workforce, and assessing their progress moving forward constitutes a roadmap for our likely progress as a nation.

References

Alba, Richard, and Victor Nee. 2003. *Remaking the American mainstream: Assimilation and contemporary immigration*. Cambridge, MA: Harvard University Press.

Anderson, Margo J. 2015. *The American census: A social history*. 2nd ed. New Haven, CT: Yale University Press.

Bean, Frank D., and Marta Tienda. 1987. *The Hispanic population of the United States*. New York, NY: Russell Sage Foundation.

Blau, Francine D., and Christopher Mackie. 2016. *The economic and fiscal consequences of immigration*. Washington, DC: National Academies Press.

Capps, Randolph, Michael E. Fix, Jason Ost, Jane Reardon-Anderson, and Jeffrey S. Passel. 2005. *The health and well-being of young children of immigrants*. Washington, DC: The Urban Institute.

Delva, Jorge, Pilar Hornwer, Ramiro Martinez, Laura Sanders, William D. Lopez, and John Doering-White. 2013. Mental health problems of children of undocumented parents in the United States: A hidden crisis. *Journal of Community Positive Practices* 13 (3): 25–35.

Farley, Reynolds. 1991. The new census question about ancestry: What did it tell us? *Demography* 28 (3): 411–29.

Fortuny, Karina, Randy Capps, Margaret Simms, and Ajay Chaudry. 2009. *Children of immigrants: National and state characteristics*. Washington, DC: The Urban Institute.

Gelatt, Julia. 2016. Immigration status and the healthcare access and health of children of immigrants. *Social Science Quarterly* 97 (3): 540–54.

Gibson, Campbell. 2017. Nativity and parentage. In *American demographic history chartbook: 1790 to 2010*. Available from http://demographicchartbook.com/.

Glass, Andrew. 2 March 2008. Puerto Ricans granted U.S. citizenship March 2, 1917. *Politico*. Available from https://www.politico.com.

Grebler, Leo, Joan W. Moore, and Ralph C. Guzman. 1970. *The Mexican-American people: The nation's second largest minority*. Glencoe, IL: Free Press.

Haub, Carl. 2012. *Changing the way U.S. Hispanics are counted*. Washington, DC: Population Reference Bureau. Available from http://www.prb.org/Publications/Articles/2012/us-census-and-hispanics.aspx.

Hersch, Joni. 2008. Profiling the new immigrant worker: The effects of skin color and height. *Journal of Labor Economics* 26 (2): 345–86.
Hersch, Joni. 2011. The persistence of skin color discrimination for immigrants. *Social Science Research* 40 (5): 1337–49.
Higham, John. 2002. *Strangers in the land: Patterns of American nativism, 1860–1925*. Rev. ed. New Brunswick, NJ: Rutgers University Press.
Levine, Daniel B., Kenneth Hill, and Robert Warren. 1985. *Immigration statistics: A story of neglect.* Washington, DC: National Academies Press.
Lieberson, Stanley, and Mary C. Waters. 1988. *From many strands: Ethnic and racial groups in contemporary America*. New York, NY: Russell Sage Foundation.
Lopez, Mark Hugo, Jeffrey S. Passel, and Molly Rohal. 2015. *Modern immigration wave brings 59 million to U.S., driving population growth and change through 2065*. Washington, DC: Pew Research Center.
Massey, Douglas S. 1995. The new immigration and ethnicity in the United States. *Population and Development Review* 21 (3): 631–52.
Massey, Douglas S. 2010. Immigration statistics for the 21st century. *The ANNALS of the American Academy of Political and Social Science* 631:124–40.
Massey, Douglas S., Jorge Durand, and Karen A. Pren. 2014. Explaining undocumented migration. *International Migration Review* 48 (4): 1028–61.
Massey, Douglas S., Jorge Durand, and Karen A. Pren. 2016. Why border enforcement backfired. *American Journal of Sociology* 121 (5): 1557–1600.
Massey, Douglas S., and Kerstin Gentsch. 2014. Undocumented migration and the wages of Mexican immigrants in the United States. *International Migration Review* 48 (2): 482–99.
Massey, Douglas S., and Karen A. Pren. 2012. Unintended consequences of U.S. immigration policy: Explaining the post-1965 surge from Latin America. *Population and Development Review* 38 (1): 1–29.
Novak, Michael. 1972. *The rise of the unmeltable ethnics: Politics and culture in the seventies*. New York, NY: Macmillan.
Passel, Jeffrey S., and D'Vera Cohn. 2016. *Overall number of U.S. unauthorized immigrants holds steady since 2009*. Washington, DC: Pew Hispanic Center.
Passel, Jeffrey S., and Paul Taylor. 2010. *Unauthorized immigrants and their U.S.-born children.* Washington, DC: Pew Research Center.
Pew Research Center on Hispanic Trends. 2015. *First- and second-generation share of the population, 1900–2015*. Washington, DC: Pew Research Center. Available from http://www.pewhispanic.org/chart/first-and-second-generation-share-of-the-population-1900-2015/.
Rumbaut, Rubén G. 2004. Ages, life stages, and generational cohorts: Decomposing the immigrant first and second generations in the United States. *International Migration Review* 38 (3): 1160–1205.
Waldstreicher, David. 2009. *Slavery's constitution: From revolution to ratification*. New York, NY: Hill and Wang.
Waters, Mary C. 1990. *Ethnic options: Choosing identities in America*. Berkeley, CA: University of California Press.
Waters, Mary C., and Marisa Gerstein Pineau. 2015. *The integration of immigrants into American society*. Washington, DC: National Academies Press.
Yoshikawa, Hirozaku, and Ariel Kalil. 2011. The effects of parental undocumented status on the developmental contexts of young children in immigrant families. *Child Development Perspectives* 5 (4): 291–97.
Zolberg, Aristide. 2006 *A nation by design: Immigration policy in the fashioning of America*. Cambridge, MA: Harvard University Press.

Social Mobility across Immigrant Generations: Recent Evidence and Future Data Requirements

By
VAN C. TRAN

This article assesses second-generation socioeconomic mobility using the most recent data available for eighteen ethnic groups from the Current Population Survey. In contrast to prior predictions of second-generation declines in mobility, this analysis finds significant progress in the second generation, both when that generation is compared to first-generation proxy parents and when compared to native peers of the same age cohort descended from what I identify as "proximal host groups." The analysis also underscores the significant data limitations that continue to plague assessments of intergenerational mobility in immigrant-origin populations, pointing to the urgent need to collect new and better data against which researchers can benchmark socioeconomic attainment for the post-1965 third generation, which will enter young adulthood in the next decade.

Keywords: immigration; assimilation; social mobility; second generation; third generation

Half a century into the post-1965 immigration flow, the "new" second generation (i.e., U.S.-born children of immigrants) has entered young and middle adulthood. In 2010, there were 20 million second-generation adults with an additional 16 million U.S.-born children of immigrants under the age of 18 (Pew Research Center 2012). By 2050, the second generation is expected to make up 18.4 percent of the total U.S. population (Pew Research Center 2012). Currently, the second generation's proportion of the total U.S. population is approaching levels first seen at the turn of the twentieth century. This growing segment of the population is a diverse group, with Latinos and Asians making up more than half of today's

Van C. Tran is an assistant professor of sociology at Columbia University. His research has focused on the integration of immigrants and their children, ethnic and racial inequality, and neighborhood gentrification in New York City.

Correspondence: vantran@columbia.edu

DOI: 10.1177/0002716218762725

second-generation adults. One key question is how the second generation will assimilate into American society and how its incorporation will reshape ethnoracial inequality.

This article assesses second-generation socioeconomic mobility using the most recent data available from the Current Population Survey (CPS) for eighteen ethnic groups. This is the first time such data have been available for a wide array of post-1965 ethnic groups, with sizable numbers of the second generation in adulthood. In contrast to prior predictions of second-generation decline, this analysis finds significant social mobility among the second generation, compared to both first-generation proxy parents and native peers of the same age cohort descended from what I identify as "proximal host groups." This is good news. At the same time, this analysis underscores the significant data limitations that continue to plague assessments of intergenerational mobility in the immigrant populations, pointing to the urgent need to collect new and better data to benchmark socioeconomic attainment among the post-1965 third generation, which will enter young adulthood in the next decades.

Assessing Second-Generation Individual Mobility

Two decades of scholarship have focused on the question of second-generation mobility in the context of changing American society. Theoretically, this body of work has grappled with the meaning and measure of assimilation in light of a more diverse U.S. mainstream (Waters and Pineau 2015; Alba and Nee 2003; Kasinitz et al. 2008). How are immigrants and their children assimilated into American society? How does their integration reshape the American mainstream? Given the racially stratified nature of American society, how does race matter in shaping second-generation mobility? How will second-generation mobility, in turn, transform the established social reconstruction of racial categories? Methodologically, ongoing data limitations have created unique challenges for empirical assessments of second-generation decline or progress (Park, Myers, and Jiménez 2014; Tran and Valdez 2017; Farley and Alba 2002). These limitations include the inability to identify the second and third generations in the main census datasets (the decennial census and the American Community Survey [ACS]), the lack of good data on parental background to benchmark intergenerational progress, the relatively small sample size for many post-1965 ethnic groups in national surveys, the heavy reliance on robust regional surveys that are not generalizable to other parts of the country, and the rarity of longitudinal data sources that track the second generation from childhood to adulthood.

The immigration literature gives us reason to suspect downward mobility in the second generation stemming from macro-structural influences such as racial minority status, segregated urban schools, concentration in disadvantaged neighborhoods, a bifurcated economy offering fewer good jobs, and rising illegality in the first generation (Portes and Rumbaut 2001; Alba, Kasinitz, and Waters 2011; Telles and Ortiz 2008; Massey, Durand, and Pren 2016). How will the second generation overcome these hurdles and achieve social mobility, especially with increasing income inequality? Should the second generation be compared to their first-generation parents or to their native peers from the proximal host groups?

While these theoretical, methodological, and substantive debates have been central to the burgeoning scholarship on assimilation, the core challenge has been a *methodological* one. Put simply, high-quality data have been sorely lacking, severely limiting the capacity for research in this field. Prior studies of second-generation individual mobility have relied on a patchwork of data sources that have unique strengths and weaknesses. These data sources include the ACS, the CPS, and three major regional surveys on the second generation. These regional surveys include the Children of Immigrants Longitudinal Study (CILS), the Immigrant Second Generation in Metropolitan New York (ISGMNY), and the Immigration and Intergenerational Mobility in Metropolitan Los Angeles (IIMMLA), all of which were funded wholly or partly by the Russell Sage Foundation. Although both ACS and CPS are nationally representative, each of these two sources has significant weaknesses. The lack of a parental birthplace question in the ACS makes it impossible to identify the true second generation as soon as they reach adulthood and leave the parental household (Rumbaut 2004). Although the CPS added the parental birthplace question in 1994, the sample size of the CPS is relatively small compared to that of the ACS. Specifically, the CPS is a monthly survey of about 60,000 U.S. households, whereas the ACS is a monthly survey sent to about 295,000 U.S. addresses. Except for the largest ethnic groups, the CPS does not provide sufficient samples of second-generation individuals to produce reliable group-level estimates. To overcome this limitation, several studies have either combined multiple years of the CPS or used panethnic categories (Duncan and Trejo 2015, 2016; Tran and Valdez 2017; Farley and Alba 2002). Furthermore, the lack of identification of parental background in the CPS makes it impossible to meaningfully compare the socioeconomic status of first-generation parents to that of their second-generation children in adulthood. The three regional second-generation surveys are more comprehensive, but are very specific in geographical scope and were costly to implement, requiring a significant investment of time, energy, and resources from dedicated teams of interdisciplinary researchers. Altogether, these sources of data have provided significant insights into the multifaceted ways in which the second generation has become integrated into American society and cover a diverse range of topics from ethnoracial identity formation, linguistic and cultural transmission, education and socioeconomic mobility, civic and political participation, intermarriage, and union formation (Portes and Rumbaut 2001; Kasinitz et al. 2008; Bean, Brown, and Bachmeier 2015; Lee and Zhou 2015). This article builds on this body of research by providing the most recent evidence of the socioeconomic mobility among the second generation.

Recent Evidence on Second-Generation Attainment

Data and methods

To examine patterns of educational attainment across generations, this article uses the most recent pooled data from the Annual Social and Economic

Supplement of the Current Population Survey (CPS ASEC). The CPS is the only data source that provides nationally representative samples of second-generation adults from selected ethnic groups in the United States. It is administered by the U.S. Census Bureau through both in-person and telephone interviews every month to monitor basic trends in the labor force. It uses a probability sample of about sixty thousand occupied households from all fifty states and the District of Columbia. The survey design adopts a 4-8-4 sampling scheme whereby households are included in the survey for the first four consecutive months and excluded for the next eight months, before returning again for the last four consecutive months. The pooling of data over the last decade from the 2008, 2010, 2012, 2014, and 2016 samples provides nonoverlapping individuals in the pooled dataset. This pooled dataset both overcomes sample size limitations and provides the largest sample to date to identify the post-1965 second generation.

Immigrant generations and ethnic groups

Generational status is based on the individual's birthplace and that of his or her parents. The first generation comprises those born outside of the United States. The second generation includes those born in the United States to two parents born outside of the United States. This category also includes Puerto Ricans born in the United States to parents who were born in Puerto Rico. For the purposes of classification of ethnic origin, I rely on both the father's and mother's country of birth. Specifically, individuals who were born in the United States to one foreign-born parent and a U.S.-born parent (i.e., the 2.5 generation) are excluded from this analysis. Those who were born in the United States to two foreign-born parents of different national origins are also excluded. As a result, this article focuses strictly on the "pure" second generation, which includes *U.S.-born individuals with both foreign-born parents from the same sending country of origin*. This decision is a strategic one because prior research has shown that ethnic attrition among the second generation and later generations is substantially higher among individuals with mixed ancestry (Duncan and Trejo 2015). More practically, classifying these mixed individuals into one ethnic origin requires the assumption that either the father's or the mother's ethnic origin is more important to their identity and experiences. Finally, the third-plus generation includes those who were born in the United States to U.S.-born parents, although the CPS cannot distinguish between third- and fourth-and-higher-generation individuals, so the term *third-plus generation* includes both groups.

This analysis focuses on eighteen second-generation and four third-plus-generation groups. The eighteen second-generation ethnic groups are identified because each group has a sample size of at least 100 in the pooled CPS dataset. The primary focus will be on second-generation individuals between the ages of 25 and 50. This cohort of individuals most resembles the post-1965 second generation. For CPS 2008, the oldest individuals in this cohort were born between 1968 and 1983. For CPS 2016, the oldest individuals in this cohort were born between 1976 and 1991. Following the lagged-birth-cohort method (Farley and Alba 2002), I compare this cohort of second-generation individuals with their proxy parents: first-generation individuals above the age of 50. I also compare outcomes among the second generation to their third-plus-generation peers in the "proximal host" groups: non-Hispanic white, non-Hispanic black, non-Hispanic Asian, and Hispanic/Latino (Mittelberg and Waters 1992).

This analysis focuses on four dichotomous measures of socioeconomic attainment: having no high school degree, having a college degree, working in a service occupation, and working in a professional or managerial occupation. The analyses proceed in two stages. First, bivariate analyses provide statistical profiles for each ethnic group by generation. Second, multivariate analyses explore the socioeconomic attainment of second-generation ethnic groups relative to third-plus-generation proximal hosts. Because the dependent variables are dichotomous, I use logistic regressions with robust standard errors and report the odds ratios. The control variables include gender, age (plus its quadratic term), region of the country (the standard four census regions), and survey year. All analyses adjust for the stratified survey design using appropriate final weights in CPS ASEC.

Descriptive and multivariate results

The combined CPS sample size includes 1,002,647 respondents from a mix of ethnoracial origins and immigrant generations. Table 1 presents the descriptive statistics on this sample by immigrant generation and age cohort. The first panel shows that only 1.9 percent of whites and 1.1 percent of blacks belong to the second generation, whereas these proportions are 11.2 percent of Hispanics and 10.5 percent of Asians. Of whites and blacks, 92.9 percent and 87.2 percent are in the third-plus generation, compared to only 28.3 percent of Hispanics and 12.4 percent of Asians. The next three panels in Table 1 provide the race and age distributions across generations. In the first generation, the age profile skews older among whites. For the other three ethnoracial groups, about half are between the ages of 25 and 50. In the second generation, the major difference is between whites and nonwhites. Whereas 47.7 percent of second-generation whites are above the age of 50, the proportions are small among blacks, Asians, and Hispanics (2.5 percent, 6.3 percent, and 5.8 percent, respectively). In contrast, almost three-quarters of the nonwhite second generation are below the age of 25. As the second generation comes of age in the next decade, this cohort of children and adolescents will emerge into young adulthood in sizable numbers. In the third-plus generation, the population is more evenly distributed across the age cohorts. In general, whites are more likely to be concentrated in the oldest cohort, whereas Hispanics and Asians are more likely to be concentrated in the youngest one.

Table 2 presents descriptive results for four measures of socioeconomic attainment for the eighteen ethnic groups, separately for the first-generation individuals above age 50 and for second-generation individuals aged 25 to 50. The results from Table 2 show clear evidence of mobility between the first and second generation for every ethnic group. Among the four white ethnic groups, Italians report the lowest starting point, with 34.9 percent of the first generation having no high school degree—similar to levels among first-generation Haitians and

TABLE 1
Ethnoracial Origin by Immigrant Generation and Age Cohorts

All Respondents	% 1st Gen.	% 2nd Gen.	% 3rd+ Gen.	% Total
White	5.2	1.9	92.9	100
Black	11.7	1.1	87.2	100
Hispanic	60.5	11.2	28.3	100
Asian	77.1	10.5	12.4	100
1st Generation	% Age (0–24)	% Age (25–50)	% Age (50+)	% Total
White	13.3	40.6	46.1	100
Black	18.0	51.0	31.2	100
Hispanic	14.2	49.5	36.3	100
Asian	15.5	55.2	29.6	100
2nd Generation	% Age (0–24)	% Age (25–50)	% Age (50+)	% Total
White	32.4	20.2	47.7	100
Black	77.6	19.8	2.5	100
Hispanic	70.2	23.5	6.3	100
Asian	71.6	22.5	5.8	100
3rd-Plus Generation	% Age (0–24)	% Age (25–50)	% Age (50+)	% Total
White	29.7	32.3	38.2	100
Black	38.8	32.9	28.3	100
Hispanic	43.3	27.7	29.0	100
Asian	57.5	27.5	14.9	100

SOURCE: CPS, ASEC (2008–2016).
NOTE: All numbers are row percentages.

Vietnamese. And yet, by the second generation, the high school dropout rates among these three groups hover around 2 to 3 percent, a marked improvement. By the second generation, whites, blacks, and Asians report high school dropout rates of less than 3 percent (with the exception of second-generation Canadians at 7.4 percent). Among Hispanics, many ethnic groups also report very low starting points in terms of education. In the first generation, 66.9 percent of Mexicans have no high school education, compared to 58.6 percent of Salvadorans and 50.4 percent of Guatemalans. In the second generation, these rates are dramatically reduced: 16.9 percent of Mexicans, 11.9 percent of Salvadorans, and 17.8 percent of Guatemalans. To be sure, the high school dropout rates are still highest among Hispanics, but the progress is remarkable, considering the lower starting points among the first-generation parents.

On college completion, second-generation Asians report the most exceptional outcomes, with about 56 to 80 percent of the sample having a college degree. In

TABLE 2
Descriptive Statistics on Second-Generation Attainment in Adulthood

	% No High School	% College Graduate	% Service Occupations	% Professional Occupations	Sample Size
1st generation ages 50+					
Canada	13.4	33.3	4.5	26.9	719
Germany	8.6	27.8	5.1	15.0	712
Italy	34.9	17.0	6.1	13.9	592
Poland	15.1	29.0	12.9	18.1	460
Haiti	32.1	13.9	22.5	11.4	574
Jamaica	23.6	23.0	21.4	16.5	837
China	23.4	40.3	11.1	22.5	2,686
India	10.6	63.6	3.3	34.2	1,504
Korea	10.2	43.5	10.0	18.2	1,241
Philippines	8.4	51.9	13.6	21.5	3,108
Vietnam	32.3	17.6	16.4	10.7	1,452
Colombia	17.1	26.5	17.2	14.8	799
Cuba	28.9	22.6	8.0	12.6	1,796
Dominican Republic	45.8	14.0	18.6	8.1	1,016
El Salvador	58.6	7.7	25.0	6.3	1,110
Guatemala	50.4	9.6	22.2	10.3	549
Mexico	66.9	6.3	17.7	5.0	9,638
Puerto Rico	43.4	11.8	7.7	8.5	2,294
2nd generation ages 25–50					
Canada	7.4	50.1	8.4	49.4	159
Germany	0.6	52.8	7.3	41.6	106
Italy	2.6	45.8	10.2	40.3	369
Poland	0.1	57.3	8.6	40.7	116
Haiti	2.0	52.5	13.3	45.6	136
Jamaica	2.0	32.8	10.2	30.5	128
China	1.2	80.9	5.4	62.3	540
India	1.9	81.7	3.4	63.2	378
Korea	0.2	71.6	14.0	51.4	234
Philippines	1.5	55.8	10.3	47.5	861
Vietnam	2.7	63.8	10.9	40.4	248
Colombia	3.6	50.4	9.7	45.5	147
Cuba	3.4	46.1	10.6	42.6	432
Dominican Republic	12.5	32.7	11.8	33.1	301
El Salvador	11.9	21.9	12.0	25.6	248
Guatemala	17.8	23.2	17.2	27.0	115
Mexico	16.9	17.2	14.5	21.2	5,053
Puerto Rico	14.0	16.0	16.9	20.0	1,278

SOURCE: CPS, ASEC (2008–2016).
NOTE: Grey shadings separate the ethnic groups into the four major racial categories (i.e., white, black, Hispanic, and Asian) to which they are assigned in the U.S. context.

the third-plus generation, this rate is 38.3 percent of whites, 21.4 percent of blacks, and 57 percent of Asians. Second-generation whites and blacks report high levels of college completion, surpassing their respective proximal host groups. Among blacks, there is a clear dichotomy, with second-generation Haitians reporting significantly better college completion rates than Jamaicans. Among Hispanics, Colombians and Cubans report the highest rates of college graduates, whereas the results among the other Hispanic groups are more mixed. To be sure, many Hispanics have yet to close the gaps with whites, but they have fared significantly better than the first generation from the same ethnic background.

Although there is a clear improvement from first to second generation, intergenerational differences are more modest for service occupations. The results for professional occupations, however, are revealing. With the exception of Mexicans, Puerto Ricans, and Vietnamese, every second-generation ethnic group has not only fared better than its first-generation proxy parents, but also better than its proximal host group. Among second-generation whites, these rates are between 40 and 49 percent, compared to only 36.9 percent for third-plus-generation whites. Among second-generation blacks, these rates are 45.6 percent for Haitians and 30.5 percent for Jamaicans, compared to 22.7 percent for third-plus-generation blacks. Second-generation Asians report some of the highest rates, with 62.3 percent among Chinese, 63.2 percent among Indians and 51.4 percent among Koreans holding a managerial and professional occupation. In contrast, these rates are lowest among Hispanics—especially Mexicans and Puerto Ricans—with only 20 percent reporting a professional occupation.

The multivariate analyses in Table 3 focus attention on second-generation attainment in comparison with third-plus-generation individuals, controlling for age, gender, region, and survey year. In comparison to native whites (i.e., the reference group), models 1 and 2 show that most second-generation whites and Asians are significantly less likely to have no high school degree and significantly more likely to have a college education. The largest differences are found among Chinese and Indians, who are six times more likely than whites to have a college degree. What is more remarkable is that there are no differences between second-generation blacks (i.e., Haitians and Jamaicans) and native whites, suggesting that the former have achieved parity with the latter. Among Hispanics, Colombians and Cubans fare better than native whites, whereas the other ethnic groups fare worse. On occupational attainment, models 3 and 4 show that the second generation has achieved parity with native whites, with few exceptions. For service occupations, Koreans and Puerto Ricans are significantly more likely than third-plus-generation whites to report working in the service sector. For professional occupations, Poles, Mexicans, and Puerto Ricans report a disadvantage compared to native whites, whereas Chinese and Indians report a clear advantage. Overall, these results show broad convergences between the second generation from diverse ethnic origins and third-plus-generation whites.

This comparison, however, is imperfect. First, the third-plus-generation category is diverse, lumping together third-generation and later-generation individuals. A tighter comparison would be between the second and the third-only

TABLE 3
Logistic Regressions on Second-Generation Attainment in Adulthood

Variables	No High School Degree Model 1	College Graduate Model 2	Service Occupations Model 3	Professional Occupations Model 4
Ethnoracial origin				
Canadian, 2nd	1.513	1.575°	1.015	1.420
	(0.756)	(0.361)	(0.358)	(0.482)
German, 2nd	0.122°	1.790°	0.519	0.777
	(0.123)	(0.461)	(0.279)	(0.225)
Italian, 2nd	0.546	1.177	1.063	1.007
	(0.177)	(0.156)	(0.269)	(0.159)
Polish, 2nd	0.017°°°	2.024°	0.820	0.576°
	(0.017)	(0.576)	(0.430)	(0.143)
Haitian, 2nd	0.409	1.484	1.572	0.940
	(0.212)	(0.299)	(0.459)	(0.246)
Jamaican, 2nd	0.399	0.683	0.951	0.717
	(0.278)	(0.147)	(0.345)	(0.231)
Chinese, 2nd	0.268°°°	6.123°°°	0.640	1.405°
	(0.095)	(0.856)	(0.147)	(0.200)
Indian, 2nd	0.373°°	6.882°°°	0.656	1.583°
	(0.137)	(1.199)	(0.222)	(0.328)
Korean, 2nd	0.044°°°	3.619°°°	1.796°	1.016
	(0.031)	(0.713)	(0.506)	(0.219)
Filipino, 2nd	0.353°°	1.863°°°	1.056	1.050
	(0.128)	(0.170)	(0.162)	(0.131)
Vietnamese, 2nd	0.577	2.664°°°	1.291	0.769
	(0.222)	(0.465)	(0.372)	(0.169)
Colombian, 2nd	0.751	1.382	0.755	0.985
	(0.470)	(0.304)	(0.237)	(0.315)
Cuban, 2nd	0.576	1.420°°	1.039	1.011
	(0.167)	(0.168)	(0.252)	(0.156)
Dominican, 2nd	3.066°°°	0.614°°	0.937	0.991
	(0.852)	(0.101)	(0.264)	(0.249)
Salvadoran, 2nd	2.920°°°	0.406°°°	0.810	0.844
	(0.743)	(0.073)	(0.189)	(0.214)
Guatemalan, 2nd	4.570°°°	0.437°°	1.154	0.705
	(1.375)	(0.133)	(0.472)	(0.275)
Mexican, 2nd	4.351°°°	0.310°°°	1.007	0.718°°°
	(0.260)	(0.015)	(0.063)	(0.037)
Puerto Rican, 2nd	3.153°°°	0.267°°°	1.345°	0.680°°
	(0.333)	(0.026)	(0.165)	(0.082)
Black, 3rd+	1.966°°°	0.440°°°	1.690°°°	0.673°°°
	(0.056)	(0.008)	(0.041)	(0.016)

(continued)

TABLE 3 (CONTINUED)

Variables	No High School Degree Model 1	College Graduate Model 2	Service Occupations Model 3	Professional Occupations Model 4
Asian, 3rd+	0.678	1.972***	1.768***	0.934
	(0.147)	(0.146)	(0.193)	(0.086)
Latino, 3rd+	3.078***	0.364***	1.299***	0.768***
	(0.118)	(0.011)	(0.047)	(0.025)
Control variables				
Age	0.909***	1.121***	0.937***	1.082***
	(0.016)	(0.010)	(0.013)	(0.013)
Age-square	1.001***	0.998***	1.001**	0.999***
	(0.000)	(0.000)	(0.000)	(0.000)
Male	1.329***	0.769***	0.595***	0.696***
	(0.029)	(0.009)	(0.011)	(0.010)
Region (ref. Northeast)				
Midwest	1.087*	0.706***	0.890***	0.894***
	(0.042)	(0.013)	(0.025)	(0.020)
South	1.378***	0.734***	0.859***	1.008
	(0.048)	(0.013)	(0.024)	(0.023)
West	0.871***	0.861***	0.906**	1.076**
	(0.035)	(0.016)	(0.890***)	(0.026)
Survey year (ref. 2008)				
2010	0.963	1.022	1.050*	1.102***
	(0.028)	(0.016)	(0.026)	(0.022)
2012	0.889***	1.112***	1.109***	1.029
	(0.027)	(0.018)	(0.027)	(0.021)
2014	0.795***	1.187***	1.123***	1.029
	(0.026)	(0.020)	(0.029)	(0.022)
2016	0.760***	1.295***	1.097***	1.096***
	(0.025)	(0.021)	(0.028)	(0.022)
Education (ref. no HS)				
High school			0.700***	1.794***
			(0.025)	(0.090)
Some college			0.577***	4.286***
			(0.021)	(0.211)
College graduate			0.214***	16.553***
			(0.009)	(0.821)
Graduate degree			0.065***	65.539***
			(0.004)	(3.633)
Constant	0.229***	0.118***	2.206**	0.026***
	(0.071)	(0.020)	(0.564)	(0.006)
N	247,008	247,008	193,262	193,262

SOURCE: CPS, ASEC (2008–2016).
NOTE: Odds ratios are reported. Robust standard errors in parentheses. The reference group for the ethnoracial origin variable is "third-plus-generation non-Hispanic whites." Total sample was restricted to respondents aged 25–50. Models 3–4 were restricted to those employed full time in the previous year.
*$p < .05$. **$p < .01$. ***$p < .001$.

generation. Second, this comparison does not account for the historical, institutional, and contextual factors that shape the context of reception and assimilation for different ethnic groups within the same racial group. Third, it does not control for parental social class and legal status, which significantly impact the Hispanic second generation.

The Rise of the Post-1965 Third Generation

Although research over the last two decades has focused on the second generation because of their theoretical importance and growing presence, assimilation is a multigenerational process and the true test of integration rests with the third generation, *not* the second generation (Alba and Nee 2003; Waters and Pineau 2015). Historically, the experiences of European ethnic groups suggest that their full integration into American life occurred by the third generation, at which point ethnic groups' socioeconomic attainment, ethnic identification, intermarriage, and residential patterns showed parity with the native white mainstream. For example, recent trends in multiracial identification and intermarriages that scholars have identified will only intensify over the next few decades with the coming of age of the third generation (Alba 2016; Lichter, Qian, and Tumin 2015; Lee and Bean 2010).

Although the third generation is still very young, early trends from the most recent CPS ASEC are telling. Among third-plus-generation Hispanics, 43.3 percent are still under the age of 25, and 27.7 percent are between the ages of 25 and 50. Among third-plus-generation Asians, 57.5 percent are still under the age of 25, and 27.5 percent are between the ages of 25 and 50. The youthful concentrations among Hispanics and Asians will translate into a significant demographic reality in the coming decades (Myers 2007). By 2020, approximately 496,000 additional third-generation Hispanics and 70,000 additional third-generation Asians will reach adulthood (Jimenez, Park, and Pedroza 2017). The ensuing decade will add 829,000 third-generation Hispanics and 118,000 third-generation Asians to these numbers. By 2030, the number of third-generation Hispanics and Asians aged 18 and older among the adult U.S. population will reach 1.7 million.

Here again, both the ACS and CPS fall significantly short. ACS data do not allow for the identification of the second or the third generation. Among adults, CPS data allow for the identification of "third-and-higher generation" individuals, but not the true third generation. As a result, the trends for this "third-and-higher-generation" category might distort the extent of social mobility. Among children, CPS data allow for the identification of the third generation and fourth-and-higher generation by identifying households that have U.S.-born children coresiding with a second-generation parent as the head of household (Jiménez, Park, and Pedroza 2017). However, because of sample size, this method limits analysis only to the largest ethnic groups (e.g., Mexicans) or to panethnic categories (i.e., Asian or Hispanic/Latino), to the exclusion of many other ethnic groups of theoretical interest.

The challenge with projecting future trends of key indicators of integration for ethnic groups using data based on children or adolescents is well-documented (Alba, Kasinitz, and Waters 2011; Kasinitz et al. 2008; Portes and Rumbaut 2001). Although aspirations for achievement are universal in adolescence, the processes of attainment, mobility, and stratification necessarily unfold over the life course from young adulthood well into middle and late adulthood in a deeply racialized and stratified opportunity structure (Bean, Brown, and Bachmeier 2015; Lee and Zhou 2015). As a result, early trends will likely underestimate both the extent of assimilation that will occur in adulthood and the significance of obstacles that might derail achievement among the second and third generations.

Unlike the 1880–1924 wave of immigration, for which the immigration hiatus between 1924 and 1965 proved crucial to the assimilation of many European ethnic groups (Alba and Nee 2003), immigrant replenishment is a key feature of post-1965 immigration (Jiménez 2010). As a result, many of these groups will include a mix of multiple generations descended from immigration cohorts that arrived in the United States at different post-1965 periods (Telles and Ortiz 2008; Waters 2014). High-quality census data with large samples from a broad range of ethnic groups are crucial for any assessment of the increasingly diverse and divergent outcomes across ethnoracial groups over time, across cohorts, and across immigrant generations.

Conclusion

As the second generation reaches adulthood, the ability to identify its members and analyze their socioeconomic progress or stagnation over time is ever more urgent. The census data sources currently available not only fall significantly short of research needs, but are also becoming rapidly inadequate for assessments of emerging trends among the third generation in the coming decades. In the long run, the addition of parental birthplace questions to the ACS will facilitate the identification of the second generation and the more precise analyses of socioeconomic mobility across immigrant generations for a broad range of ethnoracial groups. In the short run, the addition of parental socioeconomic status questions to the CPS will facilitate analyses of intergenerational mobility, albeit in a more limited way. In keeping with the spirit of a "gradual change" strategy (Prewitt 2013), the eventual addition of questions on the birthplaces of grandparents into the census will become relevant in the coming decades to enable the identification of the third generation and the rigorous analyses of ethnic attrition.

These observations are consistent with the main recommendations of two major recent reports from the National Academy of Sciences on immigrant integration and its impact on American society (Waters and Pineau 2015; Blau and Mackie 2016). Both reports agreed on the main data needs for the future and reached the same recommendations for additional questions for the ACS and CPS. On one hand, this fact alone is remarkable and points decisively to a clear consensus within the social scientific community about data needs. On the other hand, it is not surprising because immigration scholars have long recognized the significance and transformative power of the post-1965 second generation. Looking ahead, immigration scholars will need access to high-quality data to assess the unfolding lives of the children of immigrants, especially in light of the next demographic transition that is taking place as 76.4 million individuals from the Baby Boomer generation reach retirement and old age.

References

Alba, Richard. 2016. The likely persistence of a white majority. *American Prospect*, winter: 67–71.
Alba, Richard, Philip Kasinitz, and Mary C. Waters. 2011. The kids are (mostly) alright: Second-generation assimilation. *Social Forces* 89 (3): 763–74.
Alba, Richard, and Victor Nee. 2003. *Remaking the American mainstream: Assimilation and contemporary immigration*. Cambridge, MA: Harvard University Press.
Bean, Frank, Susan K. Brown, and James Bachmeier. 2015. *Parents without papers: The progress and pitfalls of Mexican American integration*. New York, NY: Russell Sage Foundation.
Blau, Francine D., and Christopher Mackie. 2016. *The economic and fiscal consequences of immigration*. Washington, DC: National Academies Press.
Duncan, Brian, and Stephen J. Trejo. 2015. Assessing the socioeconomic mobility and integration of U.S. immigrants and their descendants. *The ANNALS of the American Academy of Political and Social Science* 657:108–35.
Duncan, Brian, and Stephen J. Trejo. 2016. The complexity of immigrant generations: Implications for assessing the socioeconomic integration of Hispanics and Asians. *Industrial and Labor Relations Review*. doi:10.1177/0019793916679613.
Farley, Reynolds, and Richard Alba. 2002. The new second generation in the United States. *International Migration Review* 36:669–701.
Jiménez, Tomás R. 2010. *Replenished ethnicity: Mexican Americans, immigration, and identity*. Berkeley, CA: University of California Press.
Jiménez, Tomás R., Julie Park, and Juan Pedroza. 2017. The new third generation: Post-1965 immigration and the long march of assimilation. *International Migration Review*. doi:10.1111/imre.12343.
Kasinitz, Philip, John H. Mollenkopf, Mary C. Waters, and Jennifer Holdaway. 2008. *Inheriting the city: The children of immigrants come of age*. New York, NY, and Cambridge, MA: Russell Sage Foundation and Harvard University Press.
Lee, Jennifer, and Frank D. Bean. 2010. *The diversity paradox: Immigration and the color line in 21st-century America*. New York, NY: Russell Sage Foundation.
Lee, Jennifer, and Min Zhou. 2015. *The Asian American achievement paradox*. New York, NY: Russell Sage Foundation.
Lichter Daniel T., Zhenchao Qian, and Dimitry Tumin. 2015. Whom do immigrants marry? Emerging patterns of intermarriage and integration in the United States. *The ANNALS of the American Academy of Political* and *Social Science* 662:57–78.
Massey, Douglas S., Jorge Durand, and Karen A. Pren. 2016. Why border enforcement backfired. *American Journal of Sociology* 121 (5): 1557–1600.
Mittelberg, David, and Mary C. Waters. 1992. The process of ethnogenesis among Haitian and Israeli immigrants in the United States. *Ethnic and Racial Studies* 15 (3): 412–35.
Myers, Dowell. 2007. *Immigrants and boomers: Forging a new social contract for the future of America*. New York, NY: Russell Sage Foundation.
Park, Julie, Dowell Myers, and Tomás R. Jiménez. 2014. Intergenerational advancement of the Mexican-origin population in California and Texas relative to a changing U.S. mainstream. *International Migration Review*, summer: 1–40.

Pew Research Center. 2012. *Second-generation Americans: A portrait of adult children of immigrants*. Washington, DC: Pew Social and Demographic Trends Report.
Portes, Alejandro, and Rubén G. Rumbaut. 2001. *Legacies: The story of the immigrant second generation*. Berkeley, CA: University of California Press.
Prewitt, Kenneth. 2013. *What is your race? The flawed effort of the census to classify Americans*. Princeton, NJ: Princeton University Press.
Rumbaut, Rubén G. 2004. Ages, life stages, and generational cohorts: Decomposing the immigrant first and second generations in the United States. *International Migration Review* 38 (3): 1160–1205.
Telles, Edward E., and Vilma Ortiz. 2008. *Generations of exclusion: Mexican Americans, assimilation and race*. New York, NY: Russell Sage Foundation.
Tran, Van C., and Nicol M. Valdez. 2017. Second-generation decline or advantage? Latino assimilation in the aftermath of the great recession. *International Migration Review* 51 (1): 155–90.
Waters, Mary C. 2014. Defining difference: The role of immigrant generation and race in American and British immigration studies. *Ethnic and Racial Studies* 37 (1): 10–26.
Waters, Mary C., and Marisa Gerstein Pineau. 2015. *The integration of immigrants into American society*. Washington, DC: National Academies Press.

Tracking a Changing America across the Generations after Immigration

By
TOMÁS R. JIMÉNEZ

The post-1960s immigration boom and contemporary demographics have elevated *generation-since-immigration* as a category that is central to analysts and, more generally, to Americans as they make sense of their place in the world around them. This makes the collection of data on immigrant generations imperative if surveys are to keep up with how the nation's people think about themselves and each other. A clear portrait of contemporary assimilation, and indeed American progress, depends on possessing the right tools to paint such a portrait. That means that surveys must enable researchers to identify respondents' generation, particularly the third generation of the post-1965 immigration wave.

Keywords: immigration; assimilation; generation; identity; data

Any survey that hopes to reflect the social identities of its respondents has to keep up with the times. And these are complicated times when it comes to identity. The United States, along with other postindustrial societies, is governed by norms and institutions that now allow far greater latitude in how people identify individually (Bean, Brown, and Bachmeier 2015). Indeed, gender, sexual, race, and ethnic identities are arguably more flexible than ever (Brubaker 2016; Saperstein and Penner 2012; Schilt 2010). That dynamism poses significant challenges to surveys that aim to reflect the identities of the people answering them. The massive influx of immigrants in the last four decades only adds to the challenge. As immigrants, their children, and the society that has received them adjust to one another, notions

Tomás R. Jiménez is an associate professor of sociology and comparative studies in race and ethnicity at Stanford University. He is author of The Other Side of Assimilation: How Immigrants Change American Life *(University of California Press 2010).*

Correspondence: tjimenez@stanford.edu

DOI: 10.1177/0002716218765416

of race, ethnicity, and nation grow in complexity (Jiménez 2017). For survey designers and analysts, this requires hard choices about how to gather and analyze data that tap into group identities.

Gender, race, and ethnicity attract most of the attention regarding changes in identity, categorization, and identification. But large-scale immigration has increased the complexity of a category that is much less subject to individual choice, but nonetheless important for how individuals define themselves and others: *generation-since-immigration* (hereafter *generation*), where the first generation consists of immigrants, the second generation the children of immigrants, the third generation the grandchildren of immigrants, and so on. Tectonic shifts in the generational profile of the post-1965 wave of immigrants are already under way in the United States.[1] The shift entails the rise of a third generation whose social, political, and economic fortunes will reveal the extent and kind of assimilation among the descendants of today's largely non-European immigrants. In addition to being an important temporal marker for analysis of assimilation, generation is also a category relevant to how Americans perceive social insiders and outsiders in everyday life. In immigrant-rich contexts, generation, along with race, class, and gender, can serve as a basis upon which individuals decipher who belongs.

Yet analysts of American society are ill-equipped to make sense of generational distinctions because there is no good way in most surveys to identify a respondent's generation. And even when generation is ascertainable, it is next to impossible to identify a unique post-1965 third generation. A clear portrait of contemporary assimilation, and indeed American progress, depends on possessing the right tools with which to paint such a picture. That means that surveys must enable researchers to identify respondents' generations, and particularly the third generation of the post-1965 immigration wave.

The Centrality of Generation to the American Experience

It is incontrovertible that immigration is changing just about every aspect of American life. The numerical significance of the immigrant population relative to the overall population indicates the scale of that change. Today, immigrants make up roughly 13 percent of the population, a rate nearing historic highs (National Academies of Science, Engineering, and Medicine 2015). Immigrants and their children combine to make up one in four individuals in the United States, and in some metro regions, the first and second generations combine to make up roughly half of the population (Jiménez 2017). The effects of immigration on the racial composition of the United States are well known (Frey 2014). Indeed, attention to compositional changes resulting from immigration focus heavily on race and ethnicity, and with good reason. The United States has grown dramatically more diverse in recent decades because of the settlement of immigrants, who come overwhelmingly from Latin America, Asia, and the Caribbean (National Academies of Science, Engineering, and Medicine 2015). Inasmuch as

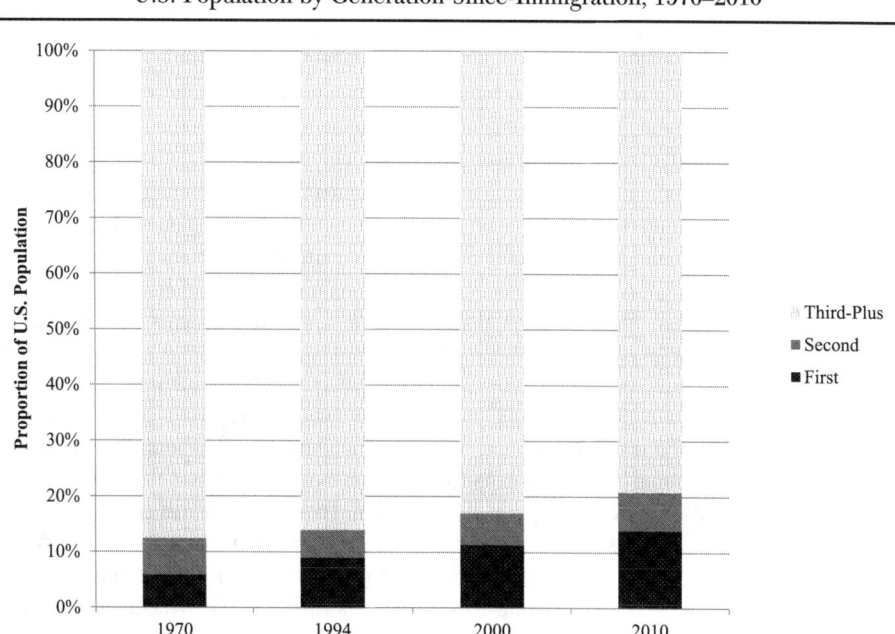

FIGURE 1
U.S. Population by Generation-Since-Immigration, 1970–2010

SOURCE: United States decennial census; Current Population Survey.
NOTE: Data for 1980 and 1990 are unavailable and thus not reported.

survey classifications of racial groups have become problematic (Prewitt 2013), large government surveys have attempted to keep up with the times by maintaining race and ethnicity[2] as categories of classification, by adopting new racial categories, and, as of 2000, by allowing respondents to check more than one racial category.

When it comes to documenting changes in the generational composition of the United States, surveys, and especially those administered by the government, have attempted but not adequately kept pace. The nation's generational profile has indeed changed dramatically. Figure 1 uses decennial census data and the Current Population Survey (CPS) to offer a generational profile of the U.S. population since 1970.

It is important to note from Figure 1 that the twentieth-century low point for the foreign-born population was 1970, when 87 percent of the American population was third generation or greater ("third-plus" generation). That figure suggests that the paradigmatic American experience of immigration was less of a defining feature of life in 1970 than at any point in the twentieth century. It was also at about that time that the grandchildren of the turn-of-the-century European immigrants were coming of age, and their income, education, intermarriage rates, and neighborhood integration indicated successful assimilation

(Alba and Nee 2003). Moreover, immigration took on a nostalgic hue in the collective identities of ethnic groups associated with that wave (Alba 1990; Waters 1990), and the descendants of that immigration wave grafted immigration onto the American national myth of origins (Jacobson 2006). With the U.S. population tilted heavily away from the first and second generations, and with the near complete assimilation of the last large wave of immigrants, the need to distinguish in surveys between different generations did not seem acute. And so 1970 was the last year that the decennial census included a question about parents' place of birth, from which analysts could distinguish between first, second, and third-plus generations. Starting in 1994, the CPS included a question about parents' place of birth, but the question has not made its way into more comprehensive government surveys, such as the census or the American Community Survey (ACS).

The large and overwhelmingly non-European immigration in the ensuing decades—the post-1965 immigration—changed the place of immigration in the American experience once again. This time, the source regions of immigrants have been decidedly non-European, with Latin America (especially Mexico), Asia, and the Caribbean sending large numbers. Not only has the most recent wave of immigrants swelled the proportion of the total population that is foreign born to near historic levels, it has also changed the nation's generational composition. Along with their second-generation children, these immigrants have grown the proportion of the total U.S. population that is either first or second generation. As Figure 1 shows, the share of the U.S. population from those generations nearly doubled between 1970 and 2010. That demographic change underscores the added importance of generation in the contemporary United States as both a temporal marker necessary for tracking patterns of assimilation and as a category that shapes how people make sense of their everyday lives.

Generation: Category of Analysis; Category of Practice

The importance of generation manifests in the way that it operates as both a category of analysis and as a category of practice. The former refers to generation as a category that social scientists use to organize populations for the sake of conducting analysis, usually of the statistical sort. The latter signifies the categories that people use in their everyday life to make sense of the world (Brubaker 2004).

Generation as a category of analysis

The presence of the large immigrant population means that adequately deciphering the contours of any social, political, and economic change entails data on generation. But among scholars, race is a favored category in analyses of differences in social and economic outcomes. For example, economic inequality unambiguously has a racial component. Blacks and Latinos generally sit at the lower end of the socioeconomic distribution, while Asians and whites anchor the high end (Massey 2007). However, examining differences in socioeconomic attainment only by comparing across racial categories misses significant generational differences *within* these categories (Alba, Jiménez, and Marrow 2014; Jiménez, Fields, and Schachter 2015). Those differences are especially important for groups with long immigration histories. Early research on immigrant populations emphasized generation as a temporal marker of assimilation, noting that with more generations in the United States, immigrant groups tended to resemble the mainstream (Warner and Srole 1945). Implicit assumptions in early assimilation theory that saw assimilation into a white, Protestant, and Anglo-Saxon notion of the American mainstream are problematic (Gordon 1964; Warner and Srole 1945; see Alba and Nee [2003] for a critique). These flaws notwithstanding, an enduring insight from these early theories related to the inevitability of generational change. Scholars ever since have measured assimilation over time using generation as the key temporal marker (National Academies of Science, Engineering, and Medicine 2015).

Mexicans, arguably the most important contemporary immigrant group and one with a long immigration history, illustrate the importance of generation for tracking assimilation patterns. Using historic U.S. decennial census data, Smith (2003, 2006) showed that there are large intergenerational differences among Mexicans in years of schooling and annual income. For example, first-generation Mexican men born between 1900 and 1905 had an average of 3.81 years of school. The second generation, born 25 years later, had an average of 7.88 years of school. The third generation, born 25 years after that, registered an average of 12.61 years of school (Smith 2006, Table 6). These quantitative findings are consistent in kind, if not degree, with trends observed among European and Asian groups whose histories in the United States go back generations (Alba and Nee 2003). Smith could calculate these generational differences because the census, prior to 1980, regularly included a question about parents' place of birth.[3] Important intergenerational differences also show up in qualitative research on Mexicans. Vasquez (2011) interviewed three generations of Mexican Americans in the same family, showing tremendous variation in mobility patterns, and ethnic consciousness across the three generations.

The large post-1965 wave of immigration highlights the continued relevance of generation for tracking assimilation. Intergenerational comparisons are central to research on post-1965 immigration, and especially diverging assessments of second-generation assimilation. There is disagreement about whether the assimilation of the Latino and black post-1965 second generation is characterized by racialization and permanent exclusion (Haller, Portes, and Lynch 2011; Portes and Rumbaut 2001), or by steady, if bumpy, progress (Alba, Kasinitz, and Waters 2011; Kasinitz et al. 2008). The data informing that debate have largely come from three nongovernmental data collection efforts: the Children of Immigrants Longitudinal Survey (CILS), the Immigrant Second Generation in Metropolitan New York (ISGMNY), and the Immigration and Intergenerational Mobility in Metropolitan Los Angeles (IIMMLA) studies. CILS sampled more than 5,000 children of immigrants in the Miami and San Diego metropolitan areas in 1992, when these children were in their early teens, and reinterviewed most of the original sample three years later, and again in 2001–2003. CILS also includes parent surveys and in-depth interviews with select survey respondents. ISGMNY is a survey and interview sample of 1.5- (arrived before the age of 12) and second-generation individuals in the New York metropolitan area. The sample also includes third-plus-generation comparison groups (whites, Puerto Ricans, and African Americans). IIMMLA focused on the mobility trajectories of the young-adult 1.5 and second generations in the Los Angeles metropolitan area. In the case of Mexicans, the sample also includes a substantial number of individuals from the third and later generations. Space constraints prevent me from laying out the findings generated from these data (see, for example, Bean, Brown, and Bachmeier 2015; Kasinitz et al. 2008; Portes and Rumbaut 2001). It suffices to say here that the major findings reveal significant differences along an array of measures between the first and second generations across groups.

As valuable as these data are, they do not capture changes across three generations of the post-1965 immigration, which are crucial to fully understand the extent and kind of contemporary assimilation. Data collection for these studies took place when the second generation of the post-1965 immigration wave was relatively young. But that is no longer the case. The leading edge of today's second generation has entered middle age, and many are themselves parents to a post-1965 "new third generation" (Jiménez, Park, and Pedroza, forthcoming). These grandchildren of the post-1965 immigrants will write the next chapter in the contemporary American immigrant assimilation story. Julie Park, Juan Pedroza, and I have conducted the first analyses of the new third generation, examining the household circumstances in which they were growing up in 2010 (Jiménez, Park, and Pedroza, forthcoming). We compared the new-third-generation household circumstances to that of a second generation in 1980. Our findings reveal the continued importance of generation as a marker of group change. Because the 1980 U.S. Census lacked a parent place-of-birth question, we had to include in our sample only U.S.-born children (age 19 and under) coresiding with foreign-born parents, age 25 to 54. We identified our 2010 third-generation sample using CPS samples from 2008 to 2013.[4] The parents' place-of-birth questions on the CPS enabled us to identify a unique third-generation (age 19 and under) coresiding with second-generation parents, age 25 to 54. We measured outcomes at the household level, including differences in parents' socioeconomic status, having intermarried parents, the presence of extended family, and the ethnic and racial labels that parents give to their children. We found that the Hispanic and Asian new third generation in 2010, compared to the second generation in 1980, has parents who are better educated, earn more, are more likely to be intermarried, and are less likely to be living with extended family. These findings point to an assimilation pattern that resembles patterns among groups with earlier immigration histories.

But there may also be important differences. We also analyzed how intermarried parents labeled their children. We found that third-generation children growing up in intermarried households with at least one Hispanic parent were *more* likely to receive a Hispanic label compared to a second generation in the same kind of household in 1980. The same was true for Asians: third-generation children growing up in an intermarried household that included at least one Asian parent were *more* often given an Asian label compared to second-generation children with intermarried parents in 1980. It is important to note that, starting in 2000, the census and the CPS gave respondents the option of checking multiple racial categories. And so while intermarried parents in 1980 were forced to select a single racial category for their children, parents in 2010 could select more than one racial category. The census and CPS treat the Hispanic category as an ethnic category, distinctive from race. Thus, parents select whether their children are Hispanic and their children's race in response to separate questions. It is possible that parents could have used the Hispanic and race categories to communicate their child's mixed ancestry, but it is impossible to know their intension from their survey responses. These caveats aside, parents continue to identify their children with the categories that reflect the origins of the immigrant generation.

The larger point from analysis of the new third generation is that among the post-1965 immigration wave, generation is an analytical category that tracks important changes within ethnic and racial groups. Moreover, generation is especially important right now because the rise of the new third generation is the best opportunity that social scientists have for gaining a fuller picture of contemporary assimilation.

Generation as a category of practice

Generation is more than a category central to analyses of group change. Generation is also a category of practice that structures how individuals categorize themselves and others in everyday life. *Intra*group identity processes centrally entail drawing distinctions among group members along generational lines. My own ethnographic research on later-generation Mexican Americans—those whose families came to the United States before 1940—in Garden City, Kansas, and Santa Maria, California, shows how Mexican Americans with deep generational roots in the United States and more recently arrived immigrants and their children distinguish each other based on generation (Jiménez 2010). The generational distinctions were animated by characteristics and behaviors that later-generation Mexican American respondents believed were associated with first- and second-generation Mexicans, and not people like themselves, whose families had "been here forever" (Jiménez 2010). Later-generation respondents saw generational differences in the degree of knowledge about Mexico, the ability to speak Spanish, the kinds of food that people eat, and tastes for popular culture. Mexican Americans in Garden City—where there have been two very distinctive waves of Mexican immigration—saw these generational differences in clearer terms than their counterparts in Santa Maria, where immigration has been more continuous. But the more relevant difference to everyday life had to do with the number of generations that individuals' families had been in the United States. Similar findings appear in other ethnographic research on generations of Mexican Americans (Macias 2006; Ochoa 2004; Vasquez 2011), Asian Americans (Tsuda 2016; Tuan 1998), and Polish Americans (Erdmans 1998).

In addition to marking differences within ethnic groups, generation is also a category of practice pertinent to *inter*group relations. The relevance of generation is particularly prominent in areas where immigrants have settled in large numbers. My ethnographic research among "established individuals"—those who are U.S.-born of U.S.-born parents—in three Silicon Valley communities illustrates the importance of generation as a marker of everyday difference that cuts through racial group distinctions. One of the communities that I studied, Cupertino, is a high-skilled immigrant gateway with large South-Asian Indian and Chinese first and second generations. The established population was largely white, but also included later-generation Chinese and Japanese Americans. Interviews with the later-generation individuals there showed that the number of generations that someone's family has been in United States was a basis for perceptions of difference and similarity. For example, respondents reported that there were few differences between established Asian American families and white families precisely because both had deep generational roots in the United States. But respondents noted significant differences between established Asian American families and those that were headed by foreign-born parents. When asked what differentiated these families, respondents said that established Chinese and Japanese Americans were more "whitewashed," which they defined by weak observance of ethnic traditions, a more relaxed approach to schooling, and greater sociability. Similar findings emerged in the other Silicon Valley locations that I studied: East Palo Alto and Berryessa (a neighborhood of San Jose) (Jiménez 2016). In all three of the locations, generational differences *within* racial groups were often just as important as markers of group distinctions as racial identity (Jiménez 2017).[5]

Measuring Generations

That generation is both a category of analysis and a category of practice implies an imperative to track generation in surveys. Accomplishing that aim is not simple. The inclusion of a parents' place-of-birth question in the CPS has allowed researchers to identify first, second, and third-plus generations. For researchers interested in post-1965 immigrant assimilation, that generational breakdown has only limited adequacy. It has allowed the documentation of progress between the adult first- and second-generations of this immigration wave, and across three-plus generations of groups with older immigration histories.

But there are at least two reasons why the CPS data are inadequate for tracking trends in immigrant integration beyond the second generation. The first is that the CPS sample is too small for the regional, metropolitan, and small-area data necessary to explain intergenerational change. When so many outcomes are linked to the places in which individuals live (Sampson 2012; Sharkey 2013), understanding intergenerational change requires data on the neighborhoods in which people grow up and the neighborhoods that they live in as adults. A second issue, and one stemming from the small sample size, is that the CPS does not enable analysts to make group distinctions beyond the largest ethnic groups. An important theme in assimilation research past and present is that assimilation outcomes between ethnic groups differ widely. Some groups, like Vietnamese, Hmong, Salvadorans, and Dominicans are too small to show up in the CPS prominently enough to permit statistical analysis. And yet these groups are important to a full understanding of American assimilation. A third issue is that the CPS forces researchers to lump all individuals who are U.S.-born of U.S.-born parents into a "third-plus-generation" category, without the ability to identify a *unique* third generation separate from those who are fourth generation and beyond. The need to identify a unique third generation comes from the demographic rise of the new third generation (Jiménez, Park, and Pedroza, forthcoming), whose outcomes will offer a fuller picture of the post-1965 immigrant integration than the one that currently relies on analyses of the first and second generations only (Alba, Kasinitz, and Waters 2011; Haller, Portes, and Lynch 2011; Kasinitz et al. 2008; Portes and Rumbaut 2001). As it stands, the only way to identify the new third generation is by selecting households from the CPS with second-generation parents who are coresiding with U.S.-born children (Jiménez, Park, and Pedroza, forthcoming). That selection strategy restricts analyses to children, leaving analysts to infer from their household circumstances what adulthood has in store. When this new third generation enters adulthood and moves out of their parents' homes, they will become part of the CPS's third-plus generation and thus be indistinguishable in the data from individuals who descend from earlier waves of immigrants of the same ethnoracial origins. The ability to adequately track the multi-intergenerational change of the post-1965 immigration will thus be lost.

What about nongovernment surveys? Surveys aimed at understanding the second generation have done a great deal to advance research on assimilation. However, these surveys are costly and tend to focus on specific regions, limiting valuable comparisons across regions.

Parents' and grandparents' place of birth

What can be done? At the very least, governmental surveys—ideally the ACS—would return to the old census practice (and current CPS practice) of asking respondents about parents' place of birth. Including that question would be a step in the right direction, but it would still not enable analysts to identify a unique third generation separate from a fourth-plus generation. In addition to a parents' place-of-birth question, including a grandparents' place-of-birth question would allow for such a distinction. I recognize that making already long surveys such as the ACS longer can hurt response and completion rates, and some respondents may not know where their grandparents were born. An intermediary step between excluding a grandparents' place-of-birth question and the current slate of questions would be to ask a simple yes-no question: Were any of your grandparents born outside of the United States? The answer to that short question would allow researchers to identify a unique third generation (the U.S. born with U.S.-born parents who answer "yes" to the grandparents' place-of-birth question would constitute the third generation), and thus yield a more precise view of assimilation among contemporary immigration waves.

At the heart of scholarly and public debates about immigration is whether today's immigrants are assimilating. It is an emotionally charged debate, and one that is more productively hashed out with good data. Contemporary immigration has elevated generation as a central category of analysis and of practice in American life, making the collection of data on generation an imperative if surveys, both government and private, are to keep up with how Americans think about themselves and each other. A better capture of generation data on surveys does more than keep up with the times. It would allow researchers to offer a fuller understanding of the times we live in.

Notes

1. The name comes from the 1965 Immigration and Nationality Act (or the Hart-Celler Act). The law overhauled the nation's immigration laws, lifting restrictive immigration quotas that had been in place since the 1920s and creating a preference system for immigration visas largely on formal scaling and family reunification.

2. The United States census offers respondents fifteen race categories, as well as the option to select multiple race boxes. The census treats Hispanics as an ethnic group.

3. Smith used synthetic cohorts, but similar generational differences among Mexicans appear in studies of nongovernmental data that match parents and their offspring (see Telles and Ortiz 2008).

4. We used data from the Minnesota Population Center's Integrated Public Use Microdata Series (IPUMS). To capture second- and third-generation households in the post-1965 immigration era, we used the 1980 PUMS 5 percent sample (Ruggles et al. 2015) and the IPUMS Current Population Survey (CPS, March Supplement) from 2008 through 2013.

5. Survey research hints at the bearing that generation has on intergroup relations as well. Schachter (Jiménez, Fields, and Schachter 2015; Schachter 2014) shows that stereotypes that native-born whites hold about Latinos, Asians, and blacks follow a clear generational gradient. U.S.-born Latinos and Asians are more positively stereotyped than their foreign-born counterparts; an inverse of that gradient holds for blacks.

References

Alba, Richard D. 1990. *Ethnic identity: The transformation of white America*. New Haven, CT: Yale University Press.
Alba, Richard, Tomás R. Jiménez, and Helen B. Marrow. 2014. Mexican Americans as a paradigm for contemporary intra-group heterogeneity. *Ethnic and Racial Studies* 37 (3): 446–66.
Alba, Richard, Philip Kasinitz, and Mary C. Waters. 2011. The kids are (mostly) alright: Second-generation assimilation, comments on Haller, Portes, and Lynch. *Social Forces* 89 (3): 763–73.
Alba, Richard, and Victor Nee. 2003. *Remaking the American mainstream: Assimilation and contemporary immigration*. Cambridge, MA: Harvard University Press.
Bean, Frank D., Susan K. Brown, and James D. Bachmeier. 2015. *Parents without papers: The progress and pitfalls of Mexican American integration*. New York, NY: Russell Sage Foundation.
Brubaker, Rogers. 2004. *Ethnicity without groups*. Cambridge, MA: Harvard University Press.
Brubaker, Rogers. 2016. *Trans: Gender and race in an age of unsettled identities*. Princeton, NJ: Princeton University Press.

Erdmans, Mary Patrice. 1998. *Opposite poles: Immigrants and ethnics in Polish Chicago, 1976-1990.* University Park, PA: Pennsylvania State University Press.

Frey, William H. 2014. *Diversity explosion: How new racial demographics are remaking America.* Washington, DC: Brookings Institution Press.

Gordon, Milton M. 1964. *Assimilation in American life: The role of race, religion, and national origins.* New York, NY: Oxford University Press.

Haller, William, Alejandro Portes, and Scott M. Lynch. 2011. Dreams fulfilled, dreams shattered: Determinants of segmented assimilation in the second generation. *Social Forces* 89 (3): 733–62.

Jacobson, Matthew Frye. 2006. *Roots too: White ethnic revival in post-civil rights America.* Cambridge, MA: Harvard University Press.

Jiménez, Tomás R. 2010. *Replenished ethnicity: Mexican Americans, immigration, and identity.* Berkeley, CA: University of California Press.

Jiménez, Tomás R. 2016. Fade to black: Multiple symbolic boundaries in "black/brown" contact. *Du Bois Review: Social Science Research on Race* 13 (1): 159–80.

Jiménez, Tomás R. 2017. *The other side of assimilation: How immigrants are changing American life.* Oakland, CA: University of California Press.

Jiménez, Tomás R., Corey Fields, and Ariela Schachter. 2015. How ethnoraciality matters: Looking inside ethnoracial groups. *Social Currents* 2 (2): 107–15.

Jiménez, Tomás R., Julie Park, and Juan Pedroza. Forthcoming. The new third generation: Post-1965 immigration and the next stage in the long march of assimilation. *International Migration Review.*

Kasinitz, Phillip, John H. Mollenkopf, Mary C. Waters, and Jennifer Holdaway. 2008. *Inheriting the city: The second generation comes of age.* Cambridge, MA, and New York, NY: Harvard University Press and Russell Sage Foundation.

Macias, Thomas. 2006. *Mestizo in America: Generations of Mexican ethnicity in the suburban Southwest.* Tucson, AZ: University of Arizona Press.

Massey, Douglas S. 2007. *Categorically unequal: The American stratification system.* New York, NY: Russell Sage Foundation.

National Academies of Science, Engineering, and Medicine. 2015. *The integration of immigrants into American society*, eds. M. C. Waters and M. G. Pineau. Washington, DC: National Academies Press.

Ochoa, Gilda. 2004. *Becoming neighbors in a Mexican American community: Power, conflict and solidarity.* Austin, TX: University of Texas Press.

Portes, Alejandro, and Rubén G. Rumbaut. 2001. *Legacies: The story of the immigrant second generation.* Berkeley, CA, and New York, NY: University of California Press and Russell Sage Foundation.

Prewitt, Kenneth. 2013. *What is your race? The census and our flawed efforts to classify Americans.* Princeton, NJ: Princeton University Press.

Ruggles, Steven, Katie Genadek, Ronald Goeken, Josiah Grover, and Matthew Sobek. 2015. Integrated Public Use Microdata Series: Version 6.0 [Machine-Readable Database]. Minneapolis, MN: University of Minnesota.

Sampson, Robert J. 2012. *Great American city: Chicago and the enduring neighborhood effect.* Chicago, IL: University of Chicago Press.

Saperstein, Aliya, and Andrew M. Penner. 2012. Racial fluidity and inequality in the United States. *American Journal of Sociology* 118 (3): 676–727.

Schachter, Ariela. 2014. Racial prejudice in an age of immigration. Paper Presented at the Stanford/ Berkeley Immigration Conference, 7 February, Stanford, CA.

Schilt, Kristen. 2010. *Just one of the guys? Transgender men and the persistence of gender inequality.* Chicago, IL: University of Chicago Press.

Sharkey, Patrick. 2013. *Stuck in place: Urban neighborhoods and the end of progress toward racial equality.* Chicago, IL: University of Chicago Press.

Smith, James P. 2003. Assimilation across the Latino generations. *American Economic Review* 93 (2): 315–19.

Smith, James P. 2006. Immigrants and the labor market. *Journal of Labor Economics* 24 (2): 203–33.

Telles, Edward E., and Vilma Ortiz. 2008. *Generations of exclusion: Mexican Americans, assimilation, and race.* New York, NY: Russell Sage Foundation.

Tsuda, Takeyuki. 2016. *Japanese American ethnicity: In search of heritage and homeland across generations.* New York, NY: New York University Press.

Tuan, Mia. 1998. *Forever foreigners or honorary whites? The Asian ethnic experience today.* New Brunswick, NJ: Rutgers University Press.
Vasquez, Jessica M. 2011. *Mexican Americans across generations: Immigrant families, racial realities.* New York, NY: New York University Press.
Warner, W. Lloyd, and Leo Srole. 1945. *The social systems of American ethnic groups.* New Haven, CT: Yale University Press.
Waters, Mary C. 1990. *Ethnic options: Choosing identities in America.* Berkeley, CA: University of California Press.

Identifying the Later-Generation Descendants of U.S. Immigrants: Issues Arising from Selective Ethnic Attrition

By
BRIAN DUNCAN
and
STEPHEN J. TREJO

Evaluating the long-term socioeconomic integration of immigrants in the United States requires analyses of differences between foreign-born and U.S.-born residents, as well as analyses across generations of the U.S.-born. Regrettably, though, standard data sources used to study these populations provide very limited information pertaining to generation. As a result, research on the U.S.-born descendants of immigrants often relies on the use of subjective measures of racial/ethnic identification. Because ethnic attachments tend to fade across generations, these subjective measures might miss a significant portion of the later-generation descendants of immigrants. Moreover, if such "ethnic attrition" is selective on socioeconomic attainment, it can distort assessments of integration and generational progress. We discuss evidence that suggests that ethnic attrition is sizable and selective for the second- and third-generation populations of key Hispanic and Asian national-origin groups, and that correcting for the resulting biases is likely to raise the socioeconomic standing of the U.S.-born descendants of most Hispanic immigrants relative to their Asian counterparts.

Keywords: racial/ethnic identification; generational mobility; immigrant integration

Historically, much of the socioeconomic mobility achieved by U.S. immigrant families has taken place across rather than within

Brian Duncan is a professor of economics at the University of Colorado Denver. His research focuses on the economics of generosity, specifically examining the conflicting motives individuals have for contributing to charitable causes. He has also written on the economic incentives of foster care and adoption, and on the intergenerational progress of the descendants of U.S. immigrants.

Stephen J. Trejo is a professor of economics at the University of Texas at Austin. His current research focuses on understanding patterns of intergenerational mobility among U.S. immigrant groups, and one strand of this work explores how selective intermarriage and ethnic identification might distort standard measures of socioeconomic attainment for the U.S.-born descendants of immigrants.

Correspondence: trejo@austin.utexas.edu

DOI: 10.1177/0002716218763293

generations (Neidert and Farley 1985; Borjas 1994; Perlmann 2005). When evaluating the long-term integration of immigrants, it is therefore important to analyze differences not just between the foreign-born and U.S.-born, but also across generations of the U.S.-born (Farley and Alba 2002; Card 2005; Smith 2006). The ideal dataset for such an analysis would include information about the family tree of each individual, enabling us to identify which individuals have ancestors who immigrated to the United States from a particular country and how many generations have elapsed since that immigration took place. Information of this sort would also allow us to characterize the complexity of each individual's immigrant roots in some detail, accounting for factors such as the specific national origins of an individual's immigrant ancestors, whether the same national origins show up on both the paternal and maternal sides of the family tree, and how far removed from the current generation are the immigrant ancestors.

Unfortunately, the large, nationally representative data sources typically employed to study U.S. immigrants and their descendants provide very limited information pertaining to immigrant generations. Microdata sources such as the decennial U.S. Census, the American Community Survey (ACS), and the Current Populations Survey (CPS) report each respondent's country of birth, thereby distinguishing foreign-born individuals (i.e., the first generation) from the U.S.-born population. Only the CPS, however, currently collects information about the countries of birth of each respondent's parents, which allows the second generation (i.e., U.S.-born individuals who have at least one foreign-born parent) to be differentiated from higher generations of U.S.-born individuals. Furthermore, none of these surveys provides information about the countries of birth of an adult respondent's grandparents, so the third generation cannot be precisely identified.

Because of these data limitations, research on the U.S.-born descendants of immigrants often must identify the populations of interest using subjective measures of racial/ethnic identification (Sakamoto, Wu, and Tzeng 2000; Snipp and Hirschman 2004; Zeng and Xie 2004; Saenz 2005; Duncan, Hotz, and Trejo 2006). In particular, this approach is typically the only feasible option for studies that examine long-term integration by distinguishing immigrant descendants in the third and higher generations (Rong and Grant 1992; Borjas 1994; Trejo 1997, 2003; Goyette and Xie 1999; Farley and Alba 2002; Grogger and Trejo 2002; Yang 2004; Smith 2006; Blau and Kahn 2007). For example, the standard definition of third- and higher-generation Mexicans Americans is U.S.-born individuals who have U.S.-born parents and who self-identify as Mexican in response to the Hispanic origin question.

A potential problem with this approach is that assimilation and intermarriage can cause ethnic attachments to fade across generations (Alba 1990; Waters 1990; Perlmann and Waters 2007; Alba and Islam 2009; Lee and Bean 2010), and therefore subjective measures of racial/ethnic identification might miss a significant portion of the later-generation descendants of immigrants. Moreover, if such "ethnic attrition" is selective on socioeconomic attainment, it can distort assessments of integration and generational progress.

Our own previous work demonstrates the salience of these issues for the specific case of Mexican Americans (Duncan and Trejo 2007, 2009, 2011). Analyzing microdata from the CPS for children living with both parents in Duncan and Trejo (2011), we compare an objective indicator of Mexican descent (based on the countries of birth of the child, his parents, and his grandparents) with the standard subjective measure of Mexican identification (based on the response to the Hispanic origin question). We find that about 30 percent of third-generation Mexican children are *not* identified as Mexican by the Hispanic origin question in the CPS, and this ethnic attrition is highly selective. In particular, the high school dropout rate of third-generation Mexican youth (ages 16 and 17) is 25 percent higher when the sample is limited to those youth subjectively identified as Mexican. Therefore, our previous research suggests that ethnic attrition is substantial among third-generation Mexicans and could produce significant downward bias in standard measures of attainment that rely on subjective ethnic identification rather than objective indicators of Mexican descent.

Extending our earlier work, which focused on Mexicans, in Duncan and Trejo (2017) we show that ethnic attrition is sizable and selective for the second- and third-generation populations of key Hispanic and Asian national-origin groups. It is important to note that these results indicate that ethnic attrition generates measurement biases that vary across groups in direction as well as magnitude, and that correcting for these biases is likely to raise the socioeconomic standing of the U.S.-born descendants of most Hispanic immigrants relative to their Asian counterparts. The results to date, however, shed more light on the direction rather than the ultimate magnitude of these measurement biases, and so at this point it is unknown whether correcting for selective ethnic attrition would produce a small or large improvement in the relative attainment of later-generation Hispanics. Below, we present in a bit more detail some of the key findings from Duncan and Trejo (2017), using updated calculations with additional years of data.

Some Evidence of Selective Ethnic Attrition

We use individual-level survey data from the CPS for all months from January 2003 through December 2016.[1] As mentioned earlier, a key feature of CPS data is their inclusion (beginning in 1994) of the information about parental countries of birth that is currently missing from the census and ACS. As a result, the CPS is now the best large-scale, nationally representative U.S. dataset for investigating how outcomes vary by immigrant generation.

Immigrant generations are defined using information on the countries of birth of the respondent, his or her parents, and (when possible, as described below) his or her grandparents. The first generation consists of foreign-born individuals (excluding those born abroad of an American parent). The second generation includes U.S.-born individuals who have at least one foreign-born parent. The third generation denotes U.S.-born individuals with two U.S.-born parents but at least one foreign-born grandparent. These immigrant generations are defined with respect to specific Hispanic (Mexico, Puerto Rico, Cuba, El Salvador, and the Dominican Republic) and Asian (China, India, Japan, Korea, and the Philippines) source countries. These particular countries were chosen because they are important sources of U.S. immigration and they yield CPS samples of reasonable size for all three generations.

Samples of first- and second-generation adults ages 25 to 59 are constructed using the information collected in the CPS regarding the countries of birth of each respondent and of each respondent's father and mother. For children living with both parents, the survey data collected from the parents reveal the countries of birth of each child's grandparents. Using this information, third-generation samples are constructed that include U.S.-born children ages 17 and younger who live in intact families and have two U.S.-born parents (ages 18 and older) but at least one grandparent born in a relevant source country.

Tables 1 and 2 show the basic patterns that emerge when the source country samples are pooled into panethnic aggregates for Hispanics and for Asians. For first-, second-, or third-generation members of a relevant Hispanic or Asian national-origin group, Table 1 reports the percentage who subjectively identify in the expected way (with subjective Hispanic identification based on responses to the CPS Hispanic origin question, and subjective Asian identification based on responses to the CPS race question).[2] Among Hispanics, these ethnic identification rates fall from 99 percent for first-generation adults to 94 percent for second-generation adults to 83 percent for third-generation children. Ethnic attrition is more prevalent and the generational gradient is steeper for Asians, with ethnic identification rates of 97 percent for the first generation, 80 percent for the second generation, and 59 percent for the third generation. More detailed tabulations show considerable variation in ethnic attrition rates across specific Hispanic and Asian national-origin groups. As a result, standard analyses that must rely on subjective racial/ethnic identification to detect the later-generation descendants of immigrants can miss large segments of the target populations.

Table 1 demonstrates that, despite nearly perfect rates of ethnic identification for first-generation adults, Hispanics and Asians exhibit substantial amounts of ethnic attrition in the second and third generations. For ethnic attrition to distort standard measures of generational progress for immigrant groups, however, it is not enough that such attrition be sizable; the attrition must also be selective on socioeconomic attainment. To provide some evidence on this issue, Table 2 reports average completed years of schooling by ethnic identification for second-generation adults and third-generation children. For third-generation children, the education measure represents the average of father's and mother's years of schooling.

Table 2 succinctly illustrates an important finding: with regard to educational attainment, ethnic attrition among the U.S.-born descendants of immigrants tends to be positively selected for Hispanics and negatively selected for Asians. For example, second-generation Hispanics who do not identify as Hispanic average almost three-quarters of a year *more* education than their counterparts who do so identify, whereas the analogous comparison among second-generation

TABLE 1
Rates of Ethnic Identification

	Source Countries	
	Hispanic	Asian
First-generation adults	98.6%	96.5%
	(0.04)	(0.1)
	[79,318]	[31,993]
Second-generation adults	93.7%	79.7%
	(0.2)	(0.5)
	[24,699]	[7,656]
Third-generation children	82.9%	58.8%
	(0.4)	(0.9)
	[9,603]	[3,068]

SOURCE: 2003–2016 CPS data.
NOTE: Reported figures are the percentage of individuals who identify as members of the relevant ethnic group (Hispanic or Asian). Standard errors are shown in parentheses, and sample sizes are shown in brackets. Hispanic source countries are Mexico, Puerto Rico, Cuba, El Salvador, and the Dominican Republic. Asian source countries are China, India, Japan, Korea, and the Philippines. First-generation adults are individuals ages 25–59 who were born in a relevant source country (excluding those born abroad of an American parent). Second-generation adults are U.S.-born individuals ages 25–59 who have at least one parent born in a relevant source country. Third-generation children are U.S.-born individuals ages 17 and younger who live in intact families and have two U.S.-born parents but at least one grandparent born in a relevant source country.

Asians yields a *deficit* of two-thirds of a year for those who do not identify as Asian. The pattern is similar among third-generation children: those of Hispanic descent who are not identified as Hispanic enjoy advantaged backgrounds (i.e., fathers and mothers with more schooling, on average) compared to their peers who are identified as Hispanic, and this selectivity runs in the opposite direction for children of Asian descent. In particular, average parental education is four-fifths of a year higher for third-generation Hispanic children not identified as Hispanic compared to those who are identified as Hispanic. In contrast, average parental education is three-fifths of a year lower for third-generation Asian children not identified as Asian compared to those who are identified as Asian.

Additional analyses in Duncan and Trejo (2017) show that mixed ethnic origins are common among third-generation Hispanic and Asian children, and that ethnic attrition predominately occurs in children with mixed parental origins. Among third-generation children with the relevant ethnicity on both the paternal and maternal sides of their family, ethnic attrition rates are low (2 percent for Hispanics and 7 percent for Asians), but these rates are dramatically higher among children whose ethnicity originates from only one side of their family (35 percent for Hispanics and 55 percent for Asians).

TABLE 2
Educational Selectivity of Ethnic Identification

	Source countries	
	Hispanic	Asian
First-generation adults		
Average education	10.02	15.04
	(0.01)	(0.02)
Second-generation adults		
Average education		
Identified as ethnic group member	12.96	15.13
	(0.02)	(0.03)
Not identified as ethnic group member	13.67	14.45
	(0.06)	(0.06)
All	13.00	14.99
	(0.02)	(0.03)
Third-generation children		
Average parental education:		
Child identified as ethnic group member	13.25	15.16
	(0.02)	(0.05)
Child not identified as ethnic group member	14.04	14.55
	(0.05)	(0.06)
All	13.38	14.91
	(0.02)	(0.04)

SOURCE: 2003–2016 CPS data.
NOTE: Reported figures are average completed years of education; for third-generation children, this measure represents the average of father's and mother's education. Standard errors are shown in parentheses. See Table 1 and the text for further information about the samples.

Conclusion

The research described here highlights the potential payoff to collecting more precise information in U.S. Census Bureau surveys on the immigrant generation and national origins of respondents. To this end, a valuable first step would be to add questions in the ACS about the countries of birth of each respondent's parents, similar to the questions currently asked in the CPS, so that second-generation status could be objectively identified for adults in ACS data. The much larger sample sizes in ACS data would permit meaningful analyses of generational progress for specific national-origin groups and by important subgroups (e.g., by age, gender, region, year, and so on) that are not currently feasible because of limited sample sizes for the relevant groups in CPS data. In addition, to permit accurate identification of adults in the third and later generations, it would be worthwhile to consider collecting at regular intervals supplemental information in large-scale surveys such as the ACS or CPS on the countries of birth of the respondent's grandparents and earlier ancestors.[3] Without additional information of this type, measurement biases arising from selective ethnic identification will continue to distort assessments of the socioeconomic attainment and integration of later-generation descendants of immigrants.

Notes

1. In Duncan and Trejo (2017), the data sample stopped in December 2013.

2. Beginning in January 2003, the CPS race question allows respondents to identify with more than one race category (in contrast, the Hispanic origin question permits only a single response). We consider individuals to identify as Asian if they respond to the CPS race question with "Asian" or "Hawaiian/Pacific Islander" (or both), even if they also give other (i.e., non-Asian) race responses. Treating multiple race responses in this way will produce conservative estimates of ethnic attrition.

3. The 1990 Census Content Reinterview Survey (1990 CRS) collected unique information on the national origins of the respondents' ancestors that might provide a model for future efforts along these lines (U.S. Census Bureau 1993). In particular, the 1990 CRS included a series of questions soliciting the countries of birth of the respondent, both of the respondent's parents, and all four of the respondent's grandparents. Additional questions asked about the birth country for "earlier generations" (i.e., great grandparents and beyond) on the father's side and on the mother's side, and those who failed to provide a foreign country in response to any of these questions were asked to name the birth country of their "ancestors who FIRST came to the United States." With this information, immigrant generation and national origins can be directly and precisely assigned for each respondent based on the countries of birth of the respondent's ancestors, even for those respondents whose families have lived in the United States for two or more generations.

References

Alba, Richard D. 1990. *Ethnic identity: The transformation of white America*. New Haven, CT: Yale University Press.

Alba, Richard D., and Tariqul Islam. 2009. The case of the disappearing Mexican Americans: An ethnic-identity mystery. *Population Research and Policy Review* 28 (2): 109–21.

Blau, Francine D., and Lawrence M. Kahn. 2007. Gender and assimilation among Mexican Americans. In *Mexican immigration to the United States*, ed. George J. Borjas, 57–106. Chicago, IL: University of Chicago Press.

Borjas, George J. 1994. Long-run convergence of ethnic skill differentials: The children and grandchildren of the great migration. *Industrial and Labor Relations Review* 47 (4): 553–73.

Card, David. 2005. Is the new immigration really so bad? *Economic Journal* 115 (507): 300–323.

Duncan, Brian, V. Joseph Hotz, and Stephen J. Trejo. 2006. Hispanics in the U.S. labor market. In *Hispanics and the future of America*, eds. Marta Tienda and Faith Mitchell. Washington, DC: National Academies Press.

Duncan, Brian, and Stephen J. Trejo. 2007. Ethnic identification, intermarriage, and unmeasured progress by Mexican Americans. In *Mexican immigration to the United States*, ed. George J. Borjas, 227–69. Chicago, IL: University of Chicago Press.

Duncan, Brian, and Stephen J. Trejo. 2009. Ancestry versus ethnicity: The complexity and selectivity of Mexican identification in the United States. In *Research in labor economics*, vol. 29, eds. Amelie F. Constant, Konstantinos Tatsiramos, and Klaus F. Zimmerman, 31–66. Bingley, UK: Emerald Publishing Group.

Duncan, Brian, and Stephen J. Trejo. 2011. Intermarriage and the intergenerational transmission of ethnic identity and human capital for Mexican Americans. *Journal of Labor Economics* 29 (2): 195–227.

Duncan, Brian, and Stephen J. Trejo. 2017. The complexity of immigrant generations: Implications for assessing the socioeconomic integration of Hispanics and Asians. *Industrial and Labor Relations Review* 70 (5): 1146–75.

Farley, Reynolds, and Richard Alba. 2002. The new second generation in the United States. *International Migration Review* 36 (3): 669–701.

Goyette, Kimberly, and Yu Xie. 1999. Educational expectations of Asian American youth: Determinants and ethnic differences. *Sociology of Education* 72 (1): 22–36.

Grogger, Jeffrey, and Stephen J. Trejo. 2002. *Falling behind or moving up? The intergenerational progress of Mexican Americans.* San Francisco, CA: Public Policy Institute of California.

Lee, Jennifer, and Frank D. Bean. 2010. *The diversity paradox: Immigration and the color line in 21st century America.* New York, NY: Russell Sage Foundation.

Neidert, Lisa J., and Reynolds Farley. 1985. Assimilation in the United States: An analysis of ethnic and generation differences in status and achievement. *American Sociological Review* 50 (6): 840–50.

Perlmann, Joel. 2005. *Italians then, Mexicans now: Immigrant origins and second-generation progress, 1890–2000.* New York, NY: Russell Sage Foundation.

Perlmann, Joel, and Mary C. Waters. 2007. Intermarriage and multiple identities. In *The New Americans: A guide to immigration since 1965*, eds. Mary C. Waters and Reed Udea, 110–23. Cambridge, MA: Harvard University Press.

Rong, Xue Lan, and Linda Grant. 1992. Ethnicity, generation, and school attainment of Asians, Hispanics, and non-Hispanic whites. *Sociological Quarterly* 33 (4): 625–36.

Saenz, Rogelio. 2005. Latinos and the changing face of America. In *The American people: Census 2000*, eds. Reynolds Farley and John Haaga, 352–79. New York, NY: Russell Sage Foundation.

Sakamoto, Arthur, Huei-Hsia Wu, and Jessie M. Tzeng. 2000. The declining significance of race among American men during the latter half of the twentieth century. *Demography* 37 (1): 41–51.

Smith, James P. 2006. Immigrants and the labor market. *Journal of Labor Economics* 24 (2): 203–33.

Snipp, C. Matthew, and Charles Hirschman. 2004. Assimilation in American society: Occupational achievement and earnings for ethnic minorities in the United States, 1970 to 1990. *Research in Social Stratification and Mobility* 22:93–117.

Trejo, Stephen J. 1997. Why do Mexican Americans earn low wages? *Journal of Political Economy* 105 (6): 1235–68.

Trejo, Stephen J. 2003. Intergenerational progress of Mexican-origin workers in the U.S. labor market. *Journal of Human Resources* 38 (3): 467–89.

U.S. Census Bureau. 1993. *Content Reinterview Survey: Accuracy of data for selected population and housing characteristics as measured by reinterview.* 1990 Census of Population and Housing, Evaluation and Research Reports, 1990 CPH-E-1. Washington, DC: U.S. Government Printing Office.

Waters, Mary C. 1990. *Ethnic options: Choosing identities in America.* Berkeley, CA: University of California Press.

Yang, Philip Q. 2004. Generational differences in educational attainment among Asian Americans. *Journal of Asian American Studies* 7 (1): 51–71.

Zeng, Zhen, and Yu Xie. 2004. Asian-Americans' earnings disadvantage reexamined: The role of place of education. *American Journal of Sociology* 109 (5): 1075–1108.

III: Diversities within Major Populations

Measuring Hispanic Origin: Reflections on Hispanic Race Reporting

By
SONYA R. PORTER
and
C. MATTHEW SNIPP

There are more than 50 million Hispanics in the United States, composing 16 percent of the population. Hispanics are also one of the fastest-growing race and ethnic groups. The American public often views and treats Hispanics as a racial group; yet 47 years after a Hispanic origin measure was added to the 1970 U.S. decennial census, and after numerous tests aimed at ameliorating racial measurement issues related to Hispanics, we continue to struggle with defining and measuring this population. In this article, we review literature about conceptual and measurement issues regarding Hispanic race reporting, evaluate public tabulations from one of the largest Census Bureau studies conducted in the 2010 Census to test strategies to improve race reporting for Hispanics, and discuss the opportunities and challenges of changing the race question on the decennial census to incorporate Hispanics.

Keywords: Hispanic origin; race; measurement

The Hispanic population is often viewed and treated as a racial group by the American public, but for federal statistics, "Hispanic" is not a racial group—it is an ethnicity that individuals of various race groups may or may not claim. The disjuncture between commonly held beliefs and the government's purposes in creating a Hispanic ethnicity decades ago has led to a state of affairs in which federal agencies continue to grapple with the meaning and

---

Sonya R. Porter is the director of research in the Center for Administrative Records Research and Applications at the U.S. Census Bureau. She conducts research on racial identification, racial measurement, and racial stratification and inequality.

C. Matthew Snipp is the Burnet C. and Mildred Finley Wohlford Professor of Humanities and Sciences at Stanford University. His recent publications deal with racial and ethnic inequality, and his other work includes publications that outline the development of the American Opportunity Study (AOS).

Correspondence: Sonya.rastogi.porter@census.gov

DOI: 10.1177/0002716218767384

measurement of this group. The confusion about how to define and measure Hispanics dates back to the 1800s and early 1900s, when Mexicans were generally measured as white but treated as nonwhite (Fredrickson 2003). Indeed, while Mexicans were supposed to be coded as white in the U.S. decennial census (Rumbaut 2011), there is evidence that enumerators recorded Mexicans as mulattos (Hochschild and Powell 2008). The first attempt to measure Mexican Americans as a distinct category was in the 1930 decennial census, in part due to increased Mexican migration (Snipp 2003) and concomitant nativism (Hochschild and Powell 2008). This was short-lived, as Mexican American groups and the Mexican government protested this change, preferring to be measured as white (Snipp 2003).

The next attempt to count Hispanics—in the 1970 decennial census long form—further underscores the difficulty of defining and measuring Hispanics. One measure was used in the decennial long form, a combination of surname, language, and birthplace; and a second measure based on nativity and origin was used in a 5 percent sample. This attempt was widely criticized as undercounting the Hispanic population (Snipp 2003). However, the decision to enumerate Hispanics came late in the decennial census planning cycle, and there was insufficient time to devise and test an alternative.

A major step to standardize the collection and tabulation of race and ethnic data across federal agencies was taken in 1977, when the Office of Management and Budget (OMB) established *Directive 15: Race and Ethnic Standards for Federal Statistics and Administrative Reporting*. Directive 15 finally established an official definition for Hispanics, but this definition did not alleviate conceptual and measurement issues.

The Directive 15 in 1977 defined four races: American Indian or Alaskan Native, Asian or Pacific Islander, black, and white; and two ethnicities: Hispanic and non-Hispanic. The definition for Hispanic was "a person of Mexican, Puerto Rican, Cuban, Central or South American or other Spanish culture or origin, regardless of race." Since then, each decennial census has had separate questions for race and Hispanic origin (see Figure 1 for the 2010 Census questions).

Results from the 1970 and 1980 censuses revealed that many Hispanics did not place themselves in one of the four race categories but reported "other" to the race question (Martin, DeMaio, and Campanelli 1990), pointing to conceptual and measurement issues related to Hispanic origin and race. This pattern persists today: for instance, in the 2010 Census, 37 percent, or 18.5 million Hispanics, checked some other race (SOR) alone (Humes, Jones, and Ramirez 2011).[1] Moreover, 6.2 million, or 13 percent of Hispanics, did not respond to the race question (Ríos, Romero, and Ramírez 2014). The Census Bureau has conducted numerous questionnaire design tests over the past 30 years to ameliorate these measurement issues. One of the largest and most promising tests was undertaken in the 2010 Census, the race and Hispanic origin Alternative

---

NOTE: This article is meant to inform interested parties of research and to encourage discussion. The views expressed are those of the authors and not necessarily those of the U.S. Census Bureau.

FIGURE 1
2010 Census Race and Hispanic Origin Questions

→ **NOTE: Please answer BOTH Question 8 about Hispanic origin and Question 9 about race. For this census, Hispanic origins are not races.**

8. **Is Person 1 of Hispanic, Latino, or Spanish origin?**
   - ☐ **No,** not of Hispanic, Latino, or Spanish origin
   - ☐ Yes, Mexican, Mexican Am., Chicano
   - ☐ Yes, Puerto Rican
   - ☐ Yes, Cuban
   - ☐ Yes, another Hispanic, Latino, or Spanish origin — *Print origin, for example, Argentinean, Colombian, Dominican, Nicaraguan, Salvadoran, Spaniard, and so on.* ↙

   [   ]

9. **What is Person 1's race?** *Mark ☒ one or more boxes.*
   - ☐ White
   - ☐ Black, African Am., or Negro
   - ☐ American Indian or Alaska Native — *Print name of enrolled or principal tribe.* ↙

   [   ]

   - ☐ Asian Indian   ☐ Japanese   ☐ Native Hawaiian
   - ☐ Chinese   ☐ Korean   ☐ Guamanian or Chamorro
   - ☐ Filipino   ☐ Vietnamese   ☐ Samoan
   - ☐ Other Asian — *Print race, for example, Hmong, Laotian, Thai, Pakistani, Cambodian, and so on.* ↙   ☐ Other Pacific Islander — *Print race, for example, Fijian, Tongan, and so on.* ↙

   [   ]

   - ☐ Some other race — *Print race.* ↙

   [   ]

10. **Does Person 1 sometimes live or stay somewhere else?**
    - ☐ No   ☐ Yes — *Mark ☒ all that apply.*
      - ☐ In college housing   ☐ For child custody
      - ☐ In the military   ☐ In jail or prison
      - ☐ At a seasonal   ☐ In a nursing home
        or second residence   ☐ For another reason

→ **If more people were counted in Question 1, continue with Person 2.**

Questionnaire Experiment (AQE). In this article, we review literature about Hispanic racial identification to shed light on conceptual and measurement issues, evaluate published tabulations from the AQE study (Compton et al. 2012), and reflect on the opportunities and challenges involved in changing how we measure Hispanics.

Previous Research

Heterogeneity within the Hispanic category

Similar to other racial groups, there is considerable heterogeneity within the Hispanic population. While most Hispanics in the United States have Mexican heritage (Ennis, Rios-Vargas, and Albert 2011), Hispanics have heritage from other places such as Cuba, Puerto Rico, the Dominican Republic, Columbia, and El Salvador. And these groups report their race differently. For instance, many Cubans report their race as white, while Dominicans are more likely to report SOR (Ennis, Rios-Vargas, and Albert 2011; Ríos, Romero, and Ramírez 2014). Hispanic groups in the United States also have varying socioeconomic profiles. For example, of the ten largest Hispanic groups in the United States, Ecuadorians and Columbians have the highest median household incomes, while Puerto Ricans and Dominicans have the lowest (Motel and Patten 2012). Hispanic groups also differ on political issues. For instance, immigration is an important issue for Mexican Americans, but not Puerto Ricans who are U.S. citizens by birth (Mora 2014).

The racial regimes that Hispanic immigrants come from have similarities as well as differences. Many Latin American countries have a racial ideology of *mestizaje* or racial mixture as well as a preference for social whitening (Roth and Kim 2013). However, the ways in which racial mixture is defined differ. For instance, in Puerto Rico, racial mixture is defined by indigenous, African, and Spanish ancestries (Allen 2015); while in Mexico, racial mixture is between Spanish and indigenous heritage (Massey and Denton 1992). Despite the ideology of racial mixture common to many Latin American countries, racial categories are enacted in different ways (Roth 2012). Duany (2005) found that Puerto Ricans use more than nineteen different categories to describe a person's skin tone and physical characteristics; while in the Dominican Republic, skin color and nationality are used to define people racially. Labels in between white and black such as *indio-claro* ("light Indian") are reserved for Dominicans, while Haitians are racialized as black (Itzigsohn and Dore-Cabral 2000).

Within the United States, the characteristics of Hispanics who report white, black, or SOR, or do not report a race, differ considerably. White Hispanics have higher incomes and live in more affluent areas compared to black Hispanics and Hispanics who report SOR (Logan 2003). The socioeconomic experiences of Hispanics who report SOR fall in between white Hispanics and black Hispanics, while black Hispanics and non-Hispanic blacks have similar economic characteristics (Logan 2003). SOR Hispanics are poorer, less educated, and less likely to be citizens than white Hispanics (Tafoya 2004). Skin tone also appears to play an important role in Hispanic race reporting: Hispanics who report white tend to have lighter skin tones than those who report black or other (Golash-Boza and Darity 2008).

Measuring Hispanic race

OMB's solution to capturing a population this diverse was to make the definition of Hispanic ambiguous (Mora 2014) and to define it as an ethnicity. However, decades of research suggest that this solution served to complicate race data collection and measurement. Conceptual and measurement issues involved in distinguishing race and Hispanic origin are evident in Hispanic race reporting. As mentioned earlier, 37 percent of Hispanics reported SOR in 2010 (Humes, Jones, and Ramirez 2011), and 13 percent did not answer the race question, compared to 4 percent of the U.S. population who did not answer the question (Ríos, Romero, and Ramírez 2014). Altogether, 50 percent of individuals who reported that they were Hispanic in the 2010 Census did not report within one of the five OMB race categories.[2] The SOR category was intended to be a small residual category; instead, it makes up 6 percent of the U.S. population and is the third largest category after white and black (Humes, Jones, and Ramirez 2011). Moreover, 97 percent of those who report only SOR are of Hispanic origin (Humes, Jones, and Ramirez 2011).[3] These patterns have persisted for more than 30 years.

The evidence of race response instability among Hispanics also points, at least in part, to racial and ethnic measurement and conceptual issues. Studies that have evaluated the quality of questions after the decennial censuses from 1990 to 2010 reveal relatively high levels of inconsistency in the white and SOR categories due to Hispanic race reporting (Dusch and Meier 2012; Singer and Ennis 2003; U.S. Census Bureau 1993). The 1990 Content Reinterview Survey report (U.S. Census Bureau 1993, 21) concluded, "It is apparent that Hispanics have difficulty in classifying themselves into the race categories presented." Studies linking the Current Population Survey to Census 2000 (del Pinal and Schmidley 2005) and Census 2000 to the 2010 Census (Liebler et al. 2017) also have revealed considerable race response shifting among Hispanics.

Several Census Bureau studies across the decades have tried to improve Hispanic race reporting by testing strategies to reduce Hispanic nonresponse to the race question, increase reporting in one of the five OMB race categories, and decrease reporting in the SOR category. Census researchers have evaluated instructions, the removal of the SOR category, and combined questionnaire designs. This extensive research led to one significant change related to Hispanic race reporting. The Census Bureau added an instruction to the 2010 Census—"For this census, Hispanic origins are not races"—and it, at least in part, reduced SOR reporting but only by about 5 percentage points from Census 2000 to the 2010 Census.

The Census Bureau also tested removing the SOR category; although this did improve reporting in the five OMB categories, it also increased item nonresponse to the race question and was never implemented in the decennial census. In planning for Census 2000, the Census Bureau tested the feasibility of a combined race and Hispanic origin question in the 1996 Race and Ethnicity Targeted Test (RAETT). This study found that a combined question significantly reduced item nonresponse.

The SOR category has become increasingly problematic over time. The growth of the Hispanic population has increased the number of persons selecting this category for their race. The growing SOR population is particularly problematic because the Census Bureau is the only federal agency permitted to use this category.[4] That is, it is not included in the official race classification promulgated by the OMB. Other federal agencies such as the National Center for Health Statistics or the Bureau of Labor Statistics publish rates and other statistics in which the denominators are based on census-derived estimates of specific racial groups. Omitting SOR Hispanics would seriously underestimate the sizes of these groups leading to upwardly biased statistical estimates. Consequently, the Census Bureau must reallocate SOR respondents to one of the OMB race categories for use by other agencies. In anticipation of the 2010 Census, there were plans to eliminate the SOR category but congressional action made this impossible. As a result, the Census Bureau has struggled with how to deal with the growing number of persons in the SOR category.

2010 Race and Hispanic Origin Alternative Questionnaire Experiment

The 2010 Census race and Hispanic AQE had several goals: (1) to reduce item nonresponse, (2) to increase reporting in the five OMB race categories (as opposed to the SOR response), (3) to elicit reporting of detailed race and ethnic groups, and (4) to increase accuracy and reliability of the data (Humes 2009). This article focuses on goals one, two, and four as they relate to Hispanic race reporting. Nonresponse to the race question is particularly acute for the Hispanic population (Ríos, Romero, and Ramírez 2014). This nonresponse significantly diminishes the quality of the data because it increases the amount of imputed data that may introduce bias and unreliability in population statistics. In the AQE, the control panel that mirrored the 2010 Census question had about a 20 percent item nonresponse rate among Hispanics, compared to less than 1 percent among non-Hispanics. In other panels of the AQE where separate race and Hispanic origin questions were used, item nonresponse rates exceeded 30 percent.

The AQE tested four experimental designs that combined race and Hispanic origin into one question (see Figure 2 for an illustration). These designs are labeled alternative control, detailed, streamlined, and very streamlined in the tables. The alternative control has the same checkboxes and write-in lines as the 2010 Census questionnaire. The detailed questionnaire maintains checkboxes that are on the 2010 Census for both race and Hispanic origin and includes write-in lines for each group. The streamlined questionnaire includes a checkbox for each race group and Hispanic origin and write-in lines for all categories. The very

FIGURE 2
Illustration of Combined Race and Hispanic Question—Streamlined

8. What is Person 1's race or origin? *Mark* ☒ *one or more boxes* **AND** *write in the specific race(s) or origin(s).*

☐ White — *Print origin(s), for example, German, Irish, Lebanese, Egyptian, and so on.* ↙

☐ Black, African Am., or Negro — *Print origin(s), for example, African American, Haitian, Nigerian, and so on.* ↙

☐ Hispanic, Latino, or Spanish origin — *Print origin(s), for example, Mexican, Mexican Am., Puerto Rican, Cuban, Argentinean, Colombian, Dominican, Nicaraguan, Salvadoran, Spaniard, and so on.* ↙

☐ American Indian or Alaska Native — *Print name of enrolled or principal tribe(s), for example, Navajo, Mayan, Tlingit, and so on.* ↙

☐ Asian — *Print origin(s), for example, Asian Indian, Chinese, Filipino, Japanese, Korean, Vietnamese, Hmong, Laotian, Thai, Pakistani, Cambodian, and so on.* ↙

☐ Native Hawaiian or Other Pacific Islander — *Print origin(s), for example, Native Hawaiian, Guamanian or Chamorro, Samoan, Fijian, Tongan, and so on.* ↙

☐ Some other race or origin — *Print race(s) or origin(s).* ↙

→ **If more people were counted in Question 1, continue with Person 2.**

streamlined questionnaire has checkboxes for each race and Hispanic origin category in one question and a separate question asks respondents to provide

TABLE 1
Item Nonresponse for the Separate Race and Hispanic Origin Question and the Combined Questions

	Separate Question			
Panel	Hispanic Origin Question	Race Question	Nonresponse to Both Questions	Combined Questions
Control	4.3 (0.32)	3.5 (0.28)	0.8 (0.12)	—
Alternative control	—	—	—	1.2 (0.14)
Detailed	—	—	—	0.7 (0.11)
Streamlined	—	—	—	0.8 (0.15)
Very streamlined	—	—	—	0.6 (0.13)

SOURCE: Table 7, Final Report, 2010 Census Race and Hispanic Origin AQE.
NOTE: Estimates are weighted with standard errors in parentheses. Responses on "Streamlined Question" represent people who responded to either the checkbox question or the write-in question.

detailed responses in write-in lines. There were two control panels in the AQE, both of which included the race and Hispanic origin questions that were used in the 2010 Census. The focus of our analysis is on the comparison between these control panels and the experimental ones.

Combined versus Separate Question Results

As indicated earlier, a high proportion of Hispanics do not respond to the race question, in part because they do not identify with the OMB categories (Gerber and Crowley 2005). Similarly, many non-Hispanics do not respond to the Hispanic origin question because they feel that the question is redundant or do not believe it applies to them (Martin and Gerber 2004). AQE results suggest that both of these issues could be ameliorated by combining the race and Hispanic origin question.

Table 1 shows item nonresponse rates for the control panels and the four combined questions. We see that item nonresponse rates for the Hispanic origin question is 4.3 percent and 3.5 percent for race. When race and Hispanic origin are combined into one question, the item nonresponse rate drops to 1.2 percent or less, which is in line with the percentage of people who did not respond to both the Hispanic origin and race question in the control panels.

Table 2 shows that a combined question reduces the proportion of those who report SOR alone. In the control panels, about 6 percent of people report SOR alone and that figure drops to less than 1 percent for all the combined questions. The item nonresponse and SOR alone results both suggest that the

TABLE 2
Weighted Distributions for All Panels

Panel	Alone								Two or More Races
	White	Black	AIAN[a]	Asian	NHPI[b]	SOR[c]	Hispanic	Invalid	
Control	72.8	10.8	0.6	4.9	0.1	5.7	NA	0.4	3.8
	(0.67)	(0.41)	(0.11)	(0.29)	(0.02)	(0.34)		(0.12)	(0.26)
Alternative control	66.3	10.9	0.3	5.2	0.1	0.1	11.5	0.5	3.9
	(0.73)	(0.39)	(0.10)	(0.32)	(0.09)	(0.02)	(0.43)	(0.14)	(0.26)
Detailed	64.7	10.5	0.5	4.8	0.1	0.1	11.3	0.5	6.8
	(0.66)	(0.38)	(0.12)	(0.28)	(0.02)	(0.05)	(0.42)	(0.13)	(0.38)
Streamlined	64.5	10.9	0.3	5.1	0.1	0.2	11.8	0.6	5.8
	(0.77)	(0.42)	(0.07)	(0.32)	(0.01)	(0.05)	(0.46)	(0.16)	(0.32)
Very streamlined	66.3	10.9	0.3	5.2	0.1	0.1	11.5	0.6	6.3
	(0.73)	(0.39)	(0.10)	(0.32)	(0.09)	(0.02)	(0.43)	(0.18)	(0.37)

SOURCE: 2010 Census Final Report Race and Hispanic Origin AQE, Table 8.
NOTE: Estimates are weighted with standard errors in parentheses. Responses come from both the race and Hispanic origin questions. The sample included only a small proportion of Native Hawaiian and Other Pacific Islanders making inferences on these groups difficult. A value of NA was given in categories that did not have a response option. The no response column has been removed so percentages in table are not 100 percent.
a. American Indian or Alaska Native.
b. Native Hawaiian or Other Pacific Islander.
c. Some Other Race.

combined question improves these two main measurement issues related to Hispanic race reporting.

A major concern about changing the questionnaire from two separate questions to a combined question is that this change will impact racial distributions. Table 2 shows 2010 Census control panel and combined question results.[5] The white alone population is lower in the combined question formats compared to the separate questions. This is expected and the results are in line with the proportion of non-Hispanic whites in the 2010 Census—64 percent. The combined questions and separate questions have very similar proportions for the black, Asian, and American Indian and Pacific Islander alone populations. The multiracial population is higher in several of the combined questions. Several factors could be contributing to this result, for instance, the term *origin* (Lavrankas, Courser, and Diaz-Castillo 2005) in the combined questions in conjunction with write-in lines could be eliciting more distant ancestries, for some of the forms Hispanics could be reporting their ethnicity and race, or some Hispanics may be reporting that they have non-Hispanic ancestry. The Census Bureau has conducted additional large-scale testing to try to understand these potential issues.

TABLE 3
Hispanic Origin Weighted Distribution

Panel	Hispanic, Latino, Spanish	Mexican, Mexican Am., Chicano	Puerto Rican	Cuban	Other Specific
Control	13.0 (0.52)	8.1 (0.43)	1.1 (0.14)	0.5 (0.08)	2.3 (0.18)
Alternative control	13.8 (0.49)	7.8 (0.37)	1.7 (0.22)	0.5 (0.06)	2.2 (0.18)
Detailed	14.5 (0.52)	7.4 (0.36)	1.6 (0.19)	0.5 (0.07)	2.6 (0.20)
Streamlined	14.1 (0.51)	6.4 (0.35)	1.1 (0.16)	0.6 (0.11)	2.7 (0.22
Very streamlined	14.3 (0.52)	7.3 (0.39)	1.1 (0.16)	0.6 (0.10)	2.3 (0.21)

SOURCE: 2010 Census Final Report Race and Hispanic Origin AQE, Table 10.
NOTE: Estimates are weighted with standard errors in parentheses.

Table 3 shows that the proportion of Hispanics in the combined question is similar to the proportion in the control format. The distributions are similar for Mexicans, Puerto Ricans, and Cubans as well.[6]

Overall, the results show that the combined question is a promising approach to measuring race and Hispanic origin. It sharply reduces item nonresponse and selection of the SOR category—two issues that have vexed the Census Bureau for more than 30 years. Furthermore, it does not appear to have much impact on the responses of other groups.

Discussion

Having accurate and reliable data for the Hispanic population is critical. Hispanics compose the largest ethnic minority population in American society, and in some areas of the country they are a numerical majority. Data about them are essential for monitoring civil rights and other pieces of key legislation. The accuracy of data for the Hispanic population has a direct bearing on the outcome of voting rights complaints. Community groups, and state and local governments that use Census Bureau data for planning and outreach will also find their efforts handicapped by inaccurate information.

Data that are subject to large errors of omission, that is, item nonresponse or potential biases due to high rates of imputation, present a serious problem for officials and policy-makers on many levels, from federal agencies to local elected office holders and community leaders. A better measure for this population is needed and we believe that the work on this problem under way at the Census Bureau is an important and significant step forward. However, it is not enough to simply be able to measure the Hispanic population. Indeed, the heterogeneity within this population needs to be addressed as well.

While Hispanics who report white, black, or SOR have very different experiences and characteristics, this reporting may also be due to skin tone or other phenotypical differences. This type of heterogeneity can be observed within most racial groups. Asians come from many different countries that speak different languages, have different cultural and religious beliefs, and have different socioeconomic backgrounds and experiences. Vietnamese, Cambodians, and Laotians who arrived in the United States as refugees come and settle under very different circumstances than Asian Indians immigrating with H-1B visas to work in the technology industries. Experiences of African Americans who are descendants of slaves differ from those of West Indians and Africans who have immigrated to the United States. For the Hispanic population, no less than any other group in American society, this heterogeneity needs to be accurately captured in the federal statistical system.

Moving from the current question format to a new combined format is likely to meet with some degree of opposition. One concern is that changes in the format might lead to a decline in the number of Hispanics enumerated. Given the existing evidence, we do not think this is a viable objection. A second objection pertains to interrupting the historical continuity of a question in place since 1980. Again, results from the 2010 AQE suggests that, substantively, this change will not mark an identifiable change in the population currently (and in the past) identified as Hispanic. The most noticeable change moving forward with the combined question is a significant improvement in the data. Retaining a demonstrably weak instrument simply for historical continuity denies the possibility of significant improvements in the data of the future. Whatever costs are connected with the loss of historical continuity, they are likely small and more than compensated by improvements in the data they produce.

Finally, there is a frequently heard complaint that the Census Bureau is changing Hispanic from an "ethnicity" into a "race" (Hispanic Research Inc. 2014). From our perspective, this is a nonissue. It arises from outdated, essentialized ideas about the constitutive qualities of race and ethnicity; that race is about biology and ethnicity is about culture. Few scholars today (see Wimmer 2013) would endorse this antiquated and obsolete distinction. The key point is that regardless of whether you designate an identity as a race or an ethnicity, how individuals recognize and respond to a survey question is more important than the theoretical baggage assigned to it post hoc. It is much more important that a question have salience and meaning to respondents, so they can respond in ways that accurately capture the social reality of their lives. In conclusion, we believe that the Census Bureau has taken an important step in this direction, and it should continue along this line of research to further refine and improve the combined question.

Notes

1. Unlike some other federal agencies, the Census Bureau is permitted to use the SOR category for respondents who do not see themselves in the five OMB race categories.

2. In 1997, Directive 15 was revised and a fifth category was added. The Asian or Pacific Islander category was split into two separate categories—"Asian" and "Native Hawaiian or Other Pacific Islander."

3. In part, these numbers are an artifact of Census Bureau processing rules. Persons who, for example, select SOR but also report they are Lebanese are reassigned to the white racial category. However, persons reporting Hispanic origins are not reassigned to a specific racial group because OMB regulations state that Hispanics "may be of any race."

4. However, other federal agencies sometimes use an "Other" category in their data collections and often do not report it.

5. The results from the AQE and 2010 Census are not directly comparable, for several technical reasons. For instance, AQE is a stratified sample and it was only fielded in mailout/mailback operations, whereas the entire census has several other modes of data collection. Still, we show 2010 Census race distributions for reference.

6. The distributional results in Tables 2 and 3 are promising; however, more research should be conducted. As mentioned previously, this study was conducted in a mailout/mailback environment, and the sample was stratified by race and Hispanic origin. The Census Bureau should test the combined question in different modes such as nonresponse follow-up to ensure distributional results hold. Also, while it was necessary for the AQE to use a stratified sample, it is possible that Hispanics who are less attached to their ancestry may report their identity differently in a combined question; thus, more research should be conducted to understand this potential impact.

References

Allen, Rueben. 2015. Alternative methods to enumerate data on race in Puerto Rico. *Social Science Quarterly* 96 (2): 608–28.

Compton, Elizabeth, Michael Bentley, Sharon Ennis, and Sonya Rastogi. 2012. 2010 census race and Hispanic origin alternative questionnaire experiment. 2010 Census Planning Memoranda Series #211. Washington, DC: U.S. Census Bureau.

del Pinal, Jorge, and Dianne Schmidley. 2005. *Matched race and Hispanic origin responses from Census 2000 and Current Population Survey February to May 2000*. Washington, DC: U.S. Census Bureau.

Duany, Jorge. 2005. The rough edges of Puerto Rican identities: Race, gender, transnationalism. *Latin American Research Review* 40 (3): 178–90.

Dusch, Gianna, and Fred Meier. 2012. *2010 Census content reinterview survey evaluation report*. Washington, DC: U.S. Census Bureau.

Ennis, Sharon R., Merarys Rios-Vargas, and Nora Albert. 2011. *The Hispanic population: 2010*. Washington DC: U.S. Census Bureau.

Fredrickson, George. M. 2003. *The historical construction of race and citizenship in the United States*. New York, NY: United Nations Research Institute for Social Development.

Gerber, Eleanor R., and Melinda Crowley. 2005. Report on cognitive testing of a shortened sequence of Hispanic origin, race, and modified ancestry questions: Content development for the 2005 National Content Test. Internal document. Washington, DC: U.S. Census Bureau.

Golash-Boza, Tanya, and William Darity Jr. 2008. Latino racial choices: The effects of skin color and discrimination on Latinos' and Latinas' racial self-identifications. *Ethnic and Racial Studies* 31 (5): 899–934.

Hispanic Research Inc. 2014. *Why doesn't the census include Hispanic as a race?* New York, NY: Hispanic Research Inc. Available from http://www.hispanicresearch.com/index.php/hispanic-market-data/faq/87-why-doesnt-the-census-include-hispanic-as-a-race.

Hochschild Jennifer L., and Brenna M. Powell. 2008. Racial reorganization and the United States Census 1850–1930: Mulattoes, half-breeds, mixed parentage, Hindoos, and the Mexican race. *Studies in American Political Development* 22 (1): 59–96.

Humes, Karen. 2009. *2010 census alternative questionnaire experiment: Race and Hispanic origin treatments*. Washington, DC: U.S. Census Bureau.

Humes, Karen, Nicholas A. Jones, and Roberto Ramirez. 2011. *Overview of race and Hispanic origin: 2010*. Washington, DC: U.S. Census Bureau.

Itzigsohn, Jose, and Carlos Dore-Cabral. 2000. Competing identities? Race, ethnicity, and panethnicity among Dominicans in the United States. *Sociological Forum* 15 (2): 225–47.

Lavrankas, Paul J., Matthew W. Courser, and Lillian Diaz-Castillo. 2005. What a difference a word can make: New research on the differences between Hispanic "origin" and Hispanic "identity" and their implications. Paper presented at the 2005 AAPOR meetings, Miami Beach, FL.

Liebler, Carolyn, Sonya R. Porter, Leticia E. Fernandez, James M. Noon, and Sharon R. Ennis. 2017. America's churning races: Race and ethnic response changes between Census 2000 and the 2010 census. *Demography* 54 (1): 259–84.

Logan, John. 2003. *How race counts for Hispanic Americans*. Albany, NY: Lewis Mumford Center for Comparative Urban and Regional Research, the University at Albany, State University of New York.

Martin, Elizabeth, Theresa J. DeMaio, and Pamela C. Campanelli. 1990. Context effects for census measures of race and Hispanic origin. Statistical Research Division Working Papers in Survey Methodology (#90-01), U.S. Census Bureau, Washington, DC.

Martin, Elizabeth, and Eleanor Gerber. 2004. Results of recent methodological research on the Hispanic origin and race questions. Paper presented at the annual meeting of the Population Association of American.

Massey, Douglass S., and Nancy A. Denton. 1992. Racial identity and the spatial assimilation of Mexicans in the United States. *Social Science Research* 21:235–60.

Mora, G. Christina. 2014. *Making Hispanics*. Chicago, IL: University of Chicago Press.

Motel, Seth, and Eileen Patten. 2012. *The 10 largest Hispanic origin groups: Characteristics, rankings, top counties*. Washington, DC: Pew Research Center.

Ríos, Merarys, Fabián Romero, and Roberto Ramírez. 2014. Race reporting among Hispanics: 2010. Population Division Working Paper #102, U.S. Census Bureau, Washington, DC.

Roth, Wendy D. 2012. *Race migrations: Latinos and the cultural transformation of race*. Stanford, CA: Stanford University Press.

Roth, Wendy D., and Nadia Y. Kim. 2013. Relocating prejudice: A transnational approach to understanding immigrants' racial attitudes. *International Migration Review* 47 (2): 330–73.

Rumbaut, Ruben. 2011. *Pigments of our imagination: The racialization of the Hispanic-Latino category*. Washington, DC: Migration Policy Institute.

Singer, Phyllis, and Sharon R. Ennis. 2003. *Census 2000 content reinterview survey: Accuracy of data for selected population and housing characteristics as measured by reinterview*. Washington, DC: U.S. Census Bureau.

Snipp, Matthew C. 2003. Racial measurement in the U.S. Census: Past practices and implications for the future. *Annual Review of Sociology* 29:563–88.

Tafoya, Sonya. 2004. *Shades of belonging: Latinos and racial identity*. Washington, DC: Pew Hispanic Center.

U.S. Census Bureau. 1993. *Content reinterview survey: Accuracy of data for selected population and housing characteristics as measured by reinterview*. Washington, DC: U.S. Census Bureau.

Wimmer, Andreas. 2013. *Ethnic boundary making: Institutions, power, networks*. New York, NY: Oxford University Press.

Latinos, Race, and the U.S. Census

By
EDWARD TELLES

We identify two dimensions of race for the Latino/Hispanic population in the United States—Latinos as one category among the various categories of the U.S. "ethno-racial pentagon" and racial or color differences among Latinos. In a major change from the previous (two-question) format, the Census Bureau recommends a one-question format for capturing ethno-racial distinctions in the 2020 census, which efficiently captures the Latino population on the first dimension and is consistent with racial classification and identification in the real world. At the same time, it nearly eliminates the problem that the two-question format fostered of classifying many Hispanics as "some other race" while maintaining a similar number of Americans classified as Hispanic or Latino. Whether the Census Bureau adopts the one- or two-question format is yet to be decided as of this writing. However, neither format is sufficient for capturing racial distinctions among the fast-growing Latino population, thus precluding effective monitoring of racial disparities in the United States.

Keywords: Hispanics; color; colorism; Afro-Latinos; ethno-racial; ethnic

In 1977, the U.S. Congress passed the Office of Management and Budget's (OMB) Directive 15, which regulates the classification of Latinos or Hispanics[1] in the census and other official surveys (Bean and Tienda 1988). OMB Directive 15 deems that Hispanics/Latinos are an ethnic but not a racial group in the U.S. Census. In census publications and in social practice, however, Hispanics or Latinos are

Edward Telles is distinguished professor of sociology at the University of California, Santa Barbara. He has authored Pigmentocracies: Ethnicity, Race and Color in Latin America *(The University of North Carolina Press 2014);* Race in Another America: The Significance of Skin Color in Brazil *(Princeton University Press 2004);* Generations of Exclusion: Mexican Americans, Assimilation and Race *(Russell Sage Foundation 2008); and many articles in leading academic journals.*

Correspondence: etelles@soc.ucsb.edu

DOI: 10.1177/0002716218766463

often treated as a separate category, whether it is called racial or ethnic, apart from black, Asian, white, and native Americans. More to the point, the Census Bureau attempts to treat race and ethnicity as separate dimensions for Hispanics since the 1980 census go against Latinos' own cognitive understandings of race and ethnicity—concepts that are often considered indistinguishable.

There are two dimensions of race and ethnicity among Hispanics, both of which are important and the census needs to adequately capture (Telles and Murguia 1990; López 2013): whether the respondent is in the category Hispanic/Latino, and how the person may be perceived in traditional "racial" terms. The first dimension is adequately captured by the current census two-question format and would be captured by a single question. The second dimension is also important, but it is inadequately captured by the census. Whether it was the Census Bureau's intent, analysts have used census data to model those two dimensions, but researchers have shown the capture of the second dimension to be woefully inadequate.

The Census Two-Question Format and the Hispanic Response

A two-question format in the census since 1980 has sought to implement the notion that Hispanics are an ethnicity and not a race. The Census Bureau assesses Hispanic ethnicity through a separate question and forces Hispanics to identify in the census's race categories, where Hispanic is not a category (Bean and Tienda 1988). The census introduced a question in the 1980 census that simply asks whether respondents are Hispanic or Latino in addition to the standard race question. Several versions of that two-question format were tried between 1980 and 2010, with changing wording of the questions and categories and order of the two questions (the 2010 version is reproduced in Alba, Beck, and Sahin, this volume). The "race" question never included the category Hispanic/Latino, and the large majority of Hispanics, faced with the available choices, chose either white or "other" (i.e., "some other race"). Less than 5 percent chose black, and far fewer chose any of the other terms.

Presumably the two-question format sought to eliminate confusion of race with ethnicity. The notion that race and ethnicity can be clearly separated is a common one and has been widely accepted. The Institute of Medicine defines race as "a sociocultural concept wherein groups of people sharing certain physical characteristics are treated differently based on stereotypical thinking, discriminatory institutions and social structures, a shared worldview, and social myths," whereas ethnicity is defined as "shared culture and way of life ... reflected in language, folkways, religious and other institutional forms" (Smedley, Stith, and

---

NOTE: The author would like to thank Emilce Santana and Richard Alba for their comments. At the time of this writing, the Office of Management and Budget (OMB) decided to retain the two-question format for the 2020 Census despite the Census Bureau's recommendations to move to the one-question format. By the time this article is published, it will likely have congressional approval to keep the old format. This decision, nevertheless, does not change my fundamental argument here.

Nelson 2003; Allen et al. 2011). However, these definitions do not seem to hold up on close inspection. So-called ethnic groups, such as Jewish Americans, have been characterized as having distinct physical features and discriminated against accordingly or discriminated against by their religion or culture (Roediger 1999), and so-called racial groups, such as African Americans, have been described as having a shared culture and way of life.

For such reasons, many analysts understand race and ethnicity as overlapping concepts (Cornell and Hartmann 2006; Hughes et al. 2006). Whereas ethnicity was traditionally defined as based on culture and specifically as social groups with common cultural attributes, Norwegian anthropologist Frederik Barth (1959/1998) redefined ethnicity as based on the salient social boundaries that humans create in their social interactions. Nearly 50 years later, Wimmer (2008) would expand Barth's classic definition and argue that race should be considered as one component of ethnicity.

Analysts have used the two questions together in their attempts to understand "racial" differences among Hispanics (Denton and Massey 1989; Logan 2010). Denton and Massey (1989), for example, examined segregation among Hispanics in Northeast metropolitan areas and assumed that those who self-identified as black are phenotypically black, those who identified as white are actually white, and those who identified as other or some other race are mixed. Logan made the same division and called these groups black Hispanics, white Hispanics, and Hispanic Hispanics. Notably the racial designations were based on self-classification, but analysis of surveys has shown that self-identified race among Hispanics does not reflect phenotypic or color differences (Landale and Oropesa 2002; Roth 2012; E. Vargas et al. 2016). Although dark and phenotypically African Hispanic respondents experience discrimination on the basis of phenotype, their racial self-identification may be a poor proxy for their racial ascription.

Note the example of Dominicans, who largely appear black. In the 2000 U.S. Census, only 13 percent of Dominicans also identified as black, and in 2010 that number increased to only 18 percent. Most Dominicans are probably considered black in the American understanding of the term (Roth 2012; Candelario 2007), but they have been routinely classified as *Indio* in Dominican identity cards (Howard 2001).[2] Since the early twentieth century, the black racial category, African culture, and blackness became associated with Haitians, which were seen as antithetical to Dominican-ness (Moya Pons 1986; Howard 2001; Candelario 2007). Only recently, have some (non-Haitian) Dominicans begun to embrace blackness and identify with black and especially mulatto categories (Howard 2001; Simmons 2009; Telles and Paschel 2014).

The Hispanic Response: Cognitive Understandings of Race and Ethnicity

The two-question format used by the census does not capture the way that Hispanics tend to think about race; the census's separate notions of race and ethnicity simply do not coincide with the lived experience/worldview of many

Hispanics (Hitlin, Brown, and Elder 2007). Social science research has found that cognitively Hispanics consider Hispanic/Latino as both race and ethnicity and, racially, that Hispanic is a group separate and in addition to black, white, Asian, and American Indian (Hitlin, Brown, and Elder 2007). This is consistent with a popular U.S. system of racial classification, which Hollinger (2006) described as America's ethno-racial pentagon. Even the Census Bureau treats Hispanics as a (de facto) fifth race, by typically publishing its reports to show Hispanic demographics as a fifth column alongside those of the four traditional (non-Hispanic) racial groups. In practice, though, Hispanics are often understood in both ethnic and racial terms, which some analysts prefer to call ethnic-racial or ethno-racial because of their overlapping and conceptually indistinguishable uses.[3] This lived experience in the United States, which contributes to understanding Hispanic as a separate race/ethnic category, is supported by the finding that, for immigrants, longer residence in the United States, or, for U.S. natives, more generations since immigration, is positively correlated with identification as Hispanic/Latino and rejection of the white racial category (Golash-Boza and Darity 2008).

Census design should obviously consider the social psychology of how respondents interpret questions, question formats, and response categories. Hispanics cognitively understand Hispanic or Latino as a race, while the census seeks to parse out race and ethnicity (Hitlin, Brown, and Elder 2007). Campbell and Rogalin (2006) find that when self-identified Hispanics were faced with a U.S. Census–style two-question format, nearly 80 percent identified as white; but when the category Latino was added to race, 78 percent of them switched to Latino. Rather than a conceptual confusion of race and ethnicity by Hispanics (see for example Mays et al. 2003), this switch is at least as much a reflection of how some analysts and the Census Bureau are out of step with popularly held notions of race and ethnicity.

The Census's Proposed One-Question Format for 2020

Based on extensive testing of questions in very large census survey trials, including the Alternative Questionnaire Experiment in 2010 and the National Contents Test in 2015, the Census Bureau has proposed the biggest change in the race and ethnicity question(s) since at least 1980: a one-question format that eliminates the Hispanic ethnic question and adds a Hispanic/Latino category in the race question (Perlman and Nevada 2015). In other words, Hispanic would be treated as a race (and possibly MENA [Middle Eastern and North African] would also become a new racial category) in addition to the traditional categories. Census Bureau analysts have found that the overall count of Hispanics is the same with either format and that the new format leads to a dramatic reduction in the selection of "other" or "some other race." Moreover, identification as black under either format remains the same, which means that there are similar undercounts of the Afro-Latino population under either format.

As of this writing, though, a sudden change is afoot. Despite years of analysis by the Census Bureau and its recommendation to create a single ethno-racial question, the OMB has recently recommended that the previous two-question format be continued into the 2020 Census (Wang 2018). However, the question itself, like all other items on the census, is subject to final approval by Congress.

Two Dimensions of Race and Ethnicity for Hispanics

Notwithstanding the Census Bureau's appropriate decision to move to a one-question format, there is still a need to capture the dimension of race among Hispanics that refers to their phenotype or racial ascription. But that cannot be done in the way the Census Bureau has envisioned. The design of such a question needs to consider how census respondents understand the item.

Dimension 1: Racialization as Hispanic/Latino

For reasons cited above, Hispanics/Latinos (and other Americans) often see themselves as a race/ethnic group regardless of the OMB directive. This is a first-order cognitive understanding of race or ethnicity. Also, much social science research reveals that Hispanics/Latinos are often treated as a group (Cobas, Duany, and Feagin 2015) and commonly considered and treated as nonwhite (Menchaca 2001; Roth 2012; Vargas 2015). And in some places, the category Hispanic has real-world understandings and consequences. Note that we also could substitute national categories for Hispanic/Latino but the census favors a single panethnic category.

Since 1980, the U.S. Census has used the panethnic category, Hispanic or Latino, whereas previously they had used national categories, particularly Mexican, Puerto Rican, and Cuban, which were the primary groups in the United States from Latin America. These three groups were regionally segregated, had differentiated interests, and their own spokespeople; but in the 1970s, driven by census, business and media interests, a coalition of these groups created a new ethnic category (Hispanic) to further their increasingly common political and economic interests (Mora 2014). While recent immigrants tend to identify with their national group, they increasingly choose the panethnic category especially with increasing time in the United States (Itzigsohn and Dore-Cabral 2000) and over subsequent generations since immigration (Golash-Boza and Darity 2008).[4]

The oft-repeated phrase by the census and some analysts that "Hispanic/Latino (like Mexican, Puerto Rican, etc.) is not a race" is anachronistic and harks back to racial science designations of "the races" and the biology books that until the 1960s essentialized this notion (Morning 2011). At the same time, these textbook notions go against other biologically based decisions by the U.S. Supreme Court and by local courts in the nineteenth century to classify Mexicans racially, as either white or a separate race (Menchaca 2001). More recently, police and other institutions continue to classify suspects and others in a scheme where

Hispanic is a major racial category. In institutions such as California prisons, inmates are "segregated by race" to diminish violence, reflecting the sharp racial boundaries of street gangs (Goodman 2008). In that highly racialized environment, Hispanics, African Americans, and whites are kept apart from each other, regardless of the insistence that Hispanics are not a race or the Census Bureau's notions and their neat preordained categories.

Race is a social construction and if members of a society deem certain individuals as belonging to a distinct race, then that view reflects the racialization of that society, whereby its members are classified in particular categories and then treated accordingly. In other words, society often distinguishes Latinos as a race apart but there is another dimension. Society, including Latinos themselves, also often racializes Latinos who appear African and those with dark skin.

Dimension 2: Racialization by color or as black, white, mestizo, and so on

Social science data show that U.S. Latinos and Latin Americans are socially ranked along a racial hierarchy of skin colors and phenotypes (Telles and Murguia 1990; Rodriguez 2000; Telles and the Project on Ethnicity and Race in Latin America [PERLA] 2014) in much the same way as there is a racial hierarchy in the United States. But that hierarchy within the Hispanic population is not adequately captured in the census. When asked about one's race and ethnicity, Hispanics/Latinos are likely to "racially" self-identify as Hispanic/Latino or under a nationality group like Mexican or Dominican. At the same time, their lived experience also reflects their treatment in American society, where phenotype, especially a black phenotype, affects their life chances. Yet they often do not identify as black even though they may be perceived as such (Candelario 2007; Roth 2012). The second dimension, which we refer to as a second-order category of race, is fluid, while the first-order identification as Hispanic is not. For example, Hannon and DeFina (2015) find in a longitudinal study that only 2 percent of respondents switched classification as Hispanic from one year to another, but fully 44 percent of Hispanics switched their second-order racial classification.

The U.S. Census is inadequately equipped to capture the phenotypic and color gradients that characterize racialization within the Hispanic population. As we previously noted, the white and black categories that have been used to make such distinctions among Latinos (Logan 2010; Denton and Massey 1989) are poorly captured by the U.S. Census. For many persons considered black Latino, Afro-Latino or Latino of African descent, black self-identification in the U.S. Census is a second-order identity. For example, Landale and Oropesa (2002) find that when asked to identify themselves by race, 47.5 percent of Puerto Ricans identified as Puerto Rican, 40.6 percent identified as Hispanic or Latino, and less than 1 percent identified as black.[5] Thus, many such persons fail to acknowledge second-order racial identity in the census. It is possible to capture this additional dimension along with the Hispanic dimension of race/ethnicity with the "mark more than one" option in the new one-question race format but often only one, "Hispanic," is checked. In the two-question option, many such persons probably choose "some other race." Moreover, the census does not capture phenotype or skin color among Latinos (or anyone else) beyond the black category. Latinos rarely identify as indigenous except in the relatively small number of cases in which they identify with an indigenous culture or speak an indigenous language.

Latinos in the United States are immigrants or descend from Latin Americans coming from twenty countries with their own, often complex, racial histories. (Latinos also include U.S.- and island-born Puerto Ricans, who are U.S. citizens, and a few who are actually descendants of Mexicans living in areas conquered by the United States [not immigrants].) Latinos/Latin Americans span a wide range of phenotypes comprising varying degrees of European, indigenous, and African ancestries, and many, perhaps most, are racially mixed. Indeed, many of the nations from which they originated (including Puerto Rico) stress racial mixture as an essential part of the national character. Despite the rhetoric of race mixture leading to homogenization and racial egalitarianism among the national populations, the origin societies are racially stratified, characterized as pigmentocracies where skin color gradients tend to align along a social and economic hierarchy (Telles, Flores, and Urrea-Giraldo 2015). While some Latin American countries tend toward the European phenotype or origins (e.g., Argentina), others toward black (Brazil and Panama), and others toward indigenous (Bolivia, Guatemala, Mexico), most have incorporated ideas of mixture based on the idea that racial distinctions are generally difficult to make because of a history of mixing. In Mexico, for example, most are considered mestizo (mixed race) yet they vary widely by skin color, which is a primary axis of stratification in Mexican society (Martínez Casas et al. 2014; Villarreal 2010). Thus, the so-called racial categories fail to capture such racialized differences.

Note that there are also racialized differences based on color or phenotype and referred to as colorism among African Americans, but African Americans are captured in a single category in the census. Skin color and other phenotypical differences result in differential treatment in schools, the labor market, the dating and marriage market, the criminal justice system, and other dimensions of society (Dixon and Telles 2017). The census thus does only an approximate job of monitoring discrimination by capturing the first order of identification, but it fails to capture the racialized dimension of phenotype variation within the black population, as it does among Hispanics.

Despite the U.S. tendency to lump all of Latin America together, the twenty nations in the region have quite diverse racial histories, understandings of race, racial terminology, and patterns of racial classification/identification (Telles and PERLA 2014; Telles and Paschel 2014). Racial conceptions, racial identification, racial variation, and racial stratification in countries where many Latino Americans originate may vary substantially. In Mexico, where 64 percent of U.S. Latinos originate, the race question may sound odd. For example, fully 20 percent of the population when asked about their race or ethnicity does not understand the question, and another 20 percent considers it to be "Mexican" (Flores and Telles, n.d.). Cuba, Puerto Rico, and the Dominican Republic compose the next largest groups. The Caribbean countries are largely of African origin yet they and the U.S.-bound emigrants they spawned have quite distinct racial histories and politics (Sawyer 2006; Duany 2005; Candelario 2007).

Racial Identification in the U.S. Census among Hispanics

The identification of about half of Hispanics as white, and an increase of "white Hispanics" from 1990 to 2010, has been used as evidence of how Hispanics are or have become white (Cohn 2014; Yancey 2003), perhaps a result of mobility or an acceptance by whites. Indeed, the Department of Justice recently reported that most persons caught illegally crossing the U.S.-Mexico border to the United States were white, based on similar information. Hispanics who are of lighter skin color are more likely to be of higher socioeconomic status (Telles and Murguia 1990; Montalvo and Codina 2001). However, Hannon and DeFina (2015), utilizing the General Social Survey, find that for Latinos of similar skin color, identifying as white is unrelated to socioeconomic status or closeness to whites, suggesting that their reasons for identifying as white are not because they have socioeconomically assimilated or acculturated but rather because of inadequate questionnaire design. On the contrary, analysts have found that among persons of similar skin color, Latinos with higher income were more likely to refuse to identify as white (Frank, Akresh, and Lu 2010; Golash-Boza and Darity 2008). Dowling (2014) finds that Mexican Americans often identify as white not because of their phenotype—many understand that they are considered nonwhite—but because of ideologies and discursive strategies about citizenship and aspirations where white is understood as American. Moreover, identification as white occurs because the current format does not offer a Hispanic category for race even though more than 40 percent choose "other," apparently rejecting the census's racial categories (Pastor 2014; Vargas 2015). Pastor (2014) notes that slight changes in wording, particularly the admonition in 2010 that "For this census, Hispanic origins are not races," led to increases in identification as white among Hispanics.

As mentioned earlier, at the other end of the white-black continuum, only 5 percent of Hispanics and about 15 percent of Dominicans select the black category, even though some argue that most Dominicans in the United States would probably be considered black (Candelario 2007; Roth 2012). As in the Dominican Republic, Brazil, Puerto Rico, and other parts of Latin America (Candelario 2007; Telles 2004; Duany 2005), many Latinos avoid the black category because black is the most stigmatized category, instead self-classifying in U.S. Census categories such as other and white. On the whole, those who do identify as black may be the more assimilated than those who are treated as black. Golash-Boza and Darity (2008) find that greater experience with color discrimination is associated with greater identification as black. However, they and others (Landale and Oropesa 2002; Hannon and DeFina 2015) find that skin color is only loosely associated with identification as black. The U.S. Census thus does not reliably capture race differences within the Hispanic population.

Conclusion

The U.S. Census has come a long way in efficiently enumerating the Hispanic/Latino population, but it has a way to go in capturing racial distinctions among it.

Racialization among Latinos or Latin Americans is often based on phenotypical differences, particularly skin color, yet these differences are often not considered consequential in the United States or the many countries of Latin America. Extensive research has shown that dark skin color and African origin negatively affect social mobility and the opportunities available to Latinos in the United States, just as they do throughout Latin America. The U.S. Census should pay more attention to ways of effectively capturing such characteristics. Considering that the phenotypically diverse Latino population is now the nation's largest minority, counting that diversity is now critical for understanding racial disparities.

The U.S. Census laudably attempts to designate Afro Latinos. However, it has not been able to fully identify that population, in either the old or the new format. In the old format, Latinos—identified in the Hispanic question—could also identify as black in the race question, and in the new format, respondents can check both the Latino/Hispanic and black categories. Indeed, the Census Bureau has found that the change from the old to the new format does not really change the number of persons that are classified as Afro-Latino. The problem has not so much to do with the census question format as with self-identifications. Latinos, even when they are seen as black, often do not identify that way. In the U.S. context, where single identities are most common, they may be seen as primarily Latino and see themselves that way; perhaps more worrisome, many see blackness as an identity to be avoided.

So how do we overcome this problem? Perhaps a long-term strategy, which has been tried by the Afro-Latino Forum in New York City, is to raise awareness and consciousness through TV spots about race in the Latino community for Hispanic media markets. By exposing Hispanics to the importance of checking off both black and Latino and by reducing the stigma of blackness, self-identification as Afro-Latino might be enhanced. The use of supplemental surveys that measure skin color and hair type also provide direct measures of observed racial status, which can be used to assess an Afro-Latino population as well as distinguish the very heterogeneous Hispanic population by phenotype. Surveys might also consider a question on reflective race like "What race do others think you are?" or "Do others ever consider you black or of African origin?" Finally, the Census Bureau should consider publishing data specifically on Afro-Latinos, while seeking to specifically improve its ability to capture that population.

The problem of identifying Afro-Latinos notwithstanding, the Census Bureau has recommended the one-question format for the ethno-racial question in the 2020 Census. This new format, which considers Hispanic or Latino one category among the various racial terms of the U.S. "ethno-racial pentagon," is more consistent with racial classification in the real world. At the same time, it nearly eliminates the problem that the old (two-question) format that fostered classifying many Hispanics in the residual "some other race" category while it maintains the number of Americans classified as Hispanic or Latino the same as in the old format. Unfortunately, as of this writing, the Trump administration, through the OMB, threatens to roll back these advances.

Notes

1. *Hispanic* and *Latino* will be used interchangeably and synonymously in this article.
2. Even though the Dominican Republic had a majority black population during the colonial period (Andrews 2004), Dominican elites glorified European and indigenous (*taino*) contributions to the nation, while they reviled and ignored African ancestry. Dominican nationalism and notions of race would develop in relation to neighboring Haiti, with which it shared a small island and a complicated history of colonization and conquest.
3. For example, Hughes et al. (2006, 764–65) refer to ethnic-racial socialization as "rooted in a group's historical experiences and in family practices that are passed down through successive generations" or "types of messages are reactive to contemporary constraints, opportunities, and social processes, including discrimination."
4. Note that both *Hispanic* and *Latino* are terms derived in the United States, though the notion of Latin American goes back to Simon Bolivar in the eighteenth century, particularly as a call for a unified Latin America during its wave of independence from Spain. The idea has also been used in other waves of Latin American unification such as by Che Guevara in the 1950s and 1960s and later in the 1970s promoted in popular music and literature. In the 1960s, ethnic identification as Latin American was widely used in Texas by Mexican Americans, presumably as a way to avoid identification with the highly stigmatized category of Mexican (Telles and Ortiz 2008).
5. Interestingly, the numbers were about the same or more for light and medium colored persons on the mainland, while the numbers were much larger and skin tone was correlated with black identification on the island.

References

Alba, Richard, Brenden Beck, and Duygu Basaran Sahin. 2018. The rise of mixed parentage: A sociological and demographic phenomenon to be reckoned with. *The ANNALS of the American Academy of Political and Social Science* (this volume).
Allen, Vincent C., Christina Lachance, Britt Rios-Ellis, and Kimberly A. Kaphingst. 2011. Issues in the assessment of "race" among Latinos: Implications for research and policy. *Hispanic Journal of Behavioral Sciences* 33 (4): 411–24.
Andrews, George R. 2004. *Afro Latin America, 1800–2000*. New York, NY: Oxford University Press.
Barth, Fredrik. 1959/1998. *Ethnic groups and boundaries: The social organization of culture difference*. Long Grove, IL: Waveland Press.
Bean, Frank D., and Marta Tienda. 1988. *Hispanic population of the United States*. New York, NY: Russell Sage Foundation.
Campbell, Mary E., and Christabel L. Rogalin. 2006. Categorical imperatives: The interaction of Latino and racial identification. *Social Science Quarterly* 87 (5): 1030–52.
Candelario, Ginetta E. B. 2007. *Black behind the ears: Dominican racial identity from museums to beauty shops*. Durham, NC: Duke University Press.
Cobas, José A., Jorge Duany, and Joe R. Feagin. 2015. *How the United States racializes Latinos: White hegemony and its consequences*. New York, NY: Routledge.
Cohn, Nate. 21 May 2014. More Hispanics declaring themselves white. *New York Times*.
Cornell, Stephen, and Douglas Hartmann. 2006. *Ethnicity and race: Making identities in a changing world*. Thousand Oaks, CA: Sage Publications.
Denton, Nancy A., and Douglas S. Massey. 1989. Racial identity among Caribbean Hispanics: The effect of double minority status on residential segregation. *American Sociological Review* 54 (5): 790–808.
Dixon, Angela, and Edward Telles. 2017. Skin color and colorism: Global research, concepts, and measurement. *Annual Review of Sociology* 43 (1): 405–24.
Dowling, Julie A. 2014. *Mexican Americans and the question of race*. Austin, TX: University of Texas Press.
Duany, Jorge. 2005. Neither white nor black: The representation of racial identity among Puerto Ricans on the island and in the U.S. mainland. In *Neither enemies nor friends*, eds. A. Dzidzienyo and S. Oboler, 173–88. New York, NY: Palgrave Macmillan.

Flores, Rene, and Edward Telles. n.d. Don't know and nationality responses in Mexican racial identification. Manuscript in preparation.
Frank, Reanne, Ilana Redstone Akresh, and Bo Lu. 2010. Latino immigrants and the U.S. racial order how and where do they fit in? *American Sociological Review* 75 (3): 378–401.
Golash-Boza, Tanya, and William Darity Jr. 2008. Latino racial choices: The effects of skin colour and discrimination on Latinos' and Latinas' racial self-identifications. *Ethnic and Racial Studies* 31 (5): 899–934.
Goodman, Philip. 2008. "It's just black, white, or Hispanic": An observational study of racializing moves in California's segregated prison reception centers. *Law & Society Review* 42 (4): 735–70.
Hannon, Lance, and Robert DeFina. 2015. Racial fluidity or ambivalence about available survey options? Controversy in the sociological meaning of changes in Latino/a racial self-identification. Working paper, Villanova University, Villanova, PA.
Hitlin, Steven, J. Scott Brown, and Glen H. Elder. 2007. Measuring Latinos: Racial vs. ethnic classification and self-understandings. *Social Forces* 86 (2): 587–611.
Hollinger, David A. 2006. *Postethnic America: Beyond multiculturalism*. New York, NY: Basic Books.
Howard, David. 2001. *Coloring the nation: Race and ethnicity in the Dominican Republic*. Oxford: Signal Books.
Hughes, Diane, James Rodriguez, Emilie P. Smith, Deborah J. Johnson, Howard C. Stevenson, and Paul Spicer. 2006. Parents' ethnic-racial socialization practices: A review of research and directions for future study. *Developmental Psychology* 42 (5): 747–70.
Itzigsohn, Jose, and Carlos Dore-Cabral. 2000. Competing identities? Race, ethnicity and panethnicity among Dominicans in the United States. *Sociological Forum* 15 (2): 225–47.
Landale, Nancy S., and Ralph Salvatore Oropesa. 2002. White, black, or Puerto Rican? Racial self-identification among mainland and island Puerto Ricans. *Social Forces* 81 (1): 231–54.
Logan, John R. 2010. How race counts for Hispanic Americans. In *The Afro-Latino reader: History and culture in the United States*, eds. Miriam Jiménez Román and Juan Flores, 471–84. Durham, NC: Duke University Press.
López, Nancy. 2013. Killing two birds with one stone? Why we need two separate questions on race and ethnicity in the 2020 census and beyond. *Latino Studies* 11 (3): 428–38.
Martínez Casas, Regina, Emiko Saldívar, René Flores, and Christina Sue. 2014. The different faces of mestizaje: Ethnicity and race in Mexico. In *Pigmentocracies: Ethnicity, race, and color in Latin America*, eds. Edward Telles and the Project on Ethnicity and Race in Latin America, 36–85. Chapel Hill, NC: University of North Carolina Press.
Mays, Vickie M., Ninez A. Ponce, Donna L. Washington, and Susan D. Cochran. 2003. Classification of race and ethnicity: implications for public health. *Annual Review of Public Health* 24:83–110.
Menchaca, Martha. 2001. *Recovering history, constructing race: The Indian, black, and white roots of Mexican Americans*. Austin, TX: University of Texas Press.
Montalvo, Frank F., and G. Edward Codina. 2001. Skin color and Latinos in the United States. *Ethnicities* 1 (3): 321–41.
Mora, G. Cristina. 2014. *Making Hispanics: How activists, bureaucrats, and media constructed a new American*. Chicago, IL: University of Chicago Press.
Morning, Ann. 2011. *The nature of race: How scientists think and teach about human difference*. Berkeley, CA: University of California Press.
Moya Pons, Frank. 1986. *El Pasado Dominicano*. Santo Domingo: Editora Corripio.
Pastor, Manuel. 29 July 2014. Are Latinos really turning white? *Huffington Post*.
Perlman, Joel, and Patrick Nevada. 2015. Ethno-racial origin in U.S. federal statistics: 1980–2020. Levy Economics Institute Working Paper 2015, Annandale-on-Hudson, NY.
Rodriguez, Clara E. 2000. *Changing race: Latinos, the census, and the history of ethnicity in the United States*. New York, NY: New York University Press.
Roediger, David R. 1999. *The wages of whiteness: Race and the making of the American working class*. New York, NY: Verso.
Roth, Wendy. 2012. *Race migrations: Latinos and the cultural transformation of race*. Stanford, CA: Stanford University Press.
Sawyer, Mark. 2006. *Racial politics in post-revolutionary Cuba*. Cambridge: Cambridge University Press.

Simmons, Kimberly Eison. 2009. *Reconstructing racial identity and the African past in the Dominican Republic.* Gainesville, FL: University Press of Florida.

Smedley, Brian D., Adrienne Y. Stith, and Alan R. Nelson. 2003. *Unequal treatment: Confronting racial and ethnic disparities in healthcare.* Institute of Medicine, Committee on Understanding and Eliminating Racial and Ethnic Disparities in Health Care. Washington, DC: National Academies Press.

Telles, Edward E. 2004. *Race in another America: The significance of skin color in Brazil.* Princeton, NJ: Princeton University Press.

Telles, Edward, René D. Flores, and Fernando Urrea-Giraldo. 2015. Pigmentocracies: Educational inequality, skin color and census ethnoracial identification in eight Latin American countries. *Research in Social Stratification and Mobility* 40:39–58.

Telles, Edward E., and Edward Murguia. 1990. Phenotypic discrimination and income differences among Mexican Americans. *Social Science Quarterly* 71 (4): 682–96.

Telles, Edward E., and Vilma Ortiz. 2008. *Generations of exclusion: Mexican-Americans, assimilation, and race.* New York, NY: Russell Sage Foundation.

Telles, Edward, and Tianna Paschel. 2014. Who is black, white, or mixed race? How skin color, status, and nation shape racial classification in Latin America. *American Journal of Sociology* 120 (3): 864–907.

Telles, Edward, and the Project on Ethnicity and Race in Latin America (PERLA). 2014. *Pigmentocracies: Ethnicity, race, and color in Latin America.* Chapel Hill, NC: University of North Carolina Press.

Vargas, Nicholas. 2015. Latino/a whitening? *Du Bois Review: Social Science Research on Race* 12 (1): 119–36.

Vargas, Edward D., Nadia C. Winston, John A. Garcia, and Gabriel R. Sanchez. 2016. Latina/o or Mexicana/o? The relationship between socially assigned race and experiences with discrimination. *Sociology of Race and Ethnicity* 2 (4): 1–18.

Villarreal, Andrés. 2010. Stratification by skin color in contemporary Mexico. *American Sociological Review* 75 (5): 652–78.

Yancey, George A. 2003. *Who is white? Latinos, Asians, and the new black/nonblack divide.* Boulder, CO: Lynne Rienner Publishers.

Wang, Hansi Lo. 26 January 2018. 2020 census to keep racial, ethnic categories used in 2010. National Public Radio.

Wimmer, Andreas. 2008. Elementary strategies of ethnic boundary making. *Ethnic and Racial Studies* 31 (6): 1025–55.

Estimating the Characteristics of Unauthorized Immigrants Using U.S. Census Data: Combined Sample Multiple Imputation

By
RANDY CAPPS,
JAMES D. BACHMEIER,
and
JENNIFER VAN HOOK

Contemporary U.S. immigration policy debates would be better informed by more accurate data about how many unauthorized immigrants reside in the country, where they reside, and the conditions in which they live. Researchers use demographic methods to generate aggregated information about the number and demographic composition of the unauthorized immigrant population. But understanding their social and economic characteristics (e.g., educational attainment, occupations) often requires identifying likely unauthorized immigrants at the individual level. We describe a new method that pools data from the Survey of Income and Program Participation (SIPP), which identifies unauthorized immigrants, with data from the American Community Survey (ACS), which does not. This method treats unauthorized status as missing data to be imputed by multiple imputation techniques. Likely unauthorized immigrants in the ACS are identified based on similarities to self-reported unauthorized immigrants in the SIPP. This process allows state and local disaggregation of unauthorized immigrant populations and analysis of subpopulations such as Deferred Action for Childhood Arrivals (DACA) applicants.

Keywords: unauthorized immigrants; undocumented immigrants; immigrant populations; demographic estimation methodologies

The unauthorized immigrant population in the United States has become a focal point for political debates and policy

Randy Capps, director of research for U.S. Programs at the Migration Policy Institute, is a leading national expert on the demography of the U.S. immigrant population. He has written numerous reports on immigrant populations at the state and local levels and recently published national-level reports on the integration outcomes for refugees resettled in the United States, the well-being of children in refugee families, the characteristics of children in unauthorized immigrant families, and the population eligible for the Obama administration's Deferred Action for Childhood Arrivals (DACA) program.

Correspondence: rcapps@migrationpolicy.org

DOI: 10.1177/0002716218767383

discussions. The public and policy-makers want to know the answer to questions such as

1. How many unauthorized immigrants are there in the country, and is the population growing or shrinking?
2. Where are unauthorized populations located throughout the country?
3. What are the characteristics of unauthorized immigrants, and what are their costs and benefits to society?
4. How many might be eligible for various immigration reform and deportation relief programs?

Accurate data about the unauthorized immigrant population are necessary to address these questions and overcome stereotypes and misinformation. The Census Bureau's two main surveys—the American Community Survey (ACS) and the Current Population Survey (CPS)—are the largest, most representative national surveys and as such offer the most accurate data on immigrant populations across the country. These two surveys have sufficient samples at the state and, in the case of the ACS, local levels to conduct sophisticated analyses of the immigrant population. Both surveys ask whether immigrants are U.S. citizens, but neither inquires about the legal status of noncitizens. The two surveys undercount immigrants, particularly unauthorized ones, but researchers have estimated the extent of the undercount and incorporated it into models that approximate the size of the unauthorized population.

Demographers have developed various methods to estimate the size and characteristics of the unauthorized immigrant population in the ACS and CPS using links to data from other sources. One method described in detail here relies on the Survey of Income and Program Participation (SIPP)—a less well-known, smaller-sample Census Bureau product that includes questions about the legal status of immigrants.

A Residual Method for Estimating the Number of Unauthorized Immigrants

Several established research institutions monitor the size and national origins of the U.S. unauthorized population, including the Office of Immigration Statistics

---

James D. Bachmeier is an assistant professor in the Department of Sociology at Temple University and a nonresident fellow at the Migration Policy Institute. His research has concentrated on patterns of international migration to the United States and the integration of immigrants and their children into American society. He is the author (with Frank D. Bean and Susan K. Brown) of Parents without Papers: The Progress and Pitfalls of Mexican American Integration *(Russell Sage Foundation 2015).*

Jennifer Van Hook is Roy C. Buck Professor of Sociology and Demography at the Pennsylvania State University, and nonresident fellow at the Migration Policy Institute. She is currently coeditor of Demography, *the flagship journal for population science. She has expertise in the demographics of immigrant populations and the socioeconomic integration of immigrants and their children, including work that seeks to estimate the size, characteristics, and dynamics of the unauthorized foreign-born population.*

at the Department of Homeland Security (DHS), the Hispanic Trends Project at the Pew Research Center (Pew), and the Center for Migration Studies (CMS). Researchers at these institutions have used a residual method that involves subtracting estimates of the lawful permanent resident (LPR) population and other legal noncitizens from the total foreign-born population (FB). These researchers obtain estimates of the foreign born from the ACS or CPS and estimates of LPRs from DHS admissions data, with adjustments for legal immigrants who died or left the country (Baker and Rytina 2013; Passel 2016). They also account for legal nonimmigrants (LNI)—which include students, H-2A agricultural workers, H-1B high-skilled workers, and other temporary visitors—as a separate group in the data.[1] The unauthorized population (UA) is estimated by subtracting the number of LPRs and LNIs from the total FB measured in the ACS or CPS:

$$UA = FB - LPR - LNI.$$

Finally, the UA estimate is adjusted upward because some unauthorized immigrants do not respond to the census, ACS, or CPS (i.e., they are undercounted).

Uses and limitations of the residual method

The residual method can be used to address several important demographic and policy questions. Chief among these is trends in the size of the unauthorized population, which can be affected by U.S. immigration enforcement policies; the state of the low-wage U.S. economy (as a stronger economy attracts more unauthorized immigrants); and the demographics, economics, and security conditions of major source countries such as Mexico, El Salvador, Guatemala, and Honduras.

Pew and CMS estimates show rapid increases in the number of unauthorized immigrants until about 10 years ago (2007, just before the Great Recession), and small declines or a steady state since then (Passel and Cohn 2016b; Warren 2016). Their residual method also shows a downward shift in the share of unauthorized immigrants from Mexico (to 52 percent in 2014 from 57 percent in 2007), offset by increases in those from Asian countries such as India and China, and those from Central America (Passel and Cohn 2016a).

The residual method is useful for answering a variety of broad demographic and policy questions, but without more fine-grained data, a host of other, more detailed policy and sociological questions may be left unanswered. The CPS and ACS offer a wealth of data to be explored: age, educational attainment, English proficiency, income, poverty, housing conditions, health coverage, and public benefits use to name a few. The ACS can also be used to identify the size and characteristics of different immigration status populations at the state and local levels. But the ACS and CPS do not differentiate legal immigrants from unauthorized immigrants; they only provide data on noncitizens more generally.

Methods for Identifying More Detailed Characteristics of Unauthorized Immigrants

Methods to identify the characteristics of unauthorized immigrants in detail can be characterized as either "logical imputation" or "statistical imputation." Though these are distinct and different approaches, there are methodological overlaps, and they are often used in combination.

Logical imputation

Logical imputation consists of two main steps. First, researchers use variables in the ACS or CPS that identify immigrants with a high likelihood of being lawful U.S. residents. Those immigrants who report themselves as naturalized U.S. citizens are considered lawful residents.[2] Noncitizens who are veterans, active-duty military personnel, or public-sector workers; those performing specialty professional licensed occupations (e.g., judges, lawyers, and police officers); and those receiving public assistance for which only lawful residents are eligible (e.g., Medicaid or other public health insurance) are classified as LPRs. LNIs can be identified more precisely by the terms of their visas. For example, foreign students must have completed high school, be enrolled full time in a university, be in the United States for short periods, and be in the right age range for university enrollment. H-1B and other high-skilled nonimmigrant workers must work in the correct occupation, be from countries comprising high shares of nonimmigrant visas, and be in the country for short periods (Bachmeier, Van Hook, and Bean 2014).

In the second step, once U.S. citizens, LPRs, and LNIs have been classified, the remaining immigrants serve as the "pool" of potential unauthorized immigrants. In this step, researchers may randomly assign immigrants in the pool as either LPRs or unauthorized so that the total number of each group hits the "control totals" assigned by the residual estimates, for example, 11.1 million in Pew's 2014 estimate (Passel and Cohn 2016b). These control totals may be specific for gender, age, country of birth, and state of residence as such variables are available in the DHS data on lawful admissions. But researchers may also go further and assign LPR or unauthorized status based on a more detailed set of variables available in the ACS/CPS and other datasets such as the SIPP—or in the case of Pew, the 1992 Legalized Population Survey (LPS).[3]

The accuracy of the first step in logical imputation depends on the accuracy of the variables used to make the logical assignments. If immigrants misread some of the relevant questions, this could bias the assignments. For example, unauthorized immigrants employed by private firms serving as contractors could misreport being federal, state, or local government employees, and be misclassified as LPRs. Those reporting Medicaid receipt could also be misclassified if they misunderstand the question; unauthorized immigrants are eligible for emergency Medicaid and for limited public insurance programs in some states and localities that could be confused with Medicaid. The authors tabulated Medicaid coverage among the roughly three thousand individuals who identified themselves as not being LPRs in the 2008 SIPP, and more than 10 percent reported Medicaid coverage. In short, the logical imputation method assumes that unauthorized status is perfectly correlated with certain measures (i.e., all noncitizens reporting government employment or Medicaid receipt are LPRs), when, in the data, these correlations may be less than perfect.

The second step of assigning members of the remaining "pool" to unauthorized or LPR status may also be subject to bias. Clearly, simple random assignment of the pool to either status may be highly inaccurate. But using old data sources like the 1992 LPS could also result in bias because the characteristics of unauthorized immigrants have changed so much over time (e.g., with a declining share originating in Mexico and residing in California and the Southwest).

Nonetheless, logical imputation is straightforward when researchers have confidence in the variables used to distinguish between lawful and unauthorized immigrants, and the methods to assign those in the remaining pool are transparent. Pew and CMS researchers have been using this method for years and have a substantial track record of public credibility.

Statistical imputation

The alternative approach, statistical imputation, is more complex and has several variations in the literature. This approach generally involves pooling two survey samples: a smaller "donor" sample that includes immigration status variables (e.g., the SIPP) and a larger "target" sample that does not have status variables (e.g., the ACS or CPS, see Figure 1). Variables in common between the two datasets (e.g., age, gender, country of birth, length of U.S. residence, educational attainment, income, and occupation or industry of employment in the U.S.) are used to identify people with common characteristics in both samples, who may then be classified as either LPRs or unauthorized based on the variables in the donor sample.

This approach, widely used in the statistics literature, has been referred to as "data fusion," and here we describe a form of data fusion known as combined-sample multiple imputation (CSMI). This method has been shown to yield relatively unbiased estimates of the characteristics of the unauthorized immigrant population under various simulated conditions and data scenarios (Van Hook et al. 2015). CSMI involves pooling two survey samples: a relatively small donor sample that includes a key analytical variable such as immigration status, and a target sample that does not include the key variable but is substantially larger and therefore capable of producing more precise estimates (Rendall et al. 2013). CSMI pools the two samples and treats the lack of the key measure in the target sample as a traditional missing data problem that is addressed using standard multiple imputation techniques.

Two conditions must be satisfied for CSMI to produce unbiased estimates (Rendall et al. 2013). First, the two pooled samples must be drawn from the same underlying population or "universe." This condition is critical because the imputation of missing information in the target sample is based on a set of multivariate associations observed in the donor sample, and in "imposing" these

FIGURE 1
Pooling Donor and Target Data to Impute Immigration Status in Large-Sample Surveys

DONOR DATA (SIPP)	TARGET DATA (ACS or CPS)
Includes variables on immigration status (LPR or not)	Does not include immigration statuts
Common analysis variables (e.g., country of birth, length of U.S. residence, educational attainment, occupation, income, health coverage)	Common analysis variables (e.g., country of birth, length of U.S. residence, educational attainment, occupation, income, health coverage)
Small sample limits analysis	Larger sample allows for greater disaggregation, analysis of smaller groups

associations on the target sample, one assumes that the associations are the same in both samples. For example, if one were to impute the legal status of immigrants nationwide using a donor sample of immigrants in California (e.g., the California Health Interview Survey [CHIS]), CSMI would impose the characteristics of unauthorized immigrants in California upon the population in the national target sample. For instance, in 2014 the estimated share of unauthorized immigrants from Mexico was 56 percent nationwide and 70 percent in California, and so using a California sample to impute the status nationally would result in overrepresentation of Mexicans in the final dataset (Migration Policy Institute 2017).[4] Similarly, if one were to use a donor sample from the 1990s to impute status in a contemporary target dataset, CSMI would impose the characteristics of unauthorized immigrants in the 1990s on the current data. During the 1990s, far fewer unauthorized immigrants lived outside California and the Southwest, and so using this method could underestimate the number living in other regions of the United States. The unauthorized population is also currently much better settled—with a much longer average length of U.S. residence—than it was in the 1990s (Passel and Cohn 2016a).

The second critical CSMI condition is that variables must be "jointly observed" in both the donor and target samples. For instance, an analysis of whether unauthorized immigrants report greater levels of daily stress compared to LPRs must include measures of stress in both the donor and the target samples. If immigration status is observed only in the donor sample and stress is observed only in the target sample, the association between legal status and reported stress is unknown, as they are never jointly observed within the same sample, and imputations will be prone to bias. Using micro-simulations, Van Hook and colleagues (2015) have shown that the bias resulting from violation of the joint observation condition can be substantial, both in magnitude and in direction, relative to the true effect in the population.

Using CSMI to impute immigration status in the ACS or CPS with a SIPP target sample

The SIPP is a nationally representative household-level panel survey that measures trends in employment, income, and public assistance receipt. The SIPP has many demographic, economic, and social measures in common with the ACS and CPS, and all three surveys are conducted by the U.S. Census Bureau. Unlike the ACS and CPS, the SIPP includes a series of detailed immigration status questions. But the SIPP has roughly only nine to ten thousand foreign-born respondents, about a third of whom are unauthorized, depending on the panel year, and therefore it does not facilitate the precise estimation of specific segments of the unauthorized population that might be of interest to researchers and policy-makers.

Beginning with the 1996 panel, the SIPP asked questions pertaining to status at U.S. entry, as well as status and citizenship at the time of the survey, making it the first and only nationally representative survey to include such questions.[5] More specifically, SIPP respondents were asked about the type of visa they used to first enter the United States: an LPR visa (green card), a temporary visa (e.g., student or H-1B), a refugee admission, or some "other" status. Those who did not enter as LPRs were asked whether they had adjusted to LPR status and, if so, the year in which they adjusted. Those who did not enter with a visa and who have not since adjusted can, by inference, be classified as neither LPRs nor lawful nonimmigrants—and are therefore unauthorized. While the SIPP collects detailed immigration status at entry, the public use dataset includes only variables for whether immigrants entered as LPRs or later adjusted. The authors are exploring the use of restricted-use SIPP data—which do differentiate LPRs from LNIs—to address this significant data gap.

The first step in CSMI is to pool the donor and target samples—the SIPP and ACS, respectively—into one dataset, and then identify and harmoniously code all variables jointly observed in the two datasets. It is at this stage in the process that the pooled sample should be examined for violations of the same universe condition. A simple first step is to examine a side-by-side comparison of profiles of characteristics of the foreign-born samples in each survey sample (see Table 1). For example, if Europeans compose 20 percent of the donor sample but only 10 percent of the target sample, an analyst should be concerned that the two samples might not represent the same underlying population. In our data comparing the 2014 SIPP with the 2014 ACS, the share of the foreign-born from Latin America and the Caribbean is very similar (52.6 percent versus 53.7 percent), as are shares from other world regions. There are more notable differences between the 2014 SIPP and ACS samples with respect to entry cohort distribution, but none large enough to elicit major concern. Relative to the SIPP samples, a larger proportion of the ACS immigrant sample entered the United States prior to 1980, and after the Great Recession, while a smaller share reported entry in the five-year period leading up to the Great Recession. These differences are all below 2 percentage points, however. More definitive, multivariate tests of the same universe condition can also be undertaken, but are not described here for sake of brevity (see Rendall et al. 2013).

TABLE 1
Region of Birth and Arrival Cohort Distribution of the U.S. Foreign-Born Population in the Survey of Income and Program Participation (SIPP) and the American Community Survey (ACS), 2014

	2014 SIPP		2014 ACS		
Region of Birth	Estimate	%	Estimate	%	Percentage Point Diff.
Region of birth					
Europe	4,909,172	11.9	4,962,319	11.7	−0.1
Asia/Pacific Islands	12,439,824	30.1	12,506,410	29.6	−0.5
Americas/Caribbean	21,725,467	52.6	22,672,548	53.7	1.1
Africa	1,681,290	4.1	1,862,824	4.4	0.3
Oceania	243,803	0.6	219,034	0.5	−0.1
Other	337,245	0.8	12,614	0.0	−0.8
Total	41,336,801	100.0	42,235,749	100.0	0.0
Arrival cohort					
Pre-1980	6,510,571	15.8	7,368,551	17.4	1.7
1980–1984	3,483,853	8.4	3,249,806	7.7	−0.7
1985–1989	3,952,646	9.6	3,887,865	9.2	−0.4
1990–1994	4,739,114	11.5	4,869,314	11.5	0.1
1995–1999	5,525,112	13.4	5,585,951	13.2	−0.1
2000–2004	6,739,172	16.3	6,726,592	15.9	−0.4
2005–2009	5,897,423	14.3	5,356,018	12.7	−1.6
2010–2014	4,488,910	10.9	5,191,652	12.3	1.4
Total	41,336,801	100.0	42,235,749	100.0	0.0

Once the two samples are pooled, harmonized, and tested for satisfying the same-universe condition, a multiple imputation model can be estimated. In general, the goal of the imputation model should be to maximize the predictive power of the model (e.g., by increasing the magnitude of model fit statistics). This can be accomplished by maximizing the number of jointly observed variables in the model as well as using as many interactions among the joint variables as the donor sample can tolerate given its sample size. The imputation step will create multiple iterations of imputed data, and, in basic terms, estimates and standard errors are derived by averaging across the imputed datasets (e.g., by running the CSMI model ten times and averaging the estimates and errors among the ten different sets of results).[6]

Strengths and limitations of CSMI using the SIPP and ACS

CSMI has allowed researchers to impute new information about the likely legal or unauthorized immigration status of noncitizens in the SIPP and ACS. Because the samples are so large in these surveys (particularly the ACS), this method has facilitated detailed analyses of the characteristics of smaller populations in smaller geographies.

CSMI also produces relatively unbiased results when compared with other methods. In a Monte Carlo simulation, CSMI was used to impute immigration status in half the 2008 SIPP sample, while the other half retained status as reported by respondents. When the half sample with imputed status was compared to the half sample with reported status, unauthorized immigrants in both samples had very similar characteristics—indicating a low level of bias in the imputation methodology (Van Hook et al. 2015).

CSMI can also be used to produce recent estimates of unauthorized immigrants' characteristics. The SIPP is updated regularly, with new panels started about every five years; the most recent panel started in 2014 and the data were released in early 2017. The ACS is conducted annually, and data are released about a year after collection.

The method also has its limitations. The public-use SIPP lacks details on immigration status: it only reports LPR status versus "other" (i.e., non-LPR status), leaving LNIs such as students and H-1B workers to be disaggregated from unauthorized immigrants using logical imputations—as described earlier in this article. The public-use SIPP, beginning in 2008, also lacks individual birth countries, instead providing broad regions of birth such as "Latin America" or "Asia." Without specific birth countries, the method may produce bias in birth countries within regions (e.g., assigning unauthorized status to more Japanese immigrants and fewer Vietnamese immigrants than should be the case, because both the Japanese and Vietnamese are classified as "Asian" immigrants in the public-use SIPP). These limitations can be overcome if researchers obtained access to the restricted-used SIPP data, but such data can only be accessed at Census Bureau data sites, and the Census Bureau requires proposals specifying the analyses to be conducted and the end uses of the data.

In addition, SIPP data are produced every few years, while ACS data are produced every year. This makes it difficult to track changes in the characteristics of unauthorized immigrants over a short period of time. For example, using the 2014 SIPP to impute immigration status in the 2013, 2014, and 2015 ACS would produce similar research findings over those three years, because the characteristics of the same groups of LPRs and unauthorized immigrants in the 2014 SIPP would be mapped onto the imputed groups in all three years of the ACS. If, for instance, LPRs gained health insurance coverage under the Affordable Care Act (ACA) between 2013 and 2015—the years during which ACS was implemented—but unauthorized immigrants did not (because they were ineligible for the ACA), the differences in coverage trends between the two groups could not be modeled using CSMI. LPRs and unauthorized immigrants would have health insurance coverage in the same proportion in 2013 as in 2015, even though one group presumably gained coverage through the ACA while the other did not.

A third limitation is the sampling and data quality of the SIPP, which has a much smaller sample size and far fewer resources for outreach and data collection than the ACS. As a result, the SIPP may not sample the immigrant population as adequately and accurately as ACS. Response rates are lower for some questions in the SIPP than the ACS—for instance, the question about year of U.S. arrival. Indeed, data from the ACS may be used to impute year of arrival in the SIPP to remedy this deficiency. Also, starting in 2014, the SIPP no longer asked about adjustment to LPR status; it only recorded LPR status at arrival. Thus, an additional step involving logical imputation or CSMI using an earlier SIPP panel is necessary to identify LPRs who adjusted their status, in addition to those who were LPRs at arrival.[7]

Uses of data on detailed characteristics of unauthorized immigrants

Using the SIPP to help impute unauthorized status in the ACS has allowed researchers to examine a wide variety of demographic trends and policy issues regarding the unauthorized population. One major area of exploration has been health coverage. At the cusp of the ACA, researchers showed a large gap in insurance coverage between unauthorized immigrants and LPRs, and the gap with naturalized citizens was even greater (Capps, Rosenblum, and Fix 2009). States with the largest unauthorized populations, which also tend to have relatively high rates of uninsurance (e.g., Texas and Florida), could see these coverage gaps increase the most (Capps et al. 2013). Estimating the number of uninsured unauthorized adults in California has been useful to assess the impact of state legislative proposals to extend Medicaid to them or allow them to purchase insurance on California's ACA exchange (Marcelli, Pastor, and Wallace 2015). The advantage of CSMI can be shown in the much smaller confidence intervals for point estimates of health insurance coverage in the 2008 ACS than the 2008 SIPP. Health coverage estimates are similar in the two surveys, but the confidence intervals are much wider in the SIPP, particularly for states with smaller populations (see Table 2). The smaller confidence intervals in the 2008 ACS data than in the SIPP facilitate cross-state comparisons of health insurance coverage for the unauthorized population.

Another area where the SIPP can be useful is in estimating the number and characteristics of LPRs who are eligible to naturalize. Estimates of the population eligible to naturalize have been published recently and offer support for organizations facilitating the naturalization process (Pastor et al. 2016). Estimating this population requires first identifying LPRs separately from other noncitizens, then flagging those who have at least five years of LPR status—or three years if married to a U.S. citizen. In addition to identifying LPRs, the SIPP includes the date when LPR status was issued.

The pooled SIPP-ACS data have also been helpful for anticipating the implications of various immigration proposals that have been advanced in recent years. During the debates over comprehensive immigration reform in Congress, the various legalization pathways in the legislation were modeled, including the total number of unauthorized immigrants with at least 10 and 20 years of U.S. residence, those with college degrees who entered as children, and those working in the agricultural sector (Rosenblum, Capps, and Yi-Ying Lin 2011). Since the Obama administration created the DACA program in 2012, annual estimates of the population eligible for the program at the national, state, and local levels have

TABLE 2
Rates of Health Insurance Coverage among Unauthorized Immigrants in Twenty U.S. States with the Largest Foreign-Born Population, Survey of Income and Program Participation (SIPP) and American Community Survey (ACS), 2008

	2008 SIPP				2008 ACS			
			95% C.I.				95% C.I.	
	N	Est.	Low	High	N	Est.	Low	High
California	591	.42	.38	.47	19,458	.45	.45	.46
New York	164	.51	.42	.61	3,854	.53	.51	.54
Texas	252	.27	.21	.33	8,614	.26	.25	.28
Florida	151	.24	.16	.31	3,308	.34	.32	.36
Illinois	137	.41	.32	.49	2,674	.45	.43	.47
New Jersey	165	.34	.26	.43	2,461	.46	.43	.48
Arizona	936	.27	.18	.36	2,030	.30	.27	.32
Massachusetts	87	.54	.42	.66	789	.75	.71	.79
Georgia	93	.18	.11	.26	2,314	.29	.26	.31
Washington	74	.35	.23	.47	954	.50	.46	.54
Virginia	67	.41	.28	.55	1,183	.47	.43	.50
Maryland	75	.31	.20	.41	1,128	.51	.47	.54
Pennsylvania	31	.55	.34	.76	585	.54	.49	.59
North Carolina	87	.14	.06	.22	1,946	.30	.28	.33
Michigan	37	.46	.28	.65	520	.51	.45	.56
Colorado	34	.27	.11	.43	812	.30	.26	.34
Nevada	32	.12	.00	.23	984	.39	.36	.42
Connecticut	26	.51	.31	.72	462	.47	.42	.53
Ohio	29	.49	.30	.69	381	.52	.46	.58
Oregon	18	.70	.48	.92	557	.43	.38	.48

NOTE: C.I. = confidence interval.

been produced (Batalova, Hooker, and Capps 2013; Hipsman, Gómez-Aguiñaga, and Capps 2016; Mathay and McHugh 2015).[8] These estimates, down to the state and local level, have been useful for planning outreach and application assistance for the DACA program and monitoring program participation. When the Obama administration considered expanding deferred action to different groups of parents of U.S. citizens and LPRs, estimates of eligible populations were also modeled (Capps and Rosenblum 2014).

Pooled SIPP-ACS data have also been useful in identifying employment and earnings patterns for immigrants by legal status. The earnings penalty for unauthorized workers was isolated from other factors such as age, educational attainment, and English proficiency (Bean, Brown, and Bachmeier 2015). In research exploring the underemployment of well-educated immigrants, the component of underemployment related to immigration status has also been isolated (Batalova,

Fix, and Bachmeier 2016). Finally, the amount that unauthorized immigrants' purchasing power and tax payments could rise if they were legalized and able to obtain higher wages has been calculated (Pastor et al. 2010).

Conclusion: The Importance of Disaggregating Unauthorized Immigrants in the Data for Sociological and Policy Analysis

Legal status is a key variable in immigrant integration, and one that is highly relevant for policy analysis. For instance, the National Academies of Science, Engineering, and Medicine recently concluded, "It is critical for researchers to have accurate and precise information about the number of people who acquire different legal statuses" (National Academies of Sciences, Engineering, and Medicine 2015, 416).

Demographers, social scientists, policy analysts, and the public rely on the CPS and ACS for timely, authoritative, and detailed information about the U.S. population including immigrants. It is unlikely that the Census Bureau would add legal status questions to either major survey, as this could depress immigrants' participation in the survey and, depending on the political climate, potentially identify and endanger small populations of unauthorized immigrants at the local level (National Academies of Sciences, Engineering, and Medicine 2015). At the same time, without information on legal status, the CPS and ACS alone are insufficient to address the many substantial policy questions that have been raised recently about immigration enforcement, legalization and deferred action programs, and health care and other benefits for unauthorized immigrants; and their economic and fiscal impacts.

While other sources such as the CHIS, LPS, and localized surveys provide information about the characteristics of unauthorized immigrants, the SIPP is the largest nationally representative and frequently updated source for these data. But the SIPP sample is too small to accurately estimate unauthorized populations. At the same time, the SIPP's data on immigration status can be pooled with CPS or ACS using multiple imputation. This method greatly increases the level of detail and geographic specificity that can be used for analysis of the unauthorized immigrant population. In this context, multiple imputation's main contributions are to allow much greater geographic disaggregation of information about unauthorized immigrants and more accurate analysis of small subpopulations—such as DACA-eligible immigrants—than would be possible in the SIPP. Multiple imputation cannot, however, be used to broaden analysis of unauthorized immigrants to include new variables, as all analysis variables must be included in both the donor (SIPP) and recipient (ACS/CPS) data.

Imputing immigration status in the ACS using the SIPP data has some methodological limitations. A large-scale national survey of immigrants, including unauthorized status alongside other indicators of interest to researchers and policy-makers, would be ideal. In the absence of better data, ongoing transparency and collaboration among data analysts and data users will lead to improvements in strategies to overcome methodological limitation and produce better estimates of key populations of interest such as unauthorized immigrants.

Notes

1. Some legal temporary migrants such as Temporary Protected Status (TPS) beneficiaries from El Salvador, Haiti, and Honduras are difficult to identify because they have many characteristics in common with unauthorized immigrants.

2. Some researchers reclassify some naturalized citizens as noncitizens—who could potentially be LPRs or unauthorized immigrants—when their answers to other questions suggest that they are not eligible for citizenship (e.g., if they have not resided in the United States for at least five years and are not married to a U.S. citizen or LPR).

3. The LPS was carried out during the late 1980s and early 1990s using a random sample of immigrants adjusting to LPR status from unauthorized status under the terms of the 1986 Immigration Reform and Control Act.

4. The Migration Policy Institute's 2014 estimate of the Mexican share of unauthorized immigrants nationwide (56 percent) differs slightly from Pew's estimate (52 percent) due to differences in the estimation methodology.

5. The most recent SIPP panels started every few years: 1996, 2001, 2004, 2008, and 2014. The years in between included quarterly interviews with the same respondents.

6. There does not appear to be a consensus with respect to the number of imputed datasets that one should create during the imputation step, and in practice, this number should be driven by considerations such as the size (number of observations) in the target sample and the observed variability across imputations. For example, if the target sample is relatively small and points estimates vary widely across imputations, then a greater number of imputations (e.g., twenty to fifty) should be created.

7. About half of LPRs receive that status at arrival, while the other half adjust to LPR status after arrival. Some who enter with nonimmigrant status—as students or H-1B workers for example—may overstay their visas, and become unauthorized immigrants. Without data on both arrival status and current status at the time of the survey, it is not possible to distinguish all LPRs from unauthorized immigrants.

8. DACA provides a reprieve from deportation and a work permit for two years, renewable, to unauthorized immigrants who entered the United States by June 2007, entered before they turned age 16, are ages 15 to 30, and have at least a high school degree or are enrolled in school.

References

Bachmeier, James D., Jennifer Van Hook, and Frank D. Bean. 2014. Can we measure immigrants' legal status? Lessons from two U.S. surveys. *International Migration Review* 48 (2): 538–66.

Baker, Bryan, and Nancy Rytina. 2013. *Estimates of the unauthorized immigrant population residing in the United States: January 2012*. Washington, DC: U.S. Department of Homeland Security, Office of Immigration Statistics. Available from https://www.dhs.gov/sites/default/files/publications/ois_ill_pe_2012_2.pdf.

Batalova, Jeanne, Michael Fix, and James D. Bachmeier. 2016. *Untapped talent: The costs of brain waste among highly skilled immigrants in the United States*. Washington, DC: Migration Policy Institute. Available from http://www.migrationpolicy.org/research/untapped-talent-costs-brain-waste-among-highly-skilled-immigrants-united-states.

Batalova, Jeanne, Sarah Hooker, and Randy Capps. 2013. *Deferred Action for Childhood Arrivals at the one-year mark: A profile of currently eligible youth and applicants*. Washington, DC: Migration Policy Institute. Available from http://www.migrationpolicy.org/research/deferred-action-childhood-arrivals-one-year-mark-profile-currently-eligible-youth-and.

Bean, Frank D., Susan K. Brown, and James D. Bachmeier. 2015. *Parents without papers: The progress and pitfalls of Mexican American integration*. New York, NY: Russell Sage Foundation.

Capps, Randy, Michael Fix, Jennifer Van Hook, and James D. Bachmeier. 2013. *A demographic, socioeconomic, and health coverage profile of unauthorized immigrants in the United States*. Washington, DC: Migration Policy Institute. Available from http://www.migrationpolicy.org/research/demographic-socioeconomic-and-health-coverage-profile-unauthorized-immigrants-united-states.

Capps, Randy, and Marc R. Rosenblum. 2014. *Executive action for unauthorized immigrants: Estimates of the populations that could receive relief*. Washington, DC: Migration Policy Institute. Available from http://www.migrationpolicy.org/research/executive-action-unauthorized-immigrants-estimates-populations-could-receive-relief.

Capps, Randy, Marc R. Rosenblum, and Michael Fix. 2009. *Immigrants and health care reform: What's really at stake?* Washington, DC: Migration Policy Institute. Available from http://www.migrationpolicy.org/research/immigrants-and-health-care-reform-whats-really-stake.

Hipsman, Faye, Bárbara Gómez-Aguiñaga, and Randy Capps. 2016. *DACA at four: Participation in the deferred action program and impacts on recipients*. Washington, DC: Migration Policy Institute. Available from http://www.migrationpolicy.org/research/daca-three-year-mark-high-pace-renewals-processing-difficulties-evident.

Marcelli, Enrico A., Manuel Pastor, and Steven P. Wallace. 2015. *Toward a healthy California: Why improving access to medical insurance for unauthorized immigrants matters for the Golden State*. San Diego, CA, and Los Angeles, CA: San Diego State University, University of Southern California Center for the Study of Immigrant Integration, and University of California Los Angeles Center for Health Policy Research. Available from http://dornsife.usc.edu/assets/sites/731/docs/Toward_A_Healthy_CA_Literature_Review_Web_Final_Dec2015A.pdf.

Mathay, Angelo, and Margie McHugh. 2015. *DACA at the three-year mark: High pace of renewals, but processing difficulties evident*. Washington, DC: Migration Policy Institute. Available from http://www.migrationpolicy.org/research/daca-four-participation-deferred-action-program-and-impacts-recipients.

Migration Policy Institute. 2017. Unauthorized immigrant population profiles. *Data Hub*. Available from http://www.migrationpolicy.org/programs/us-immigration-policy-program-data-hub/unauthorized-immigrant-population-profiles.

National Academies of Sciences, Engineering, and Medicine. 2015. *The integration of immigrants into American society*. Panel on the Integration of Immigrants into American Society, eds. Mary C. Waters and Marisa Gerstein Pineau, Committee on Population, Division of Behavioral and Social Sciences and Education. Washington, DC: National Academies Press.

Passel, Jeffrey S. 2016. *Measuring illegal immigration: How Pew Research Center counts unauthorized immigrants in the U.S.* Washington, DC: Pew Research Center. Available from http://www.pewresearch.org/fact-tank/2016/09/20/measuring-illegal-immigration-how-pew-research-center-counts-unauthorized-immigrants-in-the-u-s/.

Passel, Jeffrey S., and D'Vera Cohn. 2016a. *Overall number of U.S. unauthorized immigrants holds steady since 2009: Decline in share from Mexico mostly offset by growth from Asia, Central America and sub-Saharan Africa*. Washington, DC: Pew Research Center. Available from http://www.pewhispanic.org/2016/09/20/overall-number-of-u-s-unauthorized-immigrants-holds-steady-since-2009/.

Passel, Jeffrey S., and D'Vera Cohn. 2016b. *Unauthorized immigrant population stable for half a decade*. Washington, DC: Pew Research Center. Available from http://www.pewresearch.org/fact-tank/2016/09/21/unauthorized-immigrant-population-stable-for-half-a-decade/.

Pastor, Manuel, Justin Scoggins, Jennifer Tran, and Rhonda Ortiz. 2010. *The economic benefits of immigrant authorization in California*. Los Angeles, CA: University of Southern California Center for the Study of Immigrant Integration. Available from http://dornsife.usc.edu/assets/sites/731/docs/chirla_v10_small.pdf.

Pastor, Manuel, Justin Scoggins, Madeline Wander, and Rhonda Ortiz. 2016. *Data to inform strategy: Getting to know California's eligible-to-naturalize adult population*. Los Angeles, CA: University of Southern California Center for the Study of Immigrant Integration. Available from http://dornsife.usc.edu/assets/sites/731/docs/CSII_Data_Inform_Strategy_California_ETN_Final_July2016.pdf.

Rendall, Michael, Bonnie Ghosh-Dastidar, Margaret M. Weden, Elizabeth H. Baker, and Zafar Nazarov. 2013. Multiple imputation for combined-survey estimation with incomplete regressors in one but not both surveys. *Sociological Methods and Research* 42 (4): 483–530.

Rosenblum, Marc R., Randy Capps, and Serena Yi-Ying Lin. 2011. *Earned legalization: Effects of proposed requirements on unauthorized men, women, and children*. Washington, DC: Migration Policy Institute. Available from http://www.migrationpolicy.org/research/earned-legalization-effects-proposed-requirements-unauthorized-men-women-and-children.

Van Hook, Jennifer, James D. Bachmeier, Donna L. Coffman, and Ofer Harel. 2015. Can we spin straw into gold? An evaluation of immigrant legal status imputation approaches. *Demography* 52 (1): 329–54.

Warren, Robert. 2016. U.S. undocumented population drops below 11 million in 2014, with continued declines in the Mexican undocumented population. *Journal on Migration and Human Security* 4 (1): 1–15.

Counting America's First Peoples

By
CAROLYN A. LIEBLER

The descendants of the First Peoples of the Americas (labeled "American Indians and Alaska Natives" in the federal definition) are a particularly challenging group to count in censuses. In this article, I describe some enumeration issues and then outline what we have learned about American Indians and Alaska Natives from efforts that rely on individuals' answers to census questions on race, ancestry, ethnicity, and tribe. Those who do not report a tribe and those who change their race response from one census to another complicate these efforts. Tribal self-enumeration and indigenous data sovereignty may improve data about some portions of the population. Census and survey enumeration efforts should continue to separate the concepts of race, ancestry, and tribe lest the various subpopulations become indistinguishable in the data, making the data much less useful and possibly misleading.

Keywords: American Indians and Alaska Natives; U.S. Census; self-identification; tribe; indigenous

Descendants of America's first peoples, American Indians and Alaska Natives (AIANs), have proven difficult to count in surveys and censuses (Lujan 2014). In this article, I describe some issues that have caused these difficulties and then outline what we do know based on some of the best available data—census data. Tribes' self-enumerations could meet some of the challenges if done with sufficient resources, though a substantial proportion of self-identified AIANs would be excluded from

Carolyn A. Liebler is an associate professor of sociology at the University of Minnesota and an affiliate of the Minnesota Population Center.

NOTE: Part of this research was conducted in the Minnesota Research Data Center (NSF SES-0851417) with restricted-use data. Any opinions and conclusions expressed herein are those of the author and do not necessarily represent the views of the U.S. Census Bureau. All results have been reviewed to ensure that no confidential information is disclosed.

Correspondence: liebler@umn.edu

DOI: 10.1177/0002716218766276

FIGURE 1
Who Is "American Indian/Alaska Native"?

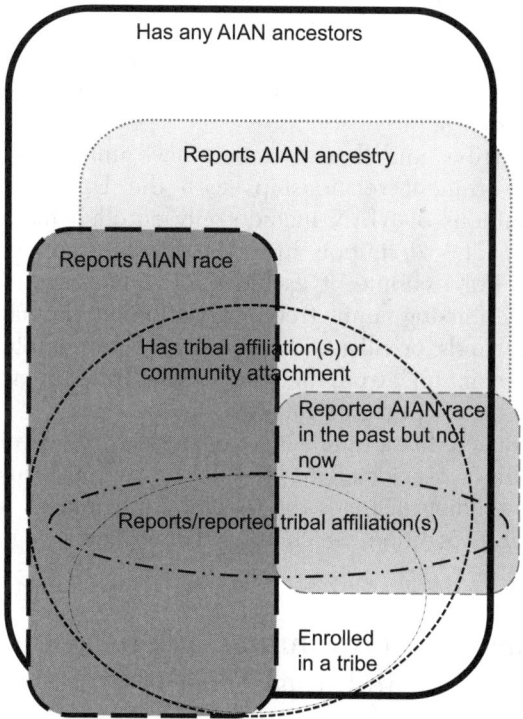

such efforts. I end by offering some suggestions for future endeavors to enumerate this important population, including the prioritization of indigenous data sovereignty[1] and the importance of distinguishing among race, ancestry, and tribe.

Who Is "American Indian/Alaska Native"?

Which individuals should be included in a count of "American Indians and Alaska Natives"? This philosophical question has a variety of answers; I have illustrated some of the possibilities in Figure 1.[2] Some definitions start with excluding people who have no AIAN ancestors, then add stipulations from there. For example, the current federal definition of who is included in the AIAN group is "a person having origins in any of the original peoples of North and South America (including Central America), and who maintains tribal affiliation or community attachment" (Office of Management and Budget 1997, 58789).

Some definitions of who is AIAN start with the principle of self-identification, which means that an AIAN is a person who reports being American Indian and/

or Alaska Native (in a race question or perhaps an ancestry question). A corollary of the principle of self-definition is that individuals should be able (though not required) to report their full self-definition, including multiple races, multiple ancestries, multiple tribes, and both Hispanic and non-Hispanic origins. Relatedly, they should have the freedom to change their response(s) over time if they change how they see themselves or revise their understanding of which answers best describe them.

Because AIAN tribes and their members have unique political status (i.e., government-to-government relationships with the United States; see Lujan 2014), some definitions of AIAN include only enrolled members of federally recognized tribes. This definition includes only a small portion of AIANs (Thornton 1997). For example, it excludes individuals with American Indian ancestors who have missing family tree information or who have ancestors from a variety of tribes, bands, or villages. Many tribes require a minimum number of ancestors ("blood quantum") from that band of that tribe for enrollment. In most cases, proving ancestors' pedigree involves finding them on a list (e.g., Dawes Rolls[3]) that was collected at a time when registering on a government list might not have seemed like a wise idea (late 1800s and early 1900s, just after the Indian Wars). Another excluding factor is the federal government's long and involved process for federal recognition, which not all tribes have navigated.[4]

Challenges to Counting American Indians and Alaska Natives

Once a definition of an AIAN is chosen, the task of finding out about this population can begin. It is important to understand AIAN enumeration issues[5] so that this fundamentally important group can be equitably included in studies and the public eye. High-quality enumeration and inclusion in studies generates useful and appropriate information for tribal, state, and federal policies. Analysts often leave AIANs out of analyses because they are a relatively small group that can be difficult to count, but AIAN people should not be left out of analyses simply for the convenience of the analyst when useful information can be compiled. If a person or a category of people are excluded from the potential benefits of research, then the risk they took as part of participation is not ethically justified.[6] Below, I outline some of the more obvious challenges to gathering high-quality information about AIAN people.

Challenge: A deficit of trust and shared resources

North American history abounds with examples of mistreatment of AIAN individuals and tribes by federal and state governments and their representatives. Although mistreatment has usually been subtle in the contemporary period, federal and state governments continue to ignore many treaties and tribal rights. Mistrust remains.

In recent years, the U.S. Census Bureau has been enhancing its efforts to consult with AIAN people, tribes, and organizations (such as the National Congress of American Indians [NCAI]) about data collection efforts (Lujan 2014; U.S. Census Bureau n.d., 2015). Not all AIANs are enrolled in tribes, so a high-quality *census* enumeration of all AIANs remains important. However, as critics point out, these efforts do not change the fact that the federal government (not tribes) has almost exclusive decision-making power because it controls most of the financial resources for enumeration and tabulation. For example, as the NCAI points out, "There has not been a comprehensive federal effort to improve the capacity of tribes to use existing data or collect tribal demographic data" (NCAI 2016, 1). This imbalance limits tribes' ability to act on their rights of sovereign self-determination. When or if a tribe has decision-making power, financial resources, and the trust of its members, it could potentially use its membership rolls, records, tribal officials, personal connections, and cultural competencies to find tribal members and encourage them to participate.

Challenge: Enumerator effects and location-related undercount

Because of the histories of tribal relocation and reservation placement, AIANs are overrepresented in very rural areas that pose challenges to standard U.S. census and survey enumeration strategies (Fallica et al. 2012; Walker et al. 2012). One challenge is that, even in the modern era, homes do not always have mailing addresses, and so a census worker must travel to them (missing some, perhaps especially, because this form of enumeration is costly). If a census worker helps the residents fill out the form, the interaction can affect how (and by whom) the questions are answered.

Most AIANs live outside of reservation areas and are rather dispersed in cities and suburbs (Keeler 2016; also see Iceland, Weinberg, and Steinmetz 2002). They are also a high-mobility group (see Lujan 2014). Without residential segregation as a clue, neighbors filling out a census form for a nonresponsive household are relatively unlikely to report AIANs as such and, instead, report them as a different race (Porter, Liebler, and Noon 2016). This dynamic adds to (and complicates) the general undercount of AIANs (Lujan 2014; Williams 2011).

Challenge: Soliciting and conveying meaningful answers on a questionnaire

A relatively high proportion of AIANs (by any definition) have mixed racial heritage (Snipp 1997) and have a wide variety of ways of reporting their identities, including using combinations of census questions on race, ancestry, tribal information, and Hispanic origins (Liebler 2010a; Snipp 1997).

Ancestry versus race: Because some people are AIAN in one definition but not another, the wording of a question can make a substantial difference in who self-identifies as AIAN. Since 1980, the Census Bureau has been asking an ancestry question—"What is this person's ancestry or ethnic origin?"—in addition to questions about race and Hispanic ethnicity. In each census year, the number and characteristics of those who report AIAN ancestry are substantially different

FIGURE 2
Reporting a Tribal Affiliation Is Not Guaranteed among Those Who Report AIAN Race

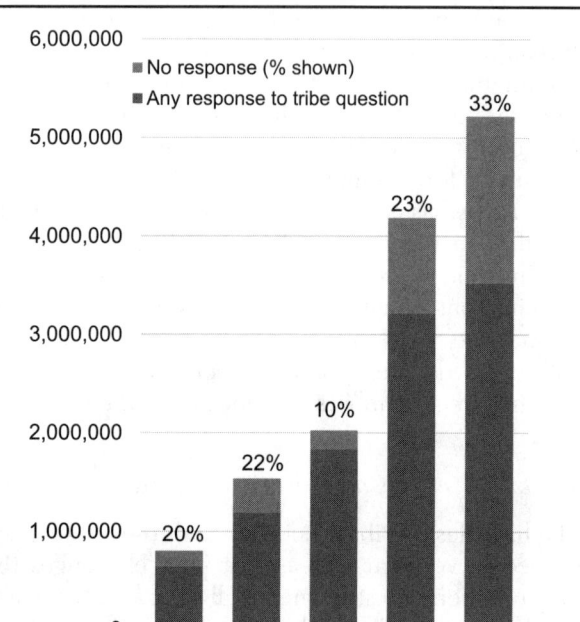

NOTE: Tribal nonresponse is less common among single-race respondents than multiple-race respondents (18 percent versus 30 percent in 2000 and 29 percent versus 37 percent in 2010).

from those who report AIAN race (Liebler 2010a; Snipp 1997); the ancestry question is tapping a different concept than the race question. Because there are so many more people who identify as having AIAN ancestry than there are racially identified AIAN people (discussed further below), the two concepts should not be mixed when creating or using data on AIANs.

Tribal affiliation or community attachment: Some concepts cannot be well captured in a questionnaire, such as the idea of "maintaining community attachment" from the federal definition (What does "attachment" mean? How much and what kind of maintenance are enough?).

A tribal identity is an important part of many people's AIAN identity, because language, symbols, history, and traditions vary by tribe, band, and village. Also, tribes are important because tribal sovereignty underlies the legal/political dimension of AIAN identity (see Robertson 2013).[7] Despite the general importance of tribe for AIAN identity, a substantial number and increasing proportion of racially identified AIANs do not report any tribal affiliation on the census. In Figure 2, I show the number of people reporting AIAN race in the census for the five censuses that included a tribal affiliation subquestion within the race question (1970–2010).[8] In 2010, about one-third of people who reported American Indian race did not give any answer at all in the boxes set aside for the respondent to "Print name of enrolled or principal tribe." As nonresponse increases, the usefulness of the information declines because the tribe information that *is* provided is from a nonrandom subsample of the total set of people affiliated with one or more tribes. See Liebler (2004) and Liebler and Zacher (2012) for more on tribal nonresponse.

Challenge: Race response change among people who ever report AIAN race

People (in all race groups) do not always keep the same race response for their entire lives (e.g., Harris and Sim 2002; Doyle and Kao 2007; Liebler et al. 2017). Thus, the set of individuals who self-identify as AIAN changes over time.[9] Response change into, and probably out of, the AIAN race response group has been going on for decades (e.g., Eschbach 1993; Liebler, Bhaskar, and Porter 2016; Liebler and Ortyl 2014; Passel 1976, 1997). Race response change can be seen even in cross-sectional data by comparing the number of people in one age/sex group to that same group a decade later (and 10 years older). For example, there were about 174,000 AIAN-race boys ages 10 to 19 in the 1980 census; and instead of this number decreasing due to deaths, 10 years later there were about 181,000 AIAN-race men ages 20 to 29. Another decade later, there were about 325,000 single- or multiple-race[10] AIAN men ages 30 to 39 (see Liebler and Ortyl [2014] for more 1990 to 2000 comparisons). This is an 86 percent net increase in population.

Because census data are cross-sectional unless linked post hoc, the amount of response change for the AIAN race response category was unknown until recently and is still being explored. Research using linked 2000 to 2010 census data shows that response change is more common among people who ever report AIAN race than it is among the larger race groups (Liebler et al. 2017). A person reported as single-race AIAN in 2000 or 2010 is often reported as multiple-race AIAN or reported as a different single race (usually white if they reported being non-Hispanic, and Some Other Race if they reported Hispanic origins) in the other year (Liebler, Bhaskar, and Porter 2016). Countervailing flows of response changes are similar in size, which hides the extent of response change in single-year data (Liebler, Bhaskar, and Porter 2016; Liebler et al. 2017). This means that comparing characteristics of the AIAN population in 2000 to the AIAN population in 2010 is like comparing the population of Minneapolis in 2000 to that in 2010—it is not safe to presume that you are comparing the same set of people. Some will be new and some will have left through processes of birth, in-migration, death, and out-migration. In the AIAN case, the in- and out-migrations are "mental migration" in the form of response change.

What the Census Data Do Tell Us about American Indians and Alaska Natives

The most comprehensive data available on AIAN people are from the U.S. Census, which has (separate) race, ancestry, tribe, and Hispanic ethnicity questions. Like all federally defined race groups, AIANs (as delineated by the census questions) are a diverse set of individuals. The various population subsets have substantially different average characteristics, which reveal different experiences and needs.

What we know from the intersection of race question responses and ancestry question responses

Research shows that people report their AIAN origins differently depending on whether they think they are being asked about their ancestry or their race. Many more people report AIAN ancestry than AIAN race. The number of people reporting AIAN race almost tripled between 1980 and 2000, growing from 1.539 million to 1.999 million to 4.319 million. In the same censuses, the number of people who reported AIAN ancestry but *not* AIAN race remained over 5 million (up to 7.1 million in 1990; see Liebler [2010a] and Gullickson and Morning [2011]). To give a more specific example: there were about 541,000 boys ages 10 to 19 in the 1980 census who were reported as having AIAN ancestry but a non-AIAN race—more than three times as many as were reported with AIAN race (about 174,000). With such a large population of ancestrally identified AIAN people relative to the racially identified population, even a small misunderstanding of race or ancestry question intentions could have serious consequences for data quality and usability to the extent that the ancestrally identified population is different than the racially identified population in substantively important ways.

Substantive differences indeed exist. Snipp (1989) and Liebler (2010a) have studied the intersection of AIAN race and ancestry responses in censuses, comparing, for example, the number and characteristics of people who report AIAN race to the number and characteristics of those who report AIAN ancestry but a different race (usually white or black). Both researchers showed clear, significant differences between groups. Ancestrally identified AIANs are, for example, more urban, more educated, and have higher incomes than racially identified AIANs in 1980–2000 (Liebler 2010a; Snipp 1989).

Another complexity involves the identity and self-identification of people with parents of different races. One might assume they would be reported as multiple-race. However, the federal definition prioritizes self-identification and the choice of how to report race and ancestry to the Census Bureau is in the hands of individuals and families. Using decennial census data from 1960 through 2010, I found that children of an AIAN parent and a non-AIAN parent were very likely to be reported as having one race and a consistent ancestry (AIAN *or* white *or* black), as opposed to being reported as multiple-race or one race and another ancestry (Liebler 2016). This pattern was distinct from patterns of identification for children in other interracial families.[11]

What we know from the intersection of race question responses and Hispanic ethnicity question responses

Hispanic AIANs are a small but growing group—they were 6 percent of the AIAN population in 1990 and 10 percent in 2000 (Liebler and Ortyl 2014, Table

S1). Some Hispanic AIANs are connected to indigenous communities in Spanish-speaking countries in South or Central America (Fox and Rivero-Salgado 2004). Others are descendants of unions between nonindigenous Hispanics and AIANs, whether long ago or recently. Previous research has not disaggregated these or other subpopulations of Hispanic AIANs.

Response change is an important issue when looking at data for Hispanic AIANs. In 2000, the Hispanic AIAN population size was two and a half times the expected size based on 1990 data—the largest increase in any race/ethnic group (Liebler and Ortyl 2014, Table S1). Linked 2000–2010 census data show that Hispanic AIANs were much more likely than non-Hispanic AIANs to change their race response across years (usually to/from Hispanic white or Hispanic Some Other Race; Liebler, Bhaskar, and Porter 2016).

What we know from the tribe subquestion response and nonresponse

AIANs have had a subquestion within the race question since 1970, asking (with varying wording) for their enrolled or principal tribe. The Census Bureau has tabulated tribe data with varying detail over the decades, although not all people answer this question, as Figure 2 illustrates. Most recently, a very detailed list of tribes has been publicly available for one subset of people—those who report only AIAN race and only one tribe. If the person reported multiple races or multiple tribes, detail is available in restricted-use microdata and in public premade tables.

Beyond its usefulness in terms of content, my research results show that there is a benefit of asking the tribal affiliation question because of how it helps disaggregate the AIAN population and allows for a more nuanced understanding of AIAN subpopulations. Giving any answer at all to the tribal affiliation question is correlated with other indicators of a connection or "thick ties" to AIAN communities (Cornell and Hartmann 2007). For example, I found that in the 1990 U.S. Census, a tribal affiliation response was more common among AIANs who spoke an AIAN language or lived in a state with a long-standing, large number of AIANs (Liebler 2004; Liebler and Zacher 2012). Interracially married AIANs who reported a tribe were more likely to report their mixed-heritage children as single-race AIAN in 2000 (Liebler 2010b). Also, those who reported a tribe were more likely to give the same race response in both 2000 and 2010 (Liebler, Bhaskar, and Porter 2016).

Nonresponse to the tribe question in 1990 was most common for "Hispanic women with low education who report no American Indian ancestry, do not live with other American Indians, and live in a metropolitan area of a 'non-Indian state'" (Liebler 2004, 310). The 2000 Census shows similar results (Liebler and Zacher 2012). Other factors predictive of tribal nonresponse are associated with survey item nonresponse that undermines all fill-in-the-blank questions (e.g., urban, large household, very old person, and/or uses a non-English language).

Better Counts of American Indians and Alaska Natives

The issues outlined here (and others discussed by Lujan 2014) might be addressed in a few ways. With training and resources, tribes could undertake high-quality censuses of the people in their populations. This would give a clear delineation of those populations (e.g., tribal members, their households, and their descendants) and would presumably address many undercount issues.

Data sovereignty for AIAN tribes is important for all data collection efforts because it has the potential to increase data quality and may be mandated by modern standards of rights and ethics.[12] AIAN data sovereignty would increase if AIAN individuals and tribes had more control over how data are collected and owned, as well as access to and support for research projects (see Kukutai and Taylor 2016). For example, outsiders collecting data on tribal land should partner with tribes from the outset of data collection efforts (at the design stage) to ensure that data collected for tribes are maximally useful to tribes themselves, then cooperate with the tribe to arrange ethical data access.

Within a project such as the census—one that has broad coverage and inclusive conceptions of "who is AIAN"—conceptualization and question wording are important for understanding and disaggregating the populations involved. There should be a clear separation between the concepts of race, ancestry, and tribal affiliation so that people with AIAN origins can figure out how to convey their self-identification clearly.

For both scientific and ethical reasons, researchers working with these data should work through complexities involved in defining the population and analysis of small population sizes so that they can include AIAN respondents in their research results. Excluding a subpopulation gives an incomplete picture of a social situation and unfairly removes the opportunity for the group to benefit from the results of the study. AIANs deserve full inclusion in the benefits of census enumeration (e.g., allocated funds) and studies aimed at understanding or improving society. With attention to questionnaire details and cooperation with the people themselves, we can make great progress in this direction.

Notes

1. Data sovereignty is the right of a sovereign nation to govern its own data in terms of collection, ownership, and application. The U.S. Indigenous Data Sovereignty Network (http://usindigenousdata.arizona.edu/) advocates for this right for American Indians and Alaska Natives, and the International Indigenous Data Sovereignty Interest Group within the Research Data Alliance has a broader scope. Also see Kukutai and Taylor (2016).

2. See Lujan (2104, 324) for additional ways to answer: "Who is AIAN?" See Roth (2016) for a broader discussion of dimensions of race and ethnicity.

3. See https://www.archives.gov/research/native-americans/dawes/tutorial/intro.html.

4. See https://www.bia.gov/WhoWeAre/AS-IA/OFA/.

5. NCAI highlights many data quality issues: http://www.ncai.org/policy-research-center/initiatives/data-quality.

6. The Belmont Report (National Commission for the Protection of Human Subjects of Biomedical and Behavioral Research 1978) explains more about this principle.

7. The National Congress of American Indians objected to a potential census question about tribal enrollment in part because of issues of tribal sovereignty; see NCAI (2016).

8. The wording of the race question has changed over the period (starting in 2000: inviting multiple race responses and AIAN identification by Central and South American indigenous people), and the tribal affiliation subquestion has also changed wording.

9. When American Indians were first included in censuses (mid-1800s), the race reported for those with mixed white and American Indian heritage depended on where the person lived (with whites or with American Indians). See Lujan (2014).

10. A person who was reported as AIAN in 1990 could have reported single-race or multiple-race AIAN, or a different race entirely, in 2000; see Liebler and Ortyl (2014).

11. Note that other interracial families have often used the ancestry and race questions together to report a child as mixed-heritage, both before and during the era when multiple race responses were invited (Liebler 2016).

12. For example, the United Nations Declaration on the Rights of Indigenous People (United Nations 2008) articles 4 and 5 emphasize rights to self-government and autonomy, both of which require appropriate data collection. Tribes may be in a better position than outside researchers to apply relevant ethical principles so as to minimize the risk of harm, have fair subject selection, and be sure the research has social value.

References

Cornell, Stephen, and Douglas Hartmann. 2007. *Ethnicity and race: Making identities in a changing world*. 2nd ed. Thousand Oaks, CA: Sage Publications.

Doyle, Jamie M., and Grace Kao. 2007. Are racial identities of multiracials stable? Changing self-identification among single and multiple race individuals. *Social Psychology Quarterly* 70 (4): 405–23.

Eschbach, Karl. 1993. Changing identification among American Indians and Alaska Natives. *Demography* 30 (4): 635–52.

Fallica, Heather, Sarah Heimel, Geoff Jackson, and Bei Zhang. 2012. *2010 Census update enumerate operations assessment: Update enumerate production, update enumerate quality control, remote update enumerate, and remote Alaska*. 2010 Census Program for Evaluations and Experiments. Washington, DC: U.S. Census Bureau.

Fox, Jonathan, and Gaspar Rivera-Salgado, eds. 2004. *Indigenous Mexican migrants in the United States*. Boulder, CO: Lynne Rienner Publishers.

Gullickson, Aaron, and Ann Morning. 2011. Choosing race: Multiracial ancestry and identification. *Social Science Research* 40:498–512.

Harris, David, and Jeremiah Joseph Sim. 2002. Who is multiracial? Assessing the complexity of lived race. *American Sociological Review* 67 (4): 614–27.

Iceland, John, Daniel H. Weinberg, and Erika Steinmetz. 2002. *Racial and ethnic residential segregation in the United States 1980–2000*. U.S. Census Bureau Series CENSR 3. Washington, DC: U.S. Government Printing Office.

Keeler, Kasey R. 2016. Indigenous suburbs: Settler colonialism, housing policy, and the erasure of American Indians from suburbia. PhD diss., University of Minnesota.

Kukutai, Tahu, and John Taylor, eds. 2016. *Indigenous data sovereignty: Toward an agenda*. Canberra, Australia: Australian National University Press.

Liebler, Carolyn A. 2004. American Indian ethnic identity: Tribal nonresponse in the 1990 Census. *Social Science Quarterly* 85 (2): 310–23.

Liebler, Carolyn A. 2010a. A group in flux: Multiracial American Indians and the social construction of race. In *Multiracial Americans and social class*, ed. Kathleen O. Korgen, 131–44. New York, NY: Routledge Press.

Liebler, Carolyn A. 2010b. Homelands and indigenous identities in a multiracial era. *Social Science Research* 39:596–609.

Liebler, Carolyn A. 2016. On the boundaries of race: Identification of mixed-heritage children in the U.S., 1960 to 2010. *Sociology of Race and Ethnicity* 2 (4): 548–68.

Liebler, Carolyn A., Renuka Bhaskar, and Sonya R. Porter. 2016. Dynamics of race: Joining, leaving, and staying in the American Indian/Alaska Native race category between 2000 and 2010. *Demography* 53 (2): 507–40.

Liebler, Carolyn A., and Timothy Ortyl. 2014. More than one million new American Indians in 2000: Who are they? *Demography* 51 (3): 1101–30.

Liebler, Carolyn A., Sonya R. Porter, Leticia E. Fernandez, James M. Noon, and Sharon R. Ennis. 2017. America's churning races: Race and ethnic response changes between Census 2000 and the 2010 census. *Demography* 54 (1): 259–84.
Liebler, Carolyn A., and Meghan Zacher. 2012. American Indians without tribes in the twenty-first century. *Ethnic and Racial Studies* 36:1910–34.
Lujan, Carol Chiago. 2014. American Indians and Alaska Natives count: The U.S. Census Bureau's efforts to enumerate the Native population. *American Indian Quarterly* 38:319–41.
National Commission for the Protection of Human Subjects of Biomedical and Behavioral Research. 1978. *The Belmont report: Ethical principles and guidelines for the protection of human subjects of research.* Bethesda, MD: National Commission.
National Congress of American Indians (NCAI). 2016. *The National Congress of American Indians Resolution #SPO-16-043: Opposing the use of a question on tribal enrollment in the 2020 Census or in the American Community Survey.* Washington, DC: NCAI.
Office of Management and Budget. 1997. Revisions to the standards for the classification of federal data on race and ethnicity. *Federal Register* 52 (210): 58782–90.
Passel, Jeffrey. 1976. Provisional evaluation of the 1970 census count of American Indians. *Demography* 13 (3): 397–409.
Passel, Jeffrey. 1997. The growing American Indian population, 1960–1990: Beyond demography. *Population Research and Policy Review* 16 (1–2): 11–31.
Porter, Sonya R., Carolyn A. Liebler, and James Noon. 2016. An outside view: What observers say about others' races and Hispanic origins. *American Behavioral Scientist* 60 (4): 465–97.
Robertson, Dwanna L. 2013. A necessary evil: Framing an American Indian legal identity. *American Indian Culture and Research Journal* 37 (4): 115–40.
Roth, Wendy. 2016. The multiple dimensions of race. *Ethnic and Racial Studies* 39 (8): 1310–38.
Snipp, C. Matthew. 1989. *American Indians: The first of this land.* New York, NY: Russell Sage Foundation.
Snipp, C. Matthew. 1997. Some observations about racial boundaries and the experiences of American Indians. *Ethnic and Racial Studies* 20:668–89.
Thornton, Russell. 1997. Tribal membership requirements and the demography of "old" and "new" Native Americans. *Population Research and Policy Review* 16 (1–2): 33–42.
United Nations. 2008. *United Nations declaration on the rights of indigenous peoples. 07-58681.* New York, NY: United Nations. Available from http://www.un.org/esa/socdev/unpfii/documents/DRIPS_en.pdf.
U.S. Census Bureau. 2015. *Tribal consultation handbook: Background materials for tribal consultations on the 2020 census.* Washington, DC: U.S. Census Bureau.
U.S. Census Bureau. n.d. *The 2010 census American Indian / Alaska Native Consultations.* Washington, DC: U.S. Census Bureau.
Walker, Shelley, Susanna Winder, Geoff Jackson, and Sarah Heimel. 2012. *2010 census non-response follow-up operations assessment.* 2010 Census Planning Memoranda Series, No. 190. Washington, DC: U.S. Census Bureau.
Williams, Jennifer D. 2011. *The 2010 Decennial Census: Background and issues.* Washington, DC: Congressional Research Service.

Accurately Counting Asian Americans Is a Civil Rights Issue

By
JENNIFER LEE,
KARTHICK
RAMAKRISHNAN,
and
JANELLE WONG

Asian Americans are the fastest-growing group in the United States, increasing from 0.7 percent in 1970 to nearly 6 percent in 2016. The U.S. Census Bureau projects that by 2065, Asian Americans will constitute 14 percent of the U.S. population. Immigration is fueling this growth: China and India have passed Mexico as the top countries sending immigrants to the United States since 2013. Today, two of three Asian Americans are foreign born—a figure that increases to nearly four of five among Asian American adults. The rise in numbers is accompanied by a rise in diversity: Asian Americans are the most diverse U.S. racial group, comprising twenty-four detailed origins with vastly different migration histories and socioeconomic profiles. In this article, we explain how the unique characteristics of Asian Americans affect their patterns of ethnic and racial self-identification, which, in turn, present challenges for accurately counting this population. We conclude by discussing policy ramifications of our findings, and explain why data disaggregation is a civil rights issue.

Keywords: Asian Americans; immigration; race; ethnicity; identity; civil rights

Asian Americans are the fastest-growing group in the United States, increasing from 0.7 percent in 1970 to nearly 6 percent in 2016.[1] The

Jennifer Lee is a professor of sociology at Columbia University. She is author or coauthor of four award-winning books: Civility in the City *(Harvard University Press 2002);* Asian American Youth *(Routledge 2004);* The Diversity Paradox *(Russell Sage Foundation 2010); and* The Asian American Achievement Paradox *(Russell Sage Foundation 2015). In her current project, she is studying how Asian ethnic groups cognitively construct the Asian American category, and how stereotypes affect group boundary formation and support for affirmative action policies.*

Karthick Ramakrishnan is a professor of public policy and political science at the University of California, Riverside, where he also serves as associate dean of the School of Public Policy and founding director of the Center for Social Innovation. He is director of the National Asian American Survey and founder of AAPIdata.com. He is the author, most recently, of The New Immigration Federalism *(Cambridge University Press 2015).*

Correspondence: lee.jennifer@columbia.edu

DOI: 10.1177/0002716218765432

U.S. Census Bureau projects that by 2065, Asian Americans will constitute about one of every seven U.S. residents, and Asian immigrants will compose the largest share (38 percent) of the foreign-born population. By contrast, Latino immigration is projected to drop to 31 percent of the total foreign-born. Since 2008, immigrants from Asia have made up the largest group of newcomers, and, since 2013, China and India have passed Mexico as the top sending countries for immigrants to the United States. The new face of U.S. immigration is Asian.

The rapid growth of Asian Americans, their majority foreign-born status, and tremendous socioeconomic diversity lead to unique patterns of ethnic and racial self-identification, which, in turn, present challenges to accurately counting this population. We discuss the best practices of counting Asian Americans, and pay particular attention to the significance of denoting national origin. Disaggregating the U.S. Asian population by national origin unveils the diverse experiences and outcomes among a group that is often perceived and studied as a monolith.

Comprising twenty-four detailed origins with vastly different migration histories, Asian Americans evince socioeconomic and political outcomes at both extremes of the spectrum, including educational attainment, median household income, health status, poverty levels, civic participation, and naturalization (Foner 2010; Kao and Tienda 1998; Kasinitz et al. 2008; Kibria 2003; Louie 2004; Min 2005; Portes and Rumbaut 2006; Ramakrishnan et al. 2012; Ramakrishnan and Shah 2017; Wong 2018; Wong et al. 2011; Zhou and Bankston 1998). For example, Indians, Chinese, and Koreans attain higher levels of education than all other U.S. groups, including native-born whites (Lee and Zhou 2015). By contrast, Cambodian, Laotian, and Hmong are less likely to complete high school than African Americans and Latinos: 40 percent of Hmong Americans do not graduate from high school, and just 14 percent have a bachelor's degree—half the national average (Ramakrishnan and Ahmad 2014).

While diversity is a hallmark of Asian Americans, it is too often eclipsed by the model minority trope, which frames Asian Americans as a homogeneous, high-achieving group. Not only is this inaccurate, but it is also detrimental, particularly for Asian ethnic groups whose experiences and outcomes do not fit this narrative (Fernández-Kelly 2016; Hsin 2016; Jiménez 2016; Lee and Zhou 2016; Tran 2016). Without an accurate and detailed count of the size, growth, and diversity of the U.S. Asian-origin population, this narrative will endure, and disadvantaged Asian ethnic groups will continue to remain invisible. Consequently, Asian Americans who direly need resources to facilitate immigrant and second-generation integration and mobility will be excluded from public policies aimed to improve socioeconomic outcomes.

Janelle Wong is a professor of American studies and Asian American studies at the University of Maryland. She is author of Immigrants, Evangelicals, and Politics in an Era of Demographic Change *(Russell Sage Foundation 2018) and* Democracy's Promise: Immigrants and American Civic Institutions *(University of Michigan Press 2006), and coauthor of two books on Asian American politics.*

NOTE: We thank the National Science Foundation (Award No: 1558986) and the Russell Sage Foundation (Award No: 93-17-07) for providing generous support for this research.

We begin this article by highlighting the unique characteristics of the Asian American population. Second, we explain why Asian Americans are more likely to identify by national origin or ethnicity than by race. For example, we explain why an individual of Korean, Indian, or Chinese origin is more likely to identify as Korean, Indian, or Chinese, respectively, than they are to identify as Asian or Asian American on the U.S. census. Third, we underscore the linguistic diversity of U.S. Asians, and unveil surprisingly high rates of limited English proficiency (LEP) and linguistic isolation, which can lead to undercounting the Asian American population. Fourth, we show how different methods of measuring ethnicity and race by the U.S. census affect the accuracy of counting this diverse population. We close by explaining why accurately counting Asian Americans—including counting by national origin—is essential to the equitable allocation of federal, state, and local funding for America's fastest growing, most diverse group.

Unique Asian American Characteristics

Three distinguishing features of the Asian-origin population are germane for considering how to best count Asian Americans, including improving ethnic, racial, and immigration statistics by the 2020 U.S. Census. First, unlike other U.S. racial groups, most Asian Americans are foreign born; two out of every three were born outside the United States—a figure that jumps to nearly four in five among Asian American adults. Second, immigration continues to be the primary driver of Asian American growth, with 61 percent of the population increase due to international migration, compared to only 22 percent for Latinos. Third, their majority foreign-born status coupled with their diversity—with respect to national origin, ethnicity, socioeconomic status, and English language proficiency—affect patterns of ethnic and racial identification differently from other U.S. groups.

Asian Americans are more likely to identify by national origin than by race

Surveys consistently show that Asian Americans are significantly more likely to identify with their national origin than their race. For example, in the 2000–2001 Pilot National Asian American Politics Survey, two-thirds of respondents identified with national origin, while only about one-fifth self-identified as Asian or Asian American (Lien, Conway, and Wong 2003). Similarly, data from the 2008 National Asian American Survey (NAAS)—a nationally representative academic survey of Asian Americans—indicate that about 75 percent identified with an ethnic group, while 33 percent identified as Asian or Asian American (Wong et al. 2011). Results from the 2012 NAAS showed even higher rates of national origin identification at 84 percent, compared to 19 percent who identified by their race. Both the 2008 and 2012 NAAS allowed respondents to self-identify with more than one category including Asian and Asian American, as well as by ethnic group (e.g., Chinese and Chinese American).

Finally, surveys that ask respondents to self-identify into mutually exclusive categories such as "Chinese/Chinese American" or "Asian/Asian American" also reveal the primacy of national origin over race: the 2012 Pew Survey of Asian Americans found that only 19 percent self-identified as Asian or Asian Americans, while the 2016 NAAS found that 21 percent self-identified with either of these panethnic labels. Thus, regardless of the survey and its question format, a clear picture emerges: Asian Americans are far more likely to identify with their national origin than with a panethnic racial label of Asian or Asian American.

Diversity among Asian Americans

That Asian Americans are more likely to identify by national origin than by race can be explained by two factors. First, the foreign born are more likely to identify by national origin or ethnicity than by race than native-born Americans (see also Imoagene 2017; Kasinitz et al. 2008; Portes and Rumbaut 2006; Waters 1999). What makes this especially germane for Asian Americans is that two-thirds are immigrants. Consequently, it comes as little surprise that Asian Americans (especially Asian immigrant adults) are less likely to identify with a U.S. racial category, and are significantly more likely to identify by ethnicity or national origin.

Second, Asian Americans are the most diverse racial group in the United States with respect to national origin, migration history, and socioeconomic and political status. While some arrive as poorly educated refugees from war-torn countries, others migrate through employer sponsored H-1B visas. The differences in migration histories manifest in socioeconomic outcomes at the extremes with respect to educational attainment, poverty levels, median household income, and political participation. For example, 72 percent of Asian Indians and 53 percent of Chinese hold a bachelor's degree or higher, yet less than 15 percent of Cambodian, Laotian, and Hmong can claim the same, as Figure 1 shows. In fact, the latter groups are much less likely than African Americans or Latinos to have high school degrees.

Asian Americans are also diverse with respect to immigrant status. About one in seven Asian immigrants is undocumented, and Asians now far outpace Mexicans and other Latinos with respect to the growth of undocumented immigrants (Ramakrishnan and Shah 2017). Thus, the diversity in national origins, migration histories, and socioeconomic and citizenship statuses further impede panethnic racial identification among Asian Americans (see also Alba, Jiménez, and Marrow 2014; Mora 2014; Okamoto and Mora 2014; Wimmer 2008).

Linguistic diversity, LEP, and linguistic isolation

Yet another hallmark of the Asian American population is its linguistic diversity and limited English language proficiency (LEP). The latter is relevant both because English language proficiency is significantly related to life outcomes

FIGURE 1
Bachelor's Degree or Higher among Asian Americans by Detailed Origin

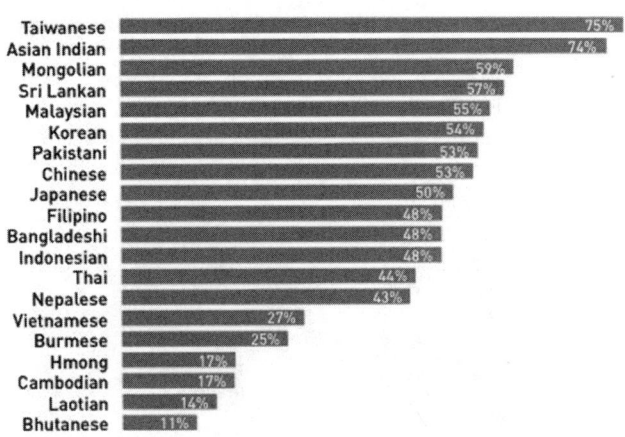

SOURCE: 2015 American Community Survey microdata.

(such as earnings, occupational status, social mobility, quality of health care, health outcomes, and the ability to participate in civic and political life), and because LEP has implications for how to most accurately count this population. In fact, Asian Americans have the highest rates of LEP of all U.S. racial groups. As Figure 2 shows, LEP rates vary by detailed origin among Asian American groups, ranging from a high of 77 and 78 percent among Burmese and Bhutanese, respectively, to a low of 27 percent for Asian Indians.

The Census Bureau categorizes someone as having LEP if they speak a language other than English at home and they speak English "less than very well." Using this definition, 35 percent of the Asian population has LEP—with 4 percent not speaking English at all, 12 percent speaking English "not well," and 19 percent speaking English "well" but short of "very well." The overall LEP figures among Asian Americans are on par with LEP rates among Latinos. Not surprisingly, nativity bears a strong relationship to English proficiency, as only 9 percent of the native-born "Asian alone" population has LEP, while the comparable figure for the foreign-born "Asian alone" population reaches 47 percent.[2]

Compared with other racial groups, Asian Americans also exhibit the highest proportion of residents who speak a language other than English at home. More than three-quarters (77 percent) of the Asian alone population speaks a language other than English at home, a figure that drops to 70 percent when we include Asian "alone or in combination with other races." By comparison, 75 percent of Latinos speak a non-English language at home, as do 43 percent of Native Hawaiians and Pacific Islanders (NHPIs), and 28 percent of American Indians and Alaska Natives.

FIGURE 2
Limited English Proficiency among Asian Americans by Detailed Origin

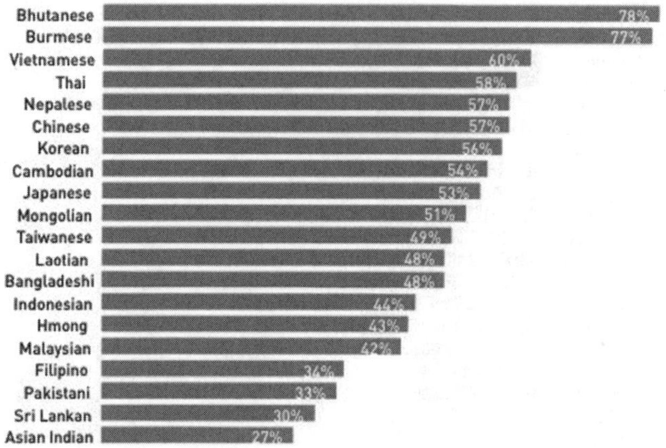

Origin	%
Bhutanese	78%
Burmese	77%
Vietnamese	60%
Thai	58%
Nepalese	57%
Chinese	57%
Korean	56%
Cambodian	54%
Japanese	53%
Mongolian	51%
Taiwanese	49%
Laotian	48%
Bangladeshi	48%
Indonesian	44%
Hmong	43%
Malaysian	42%
Filipino	36%
Pakistani	33%
Sri Lankan	30%
Asian Indian	27%

SOURCE: 2015 American Community Survey microdata.

In addition to English proficiency at the individual level, the Census Bureau also measures the extent to which households are *linguistically isolated*—meaning that there is no one in the household who is 14 years or older who speaks English exclusively or "very well." About one in every five Asian American households is linguistically isolated. This proportion is similar to the linguistic isolation among Hispanic or Latino households, and considerably higher than the proportion of NHPI households, at 6 percent, and white households at 4 percent.

Summing up, Asian Americans are significantly less likely to identify with a U.S. racial category than by their national origin. In addition, more than one-third of Asian Americans is limited English proficient, and one in five Asian American households is linguistically isolated—features that exacerbate the linguistic disadvantage for this racial group. Combined, these factors, along with their majority foreign-born status, present unique challenges to accurately counting the U.S. Asian population.

Implications for Counting Asian Americans by the U.S. Census

The goals of the U.S. census are threefold regarding collecting data on race and ethnicity in 2020: (1) increase reporting, (2) lower nonresponse rates, and (3) increase detailed reporting to more accurately reflect reporting on race and ethnicity. To achieve these goals, the U.S. Census Bureau has tested questionnaire formats and designs since the decennial census of 2010. Of most interest and concern to Asian Americans is a potential change to the ways in which individuals will report detailed-origin groups (such as "Cambodian" or "Vietnamese") under

FIGURE 3
Traditional "Checkbox" Format for Capturing Asian Detailed Origin

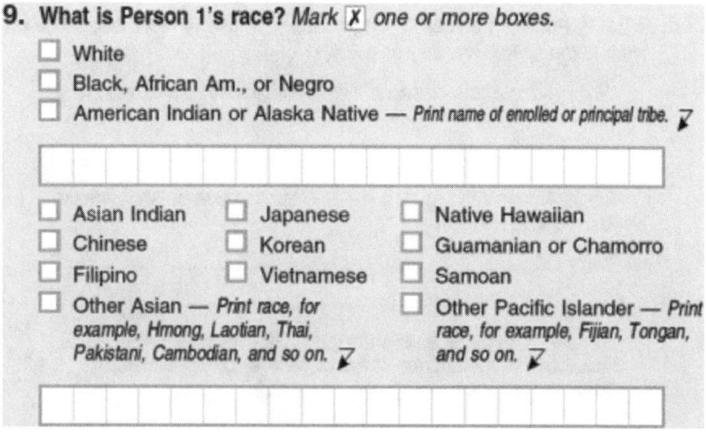

9. What is Person 1's race? *Mark ⊠ one or more boxes.*
- ☐ White
- ☐ Black, African Am., or Negro
- ☐ American Indian or Alaska Native — *Print name of enrolled or principal tribe.* ⇩

```
[                                                    ]
```

- ☐ Asian Indian   ☐ Japanese   ☐ Native Hawaiian
- ☐ Chinese   ☐ Korean   ☐ Guamanian or Chamorro
- ☐ Filipino   ☐ Vietnamese   ☐ Samoan
- ☐ Other Asian — *Print race, for example, Hmong, Laotian, Thai, Pakistani, Cambodian, and so on.* ⇩   ☐ Other Pacific Islander — *Print race, for example, Fijian, Tongan, and so on.* ⇩

```
[                                                    ]
```

SOURCE: U.S. Census.

the broader racial category of Asian. As part of their testing in 2010 and 2015, the census compared two options: a traditional format; and an alternative format.

The traditional format included a "check box" design, for which Asian Americans were offered a range of possible detailed origin groups to check off (see Figure 3). This format is a continuation from 2000 and 2010.

By contrast, the alternative format includes a "write-in" design, offering only a panethnic racial label, with a write-in option to specify detailed origin (see Figure 4). The alternative format was proposed as a way to provide more simplicity and uniformity across racial groups.

Asian American researchers (including Lee, Ramakrishnan, and Wong) underscored in meetings with census officials that the primary goal of racial identification in the U.S. census is to ensure the optimal allocation of resources based on dimensions of racial categories that are materially salient, such as educational attainment, poverty, and residential segregation. Thus, for example, measurement error in the number of whites who identify as Welsh in the United States is far less consequential than in the counts of Laotians, Cambodians, and Hmong in particular cities and counties, where public investments in language assistance and other targeted programs are at stake. Finally, as noted earlier, the uniformity of racial categories on census forms (and other government forms) is at odds with three primary goals of the U.S. census: increasing response rates, decreasing nonreponse rates, and increasing detailed reporting.

When the alternative question experiment was proposed, the presumption was that detailed-origin reporting among whites and blacks would increase because these groups had not been provided such an option before. It was not clear how much detailed-origin reporting among Asian Americans would be

FIGURE 4
Alternative Format for Race and Ethnicity Reporting: Streamlined Write-In

> **8. What is Person 1's race or origin?** *Mark ☒ one or more boxes AND write in the specific race(s) or origin(s).*
>
> ☐ White — *Print origin(s), for example, German, Irish, Lebanese, Egyptian, and so on.* ↙
>
> ☐ Black, African Am., or Negro — *Print origin(s), for example, African American, Haitian, Nigerian, and so on.* ↙
>
> ☐ Hispanic, Latino, or Spanish origin — *Print origin(s), for example, Mexican, Mexican Am., Puerto Rican, Cuban, Argentinean, Colombian, Dominican, Nicaraguan, Salvadoran, Spaniard, and so on.* ↙
>
> ☐ American Indian or Alaska Native — *Print name of enrolled or principal tribe(s), for example, Navajo, Mayan, Tlingit, and so on.* ↙
>
> ☐ Asian — *Print origin(s), for example, Asian Indian, Chinese, Filipino, Japanese, Korean, Vietnamese, Hmong, Laotian, Thai, Pakistani, Cambodian, and so on.* ↙
>
> ☐ Native Hawaiian or Other Pacific Islander — *Print origin(s), for example, Native Hawaiian, Guamanian or Chamorro, Samoan, Fijian, Tongan, and so on.* ↙
>
> ☐ Some other race or origin — *Print race(s) or origin(s).* ↙
>
> → **If more people were counted in Question 1, continue with Person 2.**

SOURCE: U.S. Census.

affected. Prior testing of a write-in strategy for Asian Americans found, however, declines in detailed-origin reporting related to factors such as LEP when only provided an open-ended write-in option to denote their national origin (Compton et al. 2013).

2010 Census Alternative Questionnaire Experiments (AQE) and 2015 National Content Test (NCT)

Two of the Census Bureau's most recent tests—the 2010 Census Alternative Questionnaire Experiments (AQE) and the 2015 National Content Test (NCT)—produced similar results for the U.S. Asian-origin population: Asian Americans are more likely to respond to (and provide national origin responses to) census questions when they are offered check boxes in combination with a write-in option (Jones and Bentley 2017; Mathews et al. 2017). Furthermore, both experiments confirmed that eliminating check boxes has clearly negative effects on detailed-origin reporting among the groups whose categories were removed. While alphabetizing examples used to illustrate Asian American detailed race groups without check boxes had little impact on response, removing a group from the list of examples significantly reduced reporting for that group.

Moreover, the alternative, streamlined format with write-in categories, yielded the lowest national origin reporting among Asian Americans of any format tested. The results from the 2010 AQE, for example, show wide variation in the rate of detailed reporting among Asian Americans from a high of 97.4 percent when Asian Americans are provided both check boxes for detailed origin as well as a write-in option, to a low of 92.6 percent when they are only provided a write-in option to denote detailed origin. While these differences in reporting may appear minimal at first glance, every percentage point of nonreporting represents the loss of data for close to 200,000 people. In addition, the combined question with detailed check boxes elicited the highest level of reporting for all racial groups tested, not just for Asian Americans.

Finally, providing detailed origin check boxes with a write-in option produced the most consistency between self-reported race and ethnicity in re-interviews, and is also the most consistent way of comparing counts of the Asian American population from 2000 and 2010. Consistency is critical to measuring progress and change, especially among rapidly growing Asian subgroups. Given these considerations, our analyses support the recommendation made by the U.S. Census Bureau: the detailed checkbox format with a write-in option is the most optimal format for the 2020 Census (see Jones and Bentley 2017; Mathews et al. 2017).

Discussion and Conclusions

Because two-thirds of the Asian American population is foreign born—a figure that reaches four-fifths among adults—Asian Americans are more likely to identify by national origin or ethnicity than by the panethnic Asian U.S. racial category. Furthermore, given the socioeconomic and linguistic diversity, coupled with high rates of LEP and linguistic isolation, Asian Americans are more likely to complete a census form (or other government forms) when they are provided with check boxes to denote their national origin combined with a write-in option. Not only does the check box plus write-in option increase response rates, but it also decreases the likelihood of nonreporting among Asian Americans and increases the likelihood of detailed reporting of national origins—the three main goals of the U.S. Census Bureau.

Collecting and reporting detailed national origin data among Asian Americans are critical for better designing federal policies and more equitably allocating federal resources, especially for members of disadvantaged Asian ethnic groups. For example, public hospitals in smaller-population counties would need a detailed count of their Asian populations to better understand the costs and benefits of providing translation services in Vietnamese, Korean, and other Asian ethnic languages. Similarly, an accurate count by national origin is essential to get the appropriate language access under Section 203 of the Voting Rights Act, which ensures that all U.S. citizens may access ballots, materials, and information about elections in a language other than English if needed. This is especially important for Asian ethnic groups who have high rates of LEP and are linguistically isolated.

Data disaggregation is also essential to identify health, educational, and economic disparities among Asian ethnic groups—a need reflected in California Governor Jerry Brown's signing of Assembly Bill (AB) 1726 into law on September 25, 2016. Spearheaded by Assembly member Rob Bonta (D-Oakland), AB 1726 directs the California Department of Public Health to collect and report disaggregated data by national origin for Asian Americans, Native Hawaiians, and Pacific Islanders on or after July 1, 2022. The University of California (UC) and California State University (CSU) have already agreed to voluntarily release disaggregated data by ethnicity on admissions, enrollment, completion, and graduation rates, which highlight the extreme diversity among Asian American students on each of these measures.

Asian American community groups hailed AB 1726 as a civil rights victory because it will help to improve the overall health, educational, and economic outcomes of Asian Americans. By requiring the Department of Public Health to disaggregate the data that it collects and reports on disease rates, health insurance coverage rates, and birth and death rates, it will allow policy-makers and community organizations to make more informed decisions about how best to serve all Asian Americans. For example, some Asian ethnic groups are more susceptible to certain health risks than others: Vietnamese men and women experience the highest rates of lung cancer among all Asian American subgroups, while Asian Indians and Pakistanis experience the lowest. Japanese and Korean men and women experience some of the highest incidences of colorectal cancer rates—about three times as high as Asian Indians and Pakistanis, according to the American Cancer Society (2016). This type of disaggregated data is necessary to identify particular health risks among Asian subgroups.

In addition, through data disaggregation, we will better understand where to target resources for outreach programs on health care access, which also varies widely among Asian ethnic groups. While 13 percent of Asian Americans lack health insurance, the rate is much higher for Koreans at 20 percent, and less than half for Japanese at 6 percent (Shah and Ramakrishnan 2017). Hence, disaggregated data are critical for health intervention and the improvement of health outcomes for Asian Americans, which can mean the difference between life and death.

Other groups, including advocates for black and Latino communities, have pressed the U.S. Census Bureau to collect detailed data on their groups as well, so that the needs of smaller ethnic groups become more visible. Whites, blacks, and Native Americans will have the option to write in their ethnicity in the upcoming 2020 census, enabling a more detailed count of these populations. Therefore, Asian Americans are not alone in their call for the collection of detailed data, but they have been leaders in this policy area.

Laws such as California's AB 1726 will provide critical data to ensure that public policy is responsive to all Asian Americans. This is especially important because the dominant narrative of Asian Americans is the model minority, which has resulted in the invisibility of disadvantaged Asian ethnic groups. It has also resulted in the exclusion of Asian Americans from policy debates and the denial of federal resources that are essential to immigrant and second-generation integration and mobility. The accuracy of counting Asian Americans—including detailed counting by national origin—is a civil rights issue; it is essential to the equitable allocation of federal, state, and local funding for America's fastest-growing, most diverse group.

Notes

1. The 2016 figure is "Asian alone" or in combination with one or more other races; see http://factfinder.census.gov/bkmk/table/1.0/en/ACS/15_1YR/B02011.

2. The "Asian alone" population refers to those who mark only an Asian ethnic category on the U.S. census. It does not include those who mark an Asian ethnic category in combination with another race. Gender differences also emerge in rates of LEP: at 48 percent, the LEP rate is slightly higher among first-generation Asian immigrant women than among first-generation men, at 45 percent.

References

Alba, Richard, Tomás R. Jiménez, and Helen Marrow. 2014. Mexican Americans as a paradigm for contemporary intragroup heterogeneity. *Ethnic and Racial Studies* 37 (3): 446–66.

American Cancer Society. 2016. *Special section: Cancer among Asian Americans, Native Hawaiians, and Pacific Islanders*. Available from https://www.cancer.org/content/dam/cancer-org/research/cancer-facts-and-statistics/annual-cancer-facts-and-figures/2016/special-section-cancer-in-asian-americans-native-hawaiians-and-pacific-islanders-cancer-facts-and-figures-2016.pdf.

Compton, Elizabeth, Michael Bentley, Sharon Ennis, and Sonya Rastogi. 2013. *2010 Census race and Hispanic origin alternative questionnaire experiment final report*. Washington, DC: U.S. Census Bureau. Available from https://www.census.gov/2010census/pdf/2010_Census_Race_HO_AQE.pdf.

Fernández-Kelly, Patricia. 2016. Fixing the cultural fallacy. *Ethnic and Racial Studies* 39 (13): 2372–78.

Foner, Nancy. 2010. Questions of success: Lessons from the last great immigration. In *Helping young refugees and immigrants succeed: Public policy, aid, and education*, eds. Gerhard Sonnert and Gerald Holton, 9–22. New York, NY: Palgrave.

Hsin, Amy. 2016. How selective migration enables socioeconomic mobility. *Ethnic and Racial Studies* 39 (13): 2379–84.

Imoagene, Onoso. 2017. *Beyond expectations*. Oakland, CA: University of California Press.

Jiménez, Tomás R. 2016. Bringing culture back in: The class origins and ethnoracial destinations of culture and achievement. *Ethnic and Racial Studies* 39 (13): 2385–90.

Jones, Nicholas A., and Michael Bentley. 2017. *Overview of 2015 national content test analysis report on race & ethnicity*. Washington, DC: U.S. Census Bureau. Available from https://www.census.gov/content/dam/Census/newsroom/press-kits/2017/2015nct_presentation_jones.pdf.

Kao, Grace, and Marta Tienda. 1998. Educational aspirations of minority youth. *American Journal of Education* 106:349–84.

Kasinitz, Philip, John H. Mollenkopf, Mary C. Waters, and Jennifer Holdaway. 2008. *Inheriting the City*. New York, NY: Russell Sage Foundation.

Kibria, Nazli. 2003. *Becoming Asian American: Second generation Chinese and Korean American identities*. Baltimore, MD: Johns Hopkins University Press.

Lee, Jennifer, and Min Zhou. 2015. *The Asian American achievement paradox*. New York, NY: Russell Sage Foundation.

Lee, Jennifer, and Min Zhou. 2016. Unraveling the link between culture and achievement. *Ethnic and Racial Studies* 39 (13): 2404–11.

Lien, Pei-te, Margaret Conway, and Janelle S. Wong. 2003. The contours and sources of ethnic identity choices among Asian Americans. *Social Science Quarterly* 84 (2): 461–81.

Louie, Vivian. 2004. *Compelled to excel: Immigration, education, and opportunity among Chinese Americans*. Stanford, CA: Stanford University Press.

Mathews, Kelly, Jessica Phelan, Nicholas A. Jones, Sarah Konya, Rachel Marks, Beverly M. Pratt, Julia Coombs, and Michael Bentley. 2017. *2015 National Content Test: Race and ethnicity analysis report*. Washington, DC: U.S. Census Bureau. Available from https://www.census.gov/programs-surveys/decennial-census/2020-census-planning-management/final-analysis/2015nct-race-ethnicity-analysis.html.

Min, Pyong Gap, ed. 2005. *Asian Americans: Contemporary trends and issues*. Thousand Oaks, CA: Sage Publications.

Mora, G. Cristina. 2014. Cross-field effects and ethnic classification: The institutionalization of Hispanic panethnicity, 1965 to 1990. *American Sociological Review* 79 (2): 183–210.

Okamoto, Dina, and G.Cristina Mora. 2014. Panethnicity. *Annual Review of Sociology* 40:219–39.

Portes, Alejandro, and Rubén G. Rumbaut. 2006. *Immigrant America: A portrait*. 3rd ed. Berkeley, CA: University of California Press.

Ramakrishnan, Karthick, and Farah Ahmad. 2014. *State of Asian Americans and Pacific Islanders*. Washington, DC: Center for American Progress. Available from http://aapidata.com/wp-content/uploads/2015/10/AAPIData-CAP-report.pdf.

Ramakrishnan, Karthick, and Sono Shah. 2017. One out of every 7 Asian immigrants is undocumented. *AAPIData*. Available from http://aapidata.com/blog/asian-undoc-1in7/.

Ramakrishnan, Karthick, Jane Junn, Taeku Lee, and Janelle Wong. 2012. National Asian American Survey, 2008 [Computer file]. ICPSR31481-v2. Ann Arbor, MI: Inter-university Consortium for Political and Social Research [distributor], 2012-07-19.

Shah, Sono, and Karthick Ramakrishnan. 2017. Why disaggregate? Disparities in AAPI health. Available from http://aapidata.com/blog/countmein-health-disparities/.

Tran, Van C. 2016. Ethnic culture and social mobility among second-generation Asian Americans. *Ethnic and Racial Studies* 39 (13): 2398–2403.

Waters, Mary C. 1999. *Black identities: West Indian immigrant dreams and American realities*. Cambridge, MA: Harvard University Press.

Wimmer, Andreas. 2008. The making and unmaking of ethnic boundaries: A multilevel process theory. *American Journal of Sociology* 113 (4): 970–1022.

Wong, Janelle S. 2018. *Immigrants, Evangelicals, and politics in an era of demographic change*. New York, NY: Russell Sage Foundation.

Wong, Janelle S., Karthick Ramakrishnan, Taeku Lee, and Jane Junn. 2011. *Asian American participation*. New York, NY: Russell Sage Foundation.

Zhou, Min, and Carl Bankston III. 1998. *Growing up American: How Vietnamese children adapt to life in the United States*. New York, NY: Russell Sage Foundation.

*IV: Some Ramifications
of Diversity*

Racial and Political Dynamics of an Approaching "Majority-Minority" United States

By
MAUREEN A. CRAIG,
JULIAN M. RUCKER,
and
JENNIFER A. RICHESON

Do demographic shifts in the racial composition of the United States promote positive changes in the nation's racial dynamics? Change in response to the nation's growing diversity is likely, but its direction and scope are less clear. This review integrates emerging social-scientific research that examines how Americans are responding to the projected changes in the racial/ethnic demographics of the United States. Specifically, we review recent empirical research that examines how exposure to information that the United States is becoming a "majority-minority" nation affects racial attitudes and several political outcomes (e.g., ideology, policy preferences), and the psychological mechanisms that give rise to those attitudes. We focus primarily on the reactions of members of the current dominant racial group (i.e., white Americans). We then consider important implications of these findings and propose essential questions for future research.

Keywords: majority-minority; demographic changes; racial/ethnic diversity; political ideology; racial attitudes

Shortly after the 2012 presidential election, pundits, strategists, and elected officials remarked that shifting societal racial demographics may have changed the electorate in favor of the Democratic Party for the foreseeable future (Center for American Progress 2012; Phillips 2016). Senator Lindsay Graham even commented that Republicans are "not generating enough angry white guys to stay in business for the long term" (Helderman and

Maureen A. Craig is an assistant professor of psychology at New York University. Her research focuses on how increasing diversity and stigma shape intergroup relations and political ideology.

Julian M. Rucker is a doctoral student in the social psychology program at Yale University. His research examines the psychological factors that influence perceptions of, and motivations to address, intergroup inequality across a variety of societal domains.

Correspondence: jennifer.richeson@yale.edu

DOI: 10.1177/0002716218766269

Cohen 2012), and the Republican Party autopsy on the election once again emphasized the need to reach out to racial and ethnic minority communities (Rubin 2013). Just four years later, of course, Donald Trump—the Republican nominee—largely rejected the recommendations of the autopsy, instead making direct and clear appeals to white American voters (Cheney 2016). Although Trump's election was certainly determined by many factors, it was, perhaps, due in part to largely unrecognized (at the time) social and political dynamics stemming from the very demographic shifts that had previously engendered enthusiasm among Democrats and pessimism among Republicans, namely, the increasing racial minority share of the national population.

The purpose of this review is to integrate the burgeoning literature on the psychological, social, and political implications of making salient projected changes in the racial/ethnic demographics of the United States. Specifically, we summarize extant empirical research on how exposure to information suggesting that white Americans are projected to become less than 50 percent of the national population around midcentury—the so-called "majority-minority" racial shift—affects racial attitudes and political outcomes such as ideology and policy preferences. We focus primarily on the reactions of members of the current dominant racial group; namely, non-Hispanic white Americans.[1] We then consider important implications of these findings and propose essential future directions for research.

Shifting Racial Demographics and Perceived Group Threat

The racial and ethnic diversity of the United States has been increasing for the past several decades (Pew Research Center 2015), a trend that is expected to continue. Indeed, recent U.S. census projections suggest that, somewhere between 2040 and 2050, the percentage of nonwhite Americans[2] in the United States will surpass that of white Americans—that is, white Americans will compose less than 50 percent of the population (U.S. Census Bureau 2015; but see Alba 2016). Since the late 1990s, media reports of this demographic shift and noteworthy milestones reflective of it—for instance, the year that the U.S. infant population became "majority-minority" (U.S. Census Bureau 2012)—have proliferated (see also Day 1996). It is in the wake of this deluge of information documenting what seems to be an inexorable march toward a "majority-minority" country that social scientists began to explore what (if any) effects this information may be having on the racial dynamics of the nation.

Jennifer A. Richeson is the Philip R. Allen Professor of Psychology and faculty fellow at the Institution for Social and Policy Studies at Yale University. Her broad research interests include the social and political dynamics of diversity, intergroup contact, and inequality.

NOTE: We are grateful for the generous feedback from Richard Alba, Kenneth Prewitt and the other participants of the Russell Sage Foundation meeting regarding racial, ethnic, and immigration statistics.

Although research on this topic is still quite young, this growing body of work finds clear evidence that many white Americans (i.e., the current racial majority) experience the impending "majority-minority" shift as a threat to their dominant (social, economic, political, and cultural) status. For instance, whites for whom a "majority-minority" future is made salient, compared with whites exposed to control information, express greater concern that their racial group's societal status in the country will decline compared with that of racial minorities (e.g., Outten et al. 2012; replicated in Craig and Richeson 2014a, 2014b, 2017b, forthcoming; see also Schildkraut and Marotta, forthcoming). Highlighting this demographic shift can also trigger more cultural threats, such as the concern that whites will no longer represent the prototypical "American" (Craig and Richeson 2017b; Danbold and Huo 2015; Zou and Cheryan 2018). In other words, salient information regarding a coming era in which whites are no longer more than 50 percent of the national population (despite remaining the largest single racial group) increases concern that the group may lose its place "at the top" of the societal racial, socioeconomic, and political status hierarchy and/or concern that the group will cease to be culturally dominant.

Shifting Racial Demographics and Intergroup Relations

Initial research examining the effects of making the "majority-minority" racial demographic shift salient for white Americans focused on the potential consequences for whites' intergroup attitudes and emotions. Given classic research noting the role of perceived threat from increasing racial/ethnic diversity in the promotion (or expression) of intergroup hostility (e.g., Blalock 1967; Blumer 1958), and research finding that white Americans who (mis)perceive greater national racial diversity tend also to hold more negative racial attitudes (e.g., Alba, Rumbaut, and Marotz 2005), it is perhaps of no surprise that salient anticipated societal demographic changes like the "majority-minority" shift also affect whites' intergroup attitudes. Indeed, experiments reveal that exposure to these anticipated changes results in increased feelings of anxiety and negative affect among white Americans (Burrow et al. 2014; Myers and Levy, this volume). Additional research finds that making anticipated national racial demographic changes salient leads both white Americans and white Canadians to express more anger and fear toward ethnic minorities and more sympathy for whites, compared with whites not exposed to these demographic shifts (Outten et al. 2012).

We have replicated and extended this work, finding that white Americans exposed to the racial shift information (relative to a number of control conditions) express greater preference for racial homophily in their social settings and interpersonal interactions, and have more negative evaluations of racial minority groups on both self-report and reaction-time measures (Craig and Richeson 2014a; see also Schildkraut and Marotta, forthcoming; Skinner and Cheadle 2016). Building on this work, Zou and Cheryan (2018) found similar effects among whites who are informed that their neighborhood will become "majority-minority" in the near future. Specifically, compared with whites who expected their neighborhood to stay majority-white, those who thought that another racial group (i.e., black, Latino, or Asian Americans) would become the majority reported being significantly more likely to move. Further, as alluded to previously, concerns about group status statistically mediated the effects of the future white minority (i.e., racial shift) information on whites' intergroup emotions, explicit racial attitudes, and desire to exit "majority-minority" neighborhoods (Craig and Richeson 2014a; Outten et al. 2012; Zou and Cheryan 2018).

In addition to the perceived threat to the socioeconomic and/or political status of the group, cultural threats in response to the declining white majority also engender racially exclusionary sentiments. Danbold and Huo (2015) found, for instance, that exposure to the projected racial demographic shift triggered fear that what it means to be the "prototypical American" will change. This cultural threat, in turn, reduced perceptions that ethnic diversity is valuable to American society and increased support for the idea that racial minorities should assimilate to mainstream American customs and practices. Similarly, Zou and Cheryan (2018) found that whites' intention to move out of their current neighborhood if it becomes majority Asian American (but, not majority black) was mediated by cultural threat—namely, the concern that foreign cultural practices will overtake white American practices in the community. Interestingly, cultural threat also seems to underlie whites' tendency to be more concerned about whites facing discrimination in a future "majority-minority" United States (Craig and Richeson 2017b).

In addition to these outcomes for intergroup emotions, attitudes, and perceptions, information about changing national racial demographics can elicit racial discrimination. Specifically, whites who read about the growth in the Hispanic population donated more money to an unknown white recipient, compared with an unknown black recipient (Abascal 2015). If nonracial information were made salient (i.e., iPhone market share growth), however, white participants donated equal amounts of money to black and white recipients. Taken together, this growing body of research suggests that communications about the changing racial demographics of the nation (or, even one's local community) readily trigger multiple concerns about the status, standing, and potential vulnerabilities of one's racial group among whites, which, in turn, promote increased favoritism toward the racial ingroup and derogation of relevant outgroups (i.e., racial minorities). In the next section, we explore the effects of these group status concerns on political outcomes.

Shifting Racial Demographics and Political Ideology, Preferences, and Behavior

Although the research on whites' reactions to anticipated racial diversity understandably began with explorations of intergroup attitudes and emotions, studies quickly moved to consider whether political ideology and behavior may also be shaped by this information. Given the rise in group status threat in response to exposure to the "majority-minority" shift information reviewed previously; the known influence of group status threat on political identity (e.g., Giles and Hertz 1994); and support for racial exclusionary policies designed to protect whites' political, economic, and social privileges (Blumer 1958; Bobo 1998; Parker and Barreto 2013), it is, again, unsurprising that highlighting this shift affects whites' political behavior (see also, Enos 2016). Indeed, whites for whom the impending racial demographic changes of the nation are salient (1) endorse more conservative positions on a variety of policy issues (Craig and Richeson 2014b, 2017b; Myers and Levy, this volume; Schildkraut and Marotta, forthcoming); (2) express more support for the Tea Party—a relatively extreme version of political conservatism (Willer, Feinberg, and Wetts 2016); and (3) reported greater support for Republican presidential candidate Donald Trump (if they also reported having higher levels of ethnic identification; Major, Blodorn, and Major-Blascovich 2016).

Moreover, studies have confirmed the mediating role of group status threat in engendering each of these outcomes. In one such experiment (Craig and Richeson 2014b), white participants were randomly assigned to be exposed to information about the projected racial demographic shift information alone (the typical racial shift treatment), or they were exposed to this information but it was followed by a statement designed to assuage participants' status threat. Specifically, participants in this *assuaged threat condition* were told that the societal status of groups—that is, their relative hierarchical position—is unlikely to change in a significantly more racially diverse United States, given group differences in educational attainment, access to resources, and so on (see Craig and Richeson [2014b] for specifics). The responses of participants in these two conditions were compared to those of participants in a control condition in which shifting racial demographics were not made salient but, rather, were changes in geographic mobility among Americans.

As shown in Figure 1, participants in the standard U.S. racial shift condition expressed greater endorsement of conservative ideology, compared with participants in the control condition, as well as compared with participants in the assuaged threat condition. That is, white participants in the assuaged threat condition endorsed conservative ideology less than participants who were exposed to the racial shift information alone. Indeed, those in the assuaged threat condition supported conservative ideology no more (or less) than did control participants. This experiment suggests, in other words, that information about the "majority-minority" racial demographic shift increases whites' sense that their racial group's societal status is in jeopardy, which, in turn, leads to greater support for politically conservative parties, policies, and candidates (see Craig and Richeson [2017b] for a replication of this effect).

Although most of the research conducted thus far has understandably focused on white Americans, the dominant majority racial group, recent work finds similar effects among racial minority participants. Specifically, Craig and Richeson (2017a) examined the effects of making salient the growth in the Hispanic population in the United States on the political ideology and policy preferences of non-Hispanic racial minorities (i.e., black, Asian, Native Americans, multiracial).

FIGURE 1
Self-Reported Political Ideology of White Americans after Exposure to Racial Demographic Shift Information Alone, with Information to Reduce the Status Threat, and Control Information

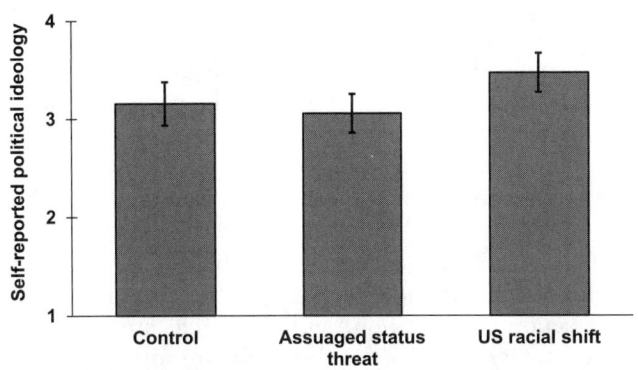

NOTE: Self-reported political ideology scale 1–7; higher numbers indicate more conservative ideology. Error bars reflect 95 percent confidence intervals about the mean.

Similar to the findings for white Americans, members of these non-Hispanic racial minority groups, on average, also endorsed politically conservative policies more strongly and identified as more conservative (or, qualitatively, less liberal) after exposure to the Hispanic growth, rather than control, information. Although the mechanism underlying these findings is not yet known, they suggest that the impacts of salient shifting demographics are not unique to whites—that is, members of dominant societal groups. They also highlight the need to examine how racial minorities are responding to the omnipresent information regarding the changing demographics of the nation (see also Abascal 2015).

Nevertheless, considered in tandem with the findings outlined previously, these results suggest that highlighting significant growth in any racial minority *outgroup* may be perceived as threatening to individuals' own racial group and, thus, promote ingroup favoring, or group defensive and/or even system protective behavior, including greater endorsement of conservative ideology (Jost et al. 2003).

Conservative Shift or Racial Resentment?

One question that is generated by the findings reviewed thus far is whether they are separable outcomes or, rather, that the findings for political conservatism reflect racial attitudes.[3] There is certainly some reason to expect that there could be shared variance in the two seemingly different outcomes (Zigerell 2015). For instance, as mentioned previously, exposure to the racial shift information increased the extent to which white Americans with higher levels of white ethnic identification expressed support for Donald Trump during the Republican primary (Major, Blodorn, and Major-Blascovich 2016). Given that Trump was not the most traditionally conservative candidate in the primary contest at the time that the data were collected, regularly engaged in explicit antiminority language and appeals, and garnered the very public support of several white supremacist groups, it is certainly likely that support for Trump's candidacy may reflect racial attitudes in addition to support for conservative principles. The same could be argued of Tea Party support (Parker and Barreto 2013; Tope, Pickett, and Chiricos 2015). In other words, some of the political outcomes that have been examined thus far may have a racial component, be it racial minority (outgroup) animus or white racial ingroup concern.

There is, however, also reason to believe that the conservatism findings and racial attitude outcomes are distinct. Most notably, research examining how exposure to the racial demographic shift (compared with control) information affects policy support (e.g., Craig and Richeson 2014b, 2017b; Major, Blodorn, and Major-Blascovich 2016) has found effects on policies that are clearly race-related (e.g., affirmative action, immigration) and those that are race-neutral (e.g., oil and gas drilling, tax rates), as well as on those that are somewhat in between (e.g., health care, defense spending; Tesler 2012). Indeed, some work has found effects of exposure to the shifting demographics on whites' support for race-neutral (taxation and public spending), but not race-related (immigration), policies (e.g., Myers and Levy, this volume). Moreover, in addition to policy support, salient racial shift information also results in greater identification with conservative ideology among whites and non-Hispanic racial minorities and even predicts the tendency for white self-described political Independents to report that they "lean Republican" when considering living in a "majority-minority" region of the country (Craig and Richeson 2014b, 2017a, 2017b). Taken together, then, there is good reason to assert that considering the increasing racial diversity of the nation results in both racial and political outcomes, although both sets of outcomes are likely to have important implications for societal racial equality.

Implications

For those most committed to progressive racial politics, the findings of recent research examining how people are responding to information about the changing racial demographics of our nation are quite sobering. This work suggests that whites experience greater concern regarding their racial group's societal rank and cultural status, which, in turn, can lead to a host of negative intergroup outcomes as well as yield greater support for politically conservative policy positions, including policies most relevant to societal racial equity (e.g., affirmative action, immigration policy, harsh criminal justice policies). The findings of this growing body of work also suggest that whites are increasingly likely to embrace an assimilative, rather than multicultural, ideology regarding racial/ethnic diversity in the United States and promote the social, political, and economic interests of whites—the racial ingroup. In other words, white identity politics (Knowles and Marshburn 2010) is likely to reemerge in overt and explicit forms (Vavreck 2017) as the racial diversity of the nation increases (see also Richeson and Craig 2011; Schildkraut 2017). Indeed, it probably already has. As mentioned previously, support for Donald Trump's candidacy for president—a candidate embraced by white nationalist and supremacist groups—was strongly predicted by concerns about the so-called "majority-minority" shift (Pew Research Center 2016) and racial resentment (Tesler 2016).

So what can be done to avoid the likelihood of increased racial tension, discrimination, and perhaps violence in the wake of the increasing diversity of the nation? One possibility is that altering the way the demographic change information is framed could reduce its most divisive effects. Consider, for instance, the "majority-minority" construct. Is there any compelling reason to think of all Americans who are not in the "non-Hispanic white" category as one group to be contrasted against non-Hispanic whites? This "us vs. them" framing is certain to facilitate the zero-sum thinking that promotes racial conflict. Similarly, it may be useful to rethink who is counted as "white" in these estimates (Alba 2016). Indeed, recent research suggests that creating a definition of white that includes, rather than excludes, anyone who identifies as having a white parent can alleviate some of the social and political effects typically found when the growing diversity of the nation is made salient (Myers and Levy, this volume). Future research is, of course, needed to understand the varied effects of employing this or other more inclusive constructions of the white category and, further, whether they will be accepted by members of the American public (see e.g., Peery and Bodenhausen 2008).

The emerging research on reactions to anticipated diversity also would benefit from being in conversation with the established body of research on the experiences people have in communities that are rapidly diversifying (e.g., Craig, Rucker, and Richeson, forthcoming). For instance, it would be useful to identify the conditions under which actual local diversity and perceived or projected diversity result in similar, rather than divergent, outcomes (see Craig and Richeson [forthcoming] for a discussion). How individuals respond to actual diversity may shape how they respond to projected diversity. For instance, whites who already live in quite diverse environments may not feel particularly threatened by these projected demographic shifts and may actually push for more inclusive social policies in response to their salience (Lee and Bean 2010; Zárate and Shaw 2010). It is also possible, however, that the effects of status and cultural threat in response to projected racial diversity on relevant policies and practices may actually change the trajectory of these population projections (Alba 2016). Given that group status and cultural threat increase support for policies that generally serve to restrict diversity (e.g., citizenship rules, immigration policy and laws, etc.), for instance, the anticipation of increasing national diversity may motivate the implementation of laws, policies, and norms that serve to slow down at least some of the factors that are currently giving rise to it.

Before we close, we should note that although the bulk of the research reviewed here examined the responses of white Americans to the growing racial diversity of the nation, additional research is needed to examine the effects of projected racial demographic shifts: (1) in more local contexts, such as neighborhoods (e.g., Zou and Cheryan 2018) and (2) on the intergroup attitudes and political behavior of members of various racial minority groups, especially depending on whether they are the current majority group in the locale, the group "moving in" or, rather, long-standing residents who are not in the numerical majority. In addition, research is needed to examine whether other emerging population trends that are beginning to garner attention are having similar social and political impacts as those found for shifting racial demographics. For instance, in *The End of White Christian America*, Robert Jones (2016) notes that white Christian Americans are already less than 50 percent of the national population, and asserts that this minority status has led to what he calls "nostalgia politics," which serves to protect the interests of the ethno-racial-religious ingroup and undermine those of relevant racial and religious outgroups. Needless to say, careful examination of these dynamics and the psychology that underlies them is paramount. In general, examination of the basic social psychological component processes—for example, categorization and perceptual biases or more social processes, such as feelings of belonging and citizenship— that are influenced by increasing societal diversity may help to elucidate the mechanism(s) underlying the downstream consequences for social and political attitudes.

Conclusion

Although the research reviewed here is relatively new, scholars, journalists, and those in positions to shape policy cannot afford to ignore it. Indeed, the relevance of race and racially motivated concerns in public opinion regarding these demographic trends is clear, and the notion that America is postracial or has overcome the racism of its past is incongruent with this social scientific literature. As the nation continues to diversify, the relevance of race, ethnicity, religion, and identity politics is likely to increase rather than fade. Indeed, it is entirely likely that some effort to assuage the identity threat and broader concerns of white (Christian) Americans is going to be necessary, but any efforts to do so will also need to avoid privileging the continued and guaranteed racial dominance of whites. Maintaining a functioning democracy in the wake of increasing racial, ethnic, and religious diversity, in other words, is likely to require the creation of a representation of America and Americans to which members of all racial, ethnic, and religious backgrounds can feel connected and included.

Notes

1. For brevity, we refer to this group hereafter as "white."
2. Reporting on these demographic changes often compares non-Hispanic whites to all other racial groups ("minorities"), including those who identify as white and some other racial group (e.g., as multiracial; see U.S. Census Bureau 2015).
3. Interestingly, in some ways this is the reverse of prior arguments regarding how racial resentment and conservative ideology are related (e.g., Feldman and Huddy 2005).

References

Abascal, Maria. 2015. Us and them: Black-white relations in the wake of Hispanic population growth. *American Sociological Review* 80 (4): 789–813.

Alba, Richard. January 2016. The likely persistence of a white majority. How Census Bureau statistics have misled thinking about the American future. *The American Prospect*. Available from http://prospect.org/article/likely-persistence-white-majority-0.

Alba, Richard, Ruben G. Rumbaut, and Karen Marotz. 2005. A distorted nation: Perceptions of racial/ethnic group sizes and attitudes toward immigrants and other minorities. *Social Forces* 84 (2): 901–19.

Blalock, Hubert M., Jr. 1967. *Toward a theory of minority-group relations*. New York, NY: Capricorn Books.

Blumer, Herbert. 1958. Race prejudice as a sense of group position. *Pacific Sociological Review* 1:3–7.

Bobo, Lawrence D. 1998. Race, interests, and beliefs about affirmative action. *American Behavioral Scientist* 41 (7): 985–1003.

Burrow, Anthony L., Maclen Stanley, Rachael Sumner, and Patrick L. Hill. 2014. Purpose in life as a resource for increasing comfort with ethnic diversity. *Personality and Social Psychology Bulletin* 40 (11): 1507–16.

Center for American Progress. December 2012. *The Obama coalition in the 2012 election and beyond*. Available from https://cdn.americanprogress.org/wp-content/uploads/2012/12/ObamaCoalition-5.pdf.

Cheney, Kyle. 3 March 2016. Trump kills GOP autopsy. Republican elders drew up a blueprint for a kinder, more inclusive Republican Party. Trump is tearing it apart. *Politico*. Available from http://www.politico.com.

Craig, Maureen A., and Jennifer A. Richeson. 2014a. More diverse yet less tolerant? How the increasingly-diverse racial landscape affects white Americans' racial attitudes. *Personality and Social Psychology Bulletin* 40 (6): 750–61.

Craig, Maureen A., and Jennifer A. Richeson. 2014b. On the precipice of a "majority-minority" America: Perceived status threat from the racial demographic shift affects white Americans' political ideology. *Psychological Science* 25 (6): 1189–97.

Craig, Maureen A., and Jennifer A. Richeson. 2017a. Hispanic population growth engenders conservative shift among non-Hispanic racial minorities. *Social Psychological and Personality Science*. doi:10.1177/1948550617712029.

Craig, Maureen A., and Jennifer A. Richeson. 2017b. Information about the U.S. racial demographic shift triggers concerns about anti-white discrimination among the prospective white "minority." *PLoS ONE* 12 (9): e0185389.

Craig, Maureen A., and Jennifer A. Richeson. Forthcoming. Majority no more? The influence of neighborhood racial diversity and national population changes on whites' perceptions of racial discrimination. *Russell Sage Foundation Journal of the Social Sciences*.

Craig, Maureen A., Julian M. Rucker, and Jennifer A. Richeson. Forthcoming. The pitfalls and promise of increasing racial diversity: Threat, contact, and race relations in the 21st century. *Current Directions in Psychological Science*.

Danbold, Felix, and Yuen J. Huo. 2015. No longer "All-American"? Whites' defensive reactions to their numerical decline. *Social Psychological and Personality Science* 6 (2): 210–18.

Day, Jennifer C. 1996. *Population projections of the United States by age, sex, race, and Hispanic origin: 1995 to 2050*. Washington, DC: U.S. Census Bureau. Available from https://www.census.gov/prod/1/pop/p25-1130.pdf.

Enos, Ryan D. 2016. What the demolition of public housing teaches us about the impact of racial threat on political behavior. *American Journal of Political Science* 60 (1): 123–42.

Feldman, Stanley, and Leonie Huddy. 2005. Racial resentment and white opposition to race-conscious programs: Principles or prejudice? *American Journal of Political Science* 49 (1): 168–83.

Giles, Michael W., and Kaenan Hertz. 1994. Racial threat and partisan identification. *American Political Science Review* 88 (2): 317–26.

Helderman, Rosalind S., and Jon Cohen. 29 August 2012. As Republican convention emphasized diversity, racial incidents intrude. *The Washington Post*.

Jones, Robert P. 2016. *The end of white Christian America*. New York, NY: Simon & Schuster.

Jost, John T., Jack Glaser, Arie W. Kruglanski, and Frank J. Sulloway. 2003. Political conservatism as motivated social cognition. *Psychological Bulletin* 129 (3): 339–75.

Knowles, Eric D., and Christopher K. Marshburn. 2010. Understanding white identity politics will be crucial to diversity science. *Psychological Inquiry* 21 (2): 134–39.
Lee, Jennifer, and Frank D. Bean. 2010. *The diversity paradox. Immigration and the color line in twenty-first century America*. New York, NY: Russell Sage Foundation.
Major, Brenda, Alison Blodorn, and Gregory Major-Blascovich. 2016. The threat of increasing diversity: Why many white Americans support Trump in the 2016 presidential election. *Group Processes and Intergroup Relations*. doi:10.1177/1368430216677304.
Myers, Dowell, and Morris Levy. 2018. Racial population projections and reactions to alternative news accounts of growing diversity. *The ANNALS of the American Academy of Political and Social Science* (this volume).
Outten, H. Robert, Michael T. Schmitt, Daniel A. Miller, and Amber L. Garcia. 2012. Feeling threatened about the future: Whites' emotional reactions to anticipated ethnic demographic changes. *Personality and Social Psychology Bulletin* 38 (1): 14–25.
Parker, Christopher S., and Matt A. Barreto. 2013. *Change they can't believe in: The Tea Party and reactionary politics in America*. Princeton, NJ: Princeton University Press.
Peery, Destiny, and Galen V. Bodenhausen. 2008. Black + white = black: Hypodescent in reflexive categorization of racially ambiguous faces. *Psychological Science* 19 (10): 973–77.
Pew Research Center. 28 September 2015. *Modern immigration wave brings 59 million to U.S., driving population growth and change through 2065: Views of immigration's impact on U.S. society mixed*. Washington, DC: Pew Research Center. Available from http://www.pewhispanic.org.
Pew Research Center. 2 June 2016. *More "warmth" for Trump among GOP voters concerned by immigrants, diversity*. Washington, DC: Pew Research Center. Available from http://www.pewresearch.org.
Phillips, Steve. 2016. *Brown is the new white: How the demographic revolution has created a new American majority*. New York, NY: The New Press.
Richeson, Jennifer A., and Maureen A. Craig. 2011. Intra-minority intergroup relations in the twenty-first century. *Daedalus* 140 (2): 166–75.
Rubin, Jennifer. 18 March 2013. GOP autopsy report goes bold. *The Washington Post*.
Schildkraut, Deborah S. 2017. White attitudes about descriptive representation in the U.S.: The roles of identity, discrimination, and linked fate. *Politics, Groups, and Identities* 5 (1): 84–106.
Schildkraut, Deborah S., and Satia A. Marotta. Forthcoming. Assessing the political distinctiveness of white millennials: How race and generation shape racial and political attitudes in a changing America. *Russell Sage Foundation Journal of the Social Sciences*.
Skinner, Allison L., and Jacob E. Cheadle. 2016. The "Obama effect"? Priming contemporary racial milestones increases implicit racial bias among whites. *Social Cognition* 34 (6): 544–58.
Tesler, Michael. 2012. The spillover of racialization into health care: How President Obama polarized public opinion by racial attitudes and race. *American Journal of Political Science* 56 (3): 690–704.
Tesler, Michael. 1 August 2016. Trump is the first modern Republican to win the nomination based on racial prejudice. *The Washington Post*.
Tope, Daniel, Justin Pickett, and Ted Chiricos. 2015. Anti-minority attitudes and Tea Party movement membership. *Social Science Research* 51:322–37.
U.S. Census Bureau. 17 May 2012. *Most children younger than 1 are minorities*. Washington, DC: U.S. Census Bureau. Available from https://www.census.gov/newsroom/releases/archives/population/cb12-90.html.
U.S. Census Bureau. 3 March 2015. *New Census Bureau report analyzes U.S. population projections*. Washington, DC: U.S. Census Bureau. Available from https://www.census.gov/newsroom/press-releases/2015/cb15-tps16.html.
Vavreck, Lynn. 8 August 2017. The political payoff of making whites feel like a minority. *New York Times*.
Willer, Robb, Matthew Feinberg, and Rachel Wetts. 2016. Threats to racial status promote Tea Party support among white Americans. Available from https://papers.ssrn.com/sol3/papers.cfm?abstract_id=2770186.
Zárate, Michael A., and Moria P. Shaw. 2010. The role of cultural inertia in reactions to immigration on the U.S./Mexico border. *Journal of Social Issues* 66 (1): 45–57.
Zigerell, Lawrence J. 2015. Distinguishing racism from ideology: A methodological inquiry. *Political Research Quarterly* 68 (3): 521–36.
Zou, Linda X., and Sapna Cheryan. 2018. Loathe thy neighbor: The effects of residential and school diversity on whites' perceptions of intergroup threats. Unpublished manuscript. University of Washington, Seattle, WA.

Racial Population Projections and Reactions to Alternative News Accounts of Growing Diversity

By
DOWELL MYERS
and
MORRIS LEVY

Projections of changes in racial demographics depend on how race is classified. The U.S. Census Bureau makes several different projections of the nation's racial demographic future, but the most publicized version projects our racial future in a way that narrows the definition of race groups to exclude people who are of mixed race or Hispanic. This definition results in projections of many fewer "whites," accelerating the impending decline of the country's white majority and perhaps heightening white audiences' anxiety about demographic change. We conducted an experiment that randomly assigned whites to read alternative news stories based on 2014 Census Bureau projections. One story emphasized growing diversity, a second emphasized the decline of the white population to minority status, and a third described an enduring white majority based on intermarriage and inclusive white identity. Much higher levels of anxiety or anger, especially among Republicans, were recorded after reading the white minority story than the alternative stories of diversity or an enduring white majority.

Keywords: race; projections; demographic change; public opinion; political psychology

How neutral are the U.S. Census Bureau's population projections from the perspective of their plural audiences? Only some are data users—researchers in academia, government, or business—while most are members of the general public who consume news reports about important findings. Demographic changes can hold particular fascination or alarm

Dowell Myers is a professor of policy, planning, and demography in the Sol Price School of Public Policy, University of Southern California. He is author of Immigrants and Boomers *(Russell Sage Foundation 2007) and other works that demonstrate a mutual benefits strategy to span demographic divides.*

Morris Levy is an assistant professor of political science at the University of Southern California. He is author of numerous articles on American and European public opinion about immigration, race, and multiculturalism.

Correspondence: dowell@usc.edu

DOI: 10.1177/0002716218766294

for the different groups being described. This article uses the Census Bureau's release of demographic projections in March 2015 to examine the interplay of choices about how to execute and communicate demographic projections and the way Americans absorb the meaning of a more diverse racial future.

When publicizing some specific projections in 2015, the Census Bureau gave top billing to an attention-grabbing headline: whites would become a minority of the U.S. population in fewer than 30 years.[1] Media coverage spanning the ideological spectrum made this the lede, casting impending decline of the white population to minority status as a simple and imminent fact, even "official."[2] What went unrecognized in the press coverage is that the Census Bureau prepares population projections that account for *six different definitions* of white racial identity. The 2000 census asked respondents to check all racial categories with which they identify and asked a Hispanic "ethnicity" question that was separate from the race question, making two basic tabulations possible. First is an "inclusive" definition of each race that counts all people who say they are of a given race, either alone, or in combination with other race choices. Importantly, this inclusive approach would be sensitive to intermarriage as a widely spreading phenomenon that is reshaping the future population (Alba, this volume). Nonetheless, for reasons to be described, the Census Bureau places emphasis on a more convenient, "exclusive" definition that focuses on single races, excluding cases that combine more than one race, and with the further restriction of excluding from the race categories people who also are of Hispanic origin or heritage. This calculus makes for the smallest count of "whites," and the resultant rapid decline to minority status for the group known as "non-Hispanic white alone." In short, how "white" is defined is crucial to the projected speed of white majority decline, indeed to whether minority status is anticipated at all.

An important question to ask, then, is what definition of "white" is the best choice for projections. Our answer considers three specific purposes for the use of racial projections, with each purpose perhaps better served by a different definition of "white." A second question to ask is how much the outlook of future minority status for whites may have changed in recent years, not only because demographic trends have shifted, but also because the white definition was revised to be narrower. The third question we address is how the definition of "white" majority may impact the attitudes and emotions of whites regarding future population changes. For answers about impacts, we employ an experimental design that tests responses to alternative ways of framing results from the Census Bureau's racial projections.

Goals and Methods of Official Race Projections

What are the goals for producing race projections?

Government agencies appear reticent to discuss the potential uses and purposes of the projections they prepare. For example, the Census Bureau offers only the following: "Projections illustrate possible courses of population change based on assumptions about future births, deaths, net international migration, and domestic migration."[3]

A broader view is offered by the Population Reference Bureau, a nongovernmental organization based in Washington, D.C., with global coverage:

> Government policymakers and planners around the world use population projections to *gauge future demand* for food, water, energy, and services, and to forecast future demographic characteristics. Population *projections can alert policymakers to major trends* that may affect economic development and *help policymakers craft policies* that can be adapted for various projection scenarios. (Population Reference Bureau 2011, emphasis added)

In practice, governments in urbanized, developed nations often adopt population projections for use in specific functions related to growth planning, such as housing and land use planning, transportation planning, health care planning, schools and higher education planning, workforce and retirement planning, and generally informing local and national policy.

While the most common use of projections is foresight about the future total growth in population, many of the functions also pertain to growth of specific age groups whose service needs vary sharply from one another (e.g., school children, retirees, etc.). The need to plan age-specific services creates demand for specific age group projections. More generally, the core demographic processes of fertility, mortality, and migration vary substantially between males and females, by age group, and by ethno-racial group. Therefore, to improve the accuracy of a total population projection, virtually all professional population projections adopt the cohort-component method of disaggregating the population by age, gender, and race (including Hispanic origin), and developing age-gender-race specific rates of behavior to apply to the corresponding subgroups of the population. This yields a set of highly disaggregated projected subgroups, whose main purpose is to produce a more accurate estimate of future total population when all the resulting subgroups are summed.

From its beginning, the United States has displayed interest in racially classifying its population in a census once every decade, with the original three categories of white, black, and indigenous Native Americans or American Indians expanded over time to more categories that form a database available to shape subsequent social policy, an evolution well described and interpreted in Prewitt (2013). Since the civil rights revolution of the 1960s, there has been legal and policy interest about *current* inequities that exist among racial groups. However, it is not apparent if any explicit governmental purposes demand information about the *future growth* in specific racial groups in the population. Nonetheless, projections of racial subgroups for future years are published as a byproduct of the cohort-component method. Even if no official uses for racial projections are suggested by the Census Bureau itself, nor by any federal agency, these projections do hold keen public interest, and so they are eagerly adopted by the press and the broader political process.

We suggest three objectives as guides for evaluating the utility of different race classification procedures used in reporting projections. These include (1) an aim of convenience or simplicity in use of the data, (2) an aim to facilitate social justice and equal opportunity policy, and (3) an aim to present a faithful portrait of how Americans view their own racial and ethnic identities and the growing racial complexity of America. The three objectives may overlap or conflict in certain ways, but we will apply them to help evaluate how well the current racial projections circulated to the press stack up against the various alternatives available from the same census data.

Which classification practices serve which objectives?

The Census Bureau has produced several variations of categorization for racial projections that are made feasible from data collected in surveys and the decennial census. All the racial variations to be discussed derive from the same total population and, therefore, share common assumptions about fertility, mortality, and migration. Whereas demographic forecasters devote their attention primarily to future assumptions regarding these input factors, what we focus on in this article are the alternative reporting classifications for projections of people in racial subgroups.

Two principal decisions have given rise to creation of multiple alternatives. The first is whether to separate or combine the information on the separate question about Hispanic origin with the information on racial subgroups. Beginning with the 1980 census, separate racial breakdowns have been produced within the Hispanic and non-Hispanic portions of the population, and sometimes combined in different arrangements, making it more complicated and varied as how to summarize the racial distribution of a given population (Myers 1992, 209–16). The second decision stems from the revision to the census data collection form first used in 2000, and thereafter, inviting respondents to check more than one category of race if so desired. (This was to allow expression of self-identity by individuals, for example, whose parents were of different racial origins.) The effect of these two decisions is to create an overlap of identification, with some people appearing in two or more racial categories and others overlapping between races and Hispanic origin.

A number of alternative tabulations are reported by the Census Bureau that simplify this complexity in different ways. In practice, two classifications emerge that demonstrate fundamentally different approaches made possible by the data collected in the census and that can be projected forward in time. These are illustrated here with data from 2015, the first year of the Census Bureau projection data produced in 2014 (see Table 1). Yet a third classification, one for equal opportunity or social justice, also will be considered, built upon elements combined from the first two.

The first classification in Table 1, which might be termed the "exclusive convenient" arrangement, is most widely used because it excludes overlapping cases and thereby sums to the population total. Although a number of configurations are possible, most commonly the Hispanic number is preserved in total and all Hispanics are subtracted from their individual race categories with which they also identify, leaving only the remainder in each race group that is non-Hispanic.

TABLE 1
Exclusive and Inclusive Racial Classifications Available in United States Population Projections, Census Bureau Vintage 2014

	Alternative Classifications				
	Convenient Exclusive			Inclusive Identity	
	Number	Share of Total Pop.		Number	Share of Total Pop.
NH whites alone	198,354	61.7%	All whites	255,682	79.6%
NH blacks alone	39,782	12.4%	All blacks	46,126	14.4%
NH AIANs alone	2,359	0.7%	All AIANs	6,618	2.1%
NH Asians alone	16,978	5.3%	All Asians	20,534	6.4%
NH NHPIs alone	549	0.2%	All NHPIs	1,486	0.5%
NH multiple races	6,593	2.1%	—		
All Hispanics	56,754	17.7%	All Hispanics	56,754	17.7%
Sum	321,369	100.0%	Sum	387,200	120.5%
Total Pop.	321,369				

NOTE: Numbers in 1000s. "Exclusive" categories report number of people who chose only a single racial or ethnic category. "Inclusive" categories permit people to appear in more than one racial or ethnic category. "NH" signifies Non-Hispanic. "Alone" indicates single race not in combination. "All" signifies inclusive-defined categories containing members selecting this group alone or in combination with other groups. "AIAN" is American Indian and Alaska Native. "NHPI" is Native Hawaiian and Pacific Islander.

Further, any non-Hispanic individuals who identify with more than one race category are removed to a category termed "multiple races." This approach restricts all population members into single categories of identity, a convenient solution for both computer programmers and data users, because everything sums to the 100 percent total of the population. This process of exclusion satisfies the first objective of convenience noted above.

In contrast, the second classification, termed here the "inclusive identity" arrangement, takes full account of the overlap across categories by tabulating people inclusively in the multiple categories they choose to select as their racial and ethnic identity. Because of "double counting," this sums to a number that is some 20 percent greater than the total population. That makes this inclusive tabulation uncomfortable for data users who wish to make a pie chart summing to the 100 percent total, even if it better reflects the true *self*-identity of population members. At different moments the same person, such as an African American who is also Hispanic, might wish to be categorized with all African Americans or, alternatively, with all Hispanics. For some purposes, it clearly is desirable to count all people of a race rather than just the non-Hispanic remainder.

In the inclusive formulation, Hispanics are counted exactly as in the first alternative (with 56.7 million) because Hispanics are the only group tabulated inclusively in the exclusive convenient alternative (Table 1). All the other groups are substantially larger in the second, inclusive alternative. Whites have the largest absolute change between the two classifications, from 198 million to 255 million, increasing from 61.7 percent to 79.6 percent of the total population in 2015.

A third classification, not shown in Table 1, derives from equal opportunity considerations, when minority groups are compared to the white group, which for that purpose is defined narrowly and exclusively as non-Hispanic and not in combination with any other racial group. Minority groups in this equal opportunity approach are defined in terms of their inclusive numbers, for example, maximizing the count of American Indians, whether they also happen to be Hispanic or may have a joint racial identity with whites or any other group. Thus, this third classification can be recognized as borrowing elements from the first two arrangements. It simply combines a category of "whites" using the narrowly restricted white definition in the exclusive convenient classification and categories for all other "minority" groups, each defined broadly as in the inclusive identity classification.

Projecting the racial future of America

As distinctions between racial categories in American society blur (e.g., Hochschild, Weaver, and Burch 2012; see also multiple contributions in this volume), projecting future numbers in fixed categories is increasingly problematic. In fact, the Census Bureau reports six alternatives in their 2014 projections (Colby and Ortman 2014), and the choice to publicize one or another has major consequences for how the public might interpret the country's demographic future. The online published data for the 2014 projections offer a full page (titled "Table 10") that shows how the same population totals can be sorted into six alternatives of ethnoracial classification, spanning years from 2015 to 2060 (too large a table to reproduce here).[4] These include sections that are Hispanic only, non-Hispanic only, and including Hispanics and non-Hispanics together. Each of those is further subdivided into tabulations of each racial group "alone" (the exclusive variation) or "alone or in combination" (the inclusive variation).

The implications of choosing among the alternative definitions could not be greater. Under the most narrow or exclusive definition, the number of people who claim an identity that is non-Hispanic and solely of white race is projected to reach a peak in 2025 of 199.8 million, after which this population will steadily decline in number. Meanwhile other groups will be growing rapidly and will surpass whites in growth. Between 2015 and 2045, Hispanics will increase in number by 73.8 percent, Asians by 82.0 percent and blacks or African Americans by 24.6 percent. Meanwhile the white population will have declined, and the nation will reach a crossing point in 2044 when the white total has fallen below 50 percent of the national population. At that time, the former minority groups, in total, will become the majority.

In contrast, under the more expansive and inclusive definition, people who claim white identity in whole or in part, and are non-Hispanic, will not arrive at minority status until 2054, fully 10 years later. And whites as a whole, regardless of Hispanic origin, will retain a three-quarters majority, 74.3 percent, of the U.S. population until at least 2060, the latest date in the projections. Other small groups are growing faster, but, of the total growth in population, the broad white majority accounts for at least 50 percent of the growth in every projection period.

Technical projections meet public audience

All projections benefit from historic perspective, because that is how people judge the future numbers. Since 2000 the Census Bureau has substantially changed its racial projections across a number of successive renditions. They revised their racial classifications and methods to accord with changes in the baseline data collection and to account for new methodologies or assumptions about future fertility, immigration, and the like (Hogan, Ortman, and Colby 2015). Accordingly, there have been substantial changes between projection series, and that could yield sometimes startling shifts in racial outcomes. In fact, these changes have generated an unintended exaggeration of the pace of future white decline.

Public perception of rapidly changing demographics is based on casual observation, as well as on reports of national trends. The sense of a greatly accelerated pace of racial change in America after 2000 was due, at least in part, to a method shift between projection series. As summarized in Table 2, the Census Bureau's projections issued in 2000 reported that the "non-Hispanic white" share of the population was projected to become a minority of the total in 2059. That was the first time this racial milestone could be detected within the 60-year horizon used in most projections. Four years later, new projections found that the "non-Hispanic white alone" share, which excludes multiracial whites, would reach minority status fully nine years sooner (2050). Four years after that, in 2008, the "non-Hispanic white alone" share was projected to fall to minority status another eight years sooner than previously expected (2042). This, in effect, communicated to lay consumers of the projections that demographic change was accelerating toward the threshold of a majority-minority society. Thereafter, the reported white decline ceased its acceleration, and the date of minority status actually shifted upward to 2044 in 2014 projections. For comparison, Table 2 also includes the much later date (2054) of white decline to minority status if the non-Hispanic white population were defined more broadly to include people who were multiracial white, either white alone or in combination with another race. And if we use the broadest definition of white, including those who are also white Hispanic, the white population retains a large majority for the rest of the century, as noted above.

By happenstance, two major historic events coincided with the finding in 2008 of a sharp acceleration in white decline. The 2008 election of Barack Obama, a Democrat, to be the nation's first nonwhite president, was an energizing moment for many Americans, and especially for African Americans and other minority groups who felt long disenfranchised. Yet it also engendered anxieties about the nation's future among some whites because it put a human and political face on the nation's racial transition that had been projected (Tesler and Sears 2010). The

TABLE 2
Changing Dates of Projected White Decline to Minority Status: Changes between Projection Series

Vintage Projection	Definition of White	Year Whites Reach Minority Status
2000	Non-Hispanic white	2059
2004	Non-Hispanic white alone	2050
2008	Non-Hispanic white alone	2042
2014	Non-Hispanic white alone	2044
2014	Non-Hispanic white alone or in combination	2054
2014	White alone or in combination	after 2060 or never

SOURCE: U.S. Census Bureau projections: for 2000: np-t5-g; for 2004: summary/natproj-tab01a; for 2008: summary-tables/np2008-t4; for 2014: NP2014-T10.

other event that unfortunately coincided in 2008 and 2009 was the severe financial crisis that spawned the deep economic anxieties of the Great Recession. The two historic events may have heightened insecurities among many in the nation's white population, now underscored by reports of their coming reduction to minority status. Any reverberations of the projections' publicity were surely unintended.[5]

In hindsight, a more consistent set of methodologies over time for classification and projection would have generated a reported pace of white decline that is more moderate and less shocking. The 14-year span between the 2000 projections of "non-Hispanic white" and the 2014 projections of "non-Hispanic white alone or in combination," amounted to only a 5-year hastening of white decline, as measured by the declining year of lost majority status from 2059 to 2054 (see Table 2). This compared to the 15-year hastening (three times faster) of lost majority in 2044 that was emphasized by the main 2014 projections of "non-Hispanic white alone."

What's the Headline, and Does It Affect Public Reactions?

Expectations of reactions to racial trends

Research on racial threat suggests that the subject of growing diversity and white decline would have particular meaning for an audience of whites. A concern is that publicity of an exaggerated decline according to the exclusive white definition can lead to divisive or discriminatory political actions by white voters who are made to feel anxious and defensive about their impending minority status.

There are at least two reasons to expect that whites would process the white minority narrative more negatively than an alternative account about racial projections that adopt the "inclusive" definition of whiteness. First, perceived zero-sum competition between groups for status and symbolic or material benefits can exacerbate feelings of threat (e.g., Bobo 1983). Public consumers of population projections often treat them as a horse race: which group is growing most, which is declining, and who will be the majority. All groups in fact may be growing, but the most common presentation is shares of a 100 percent total, and some groups are perceived as "winners" while others are projected as "losers" and may feel threatened by their loss. In the title of Kinder and Kam (2009), it is "us against them." The imminent loss of majority status, especially in a democracy where majorities ostensibly rule, could therefore augment threatened feelings and hostility from the majority group toward the groups that might overtake it. By contrast, an account of projections that casts racial groups as overlapping (the inclusive definition), with fluid boundaries, might soothe these reactions by allaying the perception of a challenge to majority status.

Second, the white minority narrative might lead to exaggerated perceptions of change and accelerated minority population growth. Members of the public are not good judges of actual racial proportions or growth rates, and they often exaggerate the prominence of growing minorities or the fate of declining whites (Alba, Rumbaut, and Marotz 2005; Wong 2007). *Population projections feed these distorted perceptions by telescoping time*—making distant changes, 40 years off, feel salient in the current year. Moreover, there is evidence that rapid growth in the size of minority populations may fuel threatened feelings even more than does the absolute size (Hopkins 2010). If the white minority narrative makes changes in the rising minority group population size seem larger and more rapid than the narrative based on inclusive accounting, we would expect it to fuel threatened feelings. Of important consequence, declining groups often retain a voting majority to act on those feelings for decades after losing a population majority, due to the typically older age and heavier voting participation of longer-established groups (Myers 2007).

Research by Craig, Rucker, and Richeson (this volume) has convincingly demonstrated that exposure to the white minority narrative is capable of inducing these threatened reactions among whites. Our inquiry seeks to gauge whether the alternative "inclusive white" narrative, which can be equally illustrated by the Census Bureau's own data, mollifies these threats. Our theoretical expectation is that it will, decreasing negative emotions such as anxiety and anger toward a news account about the race projections relative to the standard but exclusive "white minority" narrative. The inclusive narrative, we expect, makes the zero-sum implications of rising diversity less salient because whites' majority status is not imminently threatened. It also resembles an assimilationist "melting pot" narrative that still has considerable resonance in American public opinion (Citrin and Sears 2014).

If the Census Bureau projection classifications have neutral effect, the null hypothesis would be that whites feel equally threatened by both accounts. This could occur for a number of reasons. Whites may associate rising ethnic diversity with a threat to their own dominant group position irrespective of framing, or because they have already become too accustomed to the impending minority frame to be open to any alternative. Whites may also simply disbelieve the inclusive account or reject it as false. Finally, expanding the boundaries of whiteness to include previously subordinate groups, and the loss of racial exclusivity that this entails, possibly may be no less threatening to whites' group status as is the specter of becoming a minority.

Our broader research investigation, beyond what is reported here, also tested two subsidiary expectations: (1) the white minority narrative engenders more opposition to immigration and less sympathy for rapidly growing racial minority groups than does the inclusive white majority narrative, and (2) the white minority narrative promotes greater support for cuts to social services than does knowledge of the inclusive white majority narrative. Here, we confine ourselves to a summary of these findings, focusing on self-reported emotional reactions.

Experimental study

Using an experimental survey design, we tested the emotional impact of alternative narratives constructed from the 2015 Census Bureau projections. Our survey experiment, fielded in summer 2016, randomly assigned a large national sample of whites to either a control group or to one of three treatment groups, namely, to read one of three simulated news stories consisting of information and frames culled from 2015 news coverage of the Census Bureau's projections. One story presented a bare discussion of continued rises in racial diversity, without any references to majority status (*diversity*). A second foretold a persistent or continuing white majority under an inclusive definition of whiteness that counts people from mixed backgrounds as white if they so identify themselves (*inclusive*). A third resembled the dominant media treatment that emphasized the exclusive white definition and forecast a white minority by 2044 (*exclusive*).[6]

We then asked respondents whether they were familiar with the story they had seen and asked how they felt after reading it. We gauged emotional reactions to a story by asking respondents to choose an adjective that best described how they felt. The four choices were anxious, angry, hopeful, and enthusiastic. Interspersed into the rest of the survey were several questions measuring political attitudes about government spending on public goods and services, immigration, and the state of race relations in the United States, all of which the literature on racial diversity and public opinion suggested to us might be influenced by exposure to the different frames of rising diversity.

Results

Consistent with our expectation, and as illustrated in Figure 1 the *exclusive* story, forecasting a coming white minority status, makes white voters substantially more anxious than the news of growing *diversity* on its own. The rise in anxiety is especially pronounced among white Republicans, an ominous sign that fears of whites "losing control" may have played an important role in determining voters' choices in the Republican primary contests and, subsequent to our survey, in the

FIGURE 1
Emotional Reactions to News Stories by White Readers

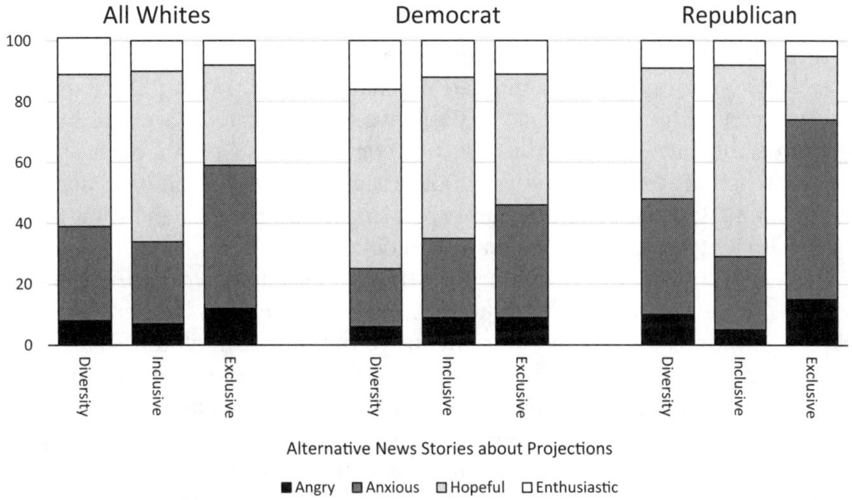

NOTE: "Exclusive" categories report number of people who chose only a single racial or ethnic category. "Inclusive" categories permit people to appear in more than one racial or ethnic category. "NH" signifies Non-Hispanic. "Alone" indicates single race, not in combination. "All" signifies inclusive-defined categories containing members selecting this group alone or in combination with other groups. "AIAN" is American Indian and Alaska Native. "NHPI" is Native Hawaiian and Pacific Islander.

general election (see, e.g., McElwee and McDaniel 2017). Reading the impending-minority, *exclusive* narrative greatly increases self-reported anxiety while dampening hopefulness, both by approximately 17 percentage points over the bare *diversity* rising narrative.

Consistent with our expectations, and central to our discussion here, the *inclusive* narrative appears to reverse these effects entirely. Not only is the level of threat lower than in the *exclusive* condition, it appears to be reassuring relative to the bare *diversity* narrative, raising the share of people who report feeling hopeful by about 6 percentage points. In effect, almost a quarter of whites in our sample who react negatively to reading the dominant press narrative about the projections, in which their group becomes a minority within 30 years, would react positively to the alternative account in which the definition of whiteness expands to include Americans with multiple racial and ethnic identities but with whites remaining in the majority.

Also notable is that the response to this *inclusive* account was especially favorable among Republicans. Republicans express considerably more negative feelings about the unelaborated *diversity* narrative than Democrats. Nearly half of Republicans acknowledged feeling negatively disposed about this account, compared to a quarter of Democrats. These partisan differences are exacerbated among respondents who read the *exclusive* account of the projections, though this account also greatly increased negativity among Democrats. Three-quarters of Republicans who read this account expressed a negative emotion, compared to 46 percent of Democrats. But Republicans' positive response to the *inclusive* narrative was overwhelming, cutting negative reactions by almost 20 points compared to the *diversity* narrative and a whopping 45 points compared to reading the *exclusive* narrative that dominated media coverage. Among Democrats, the *inclusive* account increased negativity relative to the *diversity* account but left it still appreciably lower than in the *exclusive* condition. As a result, partisan polarization in reactions to the narratives about rising diversity in the *inclusive* condition are eliminated, with Republicans expressing modestly (though insignificantly) *more* positivity toward this story than Democrats.

We found no statistically significant differences (not shown) in the emotional effects of these treatments by education, age, and gender. This indicates that accepting attitudes toward the more inclusive definition of whiteness are widely diffused through the population and not confined to the young and well educated. Negative attitudes about future minority status are also widely diffused across demographic categories among whites.

Would the reductions in threatened feelings be accompanied by shifts in racial and political attitudes? Prior research has found that threat leads to the adoption of more hostile attitudes toward the minority group as well as efforts to limit the subordinate group's numbers and economic interests (Blalock 1967; Bobo and Hutchings 1996). Indeed, respondents exposed to the *inclusive* story were more likely than those who read the *exclusive*, minority story to say that Asians and Hispanics faced racism in America (difference in means two-tailed t-test $p < .05$ in both cases), while there were no effects on perceived racism against whites or blacks. Corroborating this finding, the *inclusive* account promoted modest and marginally significant ($p < .1$) reductions in opposition to immigration relative to the *diversity* and minority narratives. And whereas the minority account increased opposition to a hypothetical school bond that would have increased property taxes to fund K–12 education, the *inclusive* majority narrative reduced opposition by nearly half a standard deviation on a *strongly agree* to *strongly disagree* scale (difference in means two-tailed t-test $p < .05$).

Conclusion

Long-range plans require long-range data, and surely trustworthy data about 40-year cumulative demographic changes could lead to vitally needed public investment decisions for current and future generations. Yet as others have shown, different characterizations of the same projections could well lead to distorted perceptions among citizen-voters about relative sizes and rates of change for different subgroups (Alba, Rumbaut, and Marotz 2005; Wong 2007). When the audience for projections consists of voters, distorted perceptions can heighten defensive reactions against perceived threat instead of promoting sound planning.

Despite the availability of a variety of racial classifications prepared by the Census Bureau, the "exclusive" alternative of nonoverlapping categories has been promoted since 2004 in projections for public consumption. That may have advantages of summing to a 100 percent total and lending greater convenience of use. But it also comports with older, now tenuous, assumptions about the rigidity and exclusivity of racial group boundaries. Projections of a population that is increasingly multiracial deserves greater use of an inclusive definition of racial identity. Our experiment shows that whites, especially Republicans, respond more favorably to the inclusive definition of whiteness that accounts for intermarriage and leaves whites in the majority rather than to the exclusive definition that shrinks them to a minority within 30 years.

The choice of racial classification may have unintended but important political repercussions on public audiences. Our research takes a first step toward the important practical aim of illuminating the consequences of different strategies for communicating demographic forecasts to the public. While demographers learn technical skills of projections, virtually no literature exists on crafting the narratives by which population projections of total growth, changing racial shares, and aging should be shared with the public, who may be the subject of study but also are a key audience. This connection is essential in a democracy because members of the public become vital actors (voters and taxpayers) who seek to shape the future in response to the projections they have learned about. More thought and care should be given to how this information is structured for sharing with the public.

Notes

1. The report is available from http://www.census.gov/newsroom/press-releases/2015/cb15-tps16.html.

2. See, for example, https://www.usnews.com/news/articles/2015/07/06/its-official-the-us-is-becoming-a-minority-majority-nation and http://www.breitbart.com/big-government/2015/06/25/census-more-minority-children-than-whites-more-whites-dying-than-being-born/, as well as the humorous take in http://www.huffingtonpost.com/entry/so-youre-about-to-become-a-minority_us_553011f0e4b04ebb92325daf.

3. See https://www.census.gov/topics/population/population-projections/about.html.

4. The full table can be observed here: Table 10, "Projections of the Population by Sex, Hispanic Origin, and Race for the United States: 2015 to 2060"; https://www.census.gov/data/tables/2014/demo/popproj/2014-summary-tables.html.

5. For example, white nationalist Richard Spencer explained prior to the first of two torch-lit rallies during 2017 in Charlottesville, VA: "What brings us together is that we are white, we are a people, we will not be replaced." Quoted in *Washington Post*, May 14, 2017.

6. For more details on these treatments and the survey instrument, please see the authors' working paper that more fully describes the survey protocol and results: "Forecasts and Frames: Narratives about Rising Racial Diversity and the Political Attitudes of U.S. Whites"; see https://dornsife.usc.edu/cf/posc/faculty_display.cfm?Person_ID=1057914.

References

Alba, Richard D. 2018. The rise of mixed parentage: A sociological and demographic phenomenon to be reckoned with. *The ANNALS of the American Academy of Political and Social Science* (this volume).

Alba, Richard D., Ruben G. Rumbaut, and Kenneth Marotz. 2005. A distorted nation: Perceptions of racial/ethnic group sizes and attitudes toward immigrants and other minorities. *Social Forces* 84 (December): 901–19.

Blalock, Hubert M. 1967. *Toward a theory of minority-group relations*. New York, NY: John Wiley and Sons.

Bobo, Lawrence. 1983. Whites' opposition to busing: Symbolic racism or realistic group conflict? *Journal of Personality and Social Psychology* 45:1196–1210.

Bobo, Lawrence, and Victor L. Hutchings. 1996. Perceptions of racial group competition: Extending Blumer's theory of group position to a multiracial social context. *American Sociological Review* 61:951–72.

Citrin, Jack, and David O. Sears. 2014. *American identity and the politics of multiculturalism*. New York, NY: Cambridge University Press.

Colby, Sandra L., and Jennifer M. Ortman. 2014. Projections of the size and composition of the U.S. population: 2014 to 2060. Current Population Reports, P25-1143. Washington, DC: U.S. Census Bureau.

Craig, Maureen A., Julian Rucker, and Jennifer A. Richeson. 2018. Approaching a "majority-minority" United States: Psychological and political impacts. *The ANNALS of the American Academy of Political and Social Science* (this volume).

Hochschild, Jennifer, Vesla M. Weaver, and Traci R. Burch. 2012. *Creating a new racial order: How immigration, multiracialism, genomics, and the young can remake race in America*. Princeton, NJ: Princeton University Press.

Hogan, Howard, Jennifer M. Ortman, and Sandra L. Colby. 2015. Projecting diversity: The methods, results, assumptions and limitations of the U.S. Census Bureau's population projections. *West Virginia Law Review* 117:1047–79.

Hopkins, Daniel J. 2010. Politicized places: Explaining where and when immigration provokes local opposition. *American Political Science Review* 104 (1): 40–60.

Kinder, Donald R., and Cindy D. Kam. 2009. *Us against them: Ethnocentric foundations of American opinion*. Chicago, IL: University of Chicago Press.

McElwee, Sean, and Jason McDaniel. 14 March 2017. Fear of diversity made people more likely to vote Trump. *The Nation*.

Myers, Dowell. 1992. *Analysis with local census data*. Boston, MA: Academic Press.

Myers, Dowell. 2007. The political lag during the demographic transition. In *Immigrants and boomers: Forging a new social contract for the future of America*. New York, NY: Russell Sage Foundation.

Population Reference Bureau. 2011. *Understanding and using population projections*. Washington, DC: Population Reference Bureau.

Prewitt, Kenneth. 2013. *What is your race? The census and our flawed efforts to classify Americans*. Princeton, NJ: Princeton University Press.

Tesler, Michael, and David O. Sears. 2010. *Obama's race: The 2008 election and the dream of a post-racial America*. Chicago, IL: University of Chicago Press.

Wong, Cara J. 2007. "Little" and "big" pictures in our heads: Race, local context, and innumeracy about racial groups in the United States. *Public Opinion Quarterly* 71 (3): 392–412.

Growing U.S. Ethnoracial Diversity: A Positive or Negative Societal Dynamic?

By
FRANK D. BEAN

Solving problems of race relations in the United States requires avoiding binary ethnoracial classifications and understanding the nature, extent, and consequences of today's diversity resulting from immigration. Recent demographic change has involved not only growth in the size of the nonwhite U.S. population but also increases in the number of new ethnoracial groups. Modest socioeconomic improvements have recently occurred among most nonwhite groups, and the rise in the number of different groups has led to some positive changes (i.e., boosting intermarriage and multiracial identification, blurring color lines among ethnoracial groups, and fostering creativity and economic growth) without diminishing social cohesion and solidarity. However, the benefits of multigroup diversity appear not to have reached many Americans who have less felt the social and economic benefits of free trade, globalization, and immigration. This underscores the need for universal policies that transcend identity- and grievance-based politics and provide security and benefits for all Americans.

Keywords: ethnoracial; diversity; immigration; integration

Nearly one-sixth of the way through the twenty-first century, the United States remains plagued by problems of *race*. Contributing to the difficulty of dealing with these problems is that we increasingly seem to disagree about what race means, vacillating between conceptualizations so broad or narrow that they are of little use. This suggests a need to

Frank D. Bean is a distinguished professor of sociology and director of the Center for Research on International Migration, University of California, Irvine. A member of the recent National Academy of Sciences/National Research Council Panel on The Integration of Immigrants into American Society, his most recent book (with Susan K. Brown and James D. Bachmeier) is Parents without Papers: The Progress and Pitfalls of Mexican American Integration *(Russell Sage Foundation 2015).*

Correspondence: fbean@uci.edu

DOI: 10.1177/0002716218765415

reexamine how we define race, classify people as belonging to particular racial groups, and incorporate race into our understandings of what the United States stands for as a country. In other words, which definitions, delineations, and narratives of race are most prevalent in the country today? What are the effects of these on the country's well-being? And which are most in need of revision? Answering these questions is not easy, and trying to do so is made harder by the millions of new immigrants who have come to the United States over the past 50 years, for whom ethnoracial designations are often especially problematic. But it is crucial that we try. Improving the country's race relations and developing solutions to other important issues of public policy depend on our doing so.

The Difficulty and Consequences of Defining Race

Following the lead of George M. Fredrickson (1988, 3), we could define race as a "consciousness of status and identity based on ancestry and color." This definition fits the black population in the United States particularly well. But in the cases of the new Latino and Asian immigrant groups, race in this sense does not by itself provide a totally suitable label because it is not clear that *color* is an attribute that can be consistently applied to immigrants from Latin America or Asia, either by natives or by these newcomers themselves. For example, some Latinos view themselves and are seen by others as white, some as brown, and some as black. Some would thus prefer the term *ethnoracial status* to refer to the ways that various peoples distinguish themselves, on the basis of ancestry and/or color.

In thinking about how immigration affects the classification of racial and ethnic groups in the United States, which in turn may itself influence racial and ethnic relations, it is fruitful to recall that immigration and race sometimes represent features of the American history that are very nearly polar opposites, at least as they have been characterized in the postwar period. Few phenomena have so captured the American imagination as immigration, and none has so contradicted American ideals as race (Cose 1992). The United States is often described as a "nation of immigrants," an idea Oscar Handlin elevated to near mythological status in claiming that the history of America was synonymous with the history of immigration (Handlin 1951/1973). Numerous books about immigration have contained in their titles some variation of the phrase "the Golden Door," emphasizing that newcomers and their descendants can achieve a better life in America than the one they had left behind (see, for example, Borjas 1999; Reimers 1985).

African Americans, however, fall into a different category. If immigration has symbolized the hopeful and uplifting side of the American experience, the practice of slavery in many of the colonies and subsequent states for the first two to three centuries after European settlers arrived has dramatized the negative and exclusionary part of the historical picture (Tocqueville 1945; Bean and Bell-Rose 1999). Whereas the weaving of many strands of immigration into the U.S. economic mainstream represents the success of the American experience, the lack of full integration in the case of the African American population represents the country's most conspicuous failure and an indication of the residual power of racial discrimination throughout American society (Fredrickson 1988; Rose 1997). Although social and economic progress among blacks has occurred, the questions of how much, when, how fast, and why are still the subjects of much debate (Hacker 1992/1995; Thernstrom and Thernstrom 1997; Frey 2014). African Americans, of course, were involuntary immigrants to the United States.

During the eighteenth century, they were the single largest immigrant group arriving in the country (Berlin 1998). Despite this, their experience cannot be understood as analogous to that of other immigrant groups. Most blacks came to the United States under chattel slavery that bound not only them but also their children to their owners for life (Morgan 1998). The modes of entry and the reception in America of immigrants from Africa were thus especially harsh and debilitating compared with the experience of immigrants from other countries. This makes it impossible to address the experience of blacks in this country as just another chapter in the story of immigration. Nor is it any less an oversimplification to view the difficulties of recent immigrants as just another chapter in the history of racism in the United States.

This reasoning lays bare the potential perils of conflating racial and ethnic status into the single term *race*, as well as the pitfalls of relying on binary distinctions in general to define and operationalize ethnoracial categories. Whatever set of categories are used, unintended consequences result. This is partly because relying on any particular classification scheme privileges the observation of certain differences over others, a tendency that is less problematic when such distinctions capture large real-world differences. For example, the use of a binary black/nonblack delineation, because of the pernicious and long-lasting negative legacies of slavery, indicates substantial black disadvantage relatively undiluted by the inclusion of other ethnoracial groups in the "black" category. A binary white/nonwhite scheme, however, which is increasingly used by many observers, is distorted by the inclusion of blacks in the nonwhite category, making nonblack disadvantaged groups appear to suffer more than is actually the case. The very usage of the category nonwhite in the absence of disaggregating nonwhites betrays an a priori assumption that today's white/nonwhite differences are as large as yesterday's black/nonblack ones.

Such usage also tends to encourage new forms of identity politics pitting whites against nonwhites, thus redirecting efforts away from addressing pressing real-world disadvantages, such as those between blacks and whites, and those between the rich and poor members of any ethnoracial group. Taking note of these problems is not to suggest that certain ways of gauging ethnoracial differences be ignored or overlooked; rather, it is (1) to underscore the importance of those "ethnoracial" classifications that most accurately reveal the largest real-world intergroup disadvantages (i.e., those most in need of amelioration), (2) to emphasize that binary classifications that gloss over national origin and other kinds of heterogeneity hamper the detection of many disadvantages, and (3) to note the potential research and policy benefits that may emerge from focusing on U.S. multicategory ethnoracial diversity.

Other current practices make it difficult to detect the latter kind of diversity effects. In using classifications of U.S. *racial groups*, analysts frequently adopt schemes that yield six exhaustive and mutually exclusive categories (and ignore the existence of multiple-race persons, by assuming that any mention of a non-white identity justifies classifying such multiracial individuals as nonwhite [Alba 2016]). This is based on respondents' self-reports to questions asking (1) whether they are Hispanic and (2) whether they are white, black, Asian, Native-American, or some other race. If respondents answer the former question by saying they are Hispanic, this is taken as their race. If they say they are not Hispanic, their race comes from answers to the latter question. The use of such categories and practices is widespread, even though doing so not only conflates a distinction between racial and ethnic groups that many scholars think should be maintained rather than obscured. Lumping all ethnoracial groups together also implicitly encourages the idea that all nonwhite groups in America (so-called people of "color") are just as disadvantaged as African Americans, even though social science research shows that this is not the case (Lee and Bean 2010).

Contemporary Ethnoracial Demographics and Social Welfare

That the size of the country's nonwhite group defined in this way has been increasing both absolutely and relatively seems to have generated concern in some quarters that the country's identity and social solidarity are weakening. Usage of such nonwhite categories for 2010 data reveals that minorities (i.e., nonwhites) composed 36.3 percent of the population. Moreover, projections suggest that each of the "new" minorities (Asians, Hispanics, and multiracial persons) will double in size by 2050. And 2011 was a "milestone" year demographically in that fewer babies were born to whites in the country than to women of all other categories combined, suggesting a future in which "whites" will be a statistical minority. This possibility seems worrisome to those who think ethnoracial minority groups, especially the large Latino and certain Asian ones, will remain disproportionately outside the middle class and thus prone to reject a common national identity and more likely to erode social cohesion.

Arrayed against such statistics, however, are others showing that nonwhite ethnoracial groups are faring notably better today on various socioeconomic integration measures than they did in 1970 (Frey 2014; National Academies of Sciences 2015), thus supporting the conclusion that growing ethnoracial diversity in the sense of the country's ethnoracial groups becoming larger in size is not inevitably leading to more widespread poverty itself. For example, many members of nonwhite groups have been gaining in average education and income and are experiencing less residential segregation from whites, often as a result of geographic mobility. This suggests notable upward mobility on the part of such groups, even African Americans, but especially among recent nonwhite immigrant groups (Lee and Bean 2010). It is also important to note that beyond the increases in the sizes of nonwhite ethnoracial groups and improvements in their socioeconomic standing, there is also the matter of growing diversity per se. In other words, the country not only has a larger nonwhite population now than formerly, this population is made up of more different subgroups than before, imparting a rising diversity of kind as well as degree to the country.

Research showing a link between this kind of ethnoracial diversity and improvements in majority attitudes toward minorities would suggest an improving climate in the country for nonwhites. In fact, studies do observe rising numbers of intermarriages (between spouses from different ethnoracial categories as defined above) and growing numbers of offspring from such marriages, which increase the number of people with multiracial parentage (Bean, Lee, and Bachmeier 2013). The degree to which people from such backgrounds see themselves in multiracial terms, of course, is a matter of self-perception and, thus, one that may vary substantially by ethnoracial category. For example, people in the South with one black and one white parent appear considerably less likely to define themselves as multiracial than is the case for people with other paired differences in racial background, suggesting that the social and temporal dynamics of black life in the United States remain more constraining than those for other groups (Lee and Bean 2010). Despite this, since 1970 evidence for blacks implies some improvement in material well-being, supporting the conclusion that notable numbers of blacks are also better off now than they were some 40 years ago (Frey 2014), even though the group as a whole continues to lag other groups, and even though a sizable number of African Americans are worse off than previously (Bean and Bell-Rose 1999).

The other two major minority populations are Latinos and Asians. They have experienced relatively rapid growth in recent decades as a result of immigration, especially when one includes the children of the immigrants in measures of their growing significance. But the groups within these panethnic categories vary in their starting points at arrival and in their experiences afterward. For example, Mexican and Central American immigrants, who make up a large fraction of Latinos, are disproportionately poorly educated, while Asian immigrants are disproportionately highly educated. This alone often contaminates comparisons among various minority groups and between minority and native groups, especially when the comparison lumps together immigrant and native-born Latinos, thus diluting Latino progress and encouraging the conclusion that their experiences and disadvantages are similar to those of blacks. But, as just noted, many blacks continue to fare much less well socioeconomically than whites, and they are viewed by whites more negatively than are Asians or native Latinos (although an exception consists of Latino unauthorized immigrants who are seen just as negatively [Hainmueller and Hopkins 2015; Schachter 2016]).

The Broader Effects of Immigration and America's Growing Diversity

Answering the question of diversity's broader implications for American society requires evidence that goes beyond simply observing growth in the sheer sizes of nonwhite groups and how well they are doing socioeconomically. Because U.S. growth in ethnoracial groups results mostly from immigration, direct assessments of the impact of immigration on society-level variables, like social cohesion and social solidarity, are particularly important. In short, what are the effects of immigration on multigroup ethnoracial diversity, and in turn, what are the effects of such diversity on social cohesion and solidarity? Both theory and research suggest these are generally positive.

Theoretically, immigrants bring with them new resources, ideas, and ways of doing things that contribute greatly to social and economic life in America. Rather than emphasizing that newcomers are essentially people of color whose mobility is limited by discriminatory treatment—an orientation that fosters anxiety narratives about immigration causing weakened social cohesion and hardened social boundaries among groups—an alternative narrative would emphasize immigration's social richness and heterogeneity and the positive consequences diversity seems to generate. In fact, ethnoracial diversity boosts people's awareness of alternative cultures and lifestyles, stimulates creativity, leads to the greater development of interpersonal and problem-solving skills, and fosters increases in innovation (Benkler 2006; Chua 2007; Grewal 2008; Herring 2009; Page 2007). Such consequences of multigroup diversity reinforce narratives about the salutary and socially enriching effects stemming from the greater diversity accompanying immigration and illustrate how immigration through diversity makes for a more resilient and vibrant society (Bean and Stevens 2003; Kasinitz et al. 2008).

Also, extensive research shows how the diversity arising from immigration affects both social cohesion and the strength of ethnoracial boundaries. Worry about negative diversity diminishing social cohesion appeared to jump in response to conjectures by Robert Putnam that the ethnic heterogeneity led natives not only to be suspicious of immigrants, but also to interact less frequently with each other, suggesting diminished social trust and solidarity in general (Putnam 2007). This widely noted possibility appeared to suggest that immigration itself exerts adverse effects on social cohesion. Since then researchers have conducted dozens of additional inquiries on the topic in the United States and Europe, concluding overwhelmingly that immigration-induced ethnoracial diversity does *not* on balance negatively influence interethnic social cohesion, except sometimes in the United States (van der Meer and Tolsma 2014; Portes and Vickstrom 2011). But this tendency went away when studies took into account the impact of prejudicial attitudes toward blacks on social cohesion. Because white Americans perceive a greater threat from and exhibit more prejudice toward blacks than toward other ethnoracial groups, whites living in areas with both large *and* immigrant and large black populations often report less social cohesion, thereby diminishing the boost in social cohesion that accompanies the diversity resulting from immigration (Bean, Lee, and Bachmeier 2013; Abascal and Baldassarri 2015).

A different way of looking at the issue of cohesion comes from examining the extent to which ethnoracial diversity breaks down boundaries between different ethnoracial groups and, thus, indirectly reflects the potential for improvements in U.S. ethnoracial relations? For instance, has diversity diminished the strength of ethnoracial color lines in the United States, including the black-white color line? Have ethnoracial heterogeneity and intermarriage contributed to boundary change? Several reasons exist for thinking that ethnoracial diversity may help to increase tolerance both for and among the members of new immigrant groups and African Americans. First, as minority immigrant groups have grown relatively larger, the probabilities of contact between the members of such groups and majority natives have increased, thus promoting more familiarity with the members of these groups, as Gordon Allport (1954) noted in his oft-cited *contact hypothesis*, especially when such groups are not seen as threatening (e.g., Pettigrew and Tropp 2006). Second, the presence of a larger number of different groups tends to diminish the significance of any single group (Lee and Bean 2010). Third, positive psychological and social dividends may result from diversity because of increased creativity, enhanced problem-solving capacities, and strengthened social resiliency, thus facilitating ties and relations across ethnoracial boundaries.

Recent research on ethnoracial intermarriage and multiracial identification is consistent with these ideas. For example, in 2010, 8.6 percent of all U.S. marriages were ethnoracially mixed (Frey 2014), and 15.1 percent of all new marriages were mixed, almost one in every seven unions (Pew Research Center 2013). Moreover, this latter figure was up from about one in eleven in 2000, a rise of more than half in one decade. Higher levels of intermarriage have also occurred in tandem with growing multiracial populations. For instance, 5.3 percent of all children aged 0 to 17 were identified as multiracial in 2010, compared to only 1.1 percent of persons aged 55 or older (Bean, Lee, and Bachmeier 2013). For whites, this figure was 6.4 percent, for blacks 14.6 percent, and for Asians 27.9 percent (comparable figures for Latinos are impossible to derive because census data do not recognize mixed Latino/non-Latino origins).

Most significant of all, research also shows that intermarriage and multiraciality are highest in those parts of the country that are the most diverse, and that this depends in part on diversity per se, rather than simply the presence of a large minority population (Bean, Lee, and Bachmeier 2013). In sum, the huge post-1965 immigration that has brought millions to the country whose ethnoracial status is neither black nor white has thus elevated ethnoracial diversity. More important, diversity appears to be creating multiple color lines, detracting from the stark emphases on black-white and white-nonwhite divides. Recent rises in intermarriage and multiracial identification— which are more pronounced among Asians and Latinos than among blacks—suggest a broad loosening of the boundaries between groups, thus setting the stage for possible increases in intergroup tolerance and social cohesion (whose implications for blacks, however, are uncertain).

Overall, U.S. minority groups are thus faring better now than they did some 40 years ago. As the growth in these groups makes for a more ethnoracially diverse America, the integration of these groups with whites is rising, a development that could serve to reduce fears that diversity is detrimental to social cohesion. In other words, the reality of diversity dynamics in the United States in recent decades suggests that growing diversity is making for a better and stronger society, although this process is not occurring as rapidly as some might like. More troublesome are other developments that threaten to derail the process. One of these is the popular inclination among young people to emphasize a binary racial classification of white and nonwhite. This, as in the case of the old black-white binary, risks the negative reification of whiteness in the former instance and blackness in the latter. It also ignores the heterogeneous nature of all groups. As Foley (2015) has cogently demonstrated, classifying many earlier immigrants to the United States as homogeneous whites has never been correct because it overlooks the remarkable diversity among those who initially came to the country as settlers, a property he argues obtains to the Mexican-origin population as well. Using dichotomies for ethnoracial analyses also does not consider that today's immigrants are arriving, like those before them, largely because their labor is needed. This need is currently increasingly because below-replacement native fertility, educational upgrading, and the aging out of the workforce of natives (Bean et al. 2012; Bean, Brown, and Bachmeier 2015), reflecting that postindustrial economies increasingly need immigration to meet the demands for labor and to sustain pension programs (Coleman 2006; Bean and Brown 2015).

Moreover, as native baby boomers continue to age and retire, workforce voids are providing prospects for both immigrant and black upward mobility (Alba 2009; Myers 2007), even as aggregate earnings stagnation reigns in the bottom two-thirds of the distribution. Many working-class whites whose families have long lived in the United States and who have not gone to college have not experienced intergenerational upward mobility, even as many immigrants coming into the country with low initial levels of education have. Paying attention to a binary ethnoracial classification that looks only at whites and nonwhites reinforces the tendency to view all nonwhites as similar to blacks, failing to give justice to the larger difficulties of African Americans and to the income stagnation of non-college-educated whites.

That the income and wealth situations of many blacks in the United States continue to lag those of third-generation ethnoracial immigrant groups suggests that the country needs a new narrative to guide the formulation of its policies regarding race. We also need policies that recognize and are directed at the disadvantages of non-black Americans that often result at least as much from their low socioeconomic status as from their ethnoracial status. In short, new ameliorative programs, like revised affirmative action programs, could target both blacks and non-college-educated persons of all ethnoracial statuses for assistance. Another special case involves unauthorized immigrants, for whom sensible legalization policies are also required because their lack of legal status now leads to such strong exclusion that both their own and their children's integration is forestalled until they have the opportunity to legalize (Bean, Brown, and Bachmeier 2015; Brown and Bean 2016).

Conclusion

Issues of race and ethnicity, along with those of social class, remain important in the United States. Although slavery caused the Civil War, a conflict that narrowly averted the breakup of the Union, its cessation ushered in Jim Crow laws almost as destructive as slavery itself (Woodward 1995). Today, the legacies of slavery and the Jim Crow era endure in the form of institutional and cultural practices that allow the disproportionate incarceration of black males and a tacit white condoning of black-targeted police violence (Alexander 2012). The recent killings by police of blacks in several U.S. cities highlight the continuation of virulent racism toward blacks. While we do not want to repeat earlier underestimations of black racism (Faust 2015), neither should we today exaggerate the extent to which harsh treatment and prejudice characterize the contemporary experiences of nonwhite U.S. immigrant groups, most of whose members show considerable integration into the country's larger socioeconomic fabric (National Academies of Sciences 2015). Overstating the extent of permanent harm to and disadvantage among today's immigrants may seem to follow from clear-cut instances of the earlier mistreatment of certain groups such as the Chinese and Japanese. However, evidence suggests that the effects of injuries from such historical injustices have now considerably waned (Foley 2015; Lee 2015), especially when viewed in comparison to the continuing contemporary difficulties of blacks. Imposing a new dichotomy, namely, a white/nonwhite one, on the country undermines recognition of the reality that growing diversity in the form of more heterogeneity is making for a better America.

Relying on rigid ethnoracial dichotomies fosters identity politics by stigmatizing one class of Americans at the expense of another, in effect implying that the members of that class alone are responsible for disadvantage. The old black-white color line helped to foster the idea that all blacks were inferior and undeserving of societal membership. The new white-nonwhite designation tends to affirm the idea that all whites are privileged and responsible for any difficulties faced by nonwhites. The result in either case is the advancement of grievance-based politics, which intrinsically (and thus inevitably) pits one faction against another, with each side blaming the other for its difficulties. This then fosters divisive zero-sum politics, which often devolve into the following form: "I want what you have. But if I can't have what you have (or don't think I can), then I don't want you to have it either." In other words, aspiration and envy can become transformed into resentment. This is especially likely to happen when the promise of upward social and economic mobility seems (or is) minimal, thus reinforcing hopelessness and producing resentment, which fuels grievance-based politics on the part of both sides.

Needless to say, all of this distracts attention from and undercuts efforts to develop more inclusive and greater opportunities for all Americans. Diversity in America today, because of immigration, derives from the presence of a large number of new national origin groups. We have seen above that the reality of this diversity in the lives of many Americans involves real and positive consequences (e.g., weaker boundaries among groups, greater social cohesion and solidarity, and more economic opportunity in the country's large metropolitan areas). However, other Americans, often those outside large metropolitan areas and in places without many immigrants, increasingly feel left behind and resentful. Seeking through grievance-based politics to stifle immigration and punish unauthorized immigrants through deportation fails to provide tangible benefits for these overlooked Americans, although it may make them feel better. And it does threaten to undercut the social and economic benefits the new diversity has brought to much of the country. What the country thus needs now more than ever is universal social and economic policies that reach all Americans in all parts of the country, especially those in the middle-class and the bottom part of the income distribution. And such policies must extend to them in real, not just in token, ways, so that they receive their fair share of the benefits of free trade and globalization.

References

Abascal, Maria, and Delia Baldassarri. 2015. Love thy neighbor? Ethnoracial diversity and trust reexamined. *American Journal of Sociology* 121 (3): 722–82.
Alba, Richard. 2009. *Blurring the color line: The new chance for a more integrated America*. Cambridge, MA: Harvard University Press.
Alba, Richard. 2016. The likely persistence of a white majority. *American Prospect* 29:67–71.
Alexander, Michelle. 2012. *The new Jim Crow: Mass incarceration in the age of colorblindness*. Rev. ed. New York, NY: New Press.
Allport, Gordon W. 1954. *The nature of prejudice*. Reading, MA: Addison-Wesley.
Bean, Frank D., and Stephanie Bell-Rose. 1999. *Immigration and opportunity: Race, ethnicity and employment in the United States*. New York, NY: Russell Sage Foundation.
Bean, Frank D., and Susan K. Brown. 2015. Demographic analyses of immigration. In *Migration theory: Talking across disciplines*, eds. Caroline B. Brettell and James F. Hollifield, 67–89. New York, NY: Routledge.
Bean, Frank D., Susan K. Brown, and James D. Bachmeier. 2015. *Parents without papers: The progress and pitfalls of Mexican-American integration*. New York, NY: Russell Sage Foundation.
Bean, Frank D., Susan K. Brown, James D. Bachmeier, Zoya Gubernskaya, and Christopher D. Smith. 2012. Luxury, necessity and anachronistic workers: Does the United States need unskilled immigrant labor? *American Behavioral Scientist* 56 (8): 1008–28.
Bean, Frank D., Jennifer Lee, and James D. Bachmeier. 2013. Immigration and the color line at the beginning of the 21st century. *Daedalus* 142 (3): 123–40.
Bean, Frank D., and Gillian Stevens. 2003. *America's newcomers and the dynamics of diversity*. New York, NY: Russell Sage Foundation Press.
Benkler, Yochai. 2006. *The wealth of networks: How social production transforms markets and freedom*. New Haven, CT: Yale University Press.
Berlin, Ira. 1998. *Many thousands gone: The first two centuries of slavery in North America*. Cambridge, MA: Belknap Press of Harvard University Press.
Borjas, George J. 1999. *Heaven's door: Immigration policy and the American economy*. Princeton, NJ: Princeton University Press.
Brown, Susan K., and Frank D. Bean. 2016. Migration status and political knowledge among Latino immigrants. *Russell Sage Foundation Journal of the Social Sciences* 2 (3): 22–41.
Chua, Amy. 2007. *Day of empire: How hyperpowers rise to global dominance—and why they fall*. New York, NY: Doubleday.
Coleman, David. 2006. Immigration and ethnic change in low-fertility countries: A third demographic transition. *Population and Development Review* 32 (3): 401–46.
Cose, Ellis. 1992. *Nation of strangers: Prejudice, politics, and the populating America*. New York, NY: HarperCollins.
Faust, Drew Gilpin. 17 December 2015. John Hope Franklin: Race and the meaning of America. *New York Review of Books*, 97–99.
Foley, Neil. 2015. *Mexicans in the making of America*. Cambridge, MA: Harvard University Press.

Fredrickson, George M. 1988. *The arrogance of race: Historical perspectives on slavery, racism, and social inequality*. Middletown, CT: Wesleyan University Press.
Frey, William H. 2014. *Diversity explosion: How new racial demographics are remaking America*. Washington, DC: Brookings Institution Press.
Grewal, David Singh. 2008. *Network power: The social dynamics of globalization*. New Haven, CT: Yale University Press.
Hacker, Andrew. 1992/1995. *Two nations: Black and white, separate, hostile, unequal*. New York, NY: Ballantine Books.
Hainmueller, Jens, and Daniel J. Hopkins. 2015. The hidden American immigration consensus: A conjoint analysis of attitudes toward immigrants. *American Journal of Political Science* 59 (3): 529–48.
Handlin, Oscar. 1951/1973. *The uprooted: The epic story of the great migrations that made the American people*. Boston, MA: Little, Brown.
Herring, Cedric. 2009. Does diversity pay? Race, gender, and the business case for diversity. *American Sociological Review* 74 (2): 208–24.
Kasinitz, Philip, John H. Mollenkopf, Mary C. Waters, and Jennifer Holdaway. 2008. *Inheriting the city: The children of immigrants come of age*. New York, NY, and Cambridge, MA: Russell Sage Foundation and Harvard University Press.
Lee, Erika. 2015. *The making of Asian America: A history*. New York, NY: Simon & Schuster.
Lee, Jennifer, and Frank D. Bean. 2010. *The diversity paradox: Immigration and the color line in 21st century America*. New York, NY: Russell Sage Foundation.
Morgan, Phillips. 1998. *Slave counterpoint: Black culture in the eighteenth-century Chesapeake and Lowcountry*. Chapel Hill, NC: University of North Carolina Press.
Myers, Dowell. 2007. *Immigrants and boomers: Forging a new social contract for the future of America*. New York, NY: Russell Sage Foundation.
National Academies of Sciences, Engineering, and Medicine. 2015. *The integration of immigrants into the United States*. Panel on Immigrant Integration, eds. M. Waters and M. G. Pineau. Washington, DC: National Academies Press. doi:10.172261/21746.
Page, Scott E. 2007. *The difference—How the power of diversity creates better groups, firms, schools, and societies*. Princeton, NJ: Princeton University Press.
Pettigrew, Thomas F., and Linda R. Tropp. 2006. A meta-analytic test of intergroup contact theory. *Journal of Personality and Social Psychology* 90 (5): 751–83.
Pew Research Center. 2013. *Intermarriage on the rise in the U.S.* Washington, DC: Pew Research Center.
Portes, Alejandro, and Erik Vickstrom. 2011. Diversity, social capital, and cohesion. *Annual Review of Sociology* 37:461–79.
Putnam, Robert D. 2007. E pluribus unum: Diversity and community in the twenty-first century: The 2006 Johan Skytte Prize Lecture. *Scandinavian Political Studies* 30 (2): 137–74.
Reimers, David M. 1985. *Still the golden door: The third world comes to America*. New York, NY: Columbia University Press.
Rose, Peter I. 1997. *Tempest-lost: Race, immigration, and the dilemmas of diversity*. New York, NY: Oxford University Press.
Schachter, Ariela. 2016. From "different" to "similar": An experimental approach to understanding assimilation. *American Sociological Review* 81 (5): 981–1013.
Thernstrom, Stephan, and Abigail Thernstrom. 1997. *America in black and white: One nation, indivisible*. New York, NY: Simon & Schuster.
Tocqueville, Alexis de. 1835/1945. *Democracy in America*. Henry Reeve, trans. New York, NY: Vintage Books.
van der Meer, Tom, and Jochem Tolsma. 2014. Ethnic diversity and its effects on social cohesion. *Annual Review of Sociology* 40:459–78.
Woodward, C. Vann. 1995. *The strange career of Jim Crow*. New York, NY: Oxford University Press.

Editors' Note

Editors' Note

In the period between the writing and the publishing of this volume, events have threatened the integrity of Census 2020. They affect what readers will take from the articles contained in this volume, and are briefly summarized here.

Start with the fact that the Census Bureau director responsible for the basic 2020 census design, including an ambitious, multiyear initiative to improve race and ethnicity statistics, announced his resignation on May 11, 2017. This was to allow President Trump to nominate a new director, who would need to supervise the significant planning effort then under way and evaluate any needed corrections to the 2020 design.

Nine months later, no director has been nominated. This hampers 2020 planning, as does severe underfunding of current planning efforts. Take, for example, a long-planned and critical end-to-end field test, sometimes labeled a dress rehearsal, which duplicates census conditions as fully as possible. It was designed to contrast three sites; it will now occur in only one site. The Census Bureau has designed an ambitious integrated communications program, which, we know from the 2000 and 2010 census experience, will substantially improve the census response rate, particularly in hard-to-count areas of the country. It is currently unfunded, and scheduled preparatory work by the contractor has been delayed; further delay will significantly reduce the scope and quality of the census public awareness campaign. As of this writing, the proposed 2018 and 2019 census budget is described as putting the Census Bureau on "life support."

Even as careful, time-tested census operations have been delayed or cut back, totally unexpected demands are being made. For example, the Department of Justice has

Correspondence: ralba@gc.cuny.edu
DOI: 10.1177/0002716218766464

requested the Census Bureau to add citizenship status to the 2020 form. This elicited strong opposition from mayors, governors, businesses, academics, advocacy groups, and a specially formed committee of prior Census Bureau directors (appointed by Republican and Democratic administrations). This broad constituency forcefully explained how a citizenship question on the decennial form will negatively affect the response rate in 2020. Cities and regions with a large number of immigrants will experience undercounting, with troubling results for political representation and public services.

To some, two years might sound like a long time to prepare for the census. It is not. The immense decennial census effort requires equally immense preparation, which is falling behind. Many informed persons already doubt that the 2020 census can match the accuracy and comprehensiveness of prior census statistics.

The phrase "failed" census has crept into current media coverage. What does that phrase mean? It means "unfair," and the mark of an unfair census is failure at the most basic level. The nation's founders had fairness firmly in mind when they allocated seats in the House *proportionate to number of residents in each state*. It works the same twenty-four decades later, a tribute to their brilliance. If some geographic areas or demographic groups are undercounted proportionate to their true numbers, they are necessarily being treated unfairly—fewer congressional seats and fewer public services. It is equally unfair to miscount whites as it is blacks, to miscount gated communities as Indian reservations.

Of immediate relevance to arguments advanced in this volume of *The ANNALS*, the proposed improvement to statistics of ethnicity and race has been taken off the table. This proposal was thoroughly tested in the 2015 National Content Test. It involved the creation of a single merged ethno-racial question (rather than the two-question format that currently separates the Hispanic ethnicity question from the race question). Census Bureau research confirms the statistical superiority of the merged question. This improvement was widely endorsed by the academic community (including the editors of and many contributors to this volume) and many other key constituencies.

It was under review by the Office of Management and Budget (OMB), and then, in mid-February 2018, it was effectively rejected with no rationale given. OMB simply instructed the Census Bureau to use the prior unimproved ethnicity/race questions in its end-to-end test. This rules out the possibility of introducing the new question in the 2020 census. The Census Bureau does not field a new census question without first testing it in an end-to-end test.

This is not a mere technicality. The rejection of the improved question will result in misleading data on one of the most consequential developments of the early twenty-first century—the rapidly growing group of young Americans who come from ethno-racially mixed families. Misleading statistics on this population group exaggerate the decline of the majority white population. As such, they will continue to roil public discussion of diversity issues.

In this, as in other features of the census, a "failed census" in 2020 has consequences. "Demography is destiny" is not a cliché at this juncture in our history.

It aptly captures a moment when many millions of Americans are struggling to comprehend and adjust to the fast-moving diversity of their country. Flawed data lead to flawed conclusions and, it follows, ill-informed actions.

—Ken Prewitt and Richard Alba